GUNS AND SOCIETY
IN COLONIAL NIGERIA

GUNS AND SOCIETY IN COLONIAL NIGERIA

Firearms, Culture, and Public Order

SAHEED ADERINTO

INDIANA UNIVERSITY PRESS

This book is a publication of

Indiana University Press
Office of Scholarly Publishing
Herman B Wells Library 350
1320 East 10th Street
Bloomington, Indiana 47405 USA

iupress.indiana.edu

© 2018 by Saheed Aderinto

All rights reserved

No part of this book may be reproduced or utilized in any form or by any means, electronic or mechanical, including photocopying and recording, or by any information storage and retrieval system, without permission in writing from the publisher. The Association of American University Presses' Resolution on Permissions constitutes the only exception to this prohibition.

The paper used in this publication meets the minimum requirements of the American National Standard for Information Sciences—Permanence of Paper for Printed Library Materials, ANSI Z39.48-1992.

Manufactured in the United States of America

Cataloging information is available from the Library of Congress.

ISBN 978-0-253-03160-0 (cloth)
ISBN 978-0-253-03161-7 (paperback)
ISBN 978-0-253-03162-4 (ebook)

1 2 3 4 5 23 22 21 20 19 18

FOR ALHAJI LATEEF ADERINTO (BABA ONIPAKO)

OJU TO R'IBI TI O FO, O DURO D'IRE
THE EYE THAT DID NOT GO BLIND UPON SIGHTING EVIL AWAITS BLESSING

ACKNOWLEDGMENTS ix

LIST OF ABBREVIATIONS xv

Introduction: *Firearms in Twentieth-Century Colonial Africa* 1

1.
"This Destructive Implement of European Ingenuity": *Firearms, the Atlantic World, and Technology Transfer in Precolonial Nigeria* 29

2.
All Firearms Are Not Made Equal: *Colonialism, Social Class, and the Emergence of a Nigerian Gun Society* 55

3.
"A Dane Gun Is Useless without Gunpowder": *The Political Economy of Nigeria's Most Popular Explosive* 93

4.
"All Europeans in This Country Should Be Able to Fire a Rifle": *Race, Leisure Shooting, and the Lethal Symbol of Imperial Domination* 119

CONTENTS

5.
Bread and Bullet: *Guns, Imperial Atrocity, and Public Disorder*   155

6.
A Fearful Weapon: *Violent Crime and Gun Accidents in Everyday Nigeria*   193

7.
"You Are to Be Robbed of Your Guns": *Firearms Regulation and the Politics of Rights and Privilege*   225

Epilogue: *Guns and the Crisis of Development in Postcolonial Nigeria*   255

BIBLIOGRAPHY   277

INDEX   293

ACKNOWLEDGMENTS

When people hear I was doing research on firearms or listened to my presentation at conferences and seminars, an important question I often get is whether my book will support gun use or not. Their curiosity is thoroughly justified. The unprecedented wave of gun violence in the second decade of the twenty-first century in the United States and in Nigeria has consistently brought to the limelight vociferous debate over the role of guns in our diverse societies. At the core of discussion about terrorism, ethno-regional agitation for secession and resource control, and ransom kidnapping, among other forms of public disorder in Nigeria, is the question of uncontrolled access to guns, the most potent tool for prosecuting violence at all levels of the society. But as this book demonstrates, the story of guns in twentieth-century colonial Nigeria transcends the seemingly irreconcilable difference between prohibition and regulation of firearms. While not contesting the obvious fact that the gun is an instrument of human destruction, I contend that it also played complex social, economic, political, and religious roles, which historians of twentieth-century colonial Africa have largely glossed over.

If it takes an entire community to raise a child in many parts of Africa, it takes more than an individual to write an academic book. Archivists Gboyega Adelowo, Eke Amadi, and Anthony Nwaneri of the Ibadan, Kaduna, and Enugu branches of the Nigerian National Archives, respectively, generously offered a lot of help in identifying and copying dozens of files used for writing this book. My good friends Adewale Adeboye, Victor

Olaoye, and Philip Olayoku not only helped search for sources but also allowed me to use their apartments as temporary repository for archival materials before being shipped to the United States. Abubakar Sadiq Musa, Bilques Yusuf, and Hauwau Yusuf liaised with my contacts at the Kaduna Archives to collect and transport archival materials to North Carolina. Without the assistance of Sara Katz and Andrew Rutledge, who reproduced documents from the National Archives of the United Kingdom, I might not have been able to compose the lead story of this book—a 1924 firearms smuggle scandal involving a popular Calabar family. Katz also supplied figure EPI.1, showing children holding toy machine guns and mimicking soldiers at a 1972 Christmas party in Benin City. When I learned I would be unable to include the cartoons in chapter 5 because of poor quality, Ganiyu Jimoh (Jimga), a talented artist and art scholar came to my help, re-creating the images as closely as possible to the originals, which were first created by Akinola Lasekan and published in the *West African Pilot* in 1949 and 1951. Xavier Moyet, the former director of the Nigeria office of the French Institute for Research in Africa (IFRA), placed the resources of his establishment at my disposal whenever I was in the southwestern part of the country. The current director of IFRA Elodie Apard gave me accommodation in the institute's guest house while I work on the final edits of the manuscript in summer of 2017. Semeeh Omoleke was so kind to allow me to stay in his apartment during my trip to Kaduna archives, and his wife, Mariya Ibrahim, and in-laws fed me for days when I visited the northern Nigerian city of Kano in 2014. Plying the very bad Onitsha-Enugu highway (like most Nigerian roads) during fieldwork in eastern Nigeria in 2014 and 2015 was uncomfortable; but Chinedu Okoye gave relief to my experience with crucial on-the-spot cultural information, which helped me to put ideas in proper historical context.

When I hired Adeyemi Afolabi, a cab driver operating on the campus of the University of Ibadan to take me to some villages in southwestern Nigeria to conduct oral interview in June 2015, I did not know I was beginning a process that would unlock the life and times of Yoruba hunters and their guns in an exciting and unexpected way. Coincidentally, Afolabi's father was a distinguished chief hunter of Alatamun village, a boundary community between Oyo and Osun states, who had spent much of his life hunting game of varying sizes across the length and breadth of southwestern Nigeria. The name of the community, Alatamun, which literally translates as "the one that shoots to hold/grab" renders an interesting perspective to the village's long history of firearms use. Afolabi introduced me to an entire community of hunters, who readily shared their stories of gun use and animal world with passion and enthusiasm. My special appreciation goes to *Oluode* (chief hunter) Kamoru Adeyemo, who coordinated interviews with his colleagues. At Mamu, another boundary community between Ogun and Oyo states, chief hunter Adegboyega Rasheed Manare, an ex-soldier shared lifetime of incredible stories of hunting, wildlife, and gun culture that cannot be found in any academic book or written archive.

Portions of this book were presented at conferences and symposia in the United States and Nigeria. In May 2013, my very good friend Adeyemi Ademowo invited me to Afe Babalola University to give an overview of the entire project. The second draft of chapter 2 was first presented at the staff and postgraduate seminar of the Department of History, Ahmadu Bello University, in June 2014, at the invitation of Zachary Gundu and Sule Muhammed. In 2015, I presented incarnations of chapters 5 and 6 at the Second Biennial International Conference of the Faculty of Arts, University of Ibadan, and at the African Studies Association meeting in San Diego, California, respectively. I thank all those who invited me and participants at these academic gatherings for their useful comments, which helped me to improve on the project. Social gatherings of great minds, aside from the office, archive, conference, and classroom, are also important sites where ideas germinate and consolidate. Rotimi Babatunde, Benson Eluma, Ropo Ewenla, Tolulope Odebunmi, Yomi Ogunsanya, Olawale Olawumi, Lanre Oladoyinbo, and Sola Olorunyomi, among other friends at the University of Ibadan Senior Staff Club, gave me a listening ear and posed provocative questions as I tested my ideas at different stages of their evolution. Abimbola Adunni Adelakun and Odebunmi also helped to transport kolanut from Nigeria—thus assisting in sustaining my fifteen years of addiction to the caffeine supplement that kept me awake to write.

My indebtedness goes to the following friends and colleagues who shelved their own work to read the book manuscript: Laurent Fourchard, Simon Heap, Giacomo Macola, Olisa Godson Muojama, Olatunji Ojo, Timothy Stapleton, William K. Storey, and Hakeem Ibikunle Tijani. I thank them for putting their diverse expertise to work in helping me rethink and restructure many portions of this book. When I got lost in the intricate web of the historiographies that this project engages, Isaac Olawale Albert,

Joseph Inikori, Brian Larkin, Jeremy Prestholdt, and Simon Wendt gladly responded to my email inquiries suggesting sources and pointing my attention to emerging trends in commodity, firearms, economic, social, and political history. Duro Adeleke and Adeola Mobolaji put their knowledge of Yoruba historical linguistics to work in helping me to understand the social context (usually lost in written text) under which the nickname (Alapafon), given to a famous murderer in 1920s Lagos emerged. The academic careers of my *ogas*—Olufunke Adeboye, Olutayo Adesina, Omoniyi Afolabi, Simon Ademola Ajayi, Gloria Chuku, Raphael Njoku, Ayodeji Olukoju, and Babatunde Sofela among others—continue to inspire me to venture into new areas of African history and develop my scholarly potential to the fullest. It has been a great pleasure working with copy editor Bob Fullilove for nine years. Fullilove has an unusual talent for catching hidden errors, carelessly tucked inside paragraphs and sentences. His patience, meticulousness, and deep theoretical questions have helped this book in a manner I cannot explain.

I have continued to enjoy the assistance of Western Carolina University, where I work. The library staff, especially Peter Johnson and Daniel Wendel, diligently worked with me to identify and secure primary and secondary sources. I thank research assistant Kyle Dreher for committing countless of hours to search for valuable data in the colonial Nigerian newspapers. My colleagues in the History Department possess an incredible congeniality, which makes teaching and writing pleasurable. I sincerely appreciate department head Mary Ella Engel's support in securing funding to cover some research travel expenses. My knowledge of firearms technology and capabilities increased when Austin Hayes, my former undergraduate student, generously allowed me to fire all the classes of nonprohibited guns discussed in this book. John Hemingway, a knowledgeable armorer, deserves special thanks for finding time to talk to me amid attending to his customers at his gun shop in Clyde, North Carolina. Not only did he help find the original copies of the various classes of guns I examined in this project, he coached me on core technology and innovation, which I carefully used in explaining the story of Nigeria's encounter with firearms.

The staff of Indiana University Press (IUP) made the publication of this book possible. I thank acquisition editors Jennika Baines, Dee Mortensen, Paige Rasmussen, and Kate Schramm for showing interest in the project months before I completed it. My special appreciation also goes to Nancy

Lila Lightfoot and Rhonda Van der Dussen at IUP, Jay Harward at Newgen North America, and copy editor Katherine Faydash for taking me through the meticulous but enjoyable production process. The critical comments I received from Matthew Heaton and Chima Korieh, who read the manuscript for the press, significantly improved both the organization and content of the book.

Olamide, my wife, and our two children (Itandayo and Itandola) are among my greatest blessings. I thank Olamide for over a decade of uncompromising love and companionship, and unquantifiable investment. By the time this book is out, Itandola will be in the first year of middle school, while Itandayo will be plowing through fourth grade. These great kids have enriched my life in an unexplainable manner—they have convinced me that I can be the kind of human, husband, father, and scholar I truly intend to be. Without my father, Alhaji Lateef Adejare Aderinto (Baba onipako), to whom I dedicate this book, I would not have had any Western education, not to talk of becoming a college professor or even writing a book. Baba onipako has experienced a lot of sadness in recent years—he lost his wife (my mother), brother (my uncle), sister (my aunt), first grandchild (my niece) and several longtime close friends and associates. I hope this book and other achievements of his children restore his dwindling strength and assure him that there is always a reason to be happy after many agonizing days. My mother, Madam Adunni Silifatu Aderinto (Iya alate), transited to the realm of the ancestress in June 2013, but her spirit has continued to guide and assure me that everything will be fine. Finally, to God be the glory.

ABBREVIATIONS

AG	Action Group
ARFT	Armed Robbery and Firearms Tribunal
AWAM	Association of West African Merchants
CID	Criminal Investigation Department
DICN	Defence Industries Corporation of Nigeria
ENG	*Eastern Nigeria Guardian*
LHC	Lagos Hunters' Club
LRC	Lagos Rifle Club
LWR	*Lagos Weekly Record*
NAE	National Archives Enugu
NAI	National Archives Ibadan
NAK	National Archives Kaduna
NAPF	Native Authority Police Force
NCNC	National Council of Nigeria and the Cameroons
NDT	*Nigerian Daily Times*
NEPU	Northern Elements Progressive Union
NPC	Northern Peoples' Congress
NPF	Nigeria Police Force
NRA	Nigerian Rifle Association
ONDIST	Onitsha District

Prof.	Province files
PWD	Public Works Department
RWAFF	Royal West African Frontier Force
SARD	Suppression of Armed Robbery Decree
SND	*Southern Nigeria Defender*
UAC	United Africa Company
UNODC	United Nations Office on Drugs and Crime
WACC	West African Challenge Cup
WAFF	West African Frontier Force
WAP	*West African Pilot*
WAPO	Wild Animal Protection Ordinance
WASPB	West African Supply and Production Board

INTRODUCTION

Firearms in Twentieth-Century Colonial Africa

On July 24, 1924, a police magistrate court in Calabar sentenced two Nigerian customs officers, Edet Mfon and Okon Ene, to twelve months in prison for trying to smuggle 143,000 rounds of ammunition (gun percussion caps) into Nigeria two weeks earlier. Their conviction also included "corruptly offering a gift" of £15 to William Prendegost, the chief officer of the SS *Zaria*, a vessel belonging to the Elder Dempster shipping company, in order to allow them to remove the ammunition ashore, even though they were not on duty on that day. The convicts' appeal to the Supreme Court was dismissed—the superior court was not convinced that they did not know that the two trunks contained contraband.[1] The circumstances that led to the prosecution of Mfon and Ene, which according to the police caused "a great excitement" in Calabar, did not begin with their attempt to use their power as customs officers to clear prohibited ammunition.[2] The foundation of their ordeal was laid thousands of miles away in the United Kingdom. On June 14, 1924, Henry Mitchell, a Liberian and fireman aboard the SS *Zaria*, met Ekpenyong Ita Hogan Bassey, a Nigerian World War I veteran and former customs officer studying in England, "in the street" of Liverpool through a friend. Bassey gave Mitchell two "very heavy" trunks containing the ammunition in question, keys to the trunks, and a letter addressed to his cousin (Ene). Mitchell claimed he did not know the contents of the trunks until they arrived in Calabar. In the letters, Bassey asked Ene to give Mitchell £3 in appreciation for helping to take the trunks on the ship and circumventing customs inspection and excise charges. The Nigerian government's detailed investigation of this case involved intercepting local and international telegrams of the Basseys, a "leading" Calabar family, and establishing their involvement in an elaborate illegal trafficking in ammunition.[3] Knowing that the police were after them, the syndicate began to code their telegram messages. Bassey did make another attempt in late 1925 to ship in more ammunition—through one Daniel Esin, a lawyer who refused to clear the consignment at the port—to the bewilderment of police authorities, who were frustrated by failed attempts to repatriate Bassey to Nigeria to face criminal charges.[4]

This saga reads like something that could take place today; the facts of the case resemble those of popular postcolonial subnationalists, terrorists, or entrepreneurial criminals seeking to import large quantities of ammunition to undermine the unity of the modern Nigerian state or to cause a massive breakdown of public order. However, this case can best be understood in the contexts of the globalization of commodity trade and of networks of cultural and human exchange made possible through the firm establishment of colonial rule. In fact, the case transcript and testimony from a wide range of people, including customs officers, sailors, family members of the convicts, and community leaders, provide uncommon insight into the conduct of international shipping and the regulations to which it was subject. In the letters Bassey addressed to Ene, which helped the government to establish criminal liability, Ene was expected to sell the ammunition and remit to Bassey's bank account "whatever he has" by the end of the month so that Bassey could pay for his bar entry examination. The market value of the 143,000 rounds of ammo was estimated by the government at £2,000.[5] The saga of Bassey, this son of a self-identified, "sufficiently wealthy" man, did not end with the failed arms-smuggling attempt. In November 1930, the UK Central Criminal Court sentenced Bassey to fourteen months in prison for forging a bachelor-of-arts degree certificate from an Africa-based college affiliated with Durham University in the United Kingdom.[6] Bassey had tried, unsuccessfully, to get senior colonial authorities in Nigeria to write a statement affirming his knowledge of "inspection, accounting, and statistics," acquired through working with the customs department for twelve years, which the legal matriculation board could then use to exempt him from taking the entry exam into the Inner Temple, one of Britain's legal-training institutions.[7] He resorted to certificate forgery when Chief Secretary of Nigeria Ward-Price insisted he would include the arms-smuggling judgment in the "statement of competence" he requested for the Inner Temple.

The 1924 arms-smuggling scandal renders an appropriate entry into the history of guns in colonial Nigeria. During the 1920s, the biggest challenge that Nigerian gun users faced was not access to nonprohibited firearms, especially Dane guns, which anyone could legally own by registering them with the government. It was that the "primitive" gun was unreliable, especially in damp weather. One of the cheapest solutions to this technological limitation was the use of percussion caps, which contained a small charge of explosives, as were common in cap guns—firearms that used a percussion lock mechanism. Cap guns were more reliable than Dane guns. But both cap guns and percussion caps were controlled or restricted imports. Nigerian blacksmiths by the 1920s could make Dane guns and cap guns, but they could not manufacture the percussion caps. Hence they relied on the international black market. Bassey and his accomplices would not have gotten into legal trouble had they tried to legally import gunpowder, shotguns, cartridges, or Dane guns, among other nonprohibited guns and ammunition. Indeed, not only were the permits to import these firearms easy to obtain; they were also in great demand and could quickly be sold off in any market. But the smuggling of percussion caps fetched more money. In his response to the Bassey case, the police commissioner E. T. Ford summed up the economic motivation for arms smuggling: "There is an enormous and a ready sale for percussion caps all over the southern provinces and there is no doubt that a considerable trade is being carried on. The profits are considerable and the risk of discovery, provided ordinary care and precaution are taken, are small." The elaborate network of waterways at the southern fringes of Nigeria—which did not have defined docks—the ample means of communication using canoes, and the "inability of the police to exercise a strict surveillance" all, according to him, facilitated firearms trafficking.[8]

This book deploys firearms as a window into a broader political, social, cultural, and economic history of colonial Nigeria. I use Nigerians' encounter with this European technology to knit together themes ranging from class, race, masculinity, and identity formation to the environment, violence, and commodification. The book engages how Nigerian societies and firearms have shaped one another across time and location. It notes that the power of the gun transcends its projectile range; the gun not only defined new ideas of citizenship, safety, and class but also shaped racial politics and played a cogent role in molding the pattern of humans' interactions with nature and the environment. The timeline of the book spans from 1900 to 1960, when Nigeria received its independence from Britain. Its geographical coverage extends across the breadth and length of Nigeria. While I emphasize that the precolonial histories of each Nigerian region shaped the politics of gun regulation in the twentieth century, there are general trends that allow me to make Nigeria-wide claims and conclusions without neglecting local or regional peculiarities.

This book is not about the intersection of firearms and military organization and warfare, which has occupied the attention of previous scholars. It is about how colonialism transformed the politics of access to firearms after the nineteenth century. The core arguments and observations in this book contravene some established ideas about the role of firearms in African history. First, I argue that there was no gun society in any part of pre-twentieth-century Africa, as suggested by some scholars.[9] Rather, a gun society emerged in Nigeria through the "liberalization of access to gun and use"—a product of significant political, cultural, and economic transformation made possible by colonial rule. Second, this book treats firearms as a commodity, defined by Igor Kopytoff as "a thing that has use value and that can be exchanged in a discrete transaction for a counterpart, the very fact of exchange [monetary or nonmonetary] indicating that the counterpart has, in the immediate context, an equivalent value."[10] I posit that historians of twentieth-century colonial Africa have overlooked guns as a vital global commodity, which possessed divergent symbolic meaning and character across locations, and from the biggest to the most micro societal spheres. I point out that a gun was not just a human instrument of destruction—it was a commodity that had a multiplier effect on several components of a society's experience. Third, although historians of Africa have adequately covered the discourse of colonial violence, they have given limited attention to how the politics of access to firearms shaped the physical and psychological encounter between colonialists and Africans, and among Africans, during the first half of the twentieth century. Here I argue that a careful engagement with the gun-bearing culture of the twentieth century yields an interesting perspective on the dynamics of violent encounters between the British and Nigerians, and among Nigerians. In other words, I put firearms squarely at the center of armed conflict and criminality. Fourth, it is important to challenge the esoteric reference to guns in Africanist literature by showing how the diverse technical capabilities of firearms shaped the politics of access to gun—a product of the colonialists' indexing of Nigerians in accordance with the real and perceived threat they posed to colonial tranquility. In the sections that follow, I integrate these arguments and observations into various themes and fields of African history.

A short terminological note is in order. The politics of ethnic identity and nationality in Nigeria, as elsewhere in Africa, is complex. I use the term *Nigerians* to mean the subjects of the British colony of Nigeria.[11] Ethnic and regional identities were not just a system of indexing; they were loaded with manifold social meanings, which I use to delineate shifting historical situations across the country. Throughout this book, flintlock guns are called *Dane guns* to keep to the term's synchronic usage. I use *guns* and *firearms* interchangeably, even though the latter also includes ammunition such as bullets, cartridges, and popular explosives such as gunpowder. The following encyclopedic definition of Nigeria's most important firearms is meant not to belittle the technological capacities of the guns, but to provide readers with a general idea of their core attributes, which dictated the politics of gun control. Additional information about the histories, technical capabilities, and social and political symbolism of each class of firearm is provided throughout the book. The Dane gun, Nigeria's most popular firearm, is a single-shot muzzle loader (loaded from the barrel's mouth). Its main ammunition included gunpowder and metal bullets, or bolts. Shotguns, in contrast, are breechloaders (loaded from the rear of the barrel). They used a cartridge or shell with premeasured pellet or shot and gunpowder. Most of colonial Nigeria's shotguns were double-barreled—hence they could fire two successive shots without reloading. Pistols and revolvers were the two most popular handheld guns, capable of firing up to six repeated shots. Some of them were automatic, thus enhancing rapidity of shooting. The rifle—which derives its name from the spiral grooves in the barrels (called rifling) that increase range and enhance accuracy—was the most advanced gun that civilians (Europeans and Africans alike) were permitted to own. These could be magazine-fed and could fire up to ten bullets.

In sum, what is important here is not just the technological capabilities of these firearms, which determined the politics of access, but also the divergent forms they assumed in response to changes in the cultural landscape in which they were found. Hence the life cycle of firearms ended not, in some cases, as a commodity, but as an object of material culture. A gun whose history started in a gunsmith's shop in Birmingham in the United Kingdom might spend years helping to prosecute a war and finish as a spiritual object and part of a cultural patrimony in the shrine dedicated to its owner in a community in southwestern Nigeria. The "life histories" of guns, like works of art and other commodities, "reveal a tangled mass of aesthetic, historical, and even political judgements, and of convictions and values that shape our attitude to objects."[12]

A Colonial African Gun Society Conceptualized

References to firearms in precolonial Africa are plenty. The role that guns played in the transatlantic slave trade before the colonial conquest of the late nineteenth century is traditionally situated as part of the broader history of Africa's relations with the Atlantic world and of technology transfer. Much of the historiography of firearms before the twentieth century involves arguments for or against the role of guns in militarism, state and empire building, and the changing landscape of power and political authority. During this period, Africa not only consumed guns in large quantities; the continent's demand had an impact on the technology of production in Europe. Thus, the history of gun technology cannot be dissociated from the dynamics of consumption, thousands of miles away from the center of production. Moreover, a sizable portion of the discourse of African resistance to colonial rule in the late nineteenth century dwells on the role of the superiority of European firearms in the defeat of African armies.[13] The year 1971 marked the beginning of serious scholarship on firearms in African historiography, with the publication of two special issues of *Journal of African History*.[14] These articles, like many studies before and after them, focus only on the years up to the 1890s.[15] Very few book-length monographs exist on the history of firearms. Until the appearance of William Storey's *Guns, Race, and Power in Colonial South Africa* in 2008, the most definitive monograph on the subject was Joseph Smaldone's 1977 study on warfare in the Sokoto Caliphate. Both books, as well as a recent work by Giacomo Macola on central Africa, focus essentially on the period before the twentieth century.[16]

Guns and Society in Colonial Nigeria is the first monograph specifically on twentieth-century colonial Africa.[17] The paucity of scholarly historical research on firearms in twentieth-century Africa leaves the impression that history ends as far as guns are concerned after the conquest of most parts of Africa in the late 1800s.[18] This study seeks to answer some fundamental questions about guns in twentieth-century colonial Africa: Did a gun society exist in colonial Nigeria? If yes, what were the structural transformations that made it possible? How did the politics of access to firearms under imperial rule define class and racial identity and perception? I invite scholars to rethink the suggestion by Shula Marks and Anthony Atmore, echoed by Macola, that a gun society existed in south and central Africa before the twentieth century.[19] Storey has refrained "from making arguments about a gun society that are difficult to confirm or contradict." While Storey's caution is understandable, I argue, on the basis of existing published works, that no African society can be said to be a gun society before the twentieth century. The question of whether there was a gun society or societies in pre-twentieth-century Africa is further compounded by the dearth of detailed conceptualizations of a gun society in previous studies. Nigeria, between 1900 and 1960, as the chapters in this book reveal, became a gun society as a result of structural transformations unleashed and consolidated by British colonialism.

This argument definitely necessitates the conceptualizing of an African gun society. It is a truism that Africans before the twentieth century used firearms for hunting, as status symbols, and for protecting their croplands, but the main uses to which this European technology was put were war and state building. A society cannot be considered a "gun society" if it used firearms predominantly for empire and state building and slave gathering—or if access to firearms was determined by powerful oligarchies, military warriors, and intermediaries who restricted them to a particular class of people according to race, ethnicity, or social class. A society in which only a few "regular" people could buy or make firearms, like any other item of trade, could not be a gun society. What pre-twentieth-century Africa had was a gun culture, not a gun society. The difference between a gun culture and a gun society is the level of interaction between a society and a gun. It is important to differentiate between a gun culture and a gun society in order to come to terms with the level of indispensability of firearms in a society. Any society that uses a gun, regardless of the purpose to which it is put, has a gun culture, but a gun society represents the peak of gun use—it is the highest stage or synergy a society can attain in its use of guns. A society becomes a gun society when it cannot do without firearms in its daily social, political, cultural, and religious life. The following questions must guide our conceptualization of an African gun society: how people acquired guns, the identity of the owners, what the guns were predominantly used for, and the visible effects of gun use in core areas of people's everyday existence.

An African gun society is still not one in which everyone, regardless of class, race, and hierarchy, could legally have unlimited access to all the types of guns they wanted or in which gun regulation by powerful institutions did not exist—there were laws preventing the use of prohibited firearms like machine guns. Rather, it is a society in which gun possession was liberalized and the largest percentage of firearms in circulation were used "productively," such as for hunting, protection of crops, and culturally symbolic ceremonial shooting—practices to which an entire community, regardless of social class, can relate. Moreover, what constitutes a "productive" tool not only is a relative matter but also is determined by the labeling agent, whether scholar or actor. For example, a gang of Lagos thieves who looted a bank with revolvers and pistols and carted away cash in the mid-1930s, and their counterparts in the hinterland who let off multiple charges of a Dane gun to scare a crowd before lifting imported textiles, among other valuables, from a local seasonal market, thought they were using their arms in a "productive" manner. They could share the proceeds of their exploits with their families, just as a hunter would spend the money he earned from selling an antelope killed with a Dane gun. Bassey would rationalize his action, which was meant to help defray the cost of studying in the United Kingdom, as "productive," even though it contravened colonial gun regulations.

A gun society is one in which shooting became an indispensable component of symbolic order, of communal rhythms and self-fashioning, and of the shifting conception of success at ceremonies and festivals—private or public, secular or religious, big or small. It is where spectacle, characterized by the pomp and pageantry of empire and aimed at reinforcing the legitimacy of colonialism during significant functions and events, and also designed to instill African loyalty to the colonial state, was incomplete without the firing of guns.[20] The use of guns for empire building and conquest faded away at the beginning of the twentieth century, for it became anachronistic. The Nigerian gun society came into existence as part of Britain's broader policies geared toward imperial tranquility and revenue generation. Thus, the liberalization of firearms regulation in colonial Nigeria was not an act of mere benevolence; it was predicated on the perception of danger informed by the social class of gun owners in relation to the type and capabilities of guns they were legally allowed to own. But the gun society did not just emerge overnight; it was built on precolonial processes, which colonialism helped to complete. This development involved the institutionalization of gun use in many aspects of social life, impossible under the precolonial politics of access controlled by powerful intermediaries and oligarchies. Nigerians across social classes, ethnicities, regions, and other categories of identity had access to firearms of different types in accordance with their needs, occupation, social status, residency, and relationship with the colonial government. Indeed, nearly all farmer-hunters in southern Nigeria had a Dane gun in the 1930s and 1940s.

Let us consider Storey's question: "At what statistical point can we say, with accuracy, that a gun society exists?"[21] I would argue that the number of guns in circulation is not necessarily the most important factor in defining a gun society, even though more Nigerians possessed nonprohibited guns (legally and illegally) between 1900 and 1960 than in any other period of its history. It was the obvious and systemic role that firearms played in shaping their society at multiple strata—from the everyday experience of a virtually unknown community in southwestern Nigeria to the weighty debates over political power and exercise of imperial authority in the Colonial Office in London. Nigeria, which imported 344 tons of gunpowder (one-fourth of all imports) for the direct consumption of its approximately eighteen million inhabitants in 1922, qualified to be called a gun society. Unlike a century earlier, when much of the gunpowder imported into what is now Nigeria went into the building and defense of empire and the capturing of slaves, the 381 tons of gunpowder Nigeria imported in 1937 were deployed productively, with significant economic and obvious daily cultural impact.[22] In the Nigerian context, these characteristics defined the gun society: (1) gun culture was firmly represented in popular artistic and dramatic production seen across the country, with strong implications for the acceptance of colonialism; (2) residents of urban centers and administrative capitals measured the passage of time with a time gun; and (3) while many communities in pre-twentieth-century Nigeria could survive without firearms, none could by the 1930s. Unlike in South Africa, where registration of arms in the nineteenth century was meant to disarm Africans, in Nigeria the registration of Dane guns was designed to generate income.[23] At a political and imperial level, a colonial society that was held together forcibly by the deployment of superior violence using highly lethal firearms also deserved the appellation of a gun society.

All guns were not made equal—so also the identity of their owners, their social status, and the perceived risk they posed to colonial peace. Possession of guns found expression in the diversity of the twentieth-century racial and social order among Africans and Europeans. The rise of the new class of educated Nigerians not only redefined precolonial notions of elitism; it also paved the way for new patterns of consumption tied to the privilege of being "enlightened" or "civilized." I use the terms *elites* and *educated* with caution, for they were not fixed social categories. A simplified pyramid of social class in colonial Nigeria—from the first-class paramount king or ruler to the laborer, and from a UK-trained lawyer to an elementary school diploma holder—can be seen in the politics of gun possession. In helping to complete the evolution of Nigeria into a gun society, the British, drawing from a late nineteenth-century international trade agreement restricting the importation of guns into the colony, made a stark demarcation between two categories of firearms—between, on the one hand, the flintlock guns, otherwise called Dane guns, and on the other hand, the "arms of precision," namely rifles, pistols, revolvers, shotguns, and cap guns. This typology of guns mirrored the relationship between the technology of firearms and the menace they posed to public peace and, more important, to the maintenance of colonial hegemony. It also dovetailed with the established colonial practices of ordering Africans in accordance by the perceived threat they posed to the status quo. Anyone could own a Dane gun and easily obtain a license, but only the "educated," popular traders and traditional rulers were allowed to bear arms of precision. Consequently, the possession of a Dane gun was treated as a "right," whereas possession of arms of precision was considered a "privilege" of social class. By 1948, the government would permanently remove the Dane gun from the list of firearms that required a license to use. This process was made possible by the realization of the extent of the systemic relationship between the society and firearms. It came with the acknowledgment of Nigeria's complete evolution as a gun society.

Consuming Guns

This book puts the overlapping literature on African commodity and economic history, and that on international trade, in the first half of the twentieth century into productive dialogue with each other. The pattern of ideas in these fields is discernible. While some authors seek to unveil the social history of commodities, others, such as those focused on exports, mining, and cash-crop agriculture, engage the contribution of Africa to local and world capitalism. Still, many rely on a dependency paradigm, examining how Africa was turned into a "dumping ground" for foreign items, many of which were produced with raw materials acquired through ruthless exploitation of the continent's natural and human resources.[24] Some scholars have gone further in treating Africa's complex global economic relations beyond dependency and exploitation. As Jeremy Prestholdt has noted, consumer goods "are uniquely able to help us perceive routes of interrelation."[25] Drawing from Marx's exposition of fetishism, Timothy Burke has noted that "commodities are able to assume independent life, that relations between things—and between people and things—accompany, conceal, or displace the actual state of relations between people."[26] Taken together, Prestholdt and Burke ask scholars to view commodities as transcending their own connection to trade or transaction and to consider how the social meaning of things (physical objects) shapes modern capitalism.[27]

This book stands at the crossroads of these perspectives on commodity, economic history, and international trade. While emphasizing that the story of firearms in the twentieth century, which scholars have heretofore largely ignored, will expand our knowledge of colonialism, the pages that follow prove that the narrative of global exploitation and dependency cannot effectively explain the dynamics of the firearms trade in twentieth-century colonial Nigeria.[28] Rather, the shifts in the colonial economy allowed for different types of firearms to respond to changing local needs within the global capitalist system. The impact of firearms liberalization was circuitous and cannot be reduced to a simple value judgment of exploitation or dependency. For, while the proliferation of Dane guns, made possible by the local blacksmiths' complete mastery of the flintlock technology, represented complete independence from foreign importation because local production matched domestic needs, Nigerians continued, throughout the colonial period, to import gunpowder, percussion caps, and shotguns, among other classes of firearms, from abroad.

It is easy to counter the notion that firearms are mainly instruments of human destruction by treating them as a commodity. Firearms and their impact were omnipresent in colonial Nigeria, for commodities and cultural evolution go hand in hand. Because Nigerians and Europeans made firearms of different types, they also created different institutions and situations to market their products. The story of firearms in colonial Nigeria is that of how cultural institutions created by humans adapt to the presence of goods they create or import, and how different genres of a particular good shape dominant cultural perceptions. The different uses to which people put firearms were a consequence of the diverse social power and social conceptions attached to guns.[29] For example, in several communities in southern Nigeria a gun that came from Europe and was clearly marked as an item of trade with a defined monetary value and maker was a ritual object, accorded a sacred and cosmological value. Gun salutes during funerals in some Nigerian cultures were meant to clear or rid diabolical spirits as the soul of the departed transcended to the world of the ancestors to begin the next phase in the unending cycle of human existence. Such unexpected subversion of foreign items is as important as the perceptions and symbolism of different types of guns, shaped by technology, innovation, globalization, and the forces of supply and demand.[30]

Firearms, like many items of trade in colonial Africa, reveal the intersection of the global and the local in the changing consumerist world. Commodities and ideas rarely respect spatial borders and national boundaries, for they have universal aspects and importance attached to them. They counter the assumption, as we have seen in Bassey's case, that human history is characterized by defined or discrete cultural and geographical space and historical peculiarity. The geo-locality of commodities obviously demonstrates that writing a history of an independent world of isolation is impossible.[31] But unlike many works on commodity exchange that overwhelmingly focus on industrial production, this book dwells on the location of consumption. I am more concerned about the utilization of firearms for one main reason—commodities do not have real impact until they arrive in places or spaces where they are domesticated. It is this aspect of domestication that is central to my narrative, for the politics of firearms control in colonial Nigeria largely bordered on the consequences of domestication.

Guns and Society in Colonial Nigeria is not just a trans-societal, social, cultural, political, and economic history of firearms in Africa's most populous country. Commodities do not have the power to speak, but the use to which they were put did affect humans in significant ways. A predominantly administrative and economic history of a commodity as seen in existing works reduces goods to mere "things," incapable of shaping the dynamics of social relations at the most micro level of a society.[32] It is possible to read massive works on the history of commodities without any information about the regular people who used them and how their encounter as consumers transformed their lives. While data about commodities (including monetary values, ship manifests, and voyages) remain important for understanding the dynamics of international trade, which also shaped major events in history, it is by putting a human face on them and the social processes they unleashed that a more nuanced history can be realized. What is more, the story of firearms in colonial Nigeria is a complex interplay of adaptation, innovation, and global dependency—three interrelated elements of firearms culture that reveal the creative ingenuity of Nigerians within the world capitalist system. And in no period in history did this become more obvious than during World War II. When the global catastrophe broke out, Nigerians had completely mastered the production of Dane guns and did not need foreign imports. However, they could not produce gunpowder in commercial quantities, which thereby allowed development of the market outside their immediate community to determine their relationship with an essential commodity. What is true about World War II is also true about the 1880s, the era of the so-called Scramble for Africa. The transformation of African-European relations during the second half of the nineteenth century went hand in hand with the manipulation of Africa's dependency on Western technology and global trade.

Colonialism integrated Africa into the world capitalist system to an unprecedented degree. Africans began consuming European-made products far more than in the centuries before the advent of colonialism. In the twentieth century, the pattern of consumption of textiles, cars, toys, movies, and electronics, among other imported consumer items, reflected prevailing social class distinctions among diverse groups of people. For many lower-, middle-, and upper-class educated colonial Nigerians, the ability to speak English and/or look dandy were not the only obvious attributes of being a modern person; another was the possession of guns. Statistics on gun ownership and the government firearms registry undoubtedly show how the possession of a shotgun rather than a Dane gun became a marker of class distinction, but this fact cannot be understood in isolation from the broader history of social change in Nigeria. It also indicates that disaggregating or classifying firearms on the basis of country of origin, type, brand name, effectiveness, and so forth, can render an unusual perspective to much bigger questions of power, access to economic resources, race, and the cultural and political institutions of colonial Nigeria. The ubiquity of advertisement of shotguns in Nigerian newspapers (one of the chief sites through which dominant notions of class differentiation were reinforced) between the 1910s and 1950s did not take place outside the consumption pattern of a section of the community. It was no accident how newspapers handled the matter of advertisements for guns—that is, why some guns were advertised in the newspapers while others were not.[33] To answer this question calls for engagement with the intersections of class, privilege, and social mobility.

One of the core themes of commodity history is how imports are integrated into specific cultural or ethnic environments—that is, how the social meanings that commodities acquire become stratified and how new conceptions of those commodities differ from or converge with the goals of manufacturers. Aside from hunting, the second most important use to which Dane guns were put in colonial Nigeria was the ceremonial salute, a practice that dictated the tempo of the political economy of gunpowder and the terms of the debate over regulation of Dane guns. The story of the sounds and noise produced with Dane guns during ceremonial shooting provides a window onto the cultural and symbolic utility of firearms, which sustained the Nigerian gun society. Gun noise itself was "consumed" or commoditized, thereby indicating a need to place African sound making in proper historical context, for the reaction of people to the boom of a gun depended on time, place, purpose, and circumstances. A gunshot announcing the birth of a new child was expected to produce a different kind of mood from one publicizing the death of an aged member of a community. Thus, noise that Africanist anthropologist and media scholar Brian Larkin defined as "interference produced by religious and cultural values, the historic configurations in which technologies and cultural forms are made manifest" (in the framework of loudspeaker and public religious sound) did not have any universal connotation.[34] A loudspeaker and a gun are two different objects. Still, they have similar characteristics in that both were European technologies, whose symbolic impact molded cultural and religious values in specific locales. The story of gun signals, communication, and noise is that of invention and reinvention of culture, which would have been impossible without global exchange. And the ability of people and communities to shape perceptions of noise went hand in hand with the transformation of the item that made it possible. Had the twentieth-century Dane gun and gunpowder trade followed the precolonial pattern, ceremonial shooting would not have become an established element of public life. It was the liberalization of firearms that made it possible for rural dwellers who were not professional hunters to buy Dane guns just to shoot during ceremonies.

Historical evolution and cultural evolution are inseparable. Africans have historically made noise or used sound objects as markers of important events, ritual feasts, ceremonies, and means of communication. Different kinds of drums and noisemaking instruments shaped salient notions of gender and power. The inroad of guns into African signal- and sound-making culture should therefore be seen as one element of cultural borrowing, domesticated to suit diverse local needs. The kind of conflict that existed between bell (religious) and drum (secular) sound in nineteenth-century France, as espoused by Alain Corbin, did not occur in Nigeria. Rather, Nigerians integrated gun noise and signals into the established repertoire of sound-making mechanisms in a complementary manner.[35] This process involved redirecting the auditory meaning of sounds produced by both new and preexisting objects by assigning secular and nonsecular connotations to them depending on context and period. Although the entry of gun sounds could have undermined the popularity of established objects, it did not totally drive them out of use.

The transformation of ceremonial shooting reflected the changing access to guns and their increasing use. During the era of the transatlantic slave trade, gunshots were fired to announce the arrival of ships. They also marked the changing phase of economic relations along the coast. Coastal European trading posts or factories did occasionally fire cannon, "to clear the political atmosphere"—that is, to reinforce their presence as a superior power in economic and political matters.[36] With time, African military aristocrats and leading political elites were honored with cannon fire. Before the twentieth century, ceremonial shooting took place only during important communal festivals. The centralization of shooting during this period fit the prevailing culture of monopolizing practices to enhance their exclusivity to the elites. The more uncommon a thing was, the more highly regarded it would be, the elites of the time probably thought. Moreover, only people close to the centers of power had regular access to guns and gunpowder. But the imposition of colonial rule not only transformed the identity of people who engaged in ceremonial shooting; it also expanded the avenues and situations in which it could take place. The reinvention of ceremonial shooting and its ubiquity in twentieth-century Nigeria meant that a cultural practice does not have to be exclusive for it to be revered. It could be popular and yet be highly valued at the same time. For a historian of colonial Africa, the transformation of gun noise clearly suggests that much of what is conceived as "customary" practice by both Europeans and Africans requires serious historicization. At what point does a practice with a foreign origin become "indigenous" or "customary"?

Colonialism and Violence

The discourse of the interrelatedness of firearms and human destruction is inescapable; colonialism was a violent enterprise. If the British Empire was created at the barrel of a gun, it was also held forcibly through the deployment of superior violence with the aid of highly lethal weapons. Africanist scholarship has invested quality energy in unveiling the dynamics of conflict between European colonizers and Africans during the first half of the twentieth century. Aside from studying specific events such as conflict over taxation, land, and political power, scholars have also engaged general trends across regions and colonial sites. Their findings have revealed the complex origins, course, and outcome of violent conflict. For one thing, much of what were labeled as "tax" riots, as J. A. Atanda, Obaro Ikime, and A. E. Afigbo have noted, were usually a product of the interplay of salient cultural, political, and economic effects of colonialism, which can best be understood by delving into the pre-European era.[37]

Surprisingly, scholarship on twentieth-century colonial Africa has paid limited attention to the role of firearms in riots, strikes, and insurgencies that exposed colonialism as an atrocious edifice. It is not enough simply to mention, as scholars often have, the obvious fact that hundreds or thousands of people died in Britain's attempts to forcibly maintain its colonies as sites of ruthless capitalist expropriation. What is more important is a critical analysis of the history and politics of access to firearms, and effective engagement with the multifold deployment of arms in the maintenance of colonial hegemony. Imperial atrocities committed during the Women's War of 1929, the General Strike of 1945, and the Enugu colliery shooting of 1949, among other sad encounters, make the discourse of firearms in colonial domination a weighty subject. The dearth of scholarship on the intersection of firearms and colonial violence is so pronounced that one can read books on the Nigeria Police Force (NPF), the Royal West African Frontier Force, and violence in colonial Nigeria by Sam Ukpabi, Tekena Tamuno, C. N. Ubah, David Killingray, and Toyin Falola, among other scholars, without finding there any critical discussion of firearms.[38] Kemi Rotimi cannot be blamed for skipping the discourse of firearms in his brilliant study of the

Native Authority Police Force, because this law enforcement body was not, unlike the NPF, allowed to use guns, for reasons I discuss in chapter 2.[39] I could not agree more with Rotimi that "colonialism was not a consensual one and that whatever legitimacy the colonial authorities possessed derived not from any set of agreed rules but from the monopoly of the means of violence."[40] Philip Tahire has attempted to make a distinction between the "militaristic" and "civil" role of the NPF.[41] This distinction is unnecessary, and it also clouds the fundamental role of the colonial police as a violent tool of imperialism. There is nothing "civil" about an institution that deployed deadly force in executing the agenda of foreign occupation. Yet one might expect a book that engages the "militaristic" role of the NPF to recognize the role of firearms.

Firearms not only caused a unique type of havoc; they tilted the equation of violence and reconfigured how people positioned and imagined their psychological oppression and powerlessness under the hegemonic colonial state. Some writers, including Frantz Fanon in *Black Skin, White Masks*, have argued that the European "civilizing" mission, as manifested in the imposition of foreign social, medical, and educational institutions, among other means of domination, helped preserve foreign colonialism in a profound manner. And those same scholars claim that an emphasis on superior firearms tends to give an undue advantage to technology in the upholding of imperialism.[42] It is impossible to deny the impact of the European "civilizing" mission in enhancing imperialism—indeed, in the case of Nigeria the British allowed the educated elites to own shotguns in the belief that these "civilized" Africans would not want to violently bring down an institution that was responsible for or that enhanced their privileged status. In addition, it is difficult for a people who had been made to think they were inferior to Europeans in terms of intelligence to want to fight a foreign domination they thought was helping them move up the ladder of civilization.[43] What is more, European political institutions (whether direct rule as seen in the French colonies or indirect rule as in the British) divided Africans across ethnicities and regions, preventing them from forging a common front against imperialism. And the ethnic groups and power structures that imperialism favored generally opposed any subversion of the status quo. As Mahmud Mamdani has noted, indirect rule, which he also refers to as "decentralized despotism," succeeded in British Africa "by tapping authoritarian possibilities in culture, and by giving culture an authoritarian bent."[44]

But we can begin to see the overwhelming importance of superior firearms in colonialism when we turn to the dynamics of armed conflict against the British. It was the technological superiority of European firearms that ordered social and political relations in favor of the colonialists. Hence, technology and society in colonial Africa must be viewed together. Nigerians grudgingly and openly accepted the "civilizing" mission and its foreign practices and institutions of domination because they feared they could lose their lives—pay the ultimate price—to British guns. A close look at the ferocity of colonial armed violence reveals that when Nigerians challenged imperialism with their Dane guns, they were convinced that all other benefits of colonial implantation and British civilization were less important than self-determination. The arguments against the overwhelming importance of superior firearms in imperialism is difficult to sustain in the face of the massive evidence available that points away from them.

Colonial gun violence must be rigorously contextualized not only from the perspective of the individuals and groups involved but also from the angles of time, place, and circumstance. To achieve this goal, I turn to the size and the training of the colonial security force. I provide a basic look at the efficacy of the Lee-Enfield rifle, the standard rifle used across the British Empire, and relate it to the state of local firearms technology and the extinction of war-making culture in the twentieth century. The most important success of colonial firearms regulation was the ability to ensure that Nigerians did not have access to war ammunition used against them by the British. I have reread the annual reports of the NPF for critical information about the mode of operation of the security apparatus of the state, which previous scholars have overlooked, and I also have reexamined the language of "right" and "privilege" of colonial subjects in debates about gun violence in the British Parliament in order to shed light on the changing meaning of colonial legitimacy between 1900 and the 1950s. The failures of the anticolonial resistance in twentieth-century Nigeria, as elsewhere in Africa, are legion, but it was the military superiority of the colonialists that proved the most important factor. In writing firearms into colonial Nigerian history, not only do I connect a number of uncharted threads about guns and violence; I also revisit some known aspects of Nigerian history to provide an alternative perspective about the real issues at stake. For example, I argue that the importance of the Enugu colliery shooting of November 1949 went beyond the conventional narratives of labor agitation, exploitation, masculinity, and workplace habit and decolonization as seen in the works of Carolyn Brown and others; it also ushered in new perceptions about guns and colonial security.[45]

It is easy to understand why colonialism was successful if one considers both that the most widely available guns (the Dane guns) were the least sophisticated firearms and that the colonial government alone had unlimited access to the most sophisticated guns (i.e., machine guns). Gunpowder, the most common and the most widely used explosive, was equally the least lethal explosive used in armed conflict. Few people directly connected with the main infrastructure of colonial political power had access to dynamite, for example, among other classes of highly dangerous explosives. Thus, liberalization of gun use came with a strong dose of unequal power distribution. And the main worry of the colonial government was not that the accumulation of Dane guns and shotguns could end British rule in Nigeria—even though colonial officers realized that occasional armed confrontation was inspired by the proliferation of guns. Rather, it was the refusal of Nigerians to pay gun license fees, like other levies and taxes, used for running the colonial state and the negative impact that violent repression of armed insurgency would have on the local and international image of the British Empire. Furthermore, nonpayment of levies meant that government could not say, in concrete terms, how many guns were in circulation—a situation that embarrassed an establishment whose policies were usually driven by numbers. Nor did the antipathy toward gun use among some colonial officers who thought that Nigerians, due to their racial inferiority, could never be responsible users of firearms ever lead to deliberalization of Dane guns during the colonial period.

The dominant trend in the discourse of colonial violence is clearly armed conflict between the government and colonial subjects. When it comes to armed conflict among Africans, one thing is certain: European colonialism did not put an end to intraethnic conflict, which was virulent in the pre-twentieth-century world. It only ensured that the ferocity of such conflict did not undermine the cardinal mission of imperialism—exploitation. My book takes on how firearms shaped conflict among Nigerians and the dispositions of both the colonial government and the Nigerian nationalists. Although the Dane gun was ineffective in prosecuting collective action by Nigerians against the British, it did prove effective in intra-Nigerian violence. Gun violence in intraethnic conflict, decolonization politics, and everyday life reveal the extent of the weaponization of Nigeria and the negative consequences of a colonial gun society. Moreover, ahistorical conclusions such as that armed robbery and gun violence in party politics are a postcolonial problem of underdevelopment have endured because of limited research on firearms. These negative consequences of gun culture date back to decades of colonial and precolonial history. The obvious adverse impact of guns is explicable in terms of a much broader discussion of negative outcomes of irresponsible technology use.

Sources and Chapter Breakdown

The lack of scholarly work on firearms in colonial Nigeria should not be taken to mean that archival materials do not exist on the subject. In the repositories of the three main archives in Nigeria, located at Ibadan, Enugu, and Kaduna, are massive volumes of untapped documents, some of which I have used in writing this book. Researchers on firearms can readily access district and provincial records. The pattern of documentation is clear. One category, which I labeled "thematic" files, focuses on correspondence among colonial officers across locations on issues related to new or proposed gun regulations and policy actions. The second group, "application to bear arms," together with the firearms registry, contains countless files of biographical information about gun owners, their guns, what they used them for, and their understanding of the notions of rights and privileges pertaining to the bearing of arms. Published and unpublished primary documents, including colonial laws, statutes, and court cases, are available in research libraries across the world; Africanist scholars including Kristin Mann and Richard L. Roberts have established these as significant tools for mapping social change in Africa.[46] In addition, practically every major colonial anthropological survey has useful information about gun culture. Their often prejudiced perspective on African culture does not override their importance in understanding Nigerian culture and customs under colonial rule.[47] As chapter 4 demonstrates, the records of the Nigerian Rifle Association, a Europeans-only gun club, as well as memoirs and travel and nature writings of colonial administrators, are a dense trove of materials on race, firearms, and imperial hunting—a critical domain where the notion of European racial superiority also was manifest.[48]

Additional Nigerian voices on firearms are clearly audible in the colonial newspapers published predominantly by Nigerians. The newspapers—

namely, the *Nigerian Pioneer, Daily Service, West African Pilot, Southern Nigeria Defender,* and *Eastern Nigeria Guardian,* among others—carried stories, news, correspondence, and comprehensive editorials regularly about different aspects of colonial gun society. These sources range from detailed transcripts of court cases and coroner's inquests of major gun accidents to criminal exploits of gun-bearing thieves to the reaction of Nigerians to indiscriminate shootings during episodes of popular unrest. Some blacksmiths and hunters, among other gun users of the colonial period, are still alive to tell their stories. Through them, a historian can piece together interesting information about the social symbolism of guns and the shifting domains in which that symbolism was reinforced. Their stories animate an inanimate object, weaving a spectrum of ideas rooted in intimate encounters with guns, aesthetics, masculinity, spirituality, and material culture into the much larger issue of gun liberalization. Together, this broad array of sources—carefully sifted, interpreted, and supplemented to highlight the multiple and contrasting voices across race and social class—provides a fascinating glimpse into a colonial gun society that did not exist before the twentieth century.

The seven chapters in this book are chronologically and thematically structured. Chapter 1 sets the tone and historical stage, offering the precolonial background to the history of firearms in Nigeria in the twentieth century. I engage the introduction of firearms to what is now Nigeria from the fifteenth century in the context of global trade and networks of cultural exchange. Many of the narratives included in this chapter focus on the role that guns played in military expansion and the heinous trade in enslaved humans. By also engaging the social history of firearms from the perspective of ceremonial shooting, religion and spirituality, and the changing notions of masculinity, this chapter advances the argument that twentieth-century colonialism helped consolidate the gun society that was already evolving.

Chapter 2 paints a portrait of a Nigerian gun society, focusing on how colonialism transformed Nigerians' encounter with firearms. During the first half of the twentieth century, the Nigerian gun society emerged through the liberalization of firearms controls. In accordance with their social class, Nigerians could possess different classes of nonprohibited firearms, which thus shaped the government's perception of dangers to peace and order. This ordering of Nigerians fit the established practice of creating differences in order to intensify divisions across social class, region, religion, and ethnicity. A chief point of focus of this chapter is the interrelatedness of guns, consumer culture, and social change. The role of guns in the society became systemic in that firearms were used for numerous economic, social, and political purposes in a manner unprecedented in the country's history. Not only did ceremonial shooting and gun salutes become established elements of public spectacle, but hunting reached its peak of popularity with the availability of firearms. This chapter also emphasizes how noise consumption or commodification became a core element of everyday life across locations, time, and situations. A brief foray into the struggles between humans and animals also calls for further serious scholarly attention to the environment and wildlife history of Nigeria.

The political economy of gunpowder and other explosives is the main theme of chapter 3. I attempt to situate the international trade in gunpowder as a significant aspect of colonial Nigerian economic and commodity history. I discuss the policies and politics of the gunpowder trade as a process of maintaining a difficult balance between the economic gains of such trade and public security. The gunpowder imported into Nigeria between the 1920s and 1960 did not go into building an empire and fighting wars. It was deployed primarily for hunting and ceremonial shooting. This chapter also considers the impact of World War II on the broader character of the Nigerian gun society. During history's deadliest war, the fecundity of gunpowder not only became more obvious than ever; it also drove a number of emergency defense and economic policies.

Chapter 4 examines the subject of race and gun ownership. My argument in this chapter is that European gun culture in Nigeria did help in consolidating the Nigerian gun society. Not only were Europeans involved in a different form of ceremonial shooting as part of imperial spectacle that supported the indigenous form, but also the goals and outcomes of game hunting were different and yet sometimes overlapped those of Nigerians. In establishing the difference between "indigenous" and "imperial" hunting from the perspective of mission, methods, and impact, I conclude that European gun use represented the symbolic domination of the human and natural world. Imperial shooting went beyond killing animals for trophy, sport, or meat. It also included rifle shooting, a Europeans-only activity that reinforced the idea of racial superiority. But beyond this, rifle shooting epitomized Europeans' presumed superior masculinity based on the assumption that Africans, given their lack of intelligence, could not be trusted with the most advanced, non-prohibited firearms. The debate over making rifle shooting a "state leisure" (like polo and horse racing) indicates that such a homogenizing category as "Europeans" needs to be disturbed to emphasize divergent social attitudes and dissimilar understandings of what constitutes safe and profitable leisure.

Chapter 5 unearths the relationship between guns and public disorder. It examines the mode of operation of the Nigeria Police Force, the efficacy of the arms it used, and its main philosophy, contrasted with the level of indigenous military culture, in order to explicate the failure of armed resistance to imperial rule. What made colonialism successful was access to superior technology of war on the part of the colonialists. This chapter engages the technology of violence used by the colonial government and by Nigerians from the perspective of efficiency and outcome, and demonstrates that colonialism survived because of the success of the British in controlling the proliferation of weapons of war such as machine guns. Major events such as the Enugu colliery shooting of 1949 and the Kano riot of 1953 tested the fundamental principles on which colonial gun society was based. I argue that the most important factor at stake in the Enugu incident was not labor agitation and reforms as scholars have affirmed; rather, it was colonial anxiety informed by the miners' access to explosives. The twenty-one miners who were gunned down in cold blood by police riflemen would not have died had security reports not indicated that terrorists intended to use mining explosives to undermine the public peace in their quest to radicalize the anticolonial movement and terminate British rule by force of arms. The nine hundred policemen mobilized to the mines were not there to quell the strike, which was peaceful.[49] Instead, they were dispatched to remove explosives that the colonial intelligence service claimed would be used by enemies of the state to bring colonialism to a halt. But colonial violence went beyond the confrontation between Nigerians and the British; it extended to relations among Nigerians. This chapter attempts to answer the question, what role did guns play in inter- and intraethnic conflict and the politics of decolonization? Answering this question involves reviewing the activities of leading political parties and how guns became a dominant symbol of political power among Nigerian leaders who blamed the British for the indiscriminate killing of fellow Nigerians.

Chapter 6 shifts focus from big issues of guns and colonial order to the grassroots and everyday misuse of guns. Gun accidents seemed inevitable—like any technology, a gun is capable of being misused. The frenzied atmosphere that accompanied ceremonial shooting and the frequent overloading of guns in an attempt to produce the loudest noise possible were two common causes of accidents. Guns require mastery and safety precautions. Yet the liberalization of gun use was not matched by proper use. Many nonprofessional hunters could be seen using guns for hunting and ceremonial shooting in contravention of indigenous practices that prepared people for the safe use of firearms. But gun accidents during hunting, among other situations, involved more than irresponsibility or the refusal to take precautions. To Nigerians, they were caused by a breakdown of the harmonious spiritual relationship between humans and the supernatural. Moreover, the criminal use of guns for robbery went hand in hand with Nigeria's firm integration into the world capitalist system. The motivations for armed robbery varied. But unemployment, the proliferation of foreign items (which could easily be fenced), and the intensification of the cash economy were among the reasons for the spate of crimes across the country. Robbery became more virulent with the use of guns, which offered advantages to someone holding one. Gun noise, which Nigerians used for ceremonies, was also deployed by thieves to instill psychological fear. The problem of armed robbery—which exposed the limitations of the colonial policing system—disturbed the very core philosophy of colonial rule. The mobilization of hunter guards to police communities, which began in the 1930s, contravened the established government policy that Nigerians should never be allowed to "police" their own communities with guns. But the realities of the time made community policing and vigilantism by hunters indispensable, and the malpractices of the guards, including extrajudicial killings and extortion, created an ambivalent situation that validated the fears of government officials.

The final chapter documents the politics of firearms regulation, or gun control. It builds on the previous chapters by emphasizing that the liberalization of gun use did not mean a total lack of control. Rather, firearms regulations and laws were regularly revised to suit the British understanding of the relationship between guns and violence, and the identity of the people or groups involved. The regional variation in the debate over Dane guns versus arms of precision mirrored the core philosophies that shaped the liberalization of arms across social class, as I discuss in chapter 2. The most important debate about Dane guns was over the need to ensure registration. Lack of registration and nonpayment of licenses defeated the purpose of liberalizing the most popular firearms. By 1948, the British finally gave up on registration of Dane guns—Nigerian could then possess them without a license. But the political volatility in the country following the Enugu colliery shooting focused government attention on arms of precision. A barrage of regulations from the 1950s tightened the possession of arms of precision that featured prominently in partisan political violence. The assumption that holders of shotguns would not use them against the government collapsed in the wake of the alleged radicalization of the labor force. By the mid-1950s, the regime of postcolonial Nigerian gun regulation began to unfold.

The epilogue connects the colonial period with the contemporary and postcolonial era. This bridging of historical timelines further emphasizes the relevance of the past to the present context. My main concern here is with examining how the postcolonial state lost complete control over the regulation of firearms. I compare and contrast the colonial and postcolonial politics of gun control from within the framework of the challenges of nation building. I argue that the proliferation of prohibited arms in postcolonial Nigeria is both the cause and the consequence of failed political leadership, manifested in crisis after crisis, ranging from the Civil War (1967–70) to ethno-religious conflict, terrorist activities, and separatist movements, to name a few. Hopes that Nigeria would emerge as a peaceful country, through the independent state's legal monopoly of violence, were disappointed. Rather, the experience of corruption at all levels, porous national borders, and crises of underdevelopment such as poverty and unemployment shaped the ways Nigerians used firearms to pursue agendas that undermined peace.

Notes

1. "Commissioner of Police vs Edet Okpo Mfon and Okon Okpo Ene," Supreme Court of Nigeria, Police Magistrate's Court, Calabar, July 18, 1924, CO 583/159/8, National Archives of the United Kingdom (hereafter cited as NAUK).

2. "Commissioner of Police Calabar-Ogoja Province to the Inspector-General of Police Lagos," March 29, 1928, CO 583/159/8, NAUK.

3. "Commissioner of Police of Calabar-Ogoja Province to the Inspector-General of Police: Rex Versus Mfon and Ene," March 29, 1928, CO 583/159/8, NAUK.

4. "Commissioner of Police Calabar-Ogoja Province to the Inspector-General of Police Lagos," March 29, 1928, CO 583/159/8, NAUK.

5. "Commissioner of Police of Calabar-Ogoja Province to the Inspector-General of Police: Rex Versus Mfon and Ene," March 29, 1928, CO 583/159/8, NAUK.

6. "Alleged Exam Forgeries," *Daily Mail*, October 21, 1930; "Act of 'Public' Mischief: Law Student with Forged Degree," *Daily Mail*, January 21, 1931.

7. "Ekpenyon Ita Hogan Bassey to the Chief Secretary, Lagos," July 21, 1925; "Bassey's Letter," June 26, 1924; Chief Secretary to the Government to E. I. H. Bassey, October 22, 1925, CO 583/159/8, NAUK.

8. "Commissioner of Police Calabar to the Inspector-General of Police Lagos," May 29, 1928, CO 583/159/8, NAUK.

9. Marks and Atmore, "Firearms in Southern Africa," 517–30; Macola, *Gun in Central Africa*.

10. Kopytoff, "Cultural Biography of Things," 68. Ross, Hinfelaar, and Pesa, *Objects of Life in Central Africa*.

11. For the evolution of Nigeria, see Tamuno, *Evolution of the Nigerian State*.

12. Kopytoff, "Cultural Biography of Things," 67.

13. Ikime, *Fall of Nigeria*; Ohadike, *Ekumeku Movement*; Dusgate, *Conquest of Northern Nigeria*; Afigbo, "Patterns of the Igbo Resistance."

14. See the following for the divergent roles that firearms played in precolonial African history: White, "Firearms in Africa"; Kea, "Firearms and Warfare"; Fisher and Rowland, "Firearms in the Central Sudan"; Echenberg, "Late Nineteenth-Century Military Technology"; Marks and Atmore, "Firearms in Southern Africa"; Gray, "Portuguese Musketeers on the Zambezi"; Atmore and Sanders, "Sotho Arms and Ammunition"; Atmore, Chirenje, and Mudenge, "Firearms in South Central Africa"; Guy, "Firearms in the Zulu Kingdom"; Miers, "Arms Trade and Government Policy"; and Richards, "Import of Firearms."

15. Storey, *Guns, Race, and Power*; Smith, *Warfare and Diplomacy*; Ajayi and Smith, *Yoruba Warfare*; Smaldone, *Warfare in the Sokoto Caliphate*; Macola, *Gun in Central Africa*; Inikori, "Import of Firearms," 339–86; Metcalf, "Why Africans Sold Slaves"; Alpern, "What Africans Got"; Caulk, "Firearms and Princely Power"; Berg, "Sacred Musket"; Law, "Horses, Firearms and Political Power"; Goody, *Technology, Tradition, and the State*.

16. Smaldone, *Warfare in the Sokoto Caliphate*; Storey, *Guns, Race, and Power*; Macola, *Gun in Central Africa*; Mavhunga, *Transient Workplaces*.

17. Macola, in *Gun in Central Africa*, dedicates just two chapters to early twentieth century gun politics. His book essentially covers the nineteenth century.

18. One of the few works on firearms in twentieth-century Africa is Dia Mwembu, "Role of Firearms in the Songye Region," 41–64.

19. Marks and Atmore, "Firearms in Southern Africa," 517–30; Macola, *Gun in Central Africa*.

20. Apter, "On Imperial Spectacle."

21. Storey, *Guns, Race, and Power*, 10.

22. *Blue Book*, "Quantity of Gunpowder Imported into Nigeria" (Lagos: Government Printer, 1939), T10.

23. Ibid.

24. The list of works in this category is not exhaustive. In addition to other works on economic and international trade in this introduction and in Chapters 1 and 3, see, among others, Inikori, *Africans and the Industrial Revolution*; Brown, "We Were All Slaves"; Freund,

Capital and Labour; Dewey and Hopkins, *Imperial Impact*; Olukoju, "United Kingdom and Political Economy"; Olukoju, "Rotgut and Revenue"; Olukoju, "Prohibition and Paternalism"; Adesina, "Modern Agriculture in Nigeria"; Heap, "Bottle of Gin"; Falola, "Salt Is Gold"; Falola, "Cassava Starch for Export"; Njoku, "Export Production Drive"; Byfield, "Feeding the Troops"; Chuku, "Crack Kernels, Crack Hitler"; Johnson, "Female Leadership"; Preteceille and Terrail, *Capitalism, Consumption and Needs*; Taussig, *Devil and Commodity Fetishism*; Thomas, *Entangled Objects*; Comaroff and Comaroff, "Goodly Beasts, Beastly Goods"; Falola and Adebayo, *Culture, Politics, and Money*; Akyeampong, *Drink, Power, and Cultural Change*; van den Bersselaar, *King of Drinks*; Richardson, "West African Consumption Patterns"; Rodney, *How Europe Underdeveloped Africa*; Hopkins, *Economic History of West Africa*; and Ross, Hinfelaar, and Pesa, *Objects of Life in Central Africa*.

25. Prestholdt, *Domesticating the World*, 4.
26. Burke, *Lifebuoy Men, Lux Women*, 5.
27. Ibid.; Prestholdt, *Domesticating the World*; McCracken, *Culture and Consumption*.
28. Hutchinson, *Nuer Dilemmas*, 103–57.
29. Hahn and Weiss, *Mobility, Meaning*; Hahn, *Consumption in Africa*; and Appadurai, *Social Life of Things*.
30. McCracken, *Culture and Consumption*.
31. Prestholdt, *Domesticating the World*, 1–2.
32. Appadurai, *Social Life of Things*.
33. For more on consumer goods and advertisement, see, among others, Jhally, *Codes of Advertising*; and Richards, *Commodity Culture of Victorian England*.
34. Larkin, *Signal and Noise*, 10.
35. Corbin, *Village Bells*.
36. Talbot, *Life in Southern Nigeria*, 293–94.
37. Ikime, *In Search of Nigerians*; Afigbo, *Warrant Chiefs*; Atanda, "Iseyin-Okeiho Rising of 1916."
38. Falola, *Colonialism and Violence in Nigeria*; Tamuno, *Police in Modern Nigeria*, 101–2; Tamuno, *Peace and Violence in Nigeria*; Ubah, *Colonial Army and Society in Northern Nigeria*; Killingray, "Maintenance of Law and Order"; Ukpabi, *Origin of the Nigerian Army*; and Thomas, *Violence and Colonial Order*. Important works on police and the army in southern and eastern Africa include Stapleton, *African Police and Soldiers*; and Parsons, *African Rank-and-File*.
39. Rotimi, *Police in a Federal State*.
40. Ibid., 131.
41. Ahire, *Imperial Policing*.
42. Fanon, *Black Skin, White Masks*.
43. Barnes, *Making Headway*; Gilman, *Difference and Pathology*; Vaughan, *Curing Their Ills*.
44. Mamdani, *Citizen and Subject*, jacket.
45. Brown, *"We Were All Slaves"*; Sklar, *Nigerian Political Parties*; Olusanya, "Zikist Movement"; Iweriebor, *Radical Politics in Nigeria*; Akpala, "Enugu Colliery Shooting"; Olorunfemi and Adesina, "Labour Unions"; Tijani, *Britain, Leftist Nationalists*; Adebiyi, "Radical Nationalism."

46. Mann and Roberts, *Law in Colonial Africa*. The full reference of all published primary documents can be found in the bibliography.

47. Temple, *Tribes, Provinces, Emirates and States*; Talbot, *Woman's Mysteries*; Basden, *Niger Ibos*; Talbot, *Life in Southern Nigeria*; Talbot, *Shadow of the Bush*; Meek, *Law and Authority*; Leonard, *Lower Niger and Its Tribes*; Talbot, *Peoples of Southern Nigeria*.

48. See chapter 4 for references to works in this category.

49. *Report of the Commission of Enquiry*, 35.

1

"THIS DESTRUCTIVE IMPLEMENT OF EUROPEAN INGENUITY"

Firearms, the Atlantic World, and Technology Transfer in Precolonial Nigeria

INTRODUCTION

This chapter lays the foundation of twentieth-century colonial Nigerian gun society. It engages the introduction of firearms to what is now Nigeria during the precolonial period, drawing on secondary literature on African economic, military, and political history. I supplement these sources with published primary documents such as the journals of European travelers and explorers like John Barbot, Richard Lander, Hugh Clapperton, and Henry Barth, the latter of whom described firearms as "this Destructive Implement of European Ingenuity" in his narrative of the impact of guns on slave raiding in Bornu, among other parts of West and North Africa, in the mid-nineteenth century.[1] The first firearms arrived in "Nigeria" as one of the numerous items of trade between Europeans and Arabs as well as Africans along both the Atlantic coast and across the Sahara. Africans, especially members of the ruling oligarchy, sought firearms not only because they proved effective in prosecuting conflict but also because they were an exotic good, possession of which accorded respect. A portion of this chapter dwells on the firearms trade during the era of the Atlantic slave trade. It reviews the arguments about the relationship between firearms and political stability espoused by scholars and notes that the advent of firearms in Africa was a component of a much larger history of technology transfer and innovation, even what we might now call globalization, in the Atlantic world. Nigerians not only adopted this European technology; they began to domesticate and incorporate it into their religious, cultural, and social experience. Thus, the social history of firearms in precolonial Nigeria presented in this chapter serves as a corrective to the conventional narrative that treats guns narrowly as mere instruments of violence.

Political, Economic, and Military History of Firearms in Precolonial Nigeria

The Portuguese are believed to have brought the first firearms to the West African coast during their explorations in the fifteenth century. By the sixteenth century, the Benin kingdom, early writers reported, tried to acquire the foreign weapons for military expansion, probably because they offered significant advantages over bows and arrows as assault and defense weapons. The earliest muskets could probably fire up to two hundred yards, three times the range of a bow and arrow. Muskets were inaccurate probably beyond fifty yards. The exoticism, noise, and potential psychological effect of the weapons offered a military advantage over enemies, especially those who lacked them.[2] Before the end of the nineteenth century, when breech-loading rifles with cartridges were introduced to Africa, the following three classes of smooth-bore muzzle loaders found their way to the continent from Europe: the matchlock, the earliest type (probably the ones represented in the Benin bronze statutory); the wheel lock, which was produced in small quantities; and the flintlock, the most popular firearm imported from the 1630s to the first half of the twentieth century.[3] Africa was thus part of the network of technology transfer in the Atlantic world. Indeed, its military needs shaped the course of firearms technology between the sixteenth and nineteenth centuries.

Writers do not agree on the extent of trade in firearms between the Portuguese and the Benin kingdom, or on the role that guns played in the latter's military success. Contemporary observers noted that the Portuguese forbade the selling of firearms to non-Christians, which included the people of the Benin kingdom. Moreover, many of the guns the Portuguese used during this period came from other parts of Europe—hence they did not themselves produce enough firearms to expend in foreign trade.[4] Writing in the late seventeenth century, Barbot stated that "the Blacks of Benin" were "no great lovers of firearms, and consequently not well skilled in the use of them." His other observation that the people occasionally killed wild boars with their javelins, and dared not try to kill lions and tigers, which were in abundance, suggests that firearms played no role in hunting.[5] Drawing on other sources produced during the sixteenth and the seventeenth centuries, R. A. Kea has argued that the "role of guns in sixteenth-century Benin military history has been overestimated." He contends that the Benin "troops did not possess the new weapon" and that their military success during this period "owed nothing to the use of firearms."[6]

However, other evidence suggests the opposite. Benin historians, including Jacob Egharevba, affirm that firearms began to play a significant role in the empire's military expansion during the reign of Oba Esigie (ca. 1504–55).[7] When the people of Benin employed some Portuguese harquebusiers in their expeditions and seized some cannon on a Portuguese ship in 1514, it was because they believed in the efficacy of firearms. They may have learned to use firearms while working with their foreign machineries. The French ships that traded with Benin in 1533 and in the 1690s, according to Alan Ryder, were "selling guns to Benin in the normal course of trade."[8] Written evidence clearly indicates that by the 1720s, the Portuguese were selling firearms to the oba (king) and that notable Benin chiefs had enough ammunition to wage constant skirmishes against their Itsekiri neighbors. After a temporary trade dispute over the Dutch request for a monopoly of trade in Benin, the Europeans resumed trade relations in 1717. They supplied the local chiefs with twenty-four guns and six hundred pounds of gunpowder. Two years earlier, the Dutch ship *Commany* arrived at the Benin River with six hundred pounds of gunpowder, among an assortment of other goods to exchange for gums, redwoods, and other local products.[9] During the same decade, the Dutch director-general presented a Benin chief with a flintlock gun of which he (the chief) was said to be "very fond."[10] By this period Europeans' firearms trade in the Benin River area had become a significant factor in the coastal economy, shaping the contours of domestic and international relations.

It is safe to say that the role of firearms in Benin's military history evolved: like most Africans encountering guns for the first time, the people struggled with the new technology, only to become highly skilled with it over time. During the late sixteenth century and much of the seventeenth, they probably did not have as much access to firearms as they wanted, but their possession of lethal weapons increased (and kept fluctuating) as trade relations between West Africa and Europe intensified. In addition, the technological transformation of firearms must have shaped attitudes toward their use, as well as toward their effects and outcomes, at different stages of the evolution and consolidation of military culture. Hence, learning and unlearning different types of firearms imported to Benin, as elsewhere in West Africa, must have produced divergent and shifting outcome from one century to another. Barbot's observation that the Benin people would not kill a lion or tiger with a firearm was probably true in the context of the hunting culture of the period. The earliest firearms were single-shot guns, which required frequent reloading and could pose greater danger to a user who missed his target. Benin hunters probably preferred arrows to hunt wild animals because they offered the opportunity of firing multiple shots more quickly than a flintlock gun. Moreover, as chapter 2 demonstrates, firearms did not play a significant role in hunting until the first half of the twentieth century in Nigeria. Rather, up to the end of the nineteenth century, they were monopolized by the military aristocrats and warriors, and deployed predominantly for warfare.[11]

Even so, the advent of firearms in West Africa initiated a phase of long sociocultural and economic relations, and technological exchange, in the Atlantic world. By the seventeenth century, Danes, English, Brandenburgers, and Dutch were selling muskets to West Africans. With time, the Dutch sales would overtake those of other Europeans. Although the Danes gave their name to the flintlock musket, which after the mid-eighteenth century was West Africa's principal weapon, most of the so-called Dane guns in fact came from Holland. Although firearms did not overtake cloth in the list of items imported from Europe, the gun did remain a significant item of international trade from the seventeenth through the nineteenth centuries. Guns represented probably one-fifth of the value of cargo shipped from England to West Africa in the eighteenth century.

Historians will never know the exact number of firearms exported to West Africa; varying estimates have been given, however. West Africa received an average of 283,000 to 394,000 guns from English suppliers and manufacturers on an annual basis in the second half of the eighteenth century up to 1807.[12] Between 1750 and 1807, yearly importation of gunpowder from Britain to West Africa varied from as low as 148,216 pounds (in 1778) to as high as 2,056,350 pounds (in 1790).[13] In all, the subcontinent received about fifty million pounds of gunpowder during the period.[14] Joseph

Inikori, relying on the records of gunmaker and British government's legislation, has revealed that guns and gunpowder were important commodities in eighteenth-century trade between Britain and West Africa.[15] "These dangerous commodities," Inikori states, "formed the backbone" of British trade with West Africa during the period. Indeed, firearms were valuable goods—a pound sterling's worth of guns had a greater purchasing power than other commodities of exchange. So valuable were guns in the West African trade that British gunmakers were constantly under pressure to produce more guns for the region. To maximize their profits, gun manufacturers shipped poorly made and finished guns to the coast of West Africa (the so-called slave guns). Indeed, the growth of Birmingham's arms industry was closely linked to the rise of guns, among other items produced in Britain for the West African trade.[16] With time, specific types of muskets acquired the names of the parts of Africa to which they were mostly shipped. In this category were the Bonny musket and Calabar gun of the second half of the eighteenth century.[17]

The most controversial topic of debate concerning the advent of guns into West Africa is not how many firearms were imported into the region from Europe; rather, it is over the role that firearms played in the heinous trade in humans.[18] Did the importation of firearms intensify slave raiding in West Africa? Historians have demonstrated that the firearms imported into Africa were used for nonmilitary purposes such as self-defense against wild animals, hunting, and ceremonial salutes, as well as status symbols.[19] However, with particular reference to Nigeria, the use of firearms for nonmilitary purposes such as ceremonial shooting did not become entrenched until the colonial period. In Senegambia, Philip Curtin did not find any correlation between firearms and slave gathering in the sixteenth and seventeenth centuries. The military culture of the area depended more on spears, javelins, and bows and arrows than on firearms.[20] Yet strong evidence, including the record of commercial transactions of a select British vessel, supports the "slave-gun cycle theory" that contends that firearm importation promoted wars and civil unrest to carry out slave gathering.[21] A vessel belonging to James Rogers and Co. of Bristol, which traded in Bonny between 1791 and 1792, exchanged a total of 1,906 guns, among other assorted goods with 334 slaves. Another vessel belonging to the same company that traded in Old Cameroons and Calabar between 1789 and 1790 exchanged 259 slaves (valued at 26,835 copper bars) for 684 guns, among other goods.[22] Regional variation in the quantity of slaves exchanged for guns and gunpowder should be expected. For one thing, the supply and demand for slaves and firearms were never static; rather, they continued to shift in accordance with the transformation of the core political and economic structures of various African locations and of international forces. By the end of the nineteenth century, the pressure to end the infamous trade probably reduced the quantity of firearms exchanged for slaves. For instance, the Aro in 1884 were exchanging four slaves for one musket, and one hundred slaves for one barrel of gunpowder and a shipload of print and handkerchiefs.[23]

Inikori and W. A. Richards have made some of the most articulate arguments about the relationship between firearms and the intensification of slave gathering.[24] They argue that firearms acquired through the sale of slaves were not used principally for gathering more slaves and that slave gatherers could have deployed their private resources to fight the battles of defense, retaliation, and aggression that were not directly related to slaving. However, Inikori posits that "where slave gathering was a state affair, the slave-gathering state may not only have waged offensive wars calculated for the capture of slaves. Its slave-gathering activities would of necessity provoke attack by its neighbors and so be forced to defend itself."[25] Inikori further contends that the violent nature of slave gathering worsened territorial and political conflict. His conclusion seems convincing—the most important slave-exporting part of West Africa, namely the Bonny area, was also one of the largest importers of firearms. The region also imported more guns for every slave exported than any other part of the West African coast.[26] Some detailed military histories of precolonial Nigerian societies validate the slave-gun cycle theory. According to Benson Osadolor, "The conditions of exchange of European firearms for slaves gave Benin warriors the opportunity to make wars successfully, and captives became the means of exchange, this completing the gun-slave cycle, which made Benin a more vigorous state, and placed it in the position of subduing her neighbors."[27] Yet, to ignore other means by which guns were acquired in large quantity is to underestimate the dynamism of precolonial political economies. When Ogunmola, an Ibadan warrior, detained Edward Roper of the Church Missionary Society in the early 1860s, he demanded the following items as ransom: two hundred kegs of gunpowder, two hundred guns, and two hundred bags of cowries (equivalent then to £200).[28]

The Yoruba wars of the 1800s best elucidate the role that firearms played in precolonial African military and political history. Although firearms were already significant in Yoruba warfare from the eighteenth century—the Oyo army that defeated the Dahomeans in 1726 was said to have made use of muskets—it was not until the next century that firearms became popular in warfare. The immense devastation of the Owu War (ca. 1817), the first major nineteenth-century Yoruba conflict, owed largely to the use of firearms. In the early nineteenth century, the Egba army predominantly carried swords (about three feet long), bows and arrows, and other arms. By 1861, all the defenders of the Egba town of Abeokuta had long Dane guns, which according to Captain Arthur Jones cost 21s. 6d. each.[29] By this era, muskets had become the major weapon among all the Yoruba groups. The impact of the Dane gun of the nineteenth century went beyond its ability to work mayhem at a relatively short distance; its noise created a terrifying atmosphere that was a significant element in the military tactics of the period. Thus, the widespread use of firearms radically transformed not only war fatalities, but military culture and warfare tactics as well. It reduced hand-to-hand battle, changing how conflict was prosecuted. The wounds inflicted by copper and iron bullets during the Ijaiye War in the 1860s, according to the Baptist missionary R. H. Stone, "tended to become gangrenous."[30] A. Mann, an Anglican missionary, also described as an "amateur surgeon," was treating between forty and sixty wounded soldiers daily in his dispensary in Ijaiye.[31]

As they did with other technologies adopted from Europe and America, the Yoruba spent several decades mastering the firing of Dane guns in order to reduce accidents and enhance marksmanship. The musket used by Yoruba soldiers in the first half of the nineteenth century constituted more serious danger to the user, if improperly handled, than to the enemy. After describing the techniques for firing arrows, Richard Lander, writing in the early 1820s, mentioned that the firearms imported from the coast "are of comparatively little use" to the Yoruba, who "know not how to handle them with effect." Shortage of ammunition intensified the burden of carrying firearms on the battlefield. In response to this, the soldiers, "to accelerate their speed," tossed their guns aside, "and their enemies eagerly lay hold of the empty muskets for their own use."[32] During the course of the nineteenth century, the Yoruba would perfect the use of firearms. For their part, soldiers did receive occasional training in marksmanship from European explorers and missionaries. With time, the Yoruba would learn to improvise gun parts and ammunition, especially when the patterns of international and domestic supply did not favor them. By the mid-nineteenth century, local blacksmiths were producing bullets or bolts of bar irons of different sizes. The stocks, or butts, on which the gun barrels were fitted were also locally manufactured. On occasion, gun barrels were imported separately; in this way, the rise of the local manufacture of firearms was enhanced by the practice of importing parts, not whole guns.

A major challenge of gun use in the nineteenth century was the large amount of gunpowder required for firing. Local manufacture of gunpowder was inhibited by the shortage of sulfur, a core ingredient. Gun users had to rely on a foreign supply, primarily from Boston, of the coarse black substance high in charcoal content. The Dane guns of the nineteenth century consumed about two handsbreadth for a charge. Many of the guns supplied to the Egba by the British littered the town because they consumed so much gunpowder that their owners abandoned them. Captain Arthur Jones's description of the fate of the abandoned arms during his visit to Abeokuta in 1861 revealed the extent of the weaponization of a community established a mere three decades earlier: "[Abandoned guns] are now lying in different parts of the City without the slightest regard being had for their preservation exposed to all the inclemency of the rainy season, whereby the carriages are part decaying, and the various accessories are either lost or broken, or afford daily amusement to the ragged or naked urchins who roam about at will." Jones, an officer of the Second West India Regiment stationed in Sierra Leone, was commissioned in 1861 to investigate the military capabilities of the Egba, whom the British planned to use as allies against Dahomey, among other enemies of Britain's emerging imperialism along the West African coast. Jones, who was wounded by a bullet while observing the Egba on the battlefield, wrote an account titled "Report on the Constitution and Military Capability of the Abbeokutan Army for Carrying on an Offensive War," which remains one of the most detailed nineteenth-century eyewitness sources of Yoruba military tactics. The availability of gunpowder thus shaped the usability of firearms. Indeed, the need to acquire gunpowder not only dictated the pattern of relations between the hinterland Yoruba people and their coastal neighbors (especially the Ijebu); it reconfigured the terms of allegiance and political alignments. One of the immediate causes of the Sixteen Years' War (1877–93), the last major war in nineteenth-century Yorubaland, was the controversy over a consignment of gunpowder from the coast.[33]

As the Yoruba wars progressed and as the popularity of the conventional Dane gun increased, so did the demand for more sophisticated firearms, needed to tilt the balance of warfare. Although artilleries were not common, the Ijaiye in the early 1860s were firing some. A major revolution in military warfare came when rifles made their way into West African markets. Historians generally agree that such breech-loading rifles as the Sniders, Martini-Henri, Mauser, Winchester, and Remington were procured for the Ekiti warriors by their kinsmen (the Ekitiparapo Society), a group of Lagos-based traders, for the prosecution of the war against the Ibadan. The superiority of rifles to the conventional Dane gun was obvious. They could fire rapidly at longer ranges and with better accuracy.[34] The use of rifles also changed the character of Yoruba warfare and military organization and gave a new bent to the disagreement among leading traders and politicians about the role of the Lagos merchants in the intensification of violence in the hinterland.[35] As a result, conventional face-to-face fighting in which belligerent groups fired at each other was considerably reduced. A special Ekitiparapo rifle corps introduced trench warfare, which wreaked destruction on the Ibadan camp. This compelled the Ibadan army to replace their bamboo walls with well-reinforced mud walls to protect against the long-range rifles.[36] Rifles temporarily tilted the balance of victory against the Ibadan, who then approached the Ijebu for a similar weapon, offering to pay between £10 and £15 for rifle and 6d. for a cartridge. These superior firearms were far more expensive than the conventional Dane gun, which sold for about 21d.

Aside from the Yoruba and the Benin, other ethnicities in modern southern Nigeria also have a long tradition of using firearms. The blunderbuss, with its bell-shaped muzzle, was probably the earliest firearm used by the Igbo. Records indicate that in the mid-sixteenth century, the Akpa, an Aro subgroup, bought these weapons from coastal traders in Calabar. The Akpa were also believed to have taught other Igbo groups how to use the imported gun. With time, the Igbo replaced the blunderbuss with the Dane gun. By the mid-nineteenth century, Abiriba, Nkwerre, and Awka blacksmiths were said to be making bullets and stocks. The Aro also sold adulterated gunpowder, mixing the imported variety with additional charcoal to increase their profits.[37]

The popularity of firearms among Nigerian ethnicities was not homogenous. The military culture of each ethnicity shaped the method and extent of domestication. According to Kenneth Dike and Felicia Ekejiuba, the Igbo did not use guns in a pronounced manner for warfare as many other ethnic groups did because of a number of economic, political, cultural, and environmental factors. First, the Aro, who continued to monopolize the sale of firearms in the region, ensured that hostile neighbors did not accumulate large consignments that could be used against them. Indeed, so expensive were the guns sold by the Aro that their use was limited to important ceremonial shooting. Second, according to the Igbo military worldview, a good warrior was the one who killed his assailant with a machete and sword at close quarters, not the one that fired a musket. It was only after a warrior had obtained a head in close fighting with a sword that he could go to war with firearms. Third, the thick vegetation of the Igbo territory limited the use of firearms, which require visibility and lack of obstruction for effectiveness.[38] Even a well-armed, gun-bearing military would easily be routed in a well-coordinated ambush by machete-wielding warriors.

These three explanations are not mutually exclusive, for military culture varied from one part of Igboland to another. The tradition among some Igbo groups forbidding the use of firearms in intraethnic conflict suggests that the people acknowledged their effectiveness and ability to cause significant damage, thereby tilting the balance of violence in an "unfair" manner.[39] One could conclude that most Igbo groups, up to the late eighteenth century, used guns as a secondary, not primary, weapon of warfare. During the nineteenth century, the use of firearms increased exponentially among the Aro—even though the machete continued to be used. The enormous havoc of the nineteenth-century Igbo wars not only led to the extermination and creation of new communities and lineages; it also transformed traditional Igbo ideals of warfare and led to the rise of merchant-warriors, "new men" who wielded political power. "A significant element of firearms" featured in the conflict among the Arondizuogu lineage groups, G. Ugo Nwokeji submitted.[40] Colonel Montenaro reported that during the conquest of the Igbo hinterland in the first decade of the twentieth century, the Aro "were well armed with sniders, rifles, chassepots, needle guns and bullets all of modern make and all in first rate order." Many of the Aro "were a good shot," he noted, and their firearms and ammunition "were preserved in a wonderful good state, locks and blocks being carefully oiled."[41]

Firearms did play a notable role in the history of other parts of southern Nigeria, especially the Niger Delta, where a few minority coastal traders held significant power. "But for this [guns] the few thousands in the Delta could not have maintained their privileged position in the Atlantic trade and played the role of economic dictators to the millions in the hinterland," Dike submitted in his seminal work, *Trade and Politics in the Niger Delta*, published in 1956.[42] Writing in 1864, Richard Burton observed that each "house" in Bonny would be able to mobilize up to 2,500 musketeers in the event of a war. He remarked further that the city-state possessed "abundance of ammunition" that could cause gargantuan damage—"bloody to the natives, and injurious, if not dangerous, to the Europeans."[43] The interaction between the environment and the needs of the military determined the kinds of firearms used in the coastal areas. In the nineteenth century, warring communities patrolled the waters and creeks with high-caliber cannon mounted on pivots in the prows of canoes. With its ability to absorb the recoil of the gun in the water, the canoe made an ideal mount.

Unlike the southern parts of modern Nigeria, where the advent of firearms points back to the fifteenth century, the North seems to have had an even longer history of encounter with guns. The earliest reference to firearms in this area can be seen in a Bornu manuscript that mentions an attempt by the Bulala to obtain firearms during their war against the Sefawa in the late twelfth century. Also, the *Kano Chronicle* tells of a Bornu prince who arrived in Kano with guns. This was during the reign of Dauda Bakon Damisa (1421–38). These early references do not suggest that guns were available in large quantity or were a vital factor in military operations and successes. The *Kano Chronicle* also records that Kano was involved in the transatlantic slave trade, exchanging humans for guns during the reign of Sharefa (1703–31).[44] The armies of Mai Idris Alooma, who reigned in Bornu from the late sixteenth to the early seventeenth centuries, were composed of Turkish musketeers. Historians do not agree on the true importance of this adopted technology to Alooma's military success. Yet, the decline of Bornu and the lack of further reference to firearms until the nineteenth century suggest that guns played a minimal role in state building. Regardless of the inconsistency of references to guns in early written records, one thing is clear—firearms were introduced to modern northern Nigeria through the Sahara, the international gateway that connected West Africa with North

Africa and southern Europe. The linguistic origin of the Hausa word for gun (*bindiga* from Kanuri) suggests that it came from Bornu.⁴⁵

The limited use of firearms in pre-nineteenth-century warfare in northern Nigerian military organizations has led some scholars to conclude that guns were incompatible with ancient modes of military tactics—namely, the cavalry. Others have rendered a motley interpretation citing numerous factors, including but not limited to the inferiority of imported guns, the difficulties and limited knowledge of repair and maintenance, unfavorable terms of trade, and limited training in handling weapons and marksmanship. Unfavorable trade relations between the middlemen who controlled the trade in firearms and the political elites also placed significant limits on the role firearms played in northern Nigeria's warfare up to the nineteenth century.⁴⁶

The Denham-Clapperton-Oudney expedition in the 1820s, the first European exploration of the central Sudan, transcended the need to gain a better knowledge of African geography, including the region's economic and political systems. The expedition distributed ammunition to the courts of the rulers of the Sokoto Caliphate and the Sudan. News of this gift spread quickly, and when Clapperton arrived in Katagum, a territory under the caliphate's control, the emir (ruler) demanded some firearms.⁴⁷ The fascination with rockets, muskets, and other classes of firearms did not end with the Clapperton's visit. Subsequent travelers recorded their interactions with local leaders concerning guns. When Barth arrived in Katsina in 1851, he temporarily allowed Emir Muhammadu Bello (r. 1844–69) to use his pistols for protection—an arrangement that attracted the attention of other chiefs, who accused him of preferential treatment. His justification for not granting the chiefs' request was that the success of his expedition depended on access to his firearms. Bello further asked Bath for "some rockets as a *magani-n-yaki* (a medicine of war), in order to frighten his enemies" and promised to keep "such a gift a secret."⁴⁸ However, Barth did not carry rockets on his expedition. His justification for this revealed his deep understanding of the nature of warfare in the Sokoto Caliphate, the elites' knowledge of the efficacy of the lethal weapon, and the safety of his party: "If we gave such to one prince, his neighbor might become fiercely hostile to us."⁴⁹

Undoubtedly, the use of firearms in modern northern Nigeria in the nineteenth century reconfigured military tactics, missions, and outcomes. It complemented established methods of warfare and other tools such as horses. As seen in the case of the southern part of the country, firearms intensified the vicious cycle of violence—wars were waged for territorial expansion and acquisition of slaves required for the gun trade. Barth, during his visit to Bornu in 1851, observed that the people embarked on an expedition against their neighbor because "the coffers and slave rooms of the great men [were] empty."[50] He noted further that if Africans "had never become acquainted" with guns, "the slave trade would never have reached those gigantic proportions which it had attained."[51] Although Africans first acquired firearms to protect themselves from their hostile neighbors, Barth remarked, "These instruments of destruction became necessary because they enabled them to hunt down less favored tribes, and, with a supply of slaves." While blaming Europeans for initiating the gun-for-slave transaction, his statement that Africans could "produce many other things which they might exchange for firearms" would find expression in the language of abolitionism and the transition from trade in humans to "legitimate" commerce.[52]

Social History of Firearms in Precolonial Nigeria

It is indisputable that many of the firearms imported to precolonial Nigeria were used for waging war. However, the imported item at various stages in its history in Nigeria went through a series of perceptual transformations. The purpose to which firearms were put also changed over time. Indeed, to associate firearms only with violence is to underestimate the creativity of Nigerians in making local or indigenous meaning out of a foreign object. Historians do not know much about the social history of firearms in precolonial Nigeria because culture—unlike the massive political and structural change that guns unleashed, which also received better documentation—operated at the grassroots level.

One aspect of the domestication of firearms is the diverse names they were given across ethnicities. This aspect of historical linguistics provides interesting insights into the history of culture contact. It also helps track the transformation in how people conceived of the "local" and the "foreign" as they adapted or responded to their technology needs. In his account of Yorubaland first collected in 1840, Osifekunde, an Ijebu man who was seized at the age of twenty and sold into slavery in the Americas around 1820, gave the following Yoruba names for different types of firearms, which he described as items "European civilization has brought": "muskets (*ibon*), gunpowder (*etou* [*etu*] *ibon*), pistol (*olewo* [*ibon ile 'wo*]), cannon (*akba* [*agba*])."[53] If these renditions of firearms reveal anything, it is that by 1820 when Osifekunde was seized, guns of different types were "popular" enough to receive local names. Moreover, Osifekunde may have updated his knowledge of Yoruba firearms culture from contacts with incoming new slaves in Brazil, where he was enslaved. The slight variation in Osifekunde's Yoruba renditions of firearms terminology (with the exception of *ibon*) also suggests the transformation of language across the Atlantic—a product of cultural interaction, or the challenge of documenting Ijebu-Yoruba words in a European language.

Osifekunde's translation of firearms terms remained relatively the same during the twentieth century. The only notable difference is between the musket (Dane gun), which was called *ibon ibile* (local or native gun), and the shotgun (*ibon ebo*, or white man's gun) by the 1920s. The justification for establishing a difference between these two popular firearms in colonial southwestern Nigeria is best explained in terms of the technological evolution that took place between 1840, when Osifekunde's account was recorded, and the 1920s. By the 1920s or earlier, the Yoruba not only produced the Dane gun in a quantity that matched local demand; they had fully domesticated and incorporated it into core elements of their social, economic, and political existence. So they treated it as a "local" firearm, or their "own gun." However, because the shotgun was newer and restricted to the educated and traditional elites, they called it the white man's gun to emphasize its exoticism or foreignness.

The Africanization and domestication of firearms into cultural codes, songs, sayings, idioms, and other forms of orality explain the creativity of Africans in making local sense of Western technology. The oral traditions that created communities, towns, and lineages (including the famous Aro and Kalabari) are replete with references to guns, rendering significant insight into the circumstances under which they came into existence.[54] Intergroup relations among some ethnicities were also forged around the story of guns. The Nkpa, an Igbo subgroup southeast of Umuahia, after learning the technique of firing the blunderbuss from the Akpa, swore an oath not to wage war against their benefactor—a pledge they kept till the demise of colonial rule.[55] In one oral tradition collected in the first decade of the twentieth century, the Eket were said to have taught the Oyubia how to use cap guns in exchange for their captured soldiers.[56] The Nkwerre received the praise name *Nkwerre opi egbe* (Nkwerre, makers of guns) from their long tradition of repairing guns in the nineteenth century.[57] The popular saying *Ope Ijaiye lo le ro yin ogun Ogunmola* (Only the Ijaiye palm trees can tell the story of Ogunmola's war) suggests the destructiveness of the Ibadan-Ijaiye War of the 1860s. The severe devastation of the Ijaiye palm trees could not have been made by a regular musket but resulted from cannon fire. What is more, when the new Snider rifle first made inroads into the Yoruba hinterland in the 1880s, the people named it *Okondo,* and the war in which it was used they called *Kiriji,* presumably from the "crack followed by a whistle which is the noise made when high-velocity bullets are fired from breech-loading rifles."[58]

Reference to firearms in folktales about animal life and nature formed a vital aspect of the worldview of some Nigerian ethnic groups, which is reinforced on a regular basis. Among the Ekoi of southern Nigeria, firearms had a place in such legends as why the sun went to the sky and why the owner of a gun shared only one leg of his game.[59] The Ekoi even had an explanation for the extinction of the lion in the bush. It is important to relate this story, recorded around 1907, for it provides an interesting perspective on indigenous hunting culture and how a European technology entered into the people's consciousness about human-animal relationships. A young teenage boy, after learning that the lion king killed his father, decides to take vengeance. Knowing well that his community's primary hunting tool, the cutlass, could not kill the dreaded animal, he exchanges a large quantity of palm kernel for a gun at the coast and ventures into the forest to call the lion to a battle. Instead of attacking his intruder, the lion king sends smaller animals to inquire about the mission of the boy. When the errand snake appears, the boy tells the animal: "I am not looking for you but my enemy *Nki* [the lion]. I could easily kill you with my machete and would not need a gun." When *Nki* eventually comes out, the boy shoots the lion king dead. He dismembers the lion and removes his father's carcass from its stomach for a proper burial. Terrified by this news, the remaining lions desert the forest in fear of being killed by a lethal weapon. Legends are difficult to believe, of course. Yet the reference to the exchange of palm kernel for a gun with Europeans at the coast and the effectiveness of a firearm in mauling one of the most dangerous animals corroborate other evidence about the advent of guns in Africa.[60]

The appropriation of firearms into nonverbal communication expanded the vocabulary of several Nigerian ethnic groups, an indication that their culture was not static, and that its invention and reinvention were shaped by complex interactions between local and foreign forces. Shortly after Adeyemi became the king of Oyo in 1876, two identical calabashes were sent from Ile-Ife, the ancestral home of the Yoruba, to signal his ascendancy. One calabash, containing cowries, beads, and cloth, among other accessories, indicated peace, tranquility, and a prosperous reign, while the other, consisting of gunpowder, bullets, razors, knives, and miniature spears and arrows, indicated war and violence. His choice of the second calabash was said to have initiated turmoil that culminated in the outbreak of the Ekitiparapo War, which paved the way for the imposition of colonialism on much of Yorubaland in the first half of the 1890s.[61]

Nonmilitary uses of firearms included gun salutes and ceremonial shooting, both popular features of European military culture brought to Africa from the sixteenth century or earlier. It is difficult to tell how the gun salute entered African military and political culture. But we do know that it was one aspect of sound making, a custom well entrenched in African culture. Musical or sound instruments of different types have historically been used for purposes that reflect the prevailing sociocultural and gendered outlook of Nigerian peoples. Sounds had both a secular and a nonsecular interpretation, and they were markers of vital rituals, tied to the wellness of the community and the passage of time and events.[62] Nigerians probably adopted gun salutes and ceremonial shooting because the sound produced with a Dane gun was louder than those from indigenous instruments or materials. Because firearms were expensive imported items used principally for warfare, though, only the elites who held military and political power were entitled to receive a gun salute. As we shall see in chapter 2, the transformation of ceremonial shooting under colonial rule speaks to an enduring cultural adaptation in the modernizing world of the twentieth century.

Samuel Johnson reported that the firing of guns and the blowing of the *Kakaki* trumpet and drumming was one activity that marked the coronation of a new king of Oyo.[63] Gun salutes also took place during the town's principal festivals (Ifa, Orun, and Bere), when the king made a public appearance.[64] In another portion of his indispensable book, Johnson provides a better view into the royal repertoire and the intensity of the noise made by the Dane guns during the Bere festival, the most solemn of the three ceremonies, which, aside from ushering in the planting season, measured the king's years on the throne:

The firing of a *feu de joie* [round of ceremonial shots] now serves to show that the ceremony is over and the parties are returning to the city. This is done in state. The Basorun [senior war chief] robes in one of the enclosures: he is attended by hundreds of horsemen and footmen, horsemen galloping backwards and forwards before him, the firing and the fifing and drumming are quite deafening. With such a right royal procession His Supernal Highness re-enters the city. On the evening of the same day, the King worships the Ogun [god of iron and warfare] which is a preliminary to every annual festival.[65]

Besides serving as a marker of significant communal events, gun firing was also used to announce the death and/or conduct the burial rites of war chiefs—similar to practices in Europe. When Ajayi Ogboriefon, a noted warrior described as the "last of those veteran generals of Ibadan, who had seen great fights," died in 1879, "the firing of musketry, volleys upon volleys announced [his death] to the public."[66] As Dike and Ekejiuba have noted, the guns sold by the Aro were so expensive that people used them only for ceremonial shooting, not warfare.[67] Gun accidents did happen during ceremonies. Accidents, as we shall see in chapter 6, were largely attributed to the improper handling of a firearm in a frenzied, carnival-like shooting atmosphere. In one oral tradition of the late nineteenth century in the Nri-Awka region, a prominent man, Ezenne Ezeanakwe, inadvertently shot and killed his friend during a funeral gun salute. The community banished him for seven years and three of his children were sold into slavery as punishment for his deed.[68]

In Africa, intrepidity and fearlessness are often significant cultural elements of "being a man." But the entry of guns added new elements to notions of masculinity as communities, ethnicities, associations, and other groupings to which people belonged defined conditions for the privilege to possess and use firearms. These conditions were usually associated with a significant phase, or rite of passage, and the fulfillment of sociocultural responsibilities. Hence, only young men who had undergone training in marksmanship and spirituality associated with the god of iron and warfare were permitted to use firearms in this changing context. Indigenous regulations on firearms defined stages in the evolution of masculinity and the mastery of cultural codes. It is a truism, as we have already seen, that when guns first made inroads into Nigeria, people encountered difficulties mastering their use. But from one decade and century to another, marksmanship was enhanced through an indigenous military and political culture tied to the changing meanings of masculinity.

Oral traditions explicate the intersection of firearms and gradations of masculinity. A short biography of Ogunmola, an Ibadan warlord of the 1860s, documented in the late nineteenth century, describes the warrior sitting on an empty keg of gunpowder challenging his superior (the Basorun) to war, while his drummer is stationed on a tree in front of his house rendering the following praise song: "Ogunmola ija 'gboro ni yio pa a dan dan dan! On yi agba gbiri gbiri gbiri! O mu agbori lowo, o n wo ona Orun yan yan yan!" (Ogunmola, of a civil fight he shall die for sure, sure, sure! He keeps kegs of powder a rolling, rolling, rolling! With a jackknife in hand he is looking heavenward steadily, steadily, steadily!).[69] To be seated on a keg of gunpowder had both practical and metaphoric meaning; it was only influential chiefs like Ogunmola who could make the kegs of gunpowder roll in preparation for war. Another praise poem of Ogunmola described him as "a nina leru bi oibo" (a man always in possession of fire [bullet] like a white man). Today, cannon, gun, and gunpowder are among the important ritual objects at Ogunmola's grave shrine at Bere, Ibadan (see figure 1.1). The reputation of Balogun Ibikunle, another prominent Ibadan warrior, went beyond his possession of a large farm. He was also described as "a lota letu Baba Osi Ibadan" (possessor of bullets and gunpowder, the Osi Ibadan).[70] Olugbode, also an Ibadan chief, received a great compliment for his lethal gun: "Baale 'Badan n ponibon Ajankoko. O n ponibon asisori" (Hail the Ibadan chief, the bearer of the poisonous *ajanlekoko* gun. The owner of the *asisori* guns).[71]

Closely connected to this is the appropriation of guns to religious and spiritual practice. The Yoruba, for instance, adopted the gun as one of the implements associated with Ogun, the god of warfare and iron, whose deification across West Africa and in the African diaspora in the Americas emerged out of the spiritual attributes of iron and of powerful people who made use of it. Ogun was a ferocious and fearless hunter, who inspired or founded many communities while living peripatetically and solitarily in the forest. A popular symbol of Yoruba masculinity, the deity combined the ambivalence of a hot temper and other dread-inspiring attributes with generosity and kindness.[72] It is difficult to know concretely when the Yoruba domesticated guns into their spirituality—linguistic, archeological, artistic, and oral traditions, among other historical sources, render conflicting accounts of the origins of Ogun, both as a concept and as a deity. Yet, one can safely suggest that it took place after the fifteenth century, when guns first appeared along the West African coast. Devotees of Ogun, especially those

Figure 1.1. Firearms at Basorun Ogunmola's grave shrine in Bere, Ibadan. Photograph by author, May 2016.

who were hunters and warriors, were expected to exhibit the core attributes of the deity, including bravery in war, skill in hunting, and moral virtue.[73] The *Ijala*, the hunter's poem performed during ceremonies and *ogun* festivals, gives some clue into the connection between spirituality, guns, and masculinity. A "real" man, in Ogun's worldview, must be able to commit suicide with a gun in order to escape public shame associated with political failure. The following *Ijala* narrates the prerequisite for becoming *Asipade*, leader of the hunter's guild:

> *Eni ti o gbonagbonagbona*
> *Ko le e J Asipade*
> *Bee le ni ti o logungun bi aroni*
> *Ko lee J Asipade*
> *Eni ti o layaa yinbonje*
> *Mo ni ko lee J Asipade wa*
> *Emi layaa yinbonje*
> *Mo le kerin loju*
> *Mo le pefon nija*
> *Mo le J Asipade*

> A person who is not ferocious
> Cannot be installed as *Asipade*
> A person who does not possess charms like *aroni*
> Cannot be installed as *Asipade*
> A person who cannot commit suicide by the gun
> I say, cannot be installed as *Asipade*
> I am brave to the point of committing suicide by the gun
> I can challenge an elephant
> I can challenge a bush cow [buffalo]
> I can be made *Asipade*.[74]

Firearms and the Conquest of Nigeria

Many studies have been conducted on the conquest of Nigeria; that is not my subject here.[75] Historians do recognize that internal factors such as political disunity among Nigerian ethnic groups, aside from superior firearms of the British, contributed to the demise of indigenous rule. Europeans' knowledge of African geography enhanced their military tactics, and the psychological impact of military defeat compelled many Nigerian groups to surrender without putting up a fight. The long period it took the British to bring the hinterland of Igboland under firm control validates the efficacy of guerrilla warfare and the indigenous peoples' dexterity with firearms. Indeed, historians can hardly be accused of romanticizing the valor of precolonial African armies in their descriptions of war episodes that terminated self-rule—the evidence of Nigerians' stiff resistance is overwhelming and hard to ignore. By emphasizing that the superiority of their firearms tilted the balance of conflict in favor of the British, a historian of Nigeria could not be accused of giving too much credit to technological factors in explaining the failure of resistance.[76] For, if the size of an army was the most determinative factor in the outcome of a military confrontation, the British could not have conquered even the small country of Sierra Leone, not to speak of massive Nigeria. The Maxim gun, designed and first produced by American-born British inventor Hiram Maxim in 1884, made British colonialism possible in Nigeria as elsewhere in Africa. A more advanced firearm than the earlier Gatling gun used during the American Civil War (1861–65), the Maxim gun was the first machine gun to deploy a fully automatic loading system with belt-fed ammunition and a water-cooled barrel.[77]

Yet a number of salient points and analyses about international trade and the politics of access to guns are worth emphasizing as we close this foundational chapter and transit to the twentieth century, this book's main period of focus. Historians generally identify Nigerians' difficulty in obtaining modern weapons as a key reason for the failure of resistance.[78] But very few historians have clearly engaged the major global developments that made access to superior firearms difficult. As Europeans' political interest in Africa grew during the latter half of the nineteenth century, so did the need to regulate Africans' access to firearms, which culminated in the Brussels Conference Act of 1890. The signatories to this act, titled the Convention Relative to the Slave Trade and Importation into Africa of Firearms, Ammunition, and Spirituous Liquors, agreed that except for flintlock unrifled guns (Dane guns) and common gunpowder, firearms should not be sold within their spheres of political and economic influence on the continent.[79]

Prohibited arms included lethal weapons such as cannon, machine guns, rockets, rifles, carbines, and revolvers. No private individual was permitted to have an armory for weapons other than "ordinary" gunpowder and flintlock muskets. Rather, public gun warehouses were to be controlled by the imperial government on behalf of the international community.

Arms could be imported only to designated ports. The purpose of these arms restrictions found expression in the spurious humanitarian agenda and language of the era: the suppression of slave raiding and the discouraging of internecine strife. But because Britain did not have strong political power in most parts of what is now Nigeria when the act came into force, implementation was left in the hands of chartered companies such as the Royal Niger Company. The presence of the British Naval Squadron in West African waterways helped enforce the Brussels Convention, among other regulations made against firearms and the slave trade. However, the convention did not put a total end to arms trafficking in the region. The French, for instance, were selling rifles to Aro traders during the late nineteenth century. The more than twenty-five thousand firearms seized during one episode of the Aro expedition in the first decade of the twentieth century could not have been acquired without the contravention of the international firearms agreement.[80] Trading companies also imported and kept Gatling guns in their outposts, for defense against local traders, in contravention of the Brussels agreement.[81] However, the illicit gun trade still could not provide the superior ammunition Nigerians needed to permanently ward off imperialism.

By the turn of the century, with the passage of the Northern Nigeria Order in Council of 1899 and Proclamation No. 10 of 1900, the enforcement of arms importation was transferred to colonial administrators. These new instruments of regulation retained the principal component of the 1890 act: prohibition on the sale of arms of precision to the "natives"—that is, residents of northern Nigeria.[82] It was not until 1901, through Proclamation No. 1, that the most comprehensive arms ordinance came into existence. This proclamation, in revising previous policy, provided conditions for the importation of certain classes of arms such as shotguns and rifles. Explicit guidelines for storing gunpowder were firmly established. All trading companies were expected to furnish the government with annual data on importation, sale, storage, and destination of guns and gunpowder.

Conclusion

The main thrust of this chapter is the role that firearms played in the economic and global history of Africa-Europe relations between the fifteenth and the late nineteenth centuries and how firearms were domesticated and incorporated into Africa's military and political culture. Ceremonial shooting, signals, and other symbolic uses to which guns were put in precolonial Nigeria tells much about the willingness of Africans to revise core elements of their religious and spiritual lives when they encountered a foreign technology. But during this period, ceremonial shooting was centralized and restricted to elites and communal events. Moreover, it is interesting to see the transition of the firearms trade in Africa from conventional commerce in the fifteenth century to "illicit" trade in the second half of the nineteenth century. This transformation cannot be explained simply from the standpoint of the extension of European imperialism to Africa. Rather, it establishes how the advancement of firearms technology from a single-shot musket in the fifteenth century to the sophisticated Maxim gun in the 1880s shaped Afro-European relations.[83] The series of international regulations on the trade in guns toward the end of the nineteenth century contributed to the emergence of the colonial Nigerian gun society, which began to take shape from the first decade of the twentieth century.

Notes

1. Barth, *Travels and Discoveries*, 2:326.
2. Smith, *Warfare and Diplomacy*, 81; Talbot, *Shadow of the Bush*, 271–72.
3. Smith, *Warfare and Diplomacy*, 83.
4. Kea, "Firearms and Warfare," 185.
5. Barbot, *Description of the Coasts*, 357–58.
6. Kea, "Firearms and Warfare," 185–86.
7. Egharevba, *Short History of Benin*, 27, 30; Osadolor, "Military System of Benin Kingdom," 87; Smith, *Kingdoms of the Yoruba*, 58–59; Ryder, *Benin and the Europeans*, 49.
8. Ryder, *Benin and the Europeans*, 114.
9. Ibid., 321.
10. Ibid., 148–50.
11. Ibid., 68; Kea, "Firearms and Warfare," 186.
12. Inikori, "Import of Firearms," 361.
13. Ibid., 344.
14. Ibid., 345.
15. Ibid., 339.
16. White, "Firearms in Africa," 181–82.
17. Inikori, "Import of Firearms," 356–57.
18. See various notes and references in Chapter 1.
19. Caulk, "Firearms and Princely Power"; Berg, "Sacred Musket."
20. Curtin, *Economic Change in Precolonial Africa*, 323–25.
21. Gemery and Hogendorn, "Technological Change," 243–58; Inikori, "Import of Firearms," 339–86.

22. Inikori, "Import of Firearms," 350–51.
23. Dike and Ekejiuba, *Aro of Southeastern Nigeria*, 239.
24. Inikori, "Import of Firearms"; Richards, "Import of Firearms."
25. Inikori, "Import of Firearms," 351.
26. Ibid., 361.
27. Osadolor, "Military System of Benin Kingdom," 27.
28. Johnson, *History of the Yorubas*, 353. For more on ransoming, see Lofkrantz and Ojo, "Slavery, Freedom."
29. Captain Arthur Jones, "Report on the Constitution and Military Capability of the Abbeokutan Army for Carrying on an Offensive War," in Ajayi and Smith, *Yoruba Warfare*, 134.
30. Ajayi and Smith, *Yoruba Warfare*, 51.
31. Ibid.
32. Lander, *Clapperton's Last Expedition to Africa*, 2:222.
33. Smith, *Warfare and Diplomacy*, 86.
34. Akintoye, *Revolution and Power Politics*, 118.
35. "Re: Letter from Latosa and Other Chiefs of Ibadan," *Lagos Observer*, July 3, 1884.
36. Akintoye, *Revolution and Power Politics*, 120–21.
37. Jackson, "Twenty Years War," 24.
38. Dike and Ekejiuba, *Aro of Southeastern Nigeria*, 171–72.
39. Jackson, "Twenty Years War," 24.
40. Nwokeji, *Slave Trade and Culture*, 191.
41. Dike and Ekejiuba, *Aro of Southeastern Nigeria*, 172–73.
42. Dike, *Trade and Politics*, 167.
43. Ibid.
44. Smaldone, *Warfare in the Sokoto Caliphate*, 95.
45. Ibid., 95–96.
46. Ibid., 94–109.
47. For additional information on the Sokoto Caliphate, see Adeleye, *Power and Diplomacy*; and Last, *Sokoto Caliphate*.
48. Barth, *Travels and Discoveries*, 1:468.
49. Ibid.
50. Ibid., 2:316.
51. Ibid., 2:326.
52. Ibid.
53. Lloyd, "Osifekunde of Ijebu," 287.
54. Jones, *Trading States*, 24–48; Talbot, *Tribes of the Niger Delta*, 6; Isichei, *History of the Igbo People*, 58, 63–65.
55. Dike and Ekejiuba, *Aro of Southeastern Nigeria*, 172.
56. Talbot, *Life in Southern Nigeria*, 262–63.
57. Dike and Ekejiuba, *Aro of Southeastern Nigeria*, 172.
58. Akintoye, *Revolution and Power Politics*, 118.
59. Talbot, *Shadow of the Bush*, 144–45, 357–59.
60. Ibid., 382–83.
61. Johnson, *History of the Yorubas*, 402–3.
62. Basden, *Niger Ibos*, 117; Meek, *Law and Authority*, 27.

63. Johnson, *History of the Yorubas*, 44.
64. Ibid., 48.
65. Ibid., 47–50.
66. Ibid., 438.
67. Dike and Ekejiuba, *Aro of Southeastern Nigeria*, 171.
68. Nwokeji, *Slave Trade and Culture*, 195.
69. Johnson, *History of the Yorubas*, 306.
70. Awe, "Oriki and Warfare in Yorubaland," 277.
71. Ibid., 289; Atilade, *Iwe Oriki Awon Orile Yoruba*, 20–23.
72. For more on Ogun, see Barnes, *Africa's Ogun*.
73. Babalola, "Portrait of Ogun," 156.
74. Ajuwon, "Ogun's Iremoje," 178–79.
75. Obaro Ikime's *Fall of Nigeria* remains the most comprehensive book on the British conquest of Nigeria. Notable regional studies include Ohadike, *Ekumeku Movement*; Dusgate, *Conquest of Northern Nigeria*; Afigbo, "Patterns of the Igbo Resistance"; Jackson, "Twenty Years War"; Aderinto, "European Invasion and African Resistance."
76. For more on the role of science and technology in imperialism, see Adas, *Machines as the Measure*.
77. Hawkey, *Amazing Hiram Maxim*; Vandervort, *Wars of Imperial Conquest*.
78. Falola, *Colonialism and Violence in Nigeria*, 18.
79. Chew, *Arming the Periphery*.
80. Dike and Ekejiuba, *Aro of Southeastern Nigeria*, 171–73.
81. Talbot, *Life in Southern Nigeria*, 293–94.
82. "Chief Assistant (Departmental)," July 27, 1907, Muri Prof., 2557/1907, NAK.
83 Markham, *Guns of the Empire*, 134.

2

ALL FIREARMS ARE NOT MADE EQUAL

Colonialism, Social Class, and the Emergence of a Nigerian Gun Society

> In the sweet early morning, while still it is dark,
> We hear from Apapa, the gun's warning bark;
> Soon the sun will be calling, for labour and play,
> The Call Birds abroad at the break of the day,
> In the heat of the noontide, we learn O'er the main,
> That the day has half gone, and we chop [eat] once again:
> At eight in the night time, the last gun bangs out,
> And we all go our ways, with what we're about.
> And so through the days, the months, and the weeks,
> We all know the hours, when Apapa gun speaks.
>
> —"The Apapa Gun," by Pillar Box, *Nigerian Pioneer*, May 12, 1922

Between the 1890s and 1910s, the colonial government in Nigeria introduced a new regime of gun ownership that gave way to a gun society by first disarming "Nigerians" and destroying the arms and ammunition they used to resist colonial conquest. This new era of gun politics, drawing inspiration from the 1890 Brussels Conference, which prohibited the importation of certain classes of guns to Africa, made a rigid distinction between flintlock guns (otherwise called Dane guns) and arms of precision, such as magazine guns, pistols, revolvers, and rifles. Shotguns and cap guns were also classified as arms of precision, even though they were not, in a practical sense. While all Nigerians, regardless of region, ethnicity, and social class, were allowed to own Dane guns, only the educated (e.g., government employees, teachers, forest guards, storekeepers, clerks, journalists, doctors, lawyers) and traditional elites were permitted to own shotguns. At the beginning of the twentieth century, no Nigerian was legally allowed to own pistols, revolvers, or rifles. But this last regulation was gradually relaxed as the century wore on. Yet, by the late 1950s, very few Nigerians legally owned rifles, revolvers, or pistols—the shotgun remained the most popular firearm among lower- and upper-class educated Nigerians, popular traders, and traditional elites. Writing in the 1950s (under the pseudonym Ian Brook), colonial officer William Ian Brinkworth made the following remarks about the intersection of firearms and social class: "The Dane gun was a primitive muzzle-loader, often nearly as tall as a man.... More sophisticated men—government clerks, traders, and lorry owners—used shot guns . . . a symbol of social status."[1] However, regional variation—shaped by history and the patterns of relations between the government and the people—also influenced the administration of gun laws, as Chapter 7 fully explicates.

As British colonialists established a Nigerian gun society through the liberalization of nonprohibited firearms, they defined the "rights" and "privileges" of gun possession. They institutionalized the possession of the Dane gun as a right partly because it was the "least" lethal of all firearms in circulation, and ownership of shotguns, rifles, pistols, revolvers, and cap guns as a privilege associated with higher status because they were considered to be more lethal; it was also assumed that "important" and "enlightened" people would not want to commit crime or undermine colonial institutions that supported or were responsible for their elevated status. Another assumption was that these guns, especially pistols, revolvers, and rifles, were best handled by "intelligent" people, not by the majority of the populace who used the "primitive" Dane guns. But the right or privilege to use firearms could be revoked if an individual or a group used guns against the government or other Nigerians. Conversely, what shaped most Nigerians' attitudes toward guns was the economic, sociocultural, and political significance of firearms, not the colonialists' construction of right and privilege. For some gun owners, such as hunters and former warriors and their descendants, possession of firearms was an inalienable right—a cultural patrimony enshrined in the character of the god of warfare and iron that they worshipped. Much of the resistance of Nigerians to firearms regulation was influenced by the desire to prevent the British from reducing a commodity that shaped people's everyday encounters with the natural environment and the spiritual world to a mere economic artifact conceived as having a serious, detrimental impact on the maintenance of law and order.

The new gun society had a racial dimension. European residents (both military and civilian) had unrestricted access to rifles, pistols, and revolvers. The fundamental principle of firearms regulation in colonial Nigeria was simple—the British ensured that Nigerians did not have legal access to highly lethal firearms like cannon and heavy explosives, which could undermine imperial rule. The fact that all guns were not manufactured the same meant that perceptions of their danger to the status quo and the social identity of their owners must have varied. Private possession of firearms became increasingly important as Nigerians placed a high premium on the boom of gunshots at communal and private ceremonies as markers of social class. What is more, as the population increased, so did human encroachment on wildlife natural habitat. Firearms proved effective in the human struggle against animals and for the control of nature. My main agenda in this chapter is to articulate the emergence of a Nigerian gun society and to look at firearms beyond their narrow conception as instruments of violence, and to demonstrate how the gun shaped new ideas and ideals of social class and colonial consumer culture.

THE DISARMING OF NIGERIANS

As previously mentioned, the standard practice after the conquest of each region and community that would later become Nigeria (as in several parts of Africa) was total disarmament of the indigenous population. This process included seizing all firearms and destroying them in public. During the conquest of the Igbo hinterland in the first decade of the twentieth century, a British military report indicated that more than twenty-five thousand rifles and Dane guns were destroyed within four months, in an area covering about six thousand square miles. Another report from the same area submitted that between December 1901 and April 1905 upward of one hundred thousand rifles and cap guns were confiscated, and five thousand people died.[2] The *Ugwu ntili egbe* (hills where guns were broken and burned) derived its name from the story of the destruction of a large stock of firearms during the colonial conquest.[3] Similarly, the British seized the following weapons from Chief Ogedengbe, an Ekitiparapo warrior, in the aftermath of the imposition of colonial rule in modern southwestern Nigeria in the mid-1890s: 126 Snider rifles, 1 Remington rifle, 20 cap guns, 101 flintlock guns,

42 kegs of gunpowder, 7 kegs of iron bullets, 237 boxes of tins, assorted cartridges, and 18 rockets.[4] Firearms control went beyond local disarmament. As the colonial government consolidated its hold in the hinterland of Nigeria, the British also increased their surveillance of international waterways, ensuring that foreign trading companies did not sell prohibited firearms to Africans, as stipulated in the international agreements discussed previously. Even the few rifles not surrendered to the government became useless after some time given the difficulty of securing ammunition from abroad.

After disarmament, colonial officers then prohibited the use of firearms until they were satisfied that the people had been completely "pacified" or accepted the legitimacy of British colonial sovereignty. This transition period lasted between a few days to several months in different communities across the country. By 1905, the image of a colonial gun society had begun to form through the efforts of Frederick Lugard. Indeed, Lugard's legacy in Nigeria transcended the introduction of the indirect rule political system—he also helped consolidate a new culture of gun ownership. To stabilize the new political units, Lugard and early colonial officers constituted the bodyguards, messengers, and trusted associates of the local chiefs, who formed the bedrock of the indirect rule system, into a law-enforcement unit that would later be known as the Native Authority Police Force (NAPF).[5] Although Lugard believed that the NAPF was "invaluable aid to the Native Authority," he did not allow its agents to carry firearms because of the fear of revolt against the government.[6] Lugard also encouraged the importation of a large quantity of Dane guns because he saw them as "less dangerous from a political point of view" than poisoned arrows.[7] In his famous *Political Memoranda* (a series of guidelines on administrative and political matters addressed to colonial officers), he further laid out his impression of the Dane gun and the bow and arrow in the context of the regional military culture and law and order: "Though I do not consider a 'Dane gun' to be so formidable a weapon as a bow and arrow in the hands of tribes who are expert bowmen, the case is different among communities in the southern provinces, where the bow and arrow has fallen out of use. There is no doubt that the possession of arms gives great confidence and prompts lawless characters to crime which they would not otherwise attempt, and occasionally leads to defiance of Government."[8] Other aspects of Lugard's order on how to deal with insurgency reinforced the military advantage made possible by superior firearms. For instance, he ordered that aside from the enlisted men of the police and army, no other persons should be used for maintaining law and order. This measure was definitely aimed at preventing infiltration, which could undermine intelligence. This directive, as Chapter 6 demonstrates, was abandoned in the wake of a rise in armed robbery in the 1930s.[9]

Lugard's comparison of the bow and arrow was based largely on the military tactic of the Sokoto Caliphate, which he had helped to conquer and several other African territories. The bow and arrow remained popular in the North, but it was going into extinction in the South given the popularity of firearms. An anthropological report on northern Nigeria published in 1919 established the efficacy of poisoned arrows. The Dukawa poisoned arrows were fairly accurate at about fifty to sixty yards—approximately the distance a good marksman could fire a Dane gun accurately. Poisoned arrows, which could also be fired with a Dane gun, were virulent when wet and fresh but less effective in the dry season.[10] The affirmation of the efficacy of poisoned arrows continued to shape the politics of gun control after the first decade of the twentieth century. In an April 1920 correspondence, Governor Hugh Clifford of Nigeria noted that Dane guns are "regarded by officers of experience as less dangerous than poisoned arrows."[11] Regardless, Lugard was one of the first British colonial soldiers to use the deadly Maxim gun, and his successors did not doubt their ability to suppress any insurgency with the Maxim gun accompanying their well-trained rifle-bearing army and police. As liberalization of nonprohibited firearms took firm root, the Nigerian gun society, which was evolving before the 1900s, came to full maturity.

Colonial gun regulations appeared better on the books than in real-life situations. Not everyone surrendered their firearms—many of the precolonial warriors continued to keep large stocks of guns in their homes. Acting Resident Harold Parsons noted in 1905, several years after Ibadan came under British rule, that the disbanded Ibadan warriors, who formed the membership of the Native Authority Police Force, "own, and daily oil, a considerable number of rifles."[12] He proposed to Lagos that the chiefs be compelled to register all arms. Similarly, after the invasion of Eket, the chiefs continued to keep huge amounts of guns for enforcing domestic trading activities. They refused to attend the meeting called by the new colonial officer, Vice Consul Henry Gallwey, unless he returned their confiscated guns, which he had destroyed. "I find these Ibibios very difficult to deal with," Gallwey reported on the defiance to disarmament in 1899.[13] Not all colonial officers believed that disarmament would bring peace. Christopher Wordsworth, who served between 1900 and 1907, thought that "peaceful, unarmed" contact had allowed him to travel peacefully through hostile communities.[14]

But beyond the relationship between arms control and colonial tranquility, the new regime of gun ownership was also influenced by economic considerations. Lugard saw the value of guns as a revenue-generating item of trade, through payment of taxes by the merchant companies that imported them.[15] He was convinced that the proliferation of arms could be monitored only by making it a legal trade and ensuring that all gun users registered their guns and paid an annual license for using them. Gun licenses, like several forms of permits, were considered a means of raising resources to run the colonial state, which the British believed must be self-sustaining, in economic terms. Lugard's policy was popular among administrators. One Captain William Ross, the resident of Oyo Province, bought and distributed 1,200 Dane guns to the people, after registering them in 1917. By the 1920s or earlier, Nigerians did not require foreign merchants to supply Dane guns—local blacksmiths had mastered the production of flintlock guns in large quantity. They could also convert the flintlock mechanism into a percussion one, which was fired with a percussion cap. But the government's limit on the importation of percussion caps, which increased the firing power and reliability of cap guns, restricted their use. Foreign importation of Dane guns dropped from 212,000 in 1932 to 83,000 in 1935.[16] However, gunpowder remained an item of international trade. Throughout the colonial period, more than 90 percent of the gunpowder used for firing Dane guns came from abroad, even though Nigerians were already experimenting with local production.

The response of district officers to a 1921 memorandum from Lagos revealed the level of proliferation of firearms. There were 1,255 and 1,470 registered Dane guns in Ede and Osogbo, respectively, in 1919.[17] However, the district officer estimated that in actuality there were about fifteen thousand guns in circulation in these towns. In Ife Division, the government did not register any new guns between 1918 and 1921, and did not collect any fees from annual registration.[18] There were at least 1,550 registered Dane guns in Ife, Ilesa, and Ila. Osogbo Division, comprising towns such as Ejigbo, Otan, Ogbomoso, Okuku, Ikirun, and Ede, among others, had about three thousand illegal guns in circulation.[19] The explanation for people's refusal to renew their licenses was apparent to most colonial officers—that is, the sudden increase of licensing fees from 1s. to 5s. Hence, while eight hundred people in Osogbo Division registered their guns in 1921, only one did so when the new fees came into effect in 1923.[20] The resident of Oyo Province estimated that there were at least fifty thousand Dane guns in his jurisdiction in 1919.[21]

Regardless, colonial officers including Lugard were convinced that the "number of guns in Egba, Yoruba, and Ijebu countries is enormous" and that serious uprisings in Iseyin-Okeiho and Abeokuta in 1916 and 1918, respectively, testified to the danger that gun liberalization posed to colonial peace.[22] Dane guns' popularity continued to increase in the North, but not at the pace of the South, where virtually every hunter-farmer had one. Regional variation in the North also applied—25 percent and 75 percent of Haraba and Maraba hunters, respectively, used Dane guns by the second half of the 1910s.[23] As chapter 7 and the preceding section in this chapter show, although colonial officers worried about the impact of the proliferation of Dane guns on public order, they never took any drastic action to outlaw them because of the cardinal role of firearms in core aspects of people's social and economic lives. Instead, by 1948, the colonial administration removed it permanently from the list of items that required a license to bear. This full liberalization of Dane guns represented a victory for hunters and farmers, among other gun owners who had long believed that bearing a Dane gun was an important component of their "native" custom, which colonial officers were undermining through the license and registration policy.

Hunting and the Expansion of Dane Gun Culture under Colonial Rule

While the colonialists treated the Dane gun as a revenue-generating item, to Nigerians it had both symbolic and material value. The use of firearms for such activities as hunting affected the environment, culture, politics, and relations between the British and Nigerians in myriad ways. Professional hunting of animals dated back centuries. But the liberalization of the firearms trade in the first half of the twentieth century and the abolition of precolonial warfare and slavery all reconfigured the domestic economy, making professional hunting one of the main occupations in rural areas. The government's outlawing of poisoned arrows for both hunting and self-defense also increased the popularity of firearms. Furthermore, the initial wave of armed robberies that followed the disbanding of local resistance armies, who suddenly found themselves idle after conquest, gave room to gradual tranquility, which directly and indirectly expanded hunting. Whereas in the precolonial period few professional hunters used firearms, in the colonial era Dane guns became the number-one hunting weapon (figure 2.1). Even among the Igbo, for whom the machete was the primary offensive weapon in precolonial times, by the 1920s a hunter was easily identified by his gun and bag. A hunter would wipe the congealed blood of each animal he killed on the stock of his gun. Indeed, the hunter's prowess was determined by the amount of congealed animal blood deposited on his gun stock.[24] The central position that hunting played in the domestic economy of each community varied. While it had an almost equal importance with farming and craft making in many communities, in Calabar and other neighboring villages the product of hunting was the "most valuable article the land produces and in return for which European goods were procured."[25]

Dane guns did not totally eliminate other traditional methods of hunting, such as by bow and arrow, trap, and dog. Neither did it obliterate the roles of the gods and goddesses or spirituality. Charms (*juju*) and indigenous knowledge of ecology continued to play a significant role in successful hunting expeditions.[26] Professional hunters must know the praise names, characters, and rules governing the killing of each animal, as chapter 6 discusses further. "The moral lesson behind the story"—the story being a pastime evening tale about a hunter who shot and killed a spirit snake that attempted to kill his young child (another animal incarnate), collected in Afikpo in the 1950s—"is that hunters do know and understand the language of animals; they know all about the secrets of the night."[27] The popularity of Dane guns among people who would not have had access to them before the twentieth century is one of the interesting dynamics of the Nigerian gun society. Farmers who did not belong to the hunter's guild acquired Dane guns to protect their crops from wild animals; the creation of cocoa plantations, which involved clearing previously uninhabited forest, increased the use of guns by farmers, who made commendable income from cash crops. Many Nigerians kept guns for ceremonial shooting and would never engage in professional or pastime hunting because of rules guiding the traditions of hunting. In many communities, one could not hunt without being initiated into the hunter's guild.

In justifying the need for a shotgun, some professional hunters complained that their Dane gun was a "disappointment," because damp gun-

Figure 2.1. Southern Nigerian Hunters, ca. 1920s. Photograph by P. A. Talbot. Reproduced by the Courtesy of the National Archives Ibadan.

powder would not let it fire, but the so-called primitive firearm served the needs of experienced hunters, partly because they were ubiquitous and far cheaper to maintain than shotguns. Local blacksmiths produced the bullets or shots from a variety of sources ranging from scrap iron to broken pots.[28] In addition, dangerous metals, including nails and poisoned slugs, could be fired from a Dane gun, which was far more resilient than a shotgun. After listing the assortment of items that a hunter loaded into his Dane gun, such as gunpowder and "whatever caught his fancy, old nails, gravels, lead shot—anything," Brinkworth then described the fatality of his shot: "Anything that got hit by that particular whiff of grape at sufficiently close quarters suffered a great deal of harm."[29] Moreover, a Dane gun, unlike a shotgun, fired a single projectile, capable of having stronger impact on targets.

A single, carefully placed Dane gun charge was capable of killing big game like elephant and hippopotamus—though not always instantaneously. Professional hunters knew that they must continue to stalk their target for hours and even days after a successful shot. The case of one Ayo Akinyemi reveals not only the circumstances under which shooting took place but also the effectiveness of Dane guns in killing big game. In his sworn affidavit of

September 6, 1956, about an accidental shooting of an elephant, Akinyemi claimed that a herd of elephants suddenly appeared to him while he was fishing at Omo River in Ijebu Province. The terrified hunter fired his Dane gun at the herd "in self-defence" and "ran away for his life."[30] When he returned to the area three days later, he found a decaying elephant about three hundred yards from where he had shot the animal. A year earlier in 1955, a government forester also "accidentally" killed an elephant with a Dane gun, a few yards from the area where Akinyemi had shot.[31]

While the Dane gun increased a hunter's confidence to hunt wild animals, it did not eliminate the danger inherent in using a firearm that could fire only one shot at a time. Unless a shot hit its target in the head or chest (close to the heart), a poorly placed shot from a Dane gun posed serious danger to the user during a confrontation with a wild animal. The need to overcome this limitation of the Dane gun led to increased training in marksmanship. The conventional wisdom concerning firing at wild animals included taking cover after each shot both to avoid angry reaction by the animal and to allow time to reload for subsequent shots, a process that could take several minutes depending on the expertise of the shooter and the environment, among other factors.

Professional hunting with the Dane gun went beyond the killing of animals for sale, medicine, ornament, or meat; it was also tied to a long history of human struggle against wild animals and for the control of the natural environment. It was during the colonial period that Nigeria lost much of its wild animal (e.g., lion, tiger, elephant, hippopotamus, leopard, fox, buffalo) population, especially those that posed serious danger to humans. On many occasions, wild animals left the forest to raid villages of their livestock, sometimes killing humans in the process. Such sensational newspaper headlines as "Expectant Mother Killed by Bush Cows," "Leopard Carries 14-Year-Old Girl While Mother Looks on Astounded," "17-Year-Old Boy Is Eaten by Wild Beast," "Lioness Devours Girl in the Area of Oloko," and "Eagle Which Killed Child Is Shot Two Years Later" reminded the people that they shared the earth with other powerful creatures.[32] In Odi, the sum of £40 was offered for any hunter who killed a buffalo that had mauled three women, reported the *West African Pilot* of July 6, 1954.[33] In Ikom Kiet, a leopard was killed after it devoured several people, including a baby girl, in 1954.[34]

Occasionally, the newspaper tied the ravaging of wild animals to the government's failure to provide public amenities such as streetlights to increase visibility at night. Some in the press even argued it was the responsibility of the government to take down the dangerous animals. This was particularly evident in the case of a notorious female leopard, known for attacking livestock in Ijeun Quarter in Abeokuta in 1916.[35] "Perhaps when some highly placed person shall have become the victim of the beast," the *Nigerian Pioneer* anticipated, "the authorities will become alert to their duties."[36] Another newspaper article reported how an "intrepid young" hunter shot a "full grown" leopard on April 30, 1916, and how young boys who set out to kill grasscutters (cane rats) lost fifteen of their eighteen hunting dogs to a leopard in Abeokuta. An experienced hunter later killed the leopard. The following published statement by the hunter who killed the leopard dramatized the battle between humans and animals, hunting techniques, and the efficacy of a Dane gun: "I went quietly round the back of him, fired and fell him. He was however, soon on his legs looking savagely round for the bold intruder. I lay on my back and reloaded, taking good care that the animal did not get to the rear of me. He soon spotted me and made a charge. I aimed at his head, fired and down came the beast, this time stone dead."[37]

In addition, the imposition of colonial rule reconstituted the geography of hunting. In precolonial times, hunting rules traditionally restricted hunters to forests within their native lands—hunters who sought hunting in another community required prior approval of the chiefs. However, the creation of new political entities such as native authorities, districts, and provinces redefined people's political affiliations and identities and broadened the area hunters could exploit to include forests hundreds of miles away from their immediate communities. The expansion of hunting opportunities not only intensified deforestation; it consistently created conflict among communities over hunting spaces.

The writings of colonial officers, travelers, and missionaries are filled with descriptions of the impact of excessive hunting on Nigerian wildlife. "Question any old hunter in hunting areas of Okpoto and Boki," the resident officer of Ogoja Province asserted about the impact of Dane gun use in his jurisdiction in 1920, "and he will tell you the supply of game is not what it was; it is becoming more difficult to get bush meat every year."[38] When he assumed his duty as the new assistant district officer in Warri Province in the 1950s, Brinkworth claimed that "chief among the things that didn't exist" in his area was shooting. "Everything that moved," he wrote exaggeratedly, "had been shot to pieces years ago by Africans armed with Dane guns."³⁹ Writing about southern Nigeria in the early 1920s, P. Amaury Talbot, a prolific anthropologist and colonial officer, wrote that "hunting is carried on more or less indiscriminately by everybody who happens to be a good shot."⁴⁰ In a detailed anthropological work on the Igbo published in 1938, missionary G. T. Basden gives a picture of the relationship between firearms and hunting and the ecology of the region: "There has been since the introduction of firearms, an unrestricted slaughter of bird and beast until they have been reduced almost to vanishing points. One may travel hundreds of miles and only occasionally see a few monkeys or a scared deer. The course of covering 100,000 miles, I doubt if more than half a dozen wild animals have crossed my path."⁴¹ An elephant hunt was a common sight at the beginning of the twentieth century, but Basden, who worked in the hinterland of Igboland for close to four decades, contended that "it is rare to hear of one at present day." He concluded that a lot of time and "arduous" hunting was required to find other classes of wild animals like the bush cow and leopard, which used to be plentiful in the past.⁴² The situation in the northern part of the country was like that in the South. Writing in the first half of the 1920s, colonial officer A. C. G. Hastings, after narrating how his rifle shot narrowly missed a lion, noted that much of the territories inhabited by humans in Kebbi used to be the natural abode of wild animals just decades before. Elephants, according to Hastings, used to feed in the marsh, close to the colonial officer's station, lions inhabited the polo grounds of Lokoja and Zungeru, and hippopotamuses swarmed in smaller rivers.⁴³

These observations of the depletion of Nigerian wildlife may have been exaggerated; nonetheless, the use of firearms did intensify the killing of wild animals, especially elephants for ivory. The ivory trade predates the establishment of colonial rule, but demand for, and hence the economic value of, this item increased with the introduction of a cash economy under British imperial power. The globalization of animal and trophy collection went hand in hand with the expansion of other sectors of the domestic and global economies. By the 1930s, several local traders, including the Nigerian Ivory Trading Company, had established a lucrative business of collecting ivories predominantly for the international market.⁴⁴ In 1907, the Royal Niger Company was bartering guns or gunpowder, or both, for tusks that weighed more than twenty-two pounds in some areas in northern Nigeria.⁴⁵ In 1952, two thousand pounds of ivory was worth about £1,000 in Lagos.⁴⁶ In January 1951, a Japanese firm, Tokyo Sales Inc., contracted a Nigerian trading company (Bright Way Stores) to supply it with two thousand pounds of ivory—a quantity that government officers described as "large" and that was the most they had ever approved.[47] An average ivory from Nigeria weighed about forty to forty-five pounds; therefore, the fulfillment of the request by Tokyo Sales would claim at least twenty-five elephants. While much Nigerian ivory was trafficked abroad, there was equally a local market for other elephant parts, some of which were used for traditional medicine. One Mallam Alli of Ibadan, in a March 1951 correspondence to the government, valued an elephant tooth, used for native medicine, at £100.[48] Trade in live animals for private and public zoos across the world directly fueled the need for guns for offensive and defensive purposes in the thick forest. So high was the application for the export of wild animal products in 1936 that the government made a newspaper announcement reminding the public of the existence of the Wild Animal Preservation Ordinance, a law meant to protect Nigerian wildlife.[49]

Nigerians killed elephants not only for ivory, medicine, and meat. The massive animals, which moved mostly in herds, posed a great threat to farmlands, not only because they consumed staple crops like yam and cassava, but also because they trampled them under foot. Even highly expensive cash crops like cocoa were not safe from the ravaging impact of elephants. The story of elephants invading and temporarily occupying farmsteads gained front-page coverage in Lagos newspapers like the *West African Pilot* and the *Daily Service* that sympathized with the agony of the country people.[50] One story published in the *Daily Service* detailed how a herd of twenty to sixty elephants caused "incalculable losses," destroying thousands of heaps of crops and forcing villagers to leave their homes.[51] Another story in the *West African Pilot* decried the "alarming" destruction caused by elephants in Auchi and urged authorities to take action to help "poor peasants."[52] Among the goriest stories of elephant atrocity, one animal killed four people in Iseyin in 1952 before returning to the forest. Its victims included a pregnant woman mauled on her way to fetch water from a stream.[53]

The descriptions in newspaper accounts and government documents relating to insecurity caused by wild animals tend to imply that Nigerians lacked the ability to control the animal world. But this is not the case—in fact, most communities had expert elephant and wildlife hunters. Nigerians' response to the conflict between humans and animals was made difficult by colonial wildlife conservation laws. From the early 1900s, the government responded to the unprecedented killing of elephants, among other wild animals, through passage of the Wild Animals Preservation Ordinance (WAPO) and creation of game reserves where hunting was prohibited. Thus, gun regulation politics and wildlife conservation, according to the secretary of the Northern Provinces in 1907, "are intimately connected."[54] Although the WAPO applied to most wild animals (lions, elephants, leopards, hippopotamuses, tigers, and exotic birds, among others), it was enforced mostly against the killing of elephants to check the trafficking in ivory. The following are the core elements of the ordinance: Before a wild animal could be killed, a district officer had to visit the community under threat and assess the level of danger. The community then organized hunters, who had to collect a permit, which normally would expire within thirty days; share the animal meat with the entire community; and deposit the ivory with the district officer, whose responsibility it was to send it to the central government treasury in Lagos for public auction.[55] Proceeds of the auction went to the government. The British imposed a deliberately expensive, onetime permit of £10, to discourage people from hunting elephants. Other hunting rules included that the hunter must not chase the elephants into the wilderness or government reserve; hence the killing must take place within the farmland being allegedly destroyed. Only adult bulls could be killed; it was an offense to kill female and young animals, regardless of the circumstances involved. Hunters, even those who were licensed, could be prosecuted if each ivory weighed less than twenty-two pounds. Hunters were required to inform their district officer of the killing of an elephant within three to seven days. From all indications, game laws turned Nigerians into poachers, even in their own communities.[56] While Nigerian hunters were prosecuted for killing wild animals, their European counterparts conceived hunting of large and small game as a legitimate form of recreation—one of the benefits of being assigned to work in tropical Africa.

But this regulation did not stop the shooting of elephants for ivory, as an underground ivory market remained in force throughout the colonial period. Hunter-farmers were unwilling to pay £10 for the right to kill elephants, which they considered an inalienable privilege to the exploitation of their community's natural endowment. Although the government did occasionally grant free licenses to hunt elephants, communities far from government offices killed elephants without government approval. Yet the felling of an elephant would rarely go unnoticed by the government because, by custom, the entire community would feast on it. The news of the killing of wild animals tended to travel fast and far. What is more, the rules for killing an elephant were hard to follow. Few hunters would wait for the animal to arrive on their farm and cause damage before shooting at it. Seasonal movements of animals in response to weather changes inhibited successful hunting by people who had game licenses. In March 1948, the *Orimolusi* (king) of Ijebu Igbo pleaded with his district officer to extend the game permit granted to his community to kill one bull elephant because hunters "reported that the elephants have left for a swampy area outside my jurisdiction during this dry season, and that they are likely to return to my area during forthcoming rainy season."[57]

One of the flawed elements of government animal conservation regulations was their overwhelming emphasis on the economic value of wild game. In fact, the cultural, medicinal, symbolic, and other aesthetic value of animals was as important as their economic value to local communities. Chiefs directly and indirectly supported the contravening of the WAPO because it disrespected the existing customary laws on big-game hunting.[58] In most local customs, the tusks, bones, and skins or hides, among other parts of wild animals, were an embodiment of cultural symbolism tied to social class, gender, and power relations. The kings and traditional elites had the prerogative, for instance, to keep the skin of lions killed within their jurisdiction. The *Oba* of Benin was entitled to one foot and one tusk of every elephant mauled, while the flesh near the kidneys belonged to the royal mother.[59] Very few chiefs would submit to the WAPO. When the resident officer of Ijebu Igbo got wind of the killing of an elephant in July 1932, he asked the *Orimolusi* to surrender the hunter for prosecution as well as the ivories. In his defense of native law, the *Orimolusi* claimed that the hunter must remain in seclusion for fourteen days "as he is bound to perform native customary ceremony relative to the killing according to the ancient orders of the Native Hunters."[60] The *Orimolusi* was willing to allow the government to measure the ivories but insisted he must keep them as the custom enshrined. When conflict over ivories emerged, the government would sell the ivories to the chiefs, at a price favorable to them.[61]

Beyond the clash between indigenous traditions of animal hunting and colonial laws, the contradiction in the regulation of big-game hunting also drove the illicit ivory trade. People could trade in ivory without government permit, but they had to ensure that the item was lawfully obtained. Only exporters of ivory required a permit. Yet there was no limit to the amount of ivory that could be exported out of Nigeria. The geographical distribution of wild animals across Nigeria was unequal for obvious reasons of diverse landscapes and habitats. For instance, in the hinterland of southwestern Nigeria, elephant hunting was popular in places such as Saki, Iganmu, Shepeteri, and Igbeti, even in the early 1950s.[62] Conversely, anthropological writings suggest that there were few elephants in the Igbo region during the 1930s.[63] Yet the WAPO did not recognize these differences, and instead sought to impose a unitary regulation for hunting animals across Nigeria's diverse ecology. In addition, conflicting information about Nigerian wildlife populations created inconsistent submission about the real and imagined dangers that the wildlife were posing to humans. While in 1917 the secretary of the Southern Provinces submitted that "the number of elephants is small at the moment," without reference to a particular region or community, a census of 169 elephants in the five communities of Bata, Diye, Iwonwo, Imeri, and Olosan in the southwest submitted by forest rangers in 1939 was considered too much for the area.[64] A local hunter, Chief Agbashan of Oban Division in the Cross-River region was said to have killed thirty-five elephants within a few months in 1907.[65] In a rare acknowledgment of the diversity of Nigeria's ecology, the acting secretary to the government in 1935 granted unrestricted permission to shoot elephants in Bama and Gwoza districts of Bornu Province because of the "serious damage that is being done by large herds of elephants."[66] But the "elephant problem" in this area seemed to continue even until the 1950s. Another elephant attack in October 1950 in the Dikwa emirate of the province drove an entire community away during the most important period—the beginning of the planting season.[67]

The transformation of human settlement patterns and ecosystems during the first half of the twentieth century largely accounted for the conflict between humans and animals. This is one aspect of West Africa's environmental history that requires serious attention. In southwestern Nigeria, the introduction of the cocoa economy reconfigured human settlement patterns as extensive acreage of predominantly uninhabited forestlands, the natural home of wild animals, was opened up for plantation. Not only were plantations established in previously uninhabited forestlands, new settlements and villages sprang up in and around cocoa plantations. Before and during World War II, the demand for wild rubber saw humans venturing deep into new forestlands, opening them up to agriculture.[68] The population boom that Nigeria witnessed in the middle of the twentieth century (from an estimated eighteen million in the early 1920s to fifty-five million in 1963) and rapid urbanization took place at the expense of the natural environment.[69] As towns became big cities, and as villages rapidly transformed into towns, so did the farm belt adjust to accommodate the growing human population that pushed deeper and deeper into the wilderness. Human interference with ecological balance intensified armed conflict for dominance of nature.

Dane guns were used for purposes other than hunting animals. They were the primary defensive and offensive weapons in popular uprisings against the colonial government and in communal conflicts. Although they were ineffective in armed resistance, because the government possessed superior weaponry like machine guns, which Nigerians were not allowed to have, they proved destructive in intra-Nigerian fighting. Moreover, Dane guns offered an advantage in non-hand-to-hand battle with thieves, intruders, or other unwanted persons. In one example, Job Udo of Uqua Eket shot Ikpa with his Dane gun while the latter was running away with items he stole from the former's compound on the night of December 4, 1951. Ikpa "collapsed and died on the spot," a newspaper crime report stated.[70] Dane guns were also the most popular firearms used by hunters who guarded communities at night. As Chapter 6 shows, the government was not favorably disposed to allowing the hunter guards in the villages to carry guns during patrol because of fear of insurgency. But large European firms in the big cities were able to secure government approval for their night guards to carry Dane guns. When Nkwere, a John Holt night guard, killed one of three invaders of the European firm's location in Benin City in September 1944, his employer gave him a ten-shilling bonus for his heroic exploits.[71]

Moreover, Dane guns—one of the most valuable economic assets and items of material culture possessed by many rural dwellers—were popular collateral for borrowing money. People who received a gun as a pawn or collateral were free to use it until their debtor returned their money in full. The gun's economic value transcended its use as a hunting weapon, or mere provider of individual livelihood; the good-luck magic, or juju, performed on Dane guns to allow them to find and hunt valuable game constituted a significant intangible community asset. The older a Dane gun, the longer its exploits in hunting valuable and exotic animals. Thus, a Dane gun known to a community to have killed a wild animal terrorizing that community was considered more valuable than a rifle, the most advanced firearm that both Nigerians and Europeans could legally possess. The popularity of guns as debt collateral increased as the government outlawed other forms of collateral such as the pawning of persons. Disagreements over "gun as pawn" or "gun as collateral" transactions regularly appeared in civil cases tried by the native courts. In one case in Tivland in 1952–53, Apev approached Iyoade (probably a native magician or doctor) to help him recover a lost item. Apev did not have the £1 that Iyoade charged for the service, so he used his Dane gun as collateral. Iyoade kept his promise and helped Apev recover his lost item. When Apev approached Iyoade with £1 to retrieve his gun, he learned that he (Iyoade) had pawned the same gun to one Ayam for £1. 12s. But the economic value of the gun had increased over the course of transfer from one person to another—Ayam claimed he spent 12s. to repair the gun and would release it only for £2. 4s. When the case came before the Tiv native court, the elders ruled that Iyoade must pay 12s. (the cost of repairing the gun), in addition to the £1. 12s. he borrowed from Ayam.[72]

The Shotgun, Social Class, and Self-Fashioning

Elite consumer attitudes reinforced the possession of the shotgun, the most liberalized of the arms of precision. Nigerians fancied the shotgun just as they did many other foreign items, such as cars. In Yorubaland, the shotgun was called *ibon oyinbo* (white man's gun), and the Dane gun *ibon ibile* (local gun). Both the shotgun and its cartridges were also more expensive than the Dane gun. In the late 1950s, an average Dane gun cost around £2, while a shotgun owned by Mathew T. Mbu, a Nigerian diplomat serving in the United Kingdom, was valued at £18. 10s.[73] Owners of shotguns also paid more for licenses and annual registration—it cost 10s. and 5s. to renew shotgun and Dane gun licenses, respectively, in the early 1930s. All classes of educated lower-, middle-, and upper-class Nigerians had shotguns—namely, government office staff members, teachers, forest guards, storekeepers, clerks, journalists, doctors, and lawyers. Other categories of shotgun owners included local entrepreneurs, like J. O. Mbadiwe, a mining contractor and owner of a popular liquor store in Kaduna.[74] In Onitsha in 1945, about two hundred people, predominantly "influential" members of the native council, owned shotguns.[75] This figure (and the ones in table 2.1 derived from yearly license renewals) is definitely on the low side—several known gun owners did not register or renew their firearms licenses.

Table 2.1. Annual registration of firearms in Ibadan Division 1950–1953

Year	Double-barrel shotgun	Single-barrel shotgun	Rifle	Pistol	Revolver	Total
1950	281	10	50	28	29	398
1951	293	28	49	18	32	420
1952	320	36	52	21	30	459
1953	252	30	31	8	26	347

Source: National Archives Ibadan (NAI), Ibadan Div. 2521.

Whereas Nigerian blacksmiths could make and repair Dane guns, very few could make shotguns, which throughout the colonial period were imported. Moreover, blacksmiths probably did not invest in shotguns because the cartridges were more expensive. Otherwise called "scatter" guns because their projectiles made a scattered impact on their target, shotguns were not, in a practical sense, "arms of precision" as classified by the government. However, they did have a marked advantage over Dane guns because, as breechloaders, they were easier to reload. This is probably why the colonial government restricted the shotgun to the educated elites, whom they thought posed only a limited armed threat to colonial rule because they were more "intelligent" than the majority of the "uncivilized" Dane gun–bearing locals. In other words, in the colonial politics of arms regulation, all Nigerians were not equal—just as in most other aspects of colonial-African encounter. A shot from the shotgun, like the Dane gun, could also be very lethal at short range. But the Dane gun could be more effective in killing big game at short distance, since its owner could fire a large quantity of dangerous metal projectiles like nails. Also, the long barrel of the Dane gun enhanced marksmanship. In contrast, shotguns used cartridges with premeasured amounts of gunpowder and pellets. The construction of the shotgun as the firearm of the elites owed in part to its shorter barrel, which made storing, transporting, and firing easier.

Other notable advantages of the shotgun over the Dane gun had to do with method of operation and consumer habits across social class. The Dane gun was a muzzle loader. Loading it created some dirt and mess as the user poured a desired quantity of gunpowder and bolts or pellets down the barrel and used a long metal rod to drive them tightly inside. A fire-inducing object (a fiber from dried palm branches) was required to ignite the charge inside the barrel when the flint struck the steel. This process not only required some level of expertise and time; it could be dangerous if improperly conducted. Conversely, the shotgun was a more user-friendly firearm. The owner inserted a cartridge from the breech or back of the gun, closed the gun, aimed at a target, and pulled the trigger. As table 2.1 illustrates, most of the shotguns in use in the 1940s and 1950s were double-barreled, which give the user the opportunity to fire two charges in quick succession. I came across a only triple-barreled shotgun twice in the arms registry and other colonial documents. Shotguns were primarily a hunting weapon for both expert and nonexpert shooters—the scattering effect of the shot enhances success in hunting small game, giving hunters some feeling of pride and control over their prey. But during the period of decolonization and the rise of bitter party politics, its use in violent conflict would usher in a new era of gun regulation.

Imperial attitudes toward security also shaped the ways in which Nigerians were allowed to purchase firearms. Unlike "ordinary" Nigerians who were required to buy their Dane guns from the trading companies such as the United Africa Company, John Holt, and others who specialized in sporting goods, the elites were allowed by the government to import their shotguns directly, in addition to buying from Nigerian-based merchants. The procedure was quite simple. A prospective importer of a shotgun first applied to the controller of customs for a permit to buy a gun from abroad, paid the custom duties when the gun arrived, and then sought the approval of his local authority for a license to bear the gun. This license was renewable on a yearly basis. The intensification of the activities of the Royal Society for the Prevention of Cruelty to Animals in Nigeria in the 1950s also popularized the use of captive-bolt weapons (also known as human-killer guns) among conservation officers, who used them to put down "hopelessly injured or unwanted" animals.[76]

The difference between a Dane gun and a shotgun transcends the colonialists' and Nigerians' construction of social class in relation to the perception of the danger that different types of firearms posed to public safety and colonial order. It also mirrored the transformation in the cultural conception of masculinity and access to firearms. During the colonial period, one could not use a Dane gun without paying regular homage or being a devotee or worshipper of the god of iron (especially Ogun among the Yoruba). It was a prerequisite. Ogun was believed not only to control the animal world and shape access or luck to hunt desired game but also to guard hunters against misfortune such as gun accidents or mauling by a wild beast. Marksmanship, even though it was part of a hunter's core training, went beyond human ingenuity and brilliance—it was viewed as a gift from the gods bestowed on humans who fulfilled covenants by performing regular sacrifices and obeying traditions. Access to Dane guns was not determined by age or socioeconomic status; rather, it was shaped by the fulfillment of rites of passage and mastery of cultural codes particular to the hunter's guild and the god of iron.[77] Among the Upila in the 1910s, "it is the ambition of every youth" to possess a Dane gun and "when that aim is gratified, a wife."[78]

Conversely, the condition for possessing a shotgun was being "educated" or "enlightened." Bearers of shotguns were not only deemed to be "civilized"; few would participate in the worship of the god of iron or respect any cultural codes associated with hunting. Most were urbanites, free from the cultural obligation imposed on the possession of a gun in the rural areas. The user-friendly nature of shotguns (described earlier) meant that long-term training was not needed. This cultural perception of firearms across social class was also shaped by the gradations of masculinity. Oral history of the colonial period collected from some Yoruba villages in summer of 2015 indicates that men who used a Dane gun felt they were superior to their shotgun-owning counterparts.[79] Hence, all guns, not to mention their bearers, occupied different rungs in the gradation and framing of masculinity.

Aside from the patterns of government gun liberalization, newspaper ads helped in consolidating the shotgun as an insignia of social class. Advertisement of shotguns, like other imported commodities, tied global commerce to the emergent elite consumerist culture in colonial Nigeria. Shotguns and their cartridges did not all have the same properties, as advertisements obviously attempted to establish. Important selling points included such attributes as high velocity and enhanced safety features. Gunmakers knew that consumers preferred smokeless shotguns and cartridges, and they tended to tailor their ad descriptions to suit that preference. Other esoteric advertisement descriptions included "strength," "satisfactory performance," and craftsmanship (figure 2.2). A beautifully and creatively finished shotgun stock crafted by an expert gunsmith was far more attractive than the industrial ones produced in large quantity without much artistic ingenuity. It was the newspaper, more than any other avenue, that brought Nigerians closer to the physical properties of shotguns, promoting sporting and gaming as rewarding activities. In addition, Nigerians did announce

L. C. Smith Long Range Shotguns.

The new Smith Long Range 12 bore 32 inch barrels chambered for 3 inch cartridges is the strongest long range hardhitting gun ever made: The immense popularity of the Smith guns is due chiefly to their great strength, durability and satisfactory performance. The longer you shoot an L. C. Smith gun the tighter it really gets. Obtainable in Lagos at moderate prices from the sole Agents.

Hunter Express Special Long Range Cartridges.

"The King of long range loads." The Hunter Express, Special Long Range Progressive Burning Smokeless Powder load has been found to add 50 yards to the range of any gun. Its penetration at long distance with bone smashing power has made the Hunter Express an all-round game load. Obtainable in 12, 16, and 410 bores and in all sizes from the Sole Agents.

The Nigerian Sporting Goods Depot
Arms and Ammunition Specialist
38, Palm Church Street, P.O. Box 657,
Lagos, Nigeria.

Figure 2.2. Advertisement of shotgun in *Eko Akete*, May 27, 1937.

their intention to buy and sell shotguns in the newspapers.[80] Much of this transaction between consumers involved used guns, cheaper than the ones sold directly by the manufactures and trading merchants.

The government firearms registry and the written application for a gun license from the early 1950s required interesting biographical information from Nigerian shotgun owners. In his application to use a double-barreled shotgun, S. A. Bamiro, the headmaster of Lagos-based Premier School and an instructor at the Teachers' Training College, stated that he earned £325 per annum and was educated at the prestigious Saint Andrew's Teacher Training College in Oyo. Bamiro indicated that he was older than forty years, had three wives, nine children, and lived in the Lagos mainland of Surulere. While not stating why he wanted a shotgun license, the last paragraph of his July 1957 letter spoke about character, which was becoming a significant criterion for granting a shotgun permit after the Enugu colliery shooting: "I have credentials to assure you that I am a responsible man."[81] With his income, Bamiro definitely belonged to the class of Nigeria's highest-earning government employees. Most middle-class Nigerians with a secondary school certificate or diploma made between £36 and £68 per year. While Bamiro did not state why he wanted a shotgun, another Surulere resident, Robert Iwedi, a journalist with nineteen years' experience with the *West African Pilot*, did. In his application, he sought a double-barreled shotgun to be used for "sporting purposes" when he visited his native home in Ahoada Division.[82]

It was not too difficult for big-city administrators to verify the claims made by applicants about occupation and socioeconomic status. From the 1940s, they kept the directory "Important Personalities" with names and addresses of professionals and civil servants such as lawyers, doctors, teachers, and politicians. Applicants who lacked reputation like Bamiro and Iwedi usually identified with well-known persons who could testify to their good character.[83] This is evident in the case of S. A. Okonkwo, a clerk with Ojukwu Transport Limited.[84] The forty-three-year-old man asked the licensing officer to obtain information about his good conduct from his boss, Chief L. Ojukwu, a prominent businessman and the father of Chukwuemeka Odumegwu Ojukwu, a military officer who would later become the leader of Biafran subnationalists in the 1960s.

What Nigerians used, or claimed to use, shotguns for mirrored the transformation in the government regulations of firearms. In the 1920s and

1930s, Nigerian elites did not have to justify why they needed shotguns—their status alone was enough to grant them permission to own firearms. They were not required to know how to use guns. As we shall see in chapter 7, firearms regulation became tighter as the government's perception of security intensified after the Enugu colliery shooting of November 1949. After being shotgun owners for a while, some Nigerians naturally wanted to upgrade, either to emulate Europeans who owned rifles or to exhibit some distinction within their social class. Like other possessors of luxury items, owners of shotguns frequently flouted their guns to seek public attention. Firearms applications clearly show that people sought guns for self-defense from both wild animals and thieves. D. A. Oyegbite, Esq., the secretary of the Okeigbo Cooperative Society and a government postal agent, wanted a double-barreled shotgun in April 1950 because he was in possession up to £4,000 in cash.[85] Reverend K. C. Edokpolo of the Church Missionary Society applied to use a rifle in June 1950 because his evangelical itinerary in the bush brought him into frequent contact with dangerous animals like buffalo. He referenced a *Daily Times* report about how a buffalo "snatched a woman from her husband" while on a bush journey to justify why he needed a rifle.[86] Another applicant, Adeusi, the *Baale* (chief) of Ikota, wanted a double-barreled shotgun because buffalos and monkeys were destroying his farm crops.[87]

Some professional local hunters who used Dane guns applied for licenses to buy rifles to hunt big game. One of them, E. A. Kinihun of Ilesa Division, who claimed to be a hunter of thirty years' experience, thought that without a rifle he "[would] not be able to hunt [elephants] successfully."[88] Gun users preferred rifles for several reasons: their appearance was unique; they were the most lethal firearm a civilian could own; they were more reliable than either shotguns or Dane guns, partly because they used enclosed metal bullets and could fire multiple shots without reloading; and their grooved barrels increased range and accuracy. One Daniel Ogundimeti claimed, "I do not trust native guns [Dane guns] . . . for they are very disappointing"—probably alluding to the fact that a damp cartridge and gunpowder could prevent a Dane gun and shotgun from firing.[89] Yet many a "big" Nigerian man had more guns than he actually needed. I. O. Egbelowa, a UAC cocoa inspector, became popular in several villages in southwestern Nigeria in the early 1950s because he was seen regularly sporting four shotguns.[90] Gun collecting was another element of class distinction that reflected the felt need among many men to exhibit superior masculinity among their peers or to imitate Europeans, most of whom had more than one gun. Gun collecting went beyond the desire to own different categories of guns, with diverse capacities (quality of stock or butt and reputation of maker were major factors).

In response to the increasing use of shotguns for interparty conflict during the era of decolonization and, more important, to reduce the amount of guns in circulation following the Enugu colliery shooting, some district officers made gun-license seekers sign an affidavit that they could be called on to undergo a test to determine their ability to use firearms safely.[91] Archival sources clearly reveal that few people were ever summoned for this test. Lewis Udobi, a foreman and long-serving staff member of the Kano Native Authority, was among the few Nigerians called for a shooting test in June 1956. Udobi failed the test. He provided a glimpse into the manner in which the test was conducted in his letter of petition to the resident of Kano Province: "At the police office, the Superintendent of Police handed a gun to me and asked me whether I have the idea of operating the gun. I said no! Upon that he asked me to loose, fix and shoot; I told him that he knows that the one who has no permit could not be allowed to handle such a gun; on face of this he told me that he will not recommend me."[92] Udobi probably refused to follow the police officer's instruction in order not to be accused of operating a gun without license. If he passed the test, that would automatically mean he had been using a gun, illegally. Udobi could have been one of the many people who were using firearms illegally but decided to obtain a license during the 1950s, when the government tightened its gun regulation policies.

Be that as it may, the shotgun culture was a paradox—there were many gun owners, but few shooters. Indeed, people bought guns not necessarily to shoot them but merely to acquire them, like any other foreign import. In the first place, the largest number of Nigerian shotgun owners were city dwellers; the urban landscape offered limited opportunity for hunting, which was the primary purpose for which the firearm was expected to be used. In fact, the government's projection in the 1920s that shotgun popularization would encourage recreational and game shooting among Nigerians did not come to pass. Rather, most shotgun owners were hesitant to substitute hunting, which posed some hazard, for other readily available forms of recreation. Even local chiefs and traditional elites rarely used their shotguns for hunting. In most communities, prevailing customary laws did not allow nonmembers of the hunters' guild to hunt with firearms, either for leisure or as a means of livelihood. It is apparent that the shotgun, aside from according its owner some degree of respect, created some sense of security as well for self-defense. An applicant for a gun license in 1952, Salawu Adefemi, who self-identified as an "independent" man (a term denoting his lack of affiliation with any political party during the turbulent era of decolonization) and a "prominent and honourable" personality of Ede, did not plan to shoot. Rather, he thought that his single-barreled gun would "surely frighten the thieves who may happen to hear of my being in its possession."[93] Government documents provide some insight into the pattern of shooting among Nigerians. In a report on firearms compiled in March 1940, the secretary to the Government of Nigeria, relying on evidence from superior police officers, claimed that many owners of shotguns did not know how to use them. The report affirmed that many "damaged guns littered" the attics of most homes.[94] This evidence does not contradict that from Nigerians themselves. M. O. Ajayi, in his letter of license renewal in 1956, expressed a desire to acquire a revolver because his shotgun, which be bought in 1940 and had never used, was damaged. He promised to learn to use his revolver if the government granted him a license.[95]

Some Nigerians did make an attempt to institutionalize recreational shooting, against all the odds. In 1915, the Nigerian Hunting Society, later known as the Lagos Hunters' Club (LHC), was formed to "develop good marksmanship and to keep together men well skilled in game-hunting."[96] The club became dormant for a long time, but was revitalized in the mid-1930s. Comprising predominantly "distinguished" Lagosian civil servants, the LHC was apparently established because the European rifle clubs and the Nigerian Rifle Association would not admit Africans. In 1936, its members included Dr. J. C. Vaughan, a founding member of the Lagos (later Nigerian) Youth Movement; Pedro Sebastian, a clerk with the Santa Anna Magistrate Court; A. A. Alakija, a politician and member of the Legislative Council; and L. A. Dada, a noted gun dealer. In 1936, the LHC claimed to have one hundred members, met twice a week, and did shooting at the Lagos suburb of Itirin (near Victoria Beach) and Ikeja. A police background report noted that the organization is "extremely well behaved" and that "it is not an easy matter to become a member"—language that suggests that its membership was selective or well controlled.[97] The LHC sought to improve its popularity by seeking the official recognition of the central government in Lagos. In September 1936, it applied to the government for a grant and for the governor to be its patron.⁹⁸ Not only did the governor refuse the LHC's request; he made a discouraging remark that "in the neighborhood of Lagos its activities must necessarily be somewhat confined."⁹⁹ As we shall see in chapter 4, recreational shooting, even among Europeans, was a highly politicized activity, for it bordered on the perception of colonial officers' safety, identity, and credible use of leisure.

The reason some gun owners did not use their guns regularly was not because they did not want to, but because of the difficulties of getting cartridges. Gun owners who ordered their cartridges directly from abroad (because they were more expensive to buy locally) waited for several months, sometimes after the expiration date of their ammunition license. They were thus compelled to obtain another ammunition license before their consignment could be released to them by the customs office in Lagos. Game shooting, like other forms of recreation, could be a difficult hobby to maintain as individuals changed environments and jobs. This is particularly true in the case of one Amanetchi, who engaged regularly in shooting when he lived in Makurdi and Lokoja. But when he assumed a new position as a charge nurse in the African hospital in Zaria in 1926, he had to stop shooting because the nature of his job compelled him to be at his station at all times. He could not leave the precinct of the hospital beyond the radius of one mile. Nevertheless, he continued to renew his license between 1926 and 1935, even though he did not use the gun, in order not to lose his gun to the government.¹⁰⁰

Leading international merchant companies like the UAC and John Holt rarely kept large stocks of cartridges, because they consumed storage space for the more marketable gunpowder. Cartridges (made with paper), like gunpowder, could also be damaged if exposed to prolonged damp conditions. Nigerians, like L. A. Sadare of Osogbo, worked to solve this problem by attempting to break the monopoly of large trading firms that supplied cartridges. Sadare's application to trade in cartridges in the "interest of the community" tied his personal economic interest to that of the larger gun society: "At the moment a lot of inconveniences are encountered by holders of shotgun licenses in this area because of the formality to be gone through before one can obtain his supply is so boring that nearly every holder of shotgun was compelled to give up shooting."¹⁰¹ In other instances, shortages of cartridges were emblematic of bigger problems that were beyond gun owners' control.¹⁰² In August 1945, members of the Calabar Shot Gun and Licence Holder Union petitioned the government for the reduction of the cost of an annual shotgun license from 10s. to 5s. because they were not using their guns due to wartime emergency regulations that was responsible for the cartridge scarcity.[103] This proposal did not receive the blessing of the government; the secretary of the Eastern Provinces wrote a memo arguing that holders of shotguns were "men of some standing" and that a "prosperous class of the community" should be able to afford the annual 10s. license.[104]

"A Noise Is a Great Thing": Signals, Ceremonial Shooting, and the Spectacle of Culture

Chapter 1 established that the tradition of gun salutes during important ceremonies such as the beginning of the planting season and a ruler's coronation started in the precolonial period. But the expansion of the gun and gunpowder trade increased not only the amount of shooting but also the avenues and circumstances under which it took place. By the 1920s, gun firing, which sustained the colonial gun society, was carried out during virtually all ceremonies—religious or secular, and from the most important affairs connected to the wellness of an entire community to private events restricted to members of a family or associations such as age grades and religious groups. Gunshots were significant signals in the symbolic order during rites of passage and ritualistic practice. In Afikpo in the 1950s, gunshots were used to announce the birth of the first child of a man and featured prominently in the initiation rites of boys.[105] In this community, the metaphoric use of a gun and its sound not only revealed the power to wreak havoc; it also denoted the phase of human childhood development when a child older than a year could move and run well—in fact, the custom is called *igba oso* (fire gun), meaning "capable of being assertive."[106] In addition, while the military class monopolized gun salutes in precolonial times, under colonial rule any gun owner could appear at the ceremony ground to add to the gun noise, which increasingly became the signifier of the success of festivals, of self-representation, and of social-class distinction. A European observer noted in the 1950s that ceremonial shooting "conferred prestige on their owners and made a lovely bang."[107] What is more, by the 1920s, both the colonial government and Nigerian ethnicities accepted gun firing at ceremonies as an integral component of "native custom." This affirmation spoke effectively to the dynamism of the Nigerian gun society.

Let us take a closer look at the space and circumstances under which ceremonial shooting took place in colonial Nigeria, including as part of funeral rites. The reconfiguration of the rights and privileges of ceremonial shooting in the first half of the twentieth century is perhaps one of the most outstanding transformations of gun firing and of burial culture in general. In the precolonial era, shooting was restricted to the funerals of the military aristocracy and of important kings and chiefs, but the demise of professional war making during the first half of the twentieth century necessitated a reinvention of this culture. The burial rites of people who did not have any military background, namely politically powerful individuals in the community or descendants of the warrior class, began to feature gun firing.[108] One such person was Chief Anasoh, a twenty-nine-year veteran of the judicial court of Amifeke town, who was described by his children as an individual "without stain about his conduct" who "showed the Government the true way to govern the then untrained inhabitants."[109] Important or "big" men were not the only ones entitled to heavy gun firing at their funerals. When Madam Ajile, a prominent centenarian and an Ibadan-based kola-nut merchant, passed away in February 1948, a "Gun Boom" announced her death, as reported in the *Southern Nigeria Defender*.[110]

The extent of shooting carried out to announce the death of people or during their burial rites varied from culture to culture. It would appear that the occupation and sociocultural association to which they belonged determined the intensity of shooting. Gunshots in honor of traditional elites and professional hunters were usually more elaborate than those for other classes. In her memoir first published in 1908, Constance Larymore, wife of a colonial officer, reported that the completion of the burial rites of the king of Ilesha in 1903 was followed by "much firing of Dane gun[s]," which she also described as "a terribly noisy performance"—an indication that the gunshots were intense.[111] Sporadic gunshots lasted throughout the funeral rites conducted (mostly at dawn) by Yoruba hunters in honor of their departed comrades. When Mazi Okpala, a member of the native court in Ndiguozu town, died in October 1943, his six sons applied to their district officer for permission to purchase gunpowder to announce the death of their patriarch. "In accordance with native law and custom," they wrote, "such a death cannot be announced without sufficient gunpowder."[112] The children of Mazi Okpala needed the government's approval to buy two kegs of gunpowder, which was more than the regulated quantity given the scarcity of the item during World War II. Regardless, even the least important person in a community was honored with gunshots during burial rites and funeral ceremonies.

Most written sources on ceremonial gun firing, including Chinua Achebe's description of the funeral rite of Chief Ezeudu, the oldest man and one of the most decorated chiefs in Umuofia, tend to paint a picture of a sporadic uncoordinated activity, whose primary aim was to create the loudest possible noise in a carnival-like atmosphere.[113] But few written sources and oral histories established that among several Nigerian ethnic groups, the manner in which guns were fired, the amount of firing, and the identity of the people involved reflected the prevailing social custom tied to the different phases of burial ceremonies, the positions held by the deceased, and the affiliations to which they belonged, among other parameters.[114] Among the Osopong of Cross River, the firing of guns for the burial of a rich person took place daily for three to four weeks at 11:00 a.m. and sunset. However, the Munshi fired only one shot, amid the beating of their wooden drum for a deceased person.[115] During the burial of members of the Egbo Society, the main Efik secret cult, the firing of guns took place after burial, not during. In fact, the community was not to know that an Egbo member was deceased until after the burial when a fourteen- to sixteen-day ceremony was held. About one hundred people armed with guns released shots into the air to accompany every mention of the good deeds of the deceased—such as helping defend the community against invaders.[116] But the clearest insight into the manner funeral shooting was conducted that I have found is in a massive anthropological work undertaken among the lower Niger ethnic groups by Major Arthur Leonard and published in 1906. The following renders a vivid picture of the symbolic order of rhythm and the intersections of social class, generation, and spirituality in Ibibio funeral rites:

> After burial, salutes are fired, the number of guns depending on the rank and wealth of deceased. In the case of a chief or king these salutes are continued for eight days, the guns being fired at intervals throughout the day and night; and in the event of his having been a grandfather they are kept up for just double that period.... This doubling of the salute to a grandfather is in fact, a bestowal of that honour to whom honour is not only due as an ancestral right and privilege, but which is the meed of him who, prior to his departure to the rest or strife of spirit land, left behind him a double reminder in two generations of the flesh—a solid memorial, which entitles him to an increased spiritual control. For ordinary people only three or

four guns are fired, according to the means of the household, and the firing is limited to four days.... In this firing of guns, both large and small, the object is not merely to honour the departed, or to announce his departure to spirit land, but to clear the road of malevolent demons, so as to ensure him a safe conduct and a journey free from molestation.[117]

By the 1920s, a lot of middle- and upper-class educated Nigerians and leading nationalists appropriated gun firing in virtually all private ceremonies—from weddings and namings to birthdays and other milestones. "Guns and Cannons Boom in Ngwo Village throughout the Nights to Honour Leader," reported the *West African Pilot* on the frenzied atmosphere that heralded the victory of the controversial Enugu mine labor leader Okwudi Ojiyi in an important legal battle.[118] Similarly, when Kingley Ozuomba Mbadiwe, a politician and president of the African Academy of Arts and Research, got married in March 1950, the honor he received went beyond the 810 congratulatory telegrams from prominent people around the world (including Governor John Macpherson of Nigeria) and the privilege of having Nnamdi Azikiwe chair his wedding banquet. His marriage procession, composed of about forty cars, was greeted by the firing of guns at every village it passed through until it arrived in Mbadiwe's family compound at Arondizuogu.[119] During the period of decolonization in the 1950s, gun salutes by local hunters at rallies became one of the measures of the popularity of political parties and nationalist leaders like Obafemi Awolowo and Azikiwe.[120]

Dane guns were the primary firearm used for ceremonial shooting. But other shooting techniques emerged in response to the popularity of the practice. Writing in 1920, the resident officer of Ogoja Province noted that "an appreciable quantity" of gunpowder was exploded in short iron tubes, usually Dane gun barrels cut to lengths of about ten inches. "A noise is a great thing," the resident officer chided about the festive mood that followed each gun boom.[121]

But gun firing transcended private and public ceremonies and festivals. It was a visible element of official British imperial culture in Nigeria. By the late 1910s, the use of time guns had complemented boggle blowing and had completely moved from the conventional domain of military barracks into the provincial and administrative headquarters. In cities like Lagos in the 1920s, time guns went off three times in a day (as this chapter's epigraph establishes) and could be heard within a two-mile radius.[122] In 1928, it cost an average of 22s. 6d. per month to purchase gunpowder for time-gun shooting carried out by soldiers or local hunters, who were hired by the government. The government temporarily suspended the Apapa gun signal for security reasons during World War II. After the end of the global hostility, Lagosians called for it to be reinstated immediately. "The public is anxiously looking forward to the time when the Gun signal will be restored . . . [it] had served to regulate our time," one Tiamiyu Ade Thompson wrote in October 1945.[123]

Time guns served as the most popular method of measuring the daily passage of time by Nigerians. Indeed, the heavy boom of the time guns, rusted cannon, and decorative firearms stationed in provincial offices reminded Nigerians of the presence of colonial power, capable of unleashing violence at any time. Paradoxically, it also gave a real and imagined sense of security to Nigerians who thought they were safe under British imperial protection.[124] A gossip column in the *Nigerian Pioneer* during World War I, titled "Alice in Wonderland" in characteristically provocative manner, made mockery of a toy gun stationed at the Race Course, Lagos's main public arena: "I wonder: If the long pop gun on the Race Course is meant as a toothpick? I also wonder: Whether it is meant for Kaiser Bill's main tooth?"[125]

Gun firing was also an important element of imperial spectacle during official ceremonies such as the opening of public facilities like schools and hospitals, Empire Day, Armistice Day, and the change of military guards and colonial administrators.[126] In addition, the ceremonies held to welcome new colonial administrators into their districts included a gun salute by local hunters. The caption of a photo of more than a dozen Dane gun–bearing local hunters who gathered to welcome T. M. Shankland, a new colonial officer, to Igarra community published in the *Daily Service* read: "There Is No War on for These Igarra Gun-Bearers: They Are the Native Hunters in 'Juju' Waistcoasts Shooting the Sky with Gun Powder Alone."[127] A nineteen-gun salute heralded the assumption of Sir James Robertson as the last British governor-general of Nigeria in June 1955.[128] And when Queen Elizabeth visited the northern region during her official tour of Nigeria in 1956, she was treated to the loudest noise ever made in peacetime with some retired World War II cannon. Moreover, the sounds of sophisticated guns that rent the air during firing practice by security forces and European rifle clubs complemented the enchantment of city life. The World War II mobilization increased the intensity of firing in places like Lagos and Kaduna, which were used as preparation camps for military service. A government-sponsored announcement published in the *West African Pilot* announced to the public that firing practice would take place for six hours daily from 10:00 a.m. to 4:00 p.m. between January 11 and 14, 1944.[129] The exhibition and mock display of huge antiaircraft guns, gun turrets from one of Britain's biggest bombers, rifles, and machine guns, among other war munitions, for fundraising during World War II increased the public's knowledge about modern warfare and intensified curiosity about developments at the war front.[130]

Conclusion

Both Nigerians and the British contributed to the emergence of the Nigerian gun society. Nigerians took advantage of the colonial government's liberalizing of the Dane gun, placing firearms at the center of valuable social, cultural, and economic activities. Ceremonial shooting and hunting would not have become dominant features of everyday life without a government gun regulation that treated Dane guns as less lethal. And the institutionalization of the shotgun as a marker of social class went hand in hand with the transformation of colonial ideals of power and privilege. The consumption patterns of guns therefore reflected the ordering of Nigerian society across ethnicity, region, and social class. The next chapter examines the gunpowder trade and its place in Nigeria's economic history and gun society.

Notes

1. Brook, *One-Eyed Man Is King*, 86.
2. Jackson, "Twenty Years War," 262.
3. Dike and Ekejiuba, *Aro of Southeastern Nigeria*, 171–72.
4. Akintoye, *Revolution and Power Politics*, 118.
5. For more on the Native Authority Police Force, see Rotimi, *Police in a Federal State*.
6. Lugard, *Political Memoranda*, 304, 325. When the question of allowing the Native Authority to carry firearms came up again in 1928, the Colonial Office ruled that this class of law-enforcement officers should not be allowed to use guns. See Rotimi, *Police in a Federal State*, 117.
7. "Secretary of the Administration of Northern Nigeria to the High Commissioner," 1907, Muri Prof., 2557/1907, NAK.
8. Lugard, *Political Memoranda*, 36–37.
9. Ibid., 250.

10. Temple, *Tribes, Provinces, Emirates and States*, 98, 301.
11. Quoted in a "Memorandum on Arms Control by Donald Cameron, Acting Governor of Nigeria, March 1921, CSO 26/03620, NAI.
12. Quoted in Watson, *"Civil Disorder Is the Disease,"* 78.
13. Jackson, "Twenty Years War," 119.
14. Ibid., 122.
15. Lugard, *Political Memoranda*, 52, 56.
16. "Conference of Residents, Northern Provinces, 1937, November 9, 1937, Kano Prof., 2496, NAK.
17. "District Officer of Ibadan Division to the Senior Resident of Oyo Province," January 24, 1924, Oyo Prof., 1792, vol. 1, NAI.
18. "District Officer of Ife Division to the Senior Resident of Oyo Province," August 19, 1924, Oyo Prof., 1792, vol. 1, NAI.
19. "Assistant District Officer of Osogbo to the Senior Resident of Oyo Province," August 7, 1926, Oyo Prof., 1792, vol. 1, NAI.
20. "Senior Resident of Oyo Province to the District Officer of Oyo," December 29, 1923, Oyo Prof., 1792, vol. 1, NAI.
21. "Resident of Oyo Province to the Secretary of Southern Provinces," November 10, 1919, Oyo Prof., 1792, vol. 1, NAI.
22. Lugard, *Political Memoranda*, 36.
23. Temple, *Tribes, Provinces, Emirates and States*, 301.
24. Basden, *Niger Ibos*, 144.
25. Talbot, *Peoples of Southern Nigeria*, 4:914.
26. Ibid., 913–16.
27. Ottenberg, *Boyhood Rituals*, 93. For a similar story among the Ibibio, see Talbot, *Woman's Mysteries*, 52–54.
28. Basden, *Niger Ibos*, 306.
29. Brook, *One-Eyed Man Is King*, 86.
30. Ayo Akinyemi (Ranger), "Killing of an Elephant on Omo River in September 1956," September 6, 1956, Ije Prof., 1129, NAI.
31. "District Officer of Ijebu to the Resident of Ijebu Province," September 12, 1955, Ije Prof., 1129, NAI.
32. From the *Nigerian Pioneer*: "Abeokuta News," March 17, 1916; Presence of Wild Animals in the Farms," November 15, 1918; and "Snake at Tinubu Square," November 21, 1919. See the following from the *Daily Service*: "Wild Cat Kills Three in Village Well," September 14, 1944; "Wild Boar Visits Railway Quarters," October 9, 1945; "Chief Killed by Leopard in Trap Set by Himself," November 17, 1945; "Wild Animal Escapes and Injures Four Persons," December 30, 1948; "Woman Killed by Strange Cow," January 1, 1949; "Buffalo Takes Lives of Two Friendly Hunters," February 2, 1949; "Expectant Mother Killed by Bush Cows," March 22, 1950; "Two Villagers Killed by Bush Cow," January 11, 1951; "Hunter Kills Leopard," March 27, 1954; "Boy, 12, Sights a Tiger," August 25, 1954. From the *WAP*: "Man Dies after Duel with Fierce Leopard," August 30, 1941; "Eagle Which Killed Child Is Shot Two Years Later," March 21, 1942; "Leopard Carries 14-Year-Old Girl while Mother Looks on Astounded," June 23, 1942; "Lioness Devours Girl in the Area of Oloko," October 23, 1942; "Crack Shot Saves Community from Ravaging Leopardess," June 15, 1943; "17-Year-Old Boy Is Eaten by Wild Beast," December 31, 1942; "Butcher Kills Three Leop-

ards at Jodome," May 7, 1945; "Ugiri Town People Attacked by Leopard," May 31, 1950; "Pet Leopard Kills African and Injures Four Europeans in Jos," April 21, 1952; "Leopard Incident in the Plateau Retold," June 19, 1952; "Two Leopards Killed by Man and Wife," March 20, 1953; "Snake Kills 18-Year-Old Woman in Bed," January 27, 1954; "Sixteen-Year-Old Girl Survives Night Attack by Leopard," June 6, 1954; "Bush Cow Kills 3: £40 Ransom Offered," July 6, 1954; and "Man Dies of Snake Bite," August 21, 1954. See also "Leopard Prowls the City of Jos," *Comet*, October 31, 1947; "Hunter Is Locked up on Top of a Tree by Two Leopards Waiting for Him," *Eastern Nigeria Guardian*, November 2, 1944.

33. "Bush Cow Kills 3."
34. "Sixteen-Year-Old Girl Survives Night Attack."
35. "That Female Leopard Again!" *Nigerian Pioneer*, June 2, 1916.
36. "Another Victim of the Leopard," *Nigerian Pioneer*, June 9, 1916.
37. "Leopards at Abeokuta," *Nigerian Pioneer*, May 19, 1916.
38. "Resident of Ogoja Province to the Secretary of the Southern Provinces," May 12, 1920, CSO 26/03620, NAI.
39. Brook, *One-Eyed Man Is King*, 86.
40. Talbot, *Peoples of Southern Nigeria*, 4:914.
41. Basden, *Niger Ibos*, 117.
42. Ibid., 117.
43. Hastings, *Nigerian Days*, 202–3.
44. "Nigerian Ivory Trading Company to the Commissioner of the Colony," February 17, 1943, Comcol, 1094, vol. 1, NAI.
45. "Resident of Muri Province to the Secretary to the Administration," July 25, 1907, Muri Prof., 2557/1907, NAK.
46. "Mohamed Nagaraba to the Administrator of the Colony," May 6, 1952, Comcol, 1094, vol. 1, NAI.
47. "R.W. Ayres to the Commissioner of the Colony," September 10, 1951, Comcol, 1094, vol. 1, NAI.
48. "Malam Alli to the Commissioner of the Colony," March 28, 1951, Comcol, 1094, vol. 1, NAI.
49. Press Notice, August 20, 1936, Comcol, 1094, vol. 1, NAI.
50. "'Troops' of Wild Elephants Ravage Farms in Ogbomoso Districts," *Daily Service*, August 24, 1951; "Stray Elephant Tramples Four People to Death in Oyo Area," *WAP*, February 19, 1952; "Elephant Menace on Crops Is Increasing," *WAP*, August 8, 1953.
51. "'Troops' of Wild Elephants Ravage Farms in Ogbomoso District."
52. "Elephant Menace on Crops Is Increasing" and "Wild Elephants Put Up Hectic Chase of Man, Wife and Child"—both in *WAP*, May 13, 1949.
53. "Stray Elephant Tramples Four People."
54. "Secretary of the Administration of Northern Nigeria to the High Commissioner," 1907, Muri Prof., 2557/1907, NAK.
55. "Secretary of Southern Provinces to the Resident of Ijebu Province," July 21, 1932, Ijebu Prof., J384, NAI.
56. "Elephant-Hunter Fined for Killing without Permit," *Daily Service*, December 28, 1946. For the story of Kenya, see Steinhart, *Black Poachers, White Hunters*.
57. "Orimolusi of Ijebu Igbo to the District Officer," March 8, 1948, Ije Prof., 1129, NAI.

58. For the impact of colonial forest reserve policies on the politics of land ownership, see Hellermann and Usuanlele, "Owner of the Land."

59. Talbot, *Peoples of Southern Nigeria*, 4:914; Temple, *Tribes, Provinces, Emirates and States*, 142; "Hunter Kills Leopard," *Daily Service*, March 27, 1954.

60. "Orimolusi to the District Officer," July 20, 1932, Ije Prof., J384, NAI.

61. "Acting District Officer of Ijebu Division to the Accountant-General," December 16, 1944, Ije Prof., 1129, NAI.

62. "Gbadamosi Amao to the Commissioner of the Colony," February 14, 1951, Comcol, 1094, vol. 1, NAI.

63. Basden, *Niger Ibos*, 117.

64. "Secretary of Southern Provinces to the Resident of Oyo Province," April 3, 1917, Oyo Prof., 1480, vol. 1, NAI.

65. Talbot, *Shadow of the Bush*, 82–83.

66. "Resident of Bornu Province to the Secretary of the Northern Provinces," May 8, 1935, SNP 17/1, 10260, vol. 13, NAK.

67. "Elephants Invade Villages in North and Cause Great Damage," *WAP*, October 21, 1950.

68. Aderinto, "Where Is the Boundary?"

69. Aluko, "How Many Nigerians?" 374.

70. "He Shot Thief Making Away with His Goods," *Daily Service*, December 5, 1951.

71. "Benin City," *WAP*, October 12, 1944.

72. Bohannan, *Justice and Judgement*, 107–8.

73. "Acting Secretary to the Prime Minister of the Federation to the Chief Administrative Officer of the Ministry of Lagos Affairs, Mines, and Power," October 31, 1957, Comcol, 29, NAI.

74. "Resident of Niger Province to the Secretary of the Northern Provinces," November 12, 1934, SNP 17/1, 10260, NAK.

75. "Deputy Controller of Palm Production to the Secretary of Eastern Provinces," June 21, 1945, CSEI/85/8651, NAE.

76. "J. A. Adebimpe to the Chief Administrative Officer," July 9, 1958, Comcol, 29, NAI.

77. Oral interview with Mr. Raufu Adeniji at Mamu on May 27, 2015.

78. Temple, *Tribes, Provinces, Emirates and States*, 250.

79. Oral interview with Mr. Oluibi Aransi at Mamu on May 28, 2015.

80. "Wanted One 12 Bore Double-Barrelled Shot Gun," *Daily Service*, November 18, 1947.

81. "S. A. Bamiro to the Arms Officer," July 26, 1957, Comcol, 29, NAI.

82. "Robert Iwedi to the Commissioner of the Colony," July 25, 1957, Comcol, 29, NAI.

83. "Olu Komolafe to the District Officer," September 1, 1956, Ilesha Div. 1/1 57, NAI.

84. "S. A. Okonkwo to the Chief Administrative Officer," August 11, 1957, Comcol, 29, NAI.

85. "D. A. Oyegbite to the District Officer of Ondo Division," April 4, 1950, Ondo Div. 1/1, 51, vol. 6, NAI.

86. "Reverend K.C. Edokpolo to the District Officer of Ondo," June 6, 1950, Ondo Div. 1/1, 51, vol. 6, NAI.

87. "Chief Okota to the District Officer of Akure-Ondo Division," December 12, 1954, Ondo Div. 1/1, 51, vol. 6, NAI.
88. "E. A. Kinihun to the District Adviser of Ilesha Division," June 17, 1958, IL, 57, vol. 6, NAI.
89. "Daniel Ogundimeti to the Assistant Registrar of Akure," January 12, 1951, Ondo Prof., 216A, NAI.
90. "I. O. Egbelowa UAC Agent—Application to Bear Arms," October 29, 1951, Ondo Prof., 216A, NAI.
91. "W. Maxwell to the Senior Superintendent of Police of Kano Province," July 5, 1956, Kano Prof., 302/S1, NAK.
92. "L. N. Udobi to the Resident of Kano Province," July 4, 1956, Kano Prof., 302/S1, NAK.
93. "Salawu Adefemi to the District Officer of Oshogbo-Oshun Division," November 8, 1952, Oshun Div. 1/1, 1571/1, vol. 2, NAI.
94. "Guns in Lagos by the Nigeria Police Force," March 25, 1940, Comcol, 1307, NAI.
95. "M. O. Ajayi to the District Adviser of Ilesha Division," June 18, 1957, IL, 57, vol. 6, NAI.
96. "Honorary Secretary of Lagos Hunters' Club to the Governor of Nigeria," September 29, 1936, Comcol, 1863, NAI.
97. "Commissioner of Police, Lagos Colony to the Commissioner of the Colony," October 19, 1936, Comcol, 1863, NAI.
98. "Honorary Secretary of the Lagos Hunters' Club to the Chief Secretary to the Government," September 29, 1936, Comcol, 1863, NAI.
99. "Acting Chief Secretary to the Government to the Honorary Secretary of the Lagos Hunters' Club," November 2, 1936, Comcol, 1863, NAI.
100. "Secretary of the Northern Provinces to the Resident of Zaria," March 18, 1935, SNP 17/1, 10260, vol. 13, NAK.
101. "L. A. Sadare to the District Officer of Oshun Division," April 25, 1953, Oshun Div. 157, vol. 11, NAI.
102. "Ilorin Hunters' Society to the District Officer of Ilorin," April 29, 1945, Ilorin Prof., 1971, NAK.
103. "Calabar Shot Gun and Licence Holder Union to the Chief Commissioner of the Eastern Provinces," August 18, 1945, CSEP/85/8651, NAE.
104. "Handwritten Memo," September 21, 1945, CSEP/85/8651, NAE.
105. Ottenberg, *Boyhood Rituals*, 7, 179.
106. Ibid., 19.
107. Brook, *One-Eyed Man Is King*, 86.
108. Talbot, *Life in Southern Nigeria*, 114, 139–69, 244.
109. "Christopher Anasoh to the Manager of UAC," July 21, 1943, ORLDIST, 3/1/409, NAE.
110. "Gun Boom to Announce Death of Popular Centenarian Madam Ajile," *SND*, February 17, 1948.
111. Larymore, *Resident's Wife in Nigeria*, 170–71.
112. "Sons of Mazi Okpala to the District Officer of Orlu," October 30, 1943, ORLDIST, 3/1/409, NAE.
113. Achebe, *Things Fall Apart*, 120–25.

114. Meek, *Law and Authority*, 33; Temple, *Tribes, Provinces, Emirates and States*, 152.

115. Talbot, *Peoples of Southern Nigeria*, 4:521, 529.

116. Talbot, *Life in Southern Nigeria*, 154–58.

117. Leonard, *Lower Niger and Its Tribes*, 175–76.

118. "Five Thousand Miners Rejoice with Okwudi Ojiyi in His Victory," *WAP*, September 9, 1950.

119. "Guns Boom in Villages at Mbadiwe's Marriage," *WAP*, March 27, 1950.

120. The manner the nationalist newspapers reported the reception giving to their patrons, like Obafemi Awolowo (*Nigeria Tribune* and *Daily Service*) and Nnamdi Azikiwe (*WAP*), with such description as the "booming of guns, the blare of trumpets, and clash of cymbals and stampede of people" fed into a prevailing political struggle among communities and ethnicities for political power. "Booming of Guns and Blare of Trumpets Herald the Arrival of Mr. Awolowo," *Daily Service*, June 9, 1954; "Photo of Hunters," *Daily Service*, August 18, 1954; "Gun Shots Announce NCNC Delegation," *WAP*, May 20, 1952; "15 Guns Are Fired in Honour of National Council Delegates," *SND*, July 17, 1946.

121. "Resident of Ogoja Province to the Secretary of the Southern Provinces," May 12, 1920, CSO 26/03620, NAI.

122. "Station Magistrate to the Officer Commanding Troops," June 28, 1928, Kano Prof., 518, NAK.

123. "Restore Apapa Gun Signal," *Daily Service*, October 22, 1945.

124. Brook, *One Eyed Man Is King*, 130–31.

125. "Alice in Wonderland," *Nigerian Pioneer*, December 15, 1916.

126. From *WAP*: "Victoria Beach Shooting Incident," July 22, 1941; "Firing at Victoria Beach," October 8, 1941; and "Guns Will Be Fired at Fire Command Today," May 18, 1945. See also "Gun-Fire Practice," *Daily Service*, August 14, 1944.

127. "Photo of Hunters," *Daily Service*, July 16, 1954.

128. "Sir James Honoured with 19-Gun Salute," *Daily Service*, June 16, 1955. See also *WAP*: "Ceremonial Parade of Police Put Off," July 16, 1947; "Fifteen Gun Salute for Northern Lieutenant Governor Taking Office," February 2, 1952.

129. "Firing Practice Will Be Held 6 Hours Daily till January 14," *WAP*, January 11, 1944.

130. *WAP*: "Lagos School Children Will See Anti-Aircraft Guns Today," July 3, 1942; and "War Weapons Just off the Secret List Are on Show by Service on the Marina," May 25, 1944.

3

"A DANE GUN IS USELESS WITHOUT GUNPOWDER"

The Political Economy of Nigeria's Most Popular Explosive

Gunpowder was the main ammunition for firing the Dane gun, the most popular firearm in colonial Nigeria. Without the liberalization of the trade in gunpowder, the Nigerian gun society would not have emerged. Hunting, which provided a means of livelihood and food, would have suffered greatly, and the firing of guns at ceremonies and festivals, which increasingly became a marker of social status, would have been negatively affected. Neither would cocoa growers, among other cash crop farmers, who used the Dane gun for self-defense against thieves and dangerous wild animals, have been able to use their firearms. Thus, gunpowder was a commodity whose impact reverberated in many areas of people's everyday lives and at different levels of their engagement with their society and the colonial state. In fact, the story of gunpowder, unlike the Dane gun, is that of global economic dependency: 99 percent of Nigeria's gunpowder came from abroad.[1] In 1923, this indispensable item accounted for one-fourth of all imported goods.[2] Thus, the history of both firearms and gunpowder cannot be disaggregated, for together they reflected the desire of the colonial government to profit from an item that was in high demand for a variety of purposes.

In addition to shedding additional light on the dynamics of Nigeria's gun society from the perspective of gunpowder trade, this chapter complements the historiography of World War II. The political and economic history of the war has examined the structural crisis of the period, which manifested in the shortage of essential imported items, including salt.[3] Rationing of foreign and locally produced items alike intensified public disorder as the government militarized markets and trading centers in response to the public's disaffection with policies that criminalized Nigerians, especially market women, for selling above the government-controlled prices.[4] As detailed as existing scholarship on the political economy of World War II in Nigeria is, the gunpowder trade and its politics have largely escaped the attention of scholars. Indeed, the importance of the gunpowder trade during the war made the item central to economic policies of the era. Like other imports, gunpowder declined as a result both of the restrictions placed on international shipments and of the mobilization of chemical industries in Europe to produce the weapons directly needed to prosecute the war.[5] But the financial problem confronting the big trading companies like John Holt, Compagnie Française de l'Afrique Occidentale (CFAO), and UAC went beyond the drop in importation and the decline in profits. It also extended to the shipments' condition—gunpowder was highly susceptible to damage by moisture. The government takeover of the magazines of the trading companies for wartime purposes deprived them of the space for storing gunpowder. Thus, on arrival at the port, gunpowder had to find its way into the hands of consumers, who were better prepared than the trading companies to prevent damage. This chapter further allows for reemphasis of some of my main, overarching argument—that the narrative of the relationship between firearms and violence cannot effectively explain the cumulative impact of the gun during the first half of the twentieth century.

International Trade and Safety Regulations

The gunpowder trade, like other foreign trade, went through a process of reconfiguration with the effective establishment of colonial rule in Nigeria. Unlike the years before the twentieth century when trading companies could sell gunpowder to local merchants, who then sold to chiefs and warriors who monopolized and used the ammunition for prosecuting wars, the consolidation of colonial rule saw the imposition of new methods and terms of trade that allowed the government to determine the quantity of gunpowder in circulation from time to time. By the early 1930s, trading companies—John Holt, UAC, G. B. Ollivant, and CFAO, among others—were licensed to import gunpowder into Nigeria. They paid around 1s. 6d. per pound of gunpowder they imported in 1937.[6]

Laws that governed the sale of gunpowder from the early twentieth century were meant to achieve two complementary goals: to increase government revenue through taxes and permits to sell gunpowder and to monitor the quantity of gunpowder in circulation in the interest of public safety. A trading company was not allowed to keep more than two tons of gunpowder in its magazine. Nigerian retailers who sought to hold more than fifty pounds were required to collect a license and adhere to safety rules. No private user of gunpowder could have more than a pound at a time. The relationship between gunpowder regulation and gun politics is not hard to see. Government would lose income from gun licenses, because gun owners would be reluctant to renew their gun permits if gunpowder was not readily available. Thus, the gunpowder trade required a difficult balance between security and economic considerations. And the chief consideration was determined by the ratio of total importation to the population of the country. In the view of the Colonial Office, the 344 tons of gunpowder that Nigeria received in 1922 would not constitute any danger, given that it amounted to only about two-thirds of an ounce per person in a country with an estimated population of eighteen million.[7] But this conclusion was flawed, for the popularity of and demand for gunpowder varied from one part of the country to another. Much of the gunpowder imported into Nigeria was consumed in the southwestern and southeastern provinces, where ceremonial shooting was widely practiced. More hunters in these regions also used firearms for hunting than did their northern counterparts.

When Governor Hugh Clifford of Nigeria visited Onitsha in October 1921, he found out that people were selling gunpowder in bottles in the open market. While not condemning the sales of gunpowder, he expressed the belief that "too many" traders were involved in the trade and that selling in bottles constituted a serious safety issue. Clifford's observation sparked a debate over whether the fifty-pound limit imposed on retailers could be reduced.[8] The responses of the resident officers across the country significantly mirrored the interplay between public safety and the importance of gunpowder to the economy. "When I was in Onitsha Province," the resident of Nupe observed about his previous station, "I saw the illegal use to which gunpowder is only too often." He recommended that people should be allowed to keep a maximum of ten pounds, only for funerals and feasts.[9] All the residents of the Northern Provinces, with the exception of those of Ilorin and Bornu, thought that fifty pounds of gunpowder was too large a quantity to be in the possession of an individual retailer.[10] For the residents in the Southern Provinces, reducing the legal limit would create two completely different outcomes. On the one hand, government would derive more income from gunpowder licenses, and on the other hand, it would increase the administrative duties of officers who must visit numerous private warehouses to ensure that they met safety standards before issuing permits.[11]

But the government was also concerned about the big trading companies' adherence to safety regulations in handling their importation. Up to the early 1920s, neither the government nor the trading firms had a magazine capable of holding more than two tons of gunpowder—a quantity far greater than the average shipment received from abroad at one time. The explosives law criminalized the storage of gunpowder with other items of trade to forestall a fire outbreak. Hence, whenever a gunpowder shipment arrived in any of the three ports permitted to handle it (Lagos, Warri, and Burutu), it was quickly transported up country. The problem of proper storage became a bigger issue in the provinces, where most of the shipment was to be sold in popular markets. Few of the trading companies were willing to build a designated gunpowder magazine that conformed to government safety standards in the hinterland, not only because it would increase their overhead cost, but also because shifting patterns of trade might render it useless. Administrators simply overlooked this contravention of the law because they also did not have proper storage facilities in which to keep confiscated gunpowder.[12] By October 1922, Lagos finally took a major step in the storage of imported gunpowder by converting an old ship, the SS *Huntsglen*, into a gunpowder hulk and placed it in the creeks of Badagry, two miles ashore, to limit the impact of a possible explosion on the general population.[13] The new hulk could hold up to thirty tons of gunpowder.

Although the colonial administration seemed to have temporarily solved the storage problem in Lagos, other ports, especially Warri and Burutu, continued to face challenges with their small magazines. When the trading company Messrs. Jannuzzelli sought government permission to import one thousand kegs of gunpowder from Hamburg via Liverpool to Warri in 1923, the secretary to the government of Nigeria suggested a private-government partnership in building a new magazine.[14] This idea seemed fair to the government, which would build a massive public warehouse, and sublet different portions, each capable of holding up to two tons of gunpowder, to the trading companies. This arrangement, the senior secretary thought, would better help the government to monitor gunpowder importation and ensure that trading companies adhered to safety rules. Moreover, the government would recoup its initial cost of building the facilities through rents paid by the trading companies. In addition, collection of customs duties would be much easier and more efficient.[15]

This entire proposed scheme seemed to contravene the explosives law. For the acting solicitor-general, the existence of several "private" warehouses each holding a maximum of two tons of gunpowder violated the existing regulations stipulating that private magazines must be located in "an isolated building."[16] Hence, there could not be more than two tons of gunpowder in a private storage facility at any given location, at any point in time. Moreover, "the greater the number of people that have access to a building of this sort," the chief legal officer affirmed, "the greater the danger of accident."[17] But closer scrutiny of the law by his political counterpart, the acting secretary of the Southern Provinces, rendered a completely different interpretation. In the first place, there was no limit to the amount of gunpowder the government could store. The two-ton limit applied only to the trading companies. His submission challenged the core safety principle of gunpowder while exposing a loophole in the existing legislation. "Let us assume for example that for the trade of a particular port," he pontificated, "the Government found it necessary to erect a public warehouse capable of holding 500 tons; it is manifestly absurd to suggest that the danger from such a building is in any way increased by subdividing the interior in such a manner as suggested in my previous minutes and to allow firms to rent such compartments as private warehouses." He was convinced that the government secretary's suggestion would guarantee the safety of the port, for he deemed it better to keep 500 tons in one place than to have 484 tons in the public warehouse and 16 tons scattered over the port in eight private warehouses each containing 2 tons.[18]

After a series of debates, the government finally settled for its previous method of repurposing abandoned ships. An old ship, the SS *Silverdale*, was converted into a gunpowder hulk with the capacity to hold up to fifty tons of gunpowder and stationed in the creeks in Warri.[19] As Warri and Lagos were solving their storage problem, new insight emerged into the growing significance of Burutu, which an agent for the Niger Company, F. Brown, noted as a port where "a great deal of powder trade is done in the Niger Provinces" and "undoubtedly the principal port in the Niger Delta."[20] The controller of customs did not doubt Brown's reaffirmation of the importance of Burutu in the gunpowder trade. But instead of accepting his offer for the government to cooperate with his company to build a magazine there, in November 1923 he acquired, for £100, another old ship—the SS *Iddo*, which was about to be destroyed by its owner, Elder Dempster—and converted it to a hulk capable of holding up to forty tons of gunpowder.[21]

As proactive as the government and trading companies appeared to be in devising safe storage arrangements for gunpowder, they could not prevent accidents caused by improper handling of the explosive. Gunpowder accidents were all but inevitable in a colonial society that lacked enough manpower to monitor how Nigerian consumers stored or used the inflammable product. In one instance in Ijasi in October 1924, a gunpowder explosion killed one Ariyo and eight others, including his wives.[22] In another case, a well-known merchant, Bolarinwale Adetunji of Ayetoro, contravened the regulation limiting the maximum capacity a retailer could hold up to fifty pounds. This accident claimed more than five homes. After another gunpowder explosion destroyed many homes and businesses in the commercial center of Agbeni in Ibadan, the *Southern Nigeria Defender* wrote an editorial calling for stricter compliance with safety regulations:

> Petrol and gun powder are highly inflammable articles and must be stored far away from where naked light is frequently used. It is by reason of their explosive nature and the danger in careless handling that only holders of permits are allowed to trade in gun powder and petrol. The slightest mistake near gun powder or petrol means danger to so many persons.... The issue of life and property cannot be sacrificed at the altar of convenience for any single person or group. It is urgent, and we submit most seriously that action [against defaulters] should be taken without any delay.[23]

Although most of the gunpowder accidents involved Nigerians, the few recorded ones involving the big European firms tended to be far more catastrophic. They also counter the notion that Africans were inherently irresponsible with gunpowder because of their lack of intelligence in handling the coarse powder. In May 1953, a CFAO store in Lagos, containing an undisclosed number of barrels of gunpowder, five hundred thousand packets of matches, and one thousand torchlight batteries, among other goods, went up in flames. The company lost about £95,000. It took ten thousand gallons of water from the Lagos lagoon, according to the *West African Pilot*, to put out the four-hundred-foot-high inferno.[24] The CFAO definitely contravened the explosives law, which prohibited storing gunpowder together with other trade items. In terms of human casualties, the Calabar accident in the store of G. B. Ollivant, also in 1953, was probably the worst. To prove to some

Nigerian traders that their gunpowder was genuine, European agents of the company were said to have lit a small quantity, which rapidly grew into a serious fire. Four Europeans and five Nigerians died in the ensuing explosion.[25]

Gunpowder accidents and the debate over the best way to store explosives were just two of the numerous sites of tension among the principal actors: the government, the trading companies, and Nigerians. Another area of conflict was fraudulent practices. Realizing the profitability of gunpowder, foreign manufacturers of the item and their Nigerian trading partners did make false weight declarations in order to reduce customs duties. When the government discovered such discrepancies, trading companies readily blamed their foreign manufacturers, who had produced and packaged the shipment. In two cases in 1936, the customs office would have lost about £32 in excise duties had it not reweighed a gunpowder consignment shipped to the UAC by Imperial Chemical Industries, its UK-based manufacturer. The government's punitive measures against fraud included seizing the underweighed consignment or imposing a fine on the importers. When the Niger Company's false declaration of gunpowder in Burutu was detected in 1936, Deputy Governor G. Whiteley let the company off the hook to compensate it for the loss of the consignment that had been stolen from the government warehouse.[26]

Gunpowder theft also caused disagreement between the government and the trading companies. Thieves targeted the government magazines because they usually held large consignments. Between July 10 and 20, 1935, gunpowder worth £480 was stolen from the government magazine at Warri.[27] Similarly, in October 1946, thirteen cases of gunpowder belonging to CFAO were carted away from the Badagry magazine.[28] Perpetrators of criminal acts against the government and against private firms remained faceless until they were apprehended and charged in court. In one instance, Richard Jedo, a government watchman in charge of the Burutu warehouse, was sentenced to two years in prison after pleading guilty to facilitating the theft of £50 of gunpowder between June and August 1940. Aside from theft, natural enemies such as ants and damp conditions damaged the gunpowder stored in government warehouses.[29] Theft and damage of gunpowder undermined the government's agenda to ensure safety. After enumerating the steps taken to reduce theft in government facilities, the inspector general of police submitted that insecurity was fueling the proliferation of illegal warehouses across the country. Many of these illegal magazines actually belonged to well-known trading companies, which preferred to pay the fines for breaking the law, if caught, than risk losing their consignment to thieves.

The challenges of the gunpowder trade went beyond fraudulent practices and theft—it extended to the crisis of policing Nigeria's international borders. Throughout the colonial era, cross-border smuggling of goods between West African colonies was common, but was abhorred by the colonial government. Smuggling further exposed the artificiality of African colonial boundaries, which were established by disregarding centuries of human interactions across regions. As the colonies were created, each site was transformed into an isolated economic and political sphere that did not exist as such before colonial rule. During his visit to Nigeria in January 1923, the lieutenant governor of Dahomey (modern Benin Republic), M. Fourn, complained about the smuggling of gunpowder from Nigeria to his colony, arguing that the quantity of gunpowder imported into Nigeria is "vastly in excess of the reasonable requirement" for local consumption. He believed that Lagos was serving as an "informal" port of entry for gunpowder into his territory, which had stricter regulations.[30] The French authorities based their accusation on the unprecedented increase in the quantity of gunpowder imported into Nigeria in the early 1920s—from 137,084 pounds in 1920 to 632,825 pounds in 1922.

This accusation compelled the government of Nigeria to investigate the pattern of importation and consumption of gunpowder in the country. The Nigerian controller of customs did not agree with the Dahomean authorities that smuggling of gunpowder was taking place between the two contiguous colonies. He attributed the difference between the 1920 and 1922 importation levels to the stability of global commerce after World War I.[31] Governor Clifford did not dispute the findings of his officers. He readily replied to his Dahomean counterparts, reiterating that local investigations "have failed to yield any evidence" of gunpowder trafficking.[32] But this internal inquiry did not end what appeared to be a political row between British and French authorities. Unsatisfied with Nigeria's explanation, the Dahomean authorities contacted the Colonial Office in London and demanded that pressure be mounted on their overseas officers to check the trafficking of gunpowder into their territory.[33] The internationalization of this disagreement compelled the controller of customs to change his tune. Not only did he admit that the earlier accusation was "probably correct"; he also identified core areas of customs policy that made smuggling of gunpowder difficult to police.

He pointed out that smuggling took place "in smaller quantities at a time" and that his men could police only "a clear and well-defined attempt." Geography and the weakness of the customs department were also important factors fueling smuggling. The controller of customs admitted that "it is not possible with the present staff to keep effective watch . . . [over] the stretch of land frontiers with innumerable paths and tracks." The core mission of Nigeria's customs department, he reiterated, was to prevent the smuggling of goods into, not from, Nigeria. On a final note, he advised the Dahomean government to establish a customs service "on similar lines with ours," noting that policing the western frontier of Nigeria "is not as simple a matter as the French authorities appear to think."[34] This response apparently brought the gunpowder trafficking controversy to an end.[35]

Trading Gunpowder for Kernel and Rubber: The Scheme

The security and economic crises of World War II tested the vulnerability of the Nigerian gun society. And the colonial government capitalized on the importance of gunpowder by "forcing" Nigerians to exchange the commodity for essential wartime materials such as rubber and palm oil. Without the "palm kernel and rubber for gunpowder" policy, a vital aspect of the political economy of the war, the British prosecution of the twentieth century's most devastating war would have encountered a setback. The loss of the Asian colonies to the Axis powers in 1942 reconfigured the pattern of Africa's economic investment in World War II as the supply of essential materials such as palm kernel and rubber derived from those parts of the British Empire dropped.[36] Consequently, economic advisers of the colonial government, representatives of the trading companies, and the West African Supply and Production Board (WASPB) realized that they could address the empire's problem of the shortage by encouraging Nigerians to exchange palm kernel and rubber for gunpowder. "Every district officer and specialist officer and all the commercial advisers," the WASPB wrote in affirmation in a secret memo, "agree[d] on the tremendous importance of gunpowder as an inducement, both for palm kernels and rubber."[37] Another report from the Association of West African Merchants (AWAM) placed the hunters at the center of the new drive for wild rubber: "It is also true that in some areas, the Ibadan division particularly, *funtumia elastica* trees [rubber tree] have been destroyed except in remote primary forest into which only the hunters dare go."[38] To enhance the effectiveness of this project of gunpowder for palm kernel and rubber, the government banned the sale of gunpowder in the Northern Provinces, restricting it to the southwestern, southeastern, and Cross River provinces, which produced palm kernel and rubber. Coincidentally, these regions consumed much of the gunpowder imported into the country.

This economic policy was a win-win situation for the colonial government, the trading companies, and the AWAM, which had some West Africans as members. The government for its own part would increase the importation of gunpowder, which would benefit the trading companies, while the rubber and palm kernel collected would meet the wartime material demands of the British Empire. But as with all colonial economic policies, Nigerians suffered from the exploitative situation the system produced. They were at the mercy of the government and the foreign merchant companies who manipulated supply to boost their own profits. However, what appeared like merely an economic policy to some colonial officers also offered important security gains at a time when administrators worried about the increasing breakdown of public order in their jurisdiction. Noting that gunpowder "takes so important a place in the life of the south eastern Nigerians," authorities thought that "there would be no misunderstanding or discontent if adequate supply of gunpowder were made proportionate to production of palm kernel."[39]

Like most wartime emergency regulation policies, the palm-kernel-for-gunpowder program received urgent executive and legal approval. The scheme involved a change in the existing laws on the quantity of gunpowder that merchant companies could hold at one time and the manner of buying and selling to the public. Instead of selling to individual retailers or groups, the government overrode its own policies and granted an entire community free license to exchange palm kernel for gunpowder at terms dictated by the government and the companies.[40] To enhance effective business transactions and prevent the emergence of multiple trading networks within each community or an underground black market economy, the transactions had to be conducted before the entire community in public, with the knowledge of notable local traders and important chiefs. In southwestern Nigeria, communities such as Shagamu, Ode, Ilishan, Ikenne, and Ayetoro, among other places, were designated as production and exchange areas for the purpose of this new economic policy. Warehouses maintained by trading firms and their African middlemen were allowed to hold more than two tons of gunpowder in order to facilitate quick distribution and prevent damage to the product.[41] New powers were delegated to political officers—namely, resident and district officers—who maintained close correspondence with trading firms to ensure that they did not undercut the government or create serious problem that could lead to a breakdown of law and order.[42]

However, the most important element of the drive was a close monitoring of the amount of gunpowder in circulation in relation to the quantity of palm kernel collected by each community. Aside from the general drop in the importation of gunpowder due to the reconfiguring of wartime shipping, the government created additional artificial scarcity of gunpowder. "But in order to be of substantial value both to the kernel and rubber drives," J. W. Wallace, the deputy controller of palm kernels for the Eastern Provinces, emphasized, "gun powder must not become too plentiful and distribution of all available supplies must be strictly controlled."[43] J. H. Mackay, Wallace's counterpart overseeing rubber supplies, put the government's agenda in strict economic terms: "Gun powder must be in a short supply and therefore in keen demand."[44] Yet the government could not totally deceive Nigerians who had had an ambivalent relationship with the produce companies. They knew the project was one of the many draconian economic policies aimed at manipulating the domestic economy in the wartime government's favor. The *Awujale* (king) of Ijebu Ode clearly asserted that "this is not a free issue of gunpowder" in his correspondence to his provincial officer.[45]

As one might expect, powerful local leaders lobbied the government and the merchant companies for the sole right to determine, on behalf of their communities, the terms of trade and the method of distributing gunpowder. One such request came from L. N. Obioha of Ndizuogu in Orlu Division, who "volunteered" to pay for "any quantity" of gunpowder allocated to his community. To convince the government that he was not trying to enrich himself, he promised a public announcement for an open market sale of the allocation, to be supervised by a government agent. The profit of the public sale, he pledged, would be paid into his local council's treasury.[46] Another chief from the same community and a council member, retired Corporal Robinson J. Nwankwo, promised to "honestly sell these [gunpowder allocations] in the open market to the satisfaction of any individual" in his letter to his district officer lobbying to collect his community's supply through Société Commerciale de l'Ouest Africain (SCOA).[47]

But this politicking was prompted by the shady practices of the government and the trading companies. To maximize the collection of palm kernel, the government and its economic agents did not fix a unitary term of trade across the production areas. Rather, the quantity of gunpowder given for palm kernel varied from one community to another, and from time to time. This is understandable, given that the production of palm kernel, like other cash crops, was seasonal. But the need to get more palm kernel for gunpowder determined the exchange formulas imposed by the government and the trading firms. In April 1943, UAC was exchanging thirty tons of palm kernel for one keg of gunpowder in Oguta and Orlu.[48] By the end of that year, SCOA, CFAO, John Holt, and G. B. Ollivant all together exchanged a total of 7,110 pounds of gunpowder for an undisclosed quantity of palm kernel.[49] Most communities in southwestern Nigeria exchanged twenty tons for one keg of gunpowder. In August 1943, a six-month supply of 24,535 pounds of gunpowder was expected to fetch the government fifty tons of palm kernel from the eastern provinces of Port Harcourt, Owerri, Onitsha, and Calabar.[50] After the exchange had been conducted, local traders then sold the item in smaller quantities in public markets. In big palm-oil-producing communities in southeastern Nigeria, a cigarette tin, the popular measure, went for 4s.1d., while twenty-five pounds sold for £8.[51]

The palm-kernel-for-gunpowder drive worked well at the beginning—except in Ibadan, where the deputy controller of palm kernels accused the district manager of the UAC of making a "deliberate attempt to sabotage the scheme."[52] Although the government and the trading firms were not necessarily on the best of terms, they worked in concert to exploit Nigerians' excessive reliance on gunpowder. But the situation cannot be reduced to a simplistic narrative of economic predation, for the scheme did help some farmers diversify their means of livelihood and avoid total bankruptcy. In the southwest, rich cocoa farmers invested in palm kernel production to cushion the effect of loss of revenue from the region's most lucrative cash crop. When the *Odemo* (king) of Ishara received the 150 pounds of gunpowder allocated to his town, he not only thanked his district officer but also he assured the government that "efforts are being doubled to reap our palm fruits and that before long you can expect a big outturn of palm kernel from this town."[53] This promise fit the customary practice of chiefs and kings pledging allegiance to the British war agenda in order not to be seen as the enemy of the colonial state during its trying times.

However, a few months into its operation, the gunpowder-for-palm-kernel program began to encounter serious problems.[54] All the checks put in place by the government seemed not to have worked, as the local agents of the trading companies manipulated commercial transactions to increase their proceeds. People accused their chiefs of hoarding and selling gunpowder on the black market, a situation that G. E. Mills, secretary of the AWAM, thought "defeats the aim of the Government."[55] What is more, while the scheme favored the trading firms and their local collaborators, such as the chiefs and rich middlemen, the ordinary consumer grumbled over the high price of gunpowder, a popular staple.[56] "Gun powder has nothing to do with kernel," declared the Abeokuta Local Merchants Committee in their protest gathering about the trade inequality and exploitation associated with the scheme. The nationalist newspapers, including the *Eastern Nigeria Guardian* and the *Daily Service*, understandably took the Nigerians' side.[57] While encouraging Nigerians to produce more palm kernel for war prosecution, they thought that the government should address the unfair trade relations and the lack of an African on the WASPB.[58]

While some communities that benefited from the scheme did complain about exploitation, others fought to be included in it. Odogbolu was not included in the program because the government did not have any record of its palm kernel production. For the year 1943–44, the town delivered thirty-five tons of palm kernel—a quantity that the UAC and the chiefs believed qualified it to take part in the project.[59] The plight of Mamu, a cocoa-producing boundary village between Ibadan Division and Ijebu Province, clearly reveals the effect of wartime economic policy on the people. After leaving cocoa production for palm oil extraction, the farmers were disappointed that the government did not recognize their efforts. They ended their petition letter with the popular sentiments of loyalty to the British Empire during the war: "We also pledge our further unremitting efforts for production of more and more PK [palm kernel] for the prosecution of the war until the allied nations trample under feet, this harsh enemy of peace Hitler and his co-belligerent."[60] Other notable challenges faced by the project were reflected in existing intercommunity political conflicts. Aredi, a community in the Ago production area, petitioned the government when it did not receive any gunpowder for its palm kernel. But it was later discovered that the chiefs of Ago-Iwoye, the biggest town in the area, withheld supplies to the Aredi community to punish its people for not recognizing Ago-Iwoye's political supremacy.[61]

Another problem of the scheme, which Wallace derogatorily labeled as a "gunpowder plot," included the adulteration of gunpowder by regional and local agents of the trading companies. While gunpowder adulteration was not unknown before the war, the need to maximize profits intensified corrupt practices as local people and the trading companies exchanged blame. In one instance, the messenger of the king of Shagamu, after returning from a CFAO distribution point with the town's allocation of gunpowder, discovered it was "damp and bad." In a joint petition letter submitted by the Shagamu town council and the farmers' association, the petitioners not only defended their messenger, whom CFAO blamed for not inspecting the consignment before leaving the location, but also highlighted the betrayed African's impression of European business practices: "If the messenger had acted wrong on this point of examination it was due either to ignorance or sense of confidence and trust that European firm could not sell out bad thing, this is how we are brought up as a race." The petition ended with a four-point discussion of the impact that bad gunpowder could have on the morale of farmers who worked hard to meet the government palm kernel quota.[62]

Whenever "gunpowder plot" accusations emerged, the government either took the side of the trading companies or clung to its widely professed but contradictory status as the "Great White Umpire" (i.e., its maintenance of a neutral position).[63] The colonial administration rarely supported Nigerians. "It would be more improper," the acting resident of Ijebu Province claimed in correspondence that finally put the Shagamu matter to rest, "for a Government officer to use any influence which he may have to require a firm to replace goods sold in good faith and which the purchaser failed to examine." He ended his letter with a paradoxical statement that reflects the conventional manner in which the government dealt with issues of this nature: "I am very distressed about what has happened but I fear that nothing can be done with the matter."[64] Yet corruption was not a one-way crime. Local farmers, too, adulterated palm kernel and declared false weights, all to raise their own profit margins.

The gunpowder-for-palm-kernel program went side by side with that of rubber. When the rubber-producing communities of Nsanarati, Ndabaya, Akwum, Mpot, Ikom, Mamfe, Bamenda, in Cross River and in the Cameroons were asked which imported item they wanted most in February 1943, they listed in order of importance: gunpowder, matches, and cloths.[65] The consumption of gunpowder in these communities dropped from 60,000 pounds in 1937–38 to 13,325 pounds in 1941–42 as a result of the war.[66] As in the palm kernel scheme, the government created artificial scarcity of gunpowder, out of the fear that people might divert it to a "more congenial and remunerative" use such as hunting, and so stop collecting rubber. In the Cross River and the Cameroons regions where rubber existed in the wild in relatively large quantity, the exchange formula was one pound of gunpowder to forty pounds of rubber. In the Western and Eastern Provinces, where rubber trees were not as plentiful, the exchange rate was one pound to twenty.[67] While a minimum of ten pounds of rubber was required for a transaction in Cross River, twenty pounds were required in places "where little rubber is available" and where tapping "represents a great effort."[68] In all, the trading companies were expected to make about fifty-one tons of gunpowder available for the rubber drive.

However, while the gunpowder-for-palm-kernel project was successful, albeit with some irregularities, the exchange for rubber encountered serious challenges. These problems reflected the overlapping, and occasionally irreconcilable, agendas of the colonial government and the merchant companies. While the government viewed rubber from a security perspective (as a raw material directly needed for producing the vehicles needed for the war effort), the UAC, John Holt, SCOA, and other companies were more concerned with maximizing their profits by putting their resources into ventures that would generate the highest return. Logistical difficulties did not help the rubber scheme. Unlike palm kernel, rubber required special storage conditions, and the merchant companies were unwilling to sacrifice the space devoted to the more profitable palm kernel. In addition, the quantity of rubber tapped was not sufficient to attract the investment of the trading companies. With the exception of the southern end of Cross River and the Cameroons, very few parts of Nigeria had rubber trees in commercial quantity. Thus, it was difficult to persuade the trading companies to consider the rubber option.

Moreover, the exchange formula of one pound of gunpowder to forty pounds of rubber was not attractive to many collectors of wild rubber, most of whom were also hunters who needed gunpowder to use their Dane guns. In Degema Division, where most rubber plantations had between five hundred and one thousand trees, collectors chose to hoard their rubber rather than exchange it for such small amounts of gunpowder.[69] Labor shortages caused by wartime rural-urban migration intensified, depriving rural communities of workers needed for agricultural purposes. Mackay, in a report titled "Gunpowder: Proposals for the Wild Rubber Drive," attributed the shortage of laborers for rubber tapping in the Western Provinces to wartime military recruitment.[70] In addition, the government appeared not to have carried out any serious feasibility study before embarking on the project. Some parts of the Northern Provinces, such as Igala Division—which Kabba Province resident R. M. Downes derogatorily labeled "a no-man's land" because it was located in an uninhabited expanse of land between north and south—was not considered for the drive even though it produced five hundred tons of rubber between April and December 1943.[71]

By the end of 1943, both the government and the trading firms had to accept a new reality. The scheme of creating artificial scarcity of gunpowder was becoming anachronistic as "heavy stocks" of gunpowder wasted away in the warehouse. Importation of gunpowder had been based largely on speculation that Nigerians would be persuaded to collect rubber if they could obtain gunpowder. In Owo Division in November 1943 the UAC had 2,560 pounds of gunpowder to exchange in a community producing just 40 pounds of rubber per month. The production of rubber in this community dropped by 94,219 pounds in the months of September and October alone, preventing the UAC from finding outlets for its gunpowder.[72] The situation in Ondo Division was by no means an exception. At the December meeting of the AWAM, the firms exchanged data that clearly demonstrated that few people were exchanging rubber for the gunpowder languishing in warehouses across the country.

Reversal of the status quo became "inescapable," to use the word of G. T. Colby, the secretary to the government who doubled as the director of supply. By December 1943, Colby began a gradual "de-restricting" of the sale of gunpowder by allowing other parts of the country that had been prevented from participating in the palm kernel and rubber scheme to buy it. He then increased the amount of gunpowder being exchanged for palm kernel and rubber across the production areas.[73] But this policy created new tensions between the government and the trading firms, which favored derestriction across the board. On June 1, 1944, an amendment to the Emergency Powers Defense Acts returned gunpowder distribution levels to those of the prewar era, nationwide, with the exception of Kabba Province, where the government decided it could still manipulate trade to get more rubber for gunpowder.

This new amendment was popular among the trading companies, which could now sell their gunpowder to prevent loss due to damage by dampness, but it generated difficulties for political officers who feared that unrestricted access to gunpowder could undermine the tenuous security situation in the country. "I do not consider for security reason," the chief commissioner of the Eastern Provinces wrote, "that all control of gunpowder should be removed." He contended that "a very considerable quantity of gunpowder could be collected there in a short time which might be highly embarrassing in the event of any political trouble."[74] Other officers based their disagreement over the lifting of the ban on gunpowder not on speculation that public peace would be undermined but on what appeared to be verifiable fact. In Ilorin, the resident claimed that the shortage of gunpowder in 1942 reduced "accidental death" from gunshot. So, when John Holt sent an "unusual quantity" of gunpowder to the region in May 1944, the resident not only decried the absence of a magazine to store it but also claimed that gun violence would undermine peace and put pressure on the coroner.[75] Here, as in several other episodes, the contradiction associated with the gunpowder trade surfaced as officers tried to balance security concerns with the significance of the item in everyday life.

Yet the lifting of the ban on gunpowder sales did not produce the anticipated result of decongesting the warehouses of the trading companies, for consumption did not return to the preregulation level. A monthly average sale of twenty-five thousand pounds in the postregulation era was also the same as during the regulation era.[76] The gravity of the situation varied from one part of the country to another. In Calabar Province, only 2,564 pounds of the total stock of 57,245 pounds were sold in the month of July 1944.[77] The economic loss went beyond the damage to the gunpowder supplies in the warehouses across the country, for if it was hard to sell a consignment at home, it would be harder still to sell new shipments arriving from abroad. In November 1944, the Port Harcourt office of CFAO shared the telegraph it received from the Imperial Chemicals Industry, its gunpowder manufacturer, advising the firm that it would be responsible for the damage to the newly manufactured gunpowder that awaited shipment at the dockyard. The AWAM, which became increasingly agitated about its members' wartime losses, shared this information with the government "to dispel the belief, if held, that Gunpowder will keep for a long period without deterioration."[78]

By November 1944, the AWAM finally succeeded in persuading the government to make another amendment to the Emergency Powers Defense Acts that governed the sale of explosives by removing the restriction of a maximum of one pound placed on the retail sale of gunpowder to consumers. Administrative officers retained the power to issue licenses because they were "more accessible than the police" and because of "their wider dispersal throughout" the country. However, they were expected "to be as liberal as possible . . . within the limits of security" when considering requests from retailers.[79] This final bold step apparently favored the big firms, which reported in March 1945 that the gunpowder trade was back to the prewar situation and that their consignments were leaving the warehouse faster than they used to. The regulation allowing Nigerians to buy more than one pound of gunpowder remained in force after World War II. Probably reacting to a rumor that the government had changed its policy by returning to prewar restrictions, an Ibadan-based lawyer, A. Odunmbaku, put out a notice in the *Southern Nigeria Defender* on June 25, 1948, advising traders that they could "sell as they like," provided that they had a permit to trade in explosives.[80] But retailers still could not buy more than fifty pounds from the trading companies at a time—the lifting of the one-pound selling limit helped ensure that they sold their gunpowder faster but did not increase the amount of supply they could hold. In the 1950s, in addition to providing written applications to sell gunpowder, traders were also required to keep monthly returns of their transactions, which the government inspected.

Explosives and the Colonial Extractive and Mining Industry

Gunpowder was Nigeria's most widely used explosive. But colonialism also brought other classes of far more dangerous explosives, such as gelignite, gelatin, and dynamite used for blasting in mining operations. The mining of solid minerals predated the establishment of colonial rule. But as Bill Freund and Carolyn Brown, among other scholars, have noted, the transformation of tin and coal mining into a capitalist venture in Nigeria came hand in hand with the establishment of colonialism and the gradual transfer of trading rights from such big imperialist companies as the Royal Niger Company to the government of Great Britain.[81] Between 1900 and 1905, tin mining in central Nigeria followed the labor-intensive format of precolonial times. H. Law, a graduate of the Royal School of Mines who established the mining settlement of Tilde in 1903, made use of six hundred carriers and twenty-five soldiers supplied by the government.[82] By the outbreak of World War I, blasting materials such as gelignite and gelatin, as well as detonators and fuses, began to play a significant role in the development of the tin extraction industry, in which about two hundred companies were involved. What is true of tin mining in central Nigeria is true also of coal, which was extracted through "shot firing" in Enugu from 1915. This process involves setting explosives and drilling holes at desired angles into the coal face. The explosives are then detonated, releasing the coal onto the floor of the mine for the miners to pack.[83] The consolidation of the mining industry as a full-fledged arm of capitalist expropriation could not have been possible without the use of blasting explosives. Aside from mining operations, colonial officers and building contractors across the country used blasting explosives in the construction of roads, bridges, and other infrastructure. Snagging of rivers with gelatin was carried out regularly to improve river flow or remove heavy obstructions like trees.

Unlike gunpowder, which the public could legally buy, blasting explosives were illegal for private individuals to possess in any quantity. Only the government and construction and mining companies that had the license to operate in Nigeria were legally allowed to use explosives.[84] Unauthorized use of blasting explosives posed greater danger to colonial security than did gunpowder. As we shall see in chapter 5, one of the bloodiest episodes in Nigerian history (the killing of twenty-one miners at Enugu in November 1949) was accentuated by the need to prevent explosives from getting into the hands of radicals, who called for a militant approach to the independence movement. The first law dealing specifically with blasting explosives was passed around 1912. Not only were explosives required to be stored on mining settlements or camps; the chief inspector of mines was obligated to ensure that storage conformed to government safety regulations. One such specification stipulated that magazines could not be within one hundred yards of human dwellings and that detonators and blasting materials had to be stored in separate compartments of the magazine. Of all the provisions of the explosives law, the most important, perhaps, was that limiting the amount a magazine could hold at one time to a maximum of five hundred pounds.

Throughout the 1920s and 1930s, legislation regulating mining explosives went through minor modifications, especially in regard to the licensing of magazines and the authority responsible for their issuance. In 1948, a major amendment completely redefined the physical and architectural properties of an acceptable magazine. In response to the intensification of seismic prospecting for crude oil in Nigeria by Shell D'Arcy Petroleum Development Company, the government permitted the use of a "floating magazine" containing up to two tons of dynamite in the waterways of southern Nigeria. For the first time, explosives meant for oil exploration could be moved on the creeks from one place to another as desired.[85] But this new development constituted some administrative challenges in terms of monitoring the location of a mobile magazine. To deal with this situation, oil companies were expected to notify both the chief inspector of mines and the district officer of their areas of operation about the location of their "floating magazines."[86] In November 1950, Shell D'Arcy's floating magazines were stationed in Gbekebo, Aboto, and Apare communities in Ondo Province.[87]

As the intensification of mining operations increased through the 1920s and 1930s, so did the deployment of explosives. Mining companies were contravening the explosives law by either possessing more than the quantity permitted or not receiving approval for the construction of magazines. The penalty for breaking the explosives law ranged from a fine of £200 to short- and long-term revocation of licenses.[88] On some occasions, poor handling of explosives led to serious accidents. When the magazine of Jos Tin Area Nigeria Limited went up in flames in September 1939 as a result of the improper storage of detonators, fifteen miners lost their lives. The government's investigation indicted the operators of the mines, who were subsequently fined £800. Explosives-related accidents also took place outside the mining settlements—blasting during the construction of roads and bridges produced casualties. In his autobiography *No Telephone to Heaven*, colonial officer Malcolm Milne narrated the challenges he confronted using explosives and detonators for snagging in the palm-oil-producing regions in the early 1940s.[89] People congregated to watch snagging operations, not only because of the loud sounds that followed detonation, but also to collect fish, which the explosions readily made available. Milne's narratives also reveal the danger that colonial officers, most of whom were not trained in the proper handling of gelatin, faced as they tried to improve or provide infrastructure in their areas of jurisdiction. His description of the fear of an explosion as he carried his entire family in his car with one thousand pounds of gelatin and detonators along the dangerous Onitsha–Port Harcourt Road is evidence not only of the poor facilities put in place to transport explosives but also of a colonial officer's recklessness.⁹⁰ "We had all been nicely poised for a powered flight to heaven should the worst have occurred," remarked Kat, Milne's wife, after the treacherous trip.⁹¹

Although private possession of blasting explosives was illegal, a black market demand for them sprang up among Nigerians who also sought to partake in the economic benefit of mining. Illegal mining flourished partly because the government refused to grant mining concessions to locals, who frequently lost their land to big foreign mining companies. Much of the illegal mining was done with shovels. But by the 1920s, administrators noted that dynamite was also being used. It was not unusual for miners to steal some explosives from government-approved magazines for their unauthorized efforts. In one of the most detailed cases of explosives theft that I have found, a consignment of one ton of dynamite belonging to Ribon Valley Tinsfields Limited was intercepted by a gang of ten men on their way to Jos on June 12, 1925. When the culprits (six of whom were former employees of the company) were arrested on June 20, more than half of the stolen dynamite had already been sold in the local black market. The speed with which the thieves were able to dispose of the stolen dynamite convinced the government of the high incidence of unauthorized mining. But more important, it heightened concerns over security and safety.⁹²

Conclusion

The gunpowder trade established how international commerce supported domestic social and economic life in Nigeria. While the colonial government benefited from it through taxes and other levies paid by importers, Nigerians used it for a variety of purposes. The economics of the gunpowder trade undoubtedly appeared to be a win-win situation for both the government and the local people; in reality, however, it was a story of the dependency of the latter. The fact that much of the gunpowder came from abroad meant that Nigerians had to yield to unfavorable economic practices imposed by the government and the big trading companies, especially during unstable periods such as World War II. Regardless, the gunpowder trade did help sustain the Nigerian gun society, shaping Nigeria's experience with firearms beyond the usual story of violence and destruction.

Notes

1. "Controller of Customs to the Chief Secretary to the Government of Nigeria," April 15, 1932, Comcol, 03452, vol. 3, NAI.
2. "Controller of Customs to the Chief Secretary to the Government of Nigeria," February 12, 1924, Comcol, 03452, vol. 2, NAI.
3. Falola, "Salt Is Gold"; Falola, "Cassava Starch for Export"; Njoku, "Export Production Drive"; Byfield, "Feeding the Troops"; Chuku, "Crack Kernels, Crack Hitler"; Johnson, "Female Leadership"; Adesina, "Colonial State's Wartime Emergency Regulations"; Byfield, "Women, Rice, and War."
4. Aderinto, "Isaac Fadoyebo"; Oyemakinde, "Pullen Marketing Scheme"; Johnson, "Female Leadership."
5. "Note on Supplies of Gunpowder," CSO/41750, NAI.
6. "Conference of Residents, Northern Provinces," November 9, 1937, Kano Prof., 2496, NAK.
7. "Memo by the Secretary of State for the Colonies," January 10, 1924, Comcol, 03452, vol. 2, NAI.
8. "Acting Chief Secretary to the Secretary of Northern Provinces," October 19, 1921, SNP, 2504/1921, NAK.
9. "Acting Resident of Nupe to the Secretary of the Northern Provinces," November 8, 1921, SNP, 2504/1921, NAK.
10. "Secretary of the Northern Provinces," April 22, 1922, SNP, 2504/1921, NAK.
11. For the involvement of the Lagos private business community in gunpowder trade regulation, see the following from the *Nigerian Pioneer*: "Gunpowder," February 9, 1923; "Minutes of a Meeting of the Lagos Chamber of Commerce Held at the Colonial Bank on Tuesday 18th September 1923," September 28, 1923; and "Gunpowder Regulations," September 28, 1923.
12. "Secretary of Southern Province to the Chief Secretary to the Government," May 2, 1922, Comcol, 03452, vol. 1, NAI.
13. "Director of Marine to the Chief Secretary to the Government," October 25, 1922, Comcol, 03452, vol. 1, NAI.
14. "Simpson & Patton to the Clerk of the Executive Council," February 26, 1923, Comcol, 03452, vol. 1, NAI.
15. "Secretary of the Southern Province to the Chief Secretary to the Government," June 16, 1923, Comcol, 03452, vol. 1, NAI.
16. "Acting Solicitor-General's Note," July 16, 1923, Comcol, 03452, vol. 1, NAI.
17. Ibid.
18. "Acting Secretary of Southern Province to the Chief Secretary to the Government," July 16, 1923, Comcol, 03452, vol. 1, NAI.
19. "Acting Secretary of Southern Province to the Chief Secretary to the Government," November 6, 1923, Comcol, 03452, vol. 1, NAI.
20. "F. Brown to the Controller of Customs," July 26, 1923, Comcol, 03452, vol. 1, NAI.
21. "Director of Marine to the Chief Secretary to the Government," November 24, 1923, Comcol, 03452, vol. 1, NAI.
22. "Fatal Gunpowder Accident," *Nigerian Pioneer*, October 10, 1924; "Explosive Blows Blacksmith's Shop," *SND*, April 10, 1948.

23. "Gunpowder and Petrol," *SND*, June 30, 1948; "Two Young Men Killed by Explosion," *Daily Service*, April 10, 1948.

24. "French Firm Loses £95,000 in Lagos Fire," *WAP*, May 18, 1953.

25. "Four Europeans Die in Gunpowder Fire," *WAP*, September 18, 1953.

26. "Deputy Governor of Nigeria to the Secretary of State for the Colonies," July 22, 1936, Comcol, 03452, vol. 2, NAI.

27. "Telegram to the Chief Secretary to the Government of Nigeria," July 27, 1935, Comcol, 03452, vol. 3, NAI.

28. "Director of Marine to the Chief Secretary to the Governor," January 14, 1947, Comcol, 03452, vol. 4, NAI.

29. "Director of Marine to the Chief Secretary to the Government," October 22, 1947, Comcol, 03452, vol. 4, NAI.

30. "Acting Secretary to the Government," January 20, 1923, Comcol, 03452, vol. 1, NAI.

31. "Controller of Customs to the Chief Secretary to the Government," February 6, 1923, Comcol, 03452, vol. 1, NAI.

32. "Governor of Nigeria to the Lieutenant-Governor," February 20, 1923, Comcol, 03452, vol. 1, NAI.

33. "Memo by the Secretary of State for the Colonies," January 10, 1924, Comcol, 03452, vol. 2, NAI.

34. "Controller of Customs to the Chief Secretary to the Government," February 12, 1924, Comcol, 03452, vol. 2, NAI.

35. "Memo by the Chief Secretary to the Government," March 7, 1924, Comcol, 03452, vol. 2, NAI.

36. Collingham, *Taste of War*, 138–40.

37. "WAWC Supply and Production Committee," May 8, 1943, CSO/41750, NAI.

38. "Association of West African Merchants," June 5, 1943, CSO/41750, NAI.

39. "WAWC Supply and Production Committee."

40. Regulations Made under the Emergency Powers (Defence Acts 1939 and 1940), No. 72 of 1943 (October 6, 1943), CSO/41750, NAI.

41. "District Agent of John Holt to the Acting Resident of Ilorin Province," April 23, 1944, CSO/41749, NAI.

42. Public Notice No. 248 of 1943, "Defence (Import, Control and Sale of Explosives Regulations, 1940)." CSO/41750, NAI.

43. "Deputy Controller of Palm Kernel Eastern Provinces to the Deputy Director of Supplies," August 6, 1943, CSO/41750, NAI.

44. J. H. Mackay, "Gunpowder," August 9, 1943, CSO/41750, vol. 2, NAI.

45. "The Awujale to the District Officer," August 2, 1943, CSO/41750, vol. 2, NAI.

46. "L. N. Obioha to the District Officer of Orlu," October 21, 1943, ORLDIST, 3/1/409, NAE.

47. "Robinson J. Nwankwo to the District Officer of Orlu," October 10, 1943, ORLDIST, 3/1/409, NAE.

48. "Assistant General Secretary of UAC to the Resident," April 19, 1943, CSO/41750, NAI.

49. "Resident of Owerri to the Superintendent of Police," April 20, 1943, CSO/41750, NAI.

50. "Deputy Controller of Palm Kernel Eastern Provinces to the Deputy Director of Supplies," August 6, 1943, CSO/41750, NAI.

51. "Assistant District Officer of Orlu to Chief Ukachukwu," October 8, 1943, ORLDIST, 3/1/409, NAE.

52. "Deputy Controller of Palm Kernels to the Director of Supply," December 24, 1943, CSO/41750, vol. 2, NAI.

53. "Odemo of Isara to the Senior District Officer," March 20, 1944, Ijebu Prof., 2639 X/2, NAI.

54. "Assistant General Manager of UAC to the Resident," April 19, 1943, CSO/41750, NAI.

55. "Secretary of the Association of West African Merchants to the Deputy Director of Supply," July 26, 1943, CSO/41750, NAI.

56. "Minutes of Local Merchants Committee Meeting Held at John Holt Abeokuta," April 17, 1944, CSO/41749, NAI.

57. "Writer Makes Suggestions for the Solution of Gun Powder Sale," July 15, 1943; and "Editorial Gun Powder Sale," July 15, 1943—both in *ENG*.

58. From the *ENG*: "Writer Makes Suggestions for the Solution to the Gun Powder Sale," July 15, 1943; "Editorial: Gun Powder Sale," July 15, 1943. From the *Daily Service*: "More Palm Kernel," June 8, 1943; "Bring in the Kernel and Groundnuts," June 9, 1943; "The Production Drive," June 9, 1943; "Palm Kernels," June 12, 1943; "Palm Kernel," June 17, 1943; "Production of Palm Kernel and Rubber," June 18, 1943; "Commissioner of the Colony Appeals to Ijesha for Increase In Production of Rubber and Palm Kernel," June 28, 1943; "The Supply Board," June 9, 1943; "Wanted an African on the Nigerian Produce Board," June 12, 1943; "African Traders and the Supply Board," June 10, 1943; "Correspondent Says Africans Are Squarely Treated by Supply Board," June 10, 1943; "Wanted an African on the Produce Board," June 14, 1943; "The Supply Board," June 16, 1943; and "The Nigerian Supply Board," June 22, 1943.

59. "United Africa Company Limited to the Senior District Officer of Ijebu Ode," February 23, 1944, Ijebu Prof., 2639 X/2, NAI.

60. "Farmers to the District Officer of Ijebu Province," March 22, 1944, Ijebu Prof., 2639 X/2, NAI.

61. "Bale to the Provincial Officer," March 3, 1944, Ijebu Prof., 2639 X/2, NAI.

62. "Secretary of Shagamu Town Council and the General Secretary of Ijebu Remo Farmers' Association," April 4, 1944, Ijebu Prof., 2639 X/2, NAI.

63. For more on conflict between African producers and big European firms, see, among others, Olukoju, "Confronting the Combines."

64. "Acting Resident of Ijebu to the Secretary of Shagamu Town Council," April 27, 1944, Ijebu Prof., 2639 X/2, NAI.

65. "Chief Conservator to the Secretary Nigeria Supply Board," February 9, 1943, CSO/41750, NAI.

66. "Deputy Director of Wild Rubber Production to the Deputy Director of Supplies," July 14, 1943, CSO/41750, NAI.

67. Ibid.

68. "Forest Officer Enugu to the Secretary of Western Provinces," July 13, 1943, CSO/41750, NAI.

69. "District Officer of Degema to the Deputy Director of Wild Rubber Production," February 15, 1944, CSO/41749, NAI.

70. "Forest Officer Enugu to the Secretary of Western Provinces," July 13, 1943, CSO/41750, vol. 2, NAI.

71. "Resident of Kabba Province to the Deputy Director of Supplies," September 1, 1943, CSO/41750, vol. 2, NAI.

72. "District Manager of UAC to the Resident of Ondo Province," November 13, 1943, CSO/41750, vol. 2, NAI.

73. GFTC Colby, "Extract from a minute by Director of Supplies," December 1943, CSO/41750, vol. 2, NAI.

74. "Acting Commissioner of Police to the Director of Supply," July 20, 1944, CSO/41750, vol. 2, NAI.

75. "Acting Resident of Ilorin Province to the Director of Supplies," May 2, 1944, CSO/41750, vol. 2, NAI.

76. "C. M. Booth and Association of West African Merchants," October 6, 1944, CSO/41750, vol. 2, NAI.

77. "Association of West African Merchants," October 1944, CSO/41750, vol. 2, NAI.

78. "T. Brady to the Director of Supplies," November 11, 1944, CSO/41750, vol. 2, NAI.

79. "Acting Chief Secretary to the Secretary Northern, Eastern and Western Provinces," November 20, 1944, CSO/41750, vol. 2, NAI.

80. "Gun Powder Dealers by A. Odunmbaku," *SND*, June 25, 1948; and "The Explosives (Import Control and Sale) Ordinance: Ammunition," *Daily Service*, January 17, 1948.

81. Freund, *Capital and Labour*; Brown, *"We Were All Slaves."*

82. Freund, *Capital and Labour*, 34–35.

83. Brown, *"We Were All Slaves,"* 114.

84. "Explosives Sold by the Niger Company Limited during 1921," SNP 144M/1921, NAK.

85. "Regulations Made under the Explosives Ordinance (133)" 1948, ONDIST 20/1/1907, NAE.

86. C. Mackay, "Seismic Cable Operation," November 30, 1953, Ondo Prof., 216/1, NAI.

87. "Senior Inspector of Mines–Western Inspectorate to the Resident of Ondo Province," November 18, 1950, Ondo Prof., 216/1, NAI.

88. "Explosives Licence No.24: Cancellation of, 1923," SNP, 408/1923, NAK.

89. Milne, *No Telephone to Heaven*, 142–53.

90. Ibid., 150.

91. Ibid.

92. "Explosives Control and Use of In Jos Area: Report on Explosives Theft," June 26, 1925, Jos Prof., 1498, NAK.

4

"ALL EUROPEANS IN THIS COUNTRY SHOULD BE ABLE TO FIRE A RIFLE"

Race, Leisure Shooting, and the Lethal Symbol of Imperial Domination

> It is, I think, one of the greatest joys in life to stroll out with a gun after the day's work is over, looking for anything that may make a suitable addition to the larder, and in Northern Nigeria there is scarcely any place where a shot-gun is not both an asset and a source of pleasure. The bags may not be large, but there is always something to shoot at, if not to shoot.
>
> —Richard Oakley, *Treks and Palavers*, 116

> I was no slaughterer at any time. I tried for the best heads, and when I had got decent ones of any species left the antelope alone, unless I came across a pair of horns that seemed to beat any that I had. I never would shoot a giraffe, which to me, is a most inoffensive creature and possesses nothing which will make a trophy.
>
> —A. C. G. Hastings, *Nigerian Days*, 182

"Large crowd gathered immediately, and it was with great difficulty that the people were dispersed," wrote the *Southern Nigeria Defender* as it attempted to describe the atmosphere at the provincial office in Oyo on April 5, 1948, when the news that Assistant District Officer J. D. Underwood had shot and killed himself with a pistol spread across the town. Earlier that day, the unmarried Underwood, who joined the Oyo administrative office in 1947, came to his office, performed some official duties, went home for lunch, and returned to the office, where the shooting occurred.[1] If Underwood's death was easily ruled as suicide, that of Theophilus Iseli, a Swiss businessman, required months of criminal investigation and a coroner's inquest. On January 27, 1951, the decomposing body of the thirty-four-year-old man was found in a secluded portion of his office at Martin Street, in Lagos, after he was declared missing two days earlier.[2] The medical examiner's report indicated that Iseli died from four gunshot wounds to the head. Two firearms, a double-barreled gun and a rifle, were recovered from the scene. Conspiracy theories emerged as the police attempted to unravel the mystery behind Iseli's death. Susanna, Iseli's Swiss wife, and a section of Lagos's Swiss community believed that Iseli's American business partner Richard Weiss and secretary Bam Gardner had conspired to kill him in order to take over his business, which specialized in buying local African produce such as rubber and ginger for the international market. Others thought that Susanna, who was known to be unhappy with her marriage, probably sent hired assassins to kill her husband. The "popular" belief in the Swiss community was that "if Theo had not married this girl [Susanna], he would not have died," the Swiss consul in Nigeria reportedly said.[3] Two other Swiss residents in Lagos allegedly mentioned that Susanna once pleaded, "Don't leave me in this country: I have no further hope here," and demanded to be returned to Switzerland because she was unhappy with her marriage.[4] Although not formally charged for the death of Iseli, Weiss and Gardner hired lawyers to defend them during the coroner's inquest, which lasted throughout the months of February and March 1951. After reviewing the testimony of nineteen people, Iseli's business transactions, and the report of medical examiner Dr. Kertetesz, the coroner ruled that Iseli had committed suicide. "Considering the evidence of the various bank managers called in," the coroner established, "the financial standing of Sotraco [Iseli's business] and the multifarious engagements the deceased had with private individuals . . . together must naturally worry any average person to death."[5]

It is difficult to say in absolute terms the nature or type of mental illness that contributed to Underwood's or Iseli's suicides.[6] But anyone familiar with the daily life of Europeans in Nigeria could presume their likely mental state. The diaries, biographies, and autobiographies of Europeans in colonial Nigeria demonstrate that most of them (especially the single men or those who were married but did not bring their wife to the colonies) lived very isolated and relatively distressed lives, attributable partly to the lack of facilities and social networks obtainable in Europe. The most important and creative solution to boredom was leisure. Anthony Kirk-Greene, a colonial administrator in Nigeria who later became a leading historian of British colonialism, has noted that his former colleagues spent their time after work in various activities ranging from horticulture and sport to writing and community service.[7] Alcohol abuse was institutionalized as one of the inevitable consequences of the African climate and a temporary relief for loneliness, and sexual liaisons between colonial officers and Nigerian women were officially unacceptable though discreet.[8] Given that the identities of European residents in Nigeria were diverse, one should also expect their sexual orientation also to be. Some Europeans in Lagos and Ibadan, according to Ian Brinkworth, who entered the colonial service in 1946 after serving in World War II, practiced homosexuality.[9] The proliferation of Europeans-only recreation facilities, sporting activities, and overseas leave packages were all meant to help officers relieve the stress of work—they were not necessarily a permanent solution to boredom, which could lead to depression.[10]

Of all the numerous pastimes, sport hunting and leisure shooting were among the most common. As the epigraphs to this chapter suggest, shooting created a high degree of personal satisfaction and entertainment, which relieved the stresses of colonial service. Indeed, few European colonial officers (especially those posted to rural communities) would claim not to have been involved in an occasional game-hunting expedition. Civilian rifle ranges managed by local branches of the Nigerian Rifle Association in the big cities and provincial capitals served the minority of European administrators and businessmen, expatriates, and others. An advertisement for Amstel beer in the *Nigerian Pioneer* in the early 1920s sums up the image of a European: it profiles colonial adventurism while justifying alcohol use in the tropics, and likening the crack of a breaking tropical tree limb to that of a rifle shot in the serious cold in Canada. The Dutch Amstel, "the beer that is brewed for abroad," and suited to the Canadian cold, would serve the needs of the tropics very well, the advertisement claims.

This chapter is about the intersection of race, leisure shooting, and imperialism in Nigerian gun society. The Nigerian gun society was made diverse by gun use among Europeans of different nationalities, Americans, and Lebanese, among other groups of non-Africans. This chapter makes two overlapping arguments. First, I posit that European gun culture in Nigeria represented a form of symbolic domination of the human and natural environment. A gun is one of the most enduring symbols of imperialism, which both the colonizers and the broader imperial establishment used in varying situations and changing contexts to affirm their superiority and legitimacy as an inevitable force of sociopolitical and economic change. The title of this chapter, a statement attributed to the assistant district officer of Ilesha, echoed the established notion that gun ownership, of not just any type of gun, but a rifle, the most advanced "light" firearm, was not a privilege but a right that every European in Nigeria must assert.[11] The expansion of the colonial service and immigration of Europeans led to the rise of a new regime of European gun culture in the empire, which was both cause and consequence of the exploitation of the natural environment. Moreover, firearms were inevitably valued as means of self-defense against both humans and animals, as Europeans of different ages, classes, and nationalities trekked thousands of miles to establish political and economic hegemony to the remotest reaches of the colonial domain. Indeed, most, if not all, European men in Nigeria, including the missionaries, bore guns. Yet because imperialism was a male-dominated enterprise, one should also expect the gun, the instrument through which it was built, to be; not surprisingly, then, very few European women used guns in Nigeria.[12] The popularity of firearms among Europeans in the early era of colonial rule owed much to the fact that military officers who later became administrative personnel were chiefly responsible for extending the empire. But as the colonial service established itself, so did the intensification of European gun culture in the colonies with the arrival of new classes of Europeans such as expatriates. At the same time, these factors diversified the Nigerian gun society.

Second, I present how European gun-bearing culture renders another viable perspective on race and racism in the Nigerian gun society. The assumption of European racial superiority was produced and reproduced on a daily basis. The laws that restricted certain classes of guns to Europeans, and that prevented Africans from shooting in European reservations and from joining European rifle clubs, were intended to sustain the assumption that Nigerians were incapable of using certain firearms or were prone to be irresponsible with dangerous weapons. Racially discriminatory gun laws thus served multiple and complementary purposes: on the one hand, to restrict highly lethal firearms like rifles to Europeans in order to maintain the notion of white superiority, and on the other hand, to ensure that Africans were not in possession of powerful weapons capable of disturbing the public peace and undermining colonial rule. Thus, all men and women, like their guns, were not equal.

Imperialism, Recreational Hunting, and Travel and Nature Writing

Nigerian historical studies on the life and times of colonial officers have revolved mainly around the exercise of imperial authority. This body of work not only tends to glorify the success of imperialism in introducing "civilization"; it also robs Africans of their own agency in the making of an idealized colonial state.[13] It is common to read about the hardships that pioneering colonial officers faced during the foundational stage of the colony, but less so about how they dominated nature and carved out an alternative lifestyle for themselves in a foreign land.[14] Colonial officers lived multiple lives outside their primary responsibility of administering the empire. Their multiple identities and lifestyles were shaped not only by the natural and human circumstances unique to Nigeria but also by their own interests in extracurricular activities. A history of European leisure, with particular focus on big- and small-game hunting, is therefore a significant correction to a historiography that overwhelmingly focuses on the exercise of political authority. Hunting was not just a pastime; it was a significant element of Western imperialism in Nigeria. As John Mackenzie has rightly observed, the "significance of hunting in the imperialism of the nineteenth and the twentieth centuries has not been fully recognised."[15] Mackenzie's observation, first made in 1988, remains valid, especially as concerns West Africa, where the literature on the intersection of imperial hunting, colonialism, wildlife conservation, and nature and travel writing is sparse.[16] Many of the existing works on these topics have focused on East and Central Africa. Regardless of region, very little Africanist literature has placed imperial hunting within the context of European gun culture.

Whether among Africans or Europeans, hunting was inseparable from firearms. Indeed, what made hunting a pleasurable activity for Europeans was both the personal fulfillment that they received from killing wild animals and the privilege to use sophisticated firearms like rifles, which few Africans were allowed to own. The rifle, more than the shotgun, the number-one firearm of most educated Africans and traditional elites, symbolized a superior imperial masculinity. More than anything else, it was the use of rifles of varying degrees of sophistication and the purpose and methods of killing large game that made imperial hunting a prime physical and symbolic element of colonial domination. The victims of colonial conquest were, therefore, not only Africa's precolonial political institutions and its cultural artifacts but also its animals and wilderness. Imperial hunting was a definite component of a complex network of social, economic, cultural, racial, and legal relationships between Nigerians and Europeans. While indigenous hunters relied on several hunting tools, including arrows, traps, and Dane guns, their imperial counterparts relied exclusively on their rifles and shotguns.[17]

The hunting practices of local and foreign hunters also varied widely. For instance, few indigenous hunters would shoot a Dane gun at a small animal like a rat, guinea fowl, or sand grouse, because its single projectile would destroy the meat and render it uneatable and because there were other alternative methods of trapping them without expending precious gunpowder, which was very expensive during crisis periods like World War II. Moreover, in indigenous hunting practice, to shoot small animals with a gun was considered unprofessional, and to some extent unethical—only an amateur who had not been initiated into the hunter's guild would do so. The Yoruba statement "Ko ni buru fun ode ko ri okete / oloungbo ko lo gbe 'bon" suggests that the worst thing that could happen to a hunter is to try to kill a cat or grasscutter with a gun—it is the height of unprofessionalism and misfortune. But imperial hunters, such as David Hunter, whose story is narrated in the last section of this chapter, would use a shotgun to kill small game, because unlike a Dane gun, it would kill the animal without rendering it uneatable.

Historians interested in the intersection of imperial hunting and firearms face a disappointing paucity of archival materials on the subject. Unlike other gun-related sporting activities such as rifle-range shooting, imperial hunting was not a well-coordinated activity promoted by the colonial government and supervised by its institutions. Rifle-range shooting managed by the Nigerian Rifle Association enjoyed better organizational structure than did game-hunting culture, partly because it did not entail the slaying of big game, most of which were protected mammals, and because it took place in the main political and administrative capital where Europeans could more easily participate. The lack of proper coordination of imperial hunting led to one devastating outcome—it made the reckless killing of large game an illegal but tolerated behavior among colonial officers. It was just one of several areas of colonial administration that the government refused to police because it was unofficially treated as one of the benefits of serving abroad. To monitor what colonial officers did with their firearms was to kill their interest in serving in remote places, where they were, for the most part, the sole political authority. Thus, the whole language of nature conservation applied only to Africans, who were expected to follow game laws.

If archival sources are silent on imperial hunting, the memoirs of colonial officers render a textual window onto firearms and the attempt to dominate the African environment and its teeming wildlife. Indeed, such memoirs represent a general body of literature aimed at Western audiences who fantasized about the abundance of wildlife on the "Coast," as West Africa was known among the colonial administrators.[18] The authors of these writings were predominantly men, although European women did make occasional reference to the use of firearms in their adventures. Constance Larymore, wife of a resident officer, accompanied her husband to several parts of modern northern Nigeria (Kano, Bidda, Keffi, Kabba, and Katagum) during 1902–3. Larymore's story is unusual: she was arguably the first wife of a colonial officer to live in northern Nigeria in the twentieth century, and she witnessed the violent conquest of many parts of the region. Her numerous references to guns in her memoir, appropriately titled *A Resident's Wife in Nigeria* and first published in 1908, revealed the role of firearms in the conquest of northern Nigeria, in burial culture, and as a significant tool of self-defense against hostile communities.[19] Similarly, when Sylvia Leith-Ross arrived in Zungeru, the capital of the Protectorate of Northern Nigeria, with her colonial officer husband in 1907, several "pagan" communities in the southern end of the former Sokoto Caliphate were still resisting colonialism. In her memoir, titled *Stepping-Stones*, she recalled touring the North with armed soldiers used for colonial conquest. In 1910, she possessed a revolver, a Dane gun, machetes, and polers' spears for self-defense against alleged cannibalism of the Mushi people.[20]

Aside from Larymore and Leith-Ross, and Lassie Fitz-Henry, another wife of a colonial officer who used guns for hunting and self-defense, it appears that firearms and wildlife did not occupy a significant space in European women's experience of Nigeria because most of them did not participate in shooting.[21] European women managed to do their part to contribute to the racial ideologies of imperialism in Nigeria—despite the fact that the colony was, up until the 1920s, considered an unsuitable place for white women because of the absence of modern amenities obtainable in Europe.[22] Not surprisingly, gleaning from available documentary sources, very few European women used guns in Nigeria. Thus, gun power was essentially white male power.

Some detailed works on the intersection of firearms and wildlife, especially *Up against It in Nigeria* (1922) by Langa Langa (H. B. Hermon-Hodge), *Nigerian Days* (1925) by A. C. G. Hastings, and *Treks and Palavers* (1938) by Richard Oakley, are important contributions to the global literature on nature and travel writing from Nigeria. If hunting was not the main reason most men enlisted in the colonial service, it nevertheless was a significant factor in keeping them there. But the relationship between imperial hunting and colonialism cannot be understood in isolation from the general Western perception and image of Africa dating to the fifteenth century. The traveling journals of European explorers from the eighteenth century gave vivid portrayals or images of the African continent replete with game animals, enjoying the abundance of a serene natural habitat.[23] In the mid-nineteenth century, books on big-game hunting written by European "naturalists" who embarked on reckless wildlife killing sprees in southern, central, and eastern Africa were canonical works among a growing population of European safari enthusiasts.[24] Moreover, the (in)famous East African safari of Theodore Roosevelt, the twenty-sixth US president, and about 250 men in 1909 did more than stock up the Smithsonian Institution with more than five hundred trophies and animal specimens for his publicly professed humanitarian and scientific purposes; it also sparked new global interest in adventure in Africa, which colonial service offered. In his book on this popular plunder, titled *African Game Trails*, Roosevelt narrated how he and his son Kermit slayed nine lions, eight elephants, thirteen rhinoceroses, and fifteen zebras, among other exotic wild animals—a remarkable record that was the envy of big-game hunters, even though they lacked the resources or means to match it.[25]

In sum, the writings on game hunting produced by non-Africans in Nigeria fit into a broader literary genre of nature writing in the nineteenth and twentieth centuries. Oakley, who first served in Zaria, Yola, among other parts of northern Nigeria when he enlisted in the colonial service in 1921, gave the following reason for joining the colonial service: "a lifelong desire to see a leopard and a giraffe in their natural setting." A proud owner of two guns, a secondhand double-barreled twelve-bore and a secondhand .303 Birmingham Small Arms Company (BSA) sporting rifle, Oakley is more specific in his choice of northern Nigeria, which he described as a "land of big games, ponies and camels, all of which have a fascination."[26] Martin Kisch received a commission into the Royal Field Artillery after completing his military training at Exeter College, Oxford, in 1904. After discovering that promotion in the army "would be slow" and that he would not be "independent for many years," he returned to college to study law and joined the colonial service in 1908 because it held the "promise of responsibility" and "adventure and sport."[27] Similarly, when Larymore's husband was notified that he would be serving at Borgu shortly after arriving in northern Nigeria in October 1902, the couple was "jubilant at the prospect of seeing some new country, especially as Borgu possessed a great reputation for good sporting."[28]

It is one thing to imagine a great sporting opportunity; it is another for that dream to come true. Not only did the officers see what they imagined—an abundance of nature and the opportunity to shoot exotic animals in their natural habitat—they also were satisfied with their pastime. Oakley was more explicit as to the importance of hunting when he stated: "Shooting . . . occasional glimpse of beautiful creatures" and "reading the footprints on the sandy bush track of animals . . . help to alleviate the sense of loneliness and to make" a colonial officer like himself "feel that after all life is worth living."[29] "Our relaxation in the evenings on the station," wrote Hastings during his first administrative tour of Bauchi and Gombe, "was mainly shooting."[30] And so elated was Hermon-Hodge after a day of shooting in Bornu around 1910 that he felt more like a "glorified thistle than anything else."[31]

The popularity of game hunting did not end with these early colonial officers of the first two decades of the twentieth century. Indeed, it continued as human interference with the natural environment intensified through the expansion of human settlement that encroached on the natural habitats of animals. After tasting the relatively exotic life of European residents in Lagos when he first arrived in Nigeria in 1937, R. T. Kerslake graciously accepted his posting as assistant district officer in remote Katsina Province. He seemed not to miss his brief encounter with the beautiful European residential quarters and clubs of Lagos when he submitted that "bush life is better." The "bush district officer," as an administrator serving in rural communities loved to call himself, wrote that he "would often go out shooting" in the late afternoon with a local hunter guide who carried bow, arrow and charms and a servant who carried his gun until he needed it.[32] When Ian Brinkworth arrived in Warri Province to commence his duty as assistant district officer in 1946, one of the first questions he asked his colleagues was, "What's the shooting like here?"[33]

Aside from leisure, colonial officers did shoot to bring down animals accused of terrorizing the community under their imperial watch. Around 1910, P. Amaury Talbot, one of colonial Nigeria's most prolific anthropologists and colonial officers, killed with his rifle an alligator believed by locals at Oron to possess a spiritual power to transform into a human.[34] The colonial officer's rifle was always useful in communities where the regular Dane gun proved ineffective in killing large animals.[35] Moreover, the laws preventing Africans from killing protected wild animals were usually overridden for colonial officers. Game animals were also a reliable source of meat for Europeans.[36] Guinea fowl was apparently the most popular small animal killed for consumption by Europeans based in the North. "Birds of all sorts were plentiful on this road, and I practically lived on them till my cartridges ran out," confessed Hermon-Hodge.[37] In another portion of his narrative, he was compelled to call for a hammock when he could no longer trek due to dysentery after eating a roan antelope that he claimed he was "tempted" to shoot while crossing the Gongola River.[38] In his diary entry for November 10, 1908, Kisch described as "excellent" his meal comprising sweet potatoes and three pigeons that he shot a day earlier.[39] Although their host communities usually supplied basic food items, including mutton, yams, sweet potatoes, maize, and eggs, the Larymores still shot bush fowl and guinea fowl for two complementary goals: "for the best of all dishes" and "game to the larder."[40] Yet not all colonial officers hunted animals for food or fun. Some, like W. R. Crocker, who served as district officer of Makurdi Division, and Larymore, shot or ordered the shooting of their dogs, horses, and ponies because of sickness and old age.[41] Crocker also shot to scare animals from disturbing his comfort. In his diary entry of May 1, 1934, he wrote: "Impossible to sleep through the heat last night. Also there were packs of scavenging dogs prowling and howling around the compound. I got up once and emptied my revolver into the air with the hopes of scaring them off."[42]

The type of animals colonial officers killed was largely determined, as one would expect, by the natural habitat of their place of assignment. Lions, elephants, rhinoceroses, tigers, and leopards were among the most popular big game that hunters killed. Roan antelopes were also choice targets among northern colonial officers. The reason for this is not hard to understand. Except for in some parts of northern Nigeria such as Katagum, where Crocker wrote that people did not eat it, the antelope was not found in large number in most parts of northern Nigeria. During one of his hunting expeditions, Oakley stalked a roan antelope for two hours. Another rare animal was the gazelle, which Hermon-Hodge remarked was a "forbidden fruit" among the people. Thus, scarcity drove interest. Rare wild animals provided the opportunity for prolonged outdoor adventure into the deep thick forest, with all the corresponding dangers that imperial hunters internalized as an inevitable aspect of their daily life on the "dark" continent. Writings about hunting are replete with exaggerations and misrepresentations as writers consistently tried to enliven their romantic tales of African wildlife.

The popularity of game shooting among colonial officers in Nigeria should not be taken to mean that they were expert shooters. To the contrary, with the exception of military officers turned administrative officials, few administrators had experience shooting a rifle before they came to Nigeria. Fewer still had participated in game shooting because it was limited to the upper classes who owned the estates on which it could take place. "I had of course, never done any 'beef' shooting before, and was naturally very excited," confessed Hermon-Hodge during his trip from Lokoja to Bauchi, his first place of assignment, in 1909.[43] Even Rex Niven, a World War I veteran, who always had a Mannlicher-Schönauer rifle and a double-barreled shotgun whenever on tour, thought he was "young and inexperienced" as a hunter when he tried to kill a leopard accused of terrorizing a community during his assignment in Kabba Province around 1922.[44] John Smith was among the last major recruits of the colonial office for Nigeria when he arrived in the country in 1951. "The most foolish thing I did was to join a hunting expedition," the new inductee into game hunting confessed. However, he would later develop a keen interest. Not only did he buy a shotgun; he borrowed a rifle as well, "for there was plenty of game.... I looked forward to learning from experienced hunters," he remarked.[45] By the time he arrived in Hadieja, the capital of the northern division of Kano Province, famed for its excellent goose and duck shooting, in 1952, Smith had become a shooting enthusiast. The following description of his shooting episode blends poetic representation of nature with humanity's undue interference with it:

> It was a magnificent sight to see the thousands of birds gathered on the many lakes. With their fringe of reeds and low horizon these reminded me of the smaller Broads in Norfolk. As flight after flight swept over at dusk it was almost impossible to miss. The temptation was to shoot for more than one could dispose of. To stand, gun in hand, as sun went down and moon came up and hear the whistling teals before I could clearly see them was unforgettable.[46]

Some officers, after years of hunting in Nigeria, could not boast of being a good marksman or stalker—even though they arrogantly believed that possession of a rifle would automatically translate to successful hunting. Indeed, many local professional hunters armed with Dane guns were better marksmen than the colonial officers were. For one thing, officers needed the local hunters for crucial information about the animals' ecology. After several years of hunting in northern Nigeria, Oakley claimed that he "remained a novice to the end."[47] Hastings admitted that he was "neither a good nor a bad shot, just average."[48] He never saw a lion in the wild until around 1923. When his rifle shot narrowly missed the lion, from which he was just about twenty yards away, Hastings received some coaching from experienced local lion hunters that he should have shot "quickly in the first place, more steadily in the second."[49] But unlike many other writers who tended to minimize their hunting failures, Hastings seemed humble in admitting that his hunting error was "typical of the sort of shooting we get in Nigeria," that a colonial administrator was first and foremost a "political officer," and that game hunting was just a secondary activity—an opportunity presented by the environment where they served.[50] Shooting mistakes, caused by reasons ranging from jamming of bullets and poor visibility, to naïveté, exhaustion, and failure to take caution, were not only common during hunting; they inflicted injuries to colonial officers and members of their hunting parties.[51] One thing colonial officials' narratives about hunting make abundantly clear is that mere possession of a rifle did not make one a great game hunter—knowledge of ecology played a crucial role in every successful hunting exercise. Hastings added two others factors: namely, luck in finding big game and a good position from which to discharge bullets.

Of all autobiographical writings about imperial hunting in Nigeria, those by Hastings, Oakley, and Hermon-Hodge stand out clearly for their in-depth discussion of the relationship between firearms and hunting. So obsessed were these three men that they used African charms in hunting and professed the efficacy of juju.[52] They render vivid information about Nigerian geography, environment, and domestic hunting practices. Their books even contain photos of their trophies, which include the heads, ivories, and feet of their notable kills, and served as advice manuals on hunting. They advised prospective hunters on the best time to hunt, how best to shoot, the most appropriate ammunition to use, and the entire African game culture. Hermon-Hodge grouped his advice for European hunters into six interrelated parts: "Huntermen," "Shooting on Trek," "Arms," "Ammunition," "Position," and "Skinning."[53] He concludes that quality shooting depends on "fitness, keenness, and freshness."[54] After itemizing the various calibers of hunting guns, he recommends a .375 rifle, specifically the BSA Express, manufactured by the Birmingham Small Arms Company, which he praises for being "light, and beautifully balanced." "With it I have shot nearly every kind of big game from elephant downwards," the boastful Hermon-Hodge claims.[55] These authors' narratives, often presented in melodramatic language, capture the uneasy confrontation between the hunter and his prey. The following description, from Hastings's account of his encounter with a hippopotamus in the Gongola River, made a hero out of the hunter and his rifle:

> The light grew stronger and presently he came up to breathe, and I fired just below his ear tip, apparently without effect. Again he sank, but probably being shaken, emerged soon after, making through the shallows for a patch of thick reeds, where he turned, facing us and opening his cavern of a mouth in anger. Another shot into his great jaws made him turn and crash away into his reeds, while polers, now wildly excited swung the barge round the point of sand to intercept him on the other side. . . . He was mad with rage by now and made for us with gaping mouth which looked large enough to take the whole barge, as he came lumbering along towards me; and I remembered wondering, as I fired hurriedly into his mouth, whether such a mass of flesh could be stopped at all by the Mannlicher bullet. That shot anyway did not, and he got within 10 feet of the side of the barge when another bullet took him in the neck.[56]

Hastings's last bullet forced the big animal to sink into the water; its lifeless body was found floating the next day. Two villages shared the animal meat that weighed about two tons. So highly consumed was the animal that, according to Hastings, "there was not enough to feed a puppy, and the disappointed vultures hopped and searched in vain about the sand."⁵⁷ Hastings, however, kept the teeth and a square of hide for himself.

Hermon-Hodge gave a similar description of a serious hunting battle with an elephant in Bornu on March 13, 1910. He ends his five-page account of the shooting encounter with a statement that tends to uphold the advantage of shooting large animals beyond the narrow interest of the colonial officer: "But news in the Dark Continent travels like lightning—especially news of meat in famine time—and within half an hour the horizon was dotted with black figures who swarmed like mosquitoes to the prospective banquet. Forming a huge human semicircle, they converged on the silent watchers, brandishing sticks, and knives, yelling songs of triumph, and ever increasing in number."⁵⁸ Like Hastings, Hermon-Hodge kept the ivories of the elephant weighing 121 pounds and the front foot that he claimed broke the era's regional trophy weight record.

Nature writings reveal that Europeans engaged in reckless shooting and disobeyed prevailing wild animal protection regulations. Colonial officers were able to get away with breaking animal conservation laws in part because many of them served in remote districts where they were the sole colonial political authority. In other words, someone further up the political hierarchy would have to act, for a European to be charged for breaking game laws. In her biography of Lord Frederick Lugard, Margery Perham noted that Lugard dismissed a political officer in the first decade of the twentieth century for killing three giraffes without a license. Perham's description of Lugard as a "lonely eminence in a new country" suggests that acts of indiscipline were widespread among colonial administrators during the early period of colonial rule, when "inexperienced" officers committed atrocities in their quest to fulfill their fantasy of a continent waiting to be plundered.⁵⁹ Regardless, imperial shooting contributed to the traffic in ivory, among other animal trophies. Boastful stories of the size and weight of trophies, as we have seen in the case of Hermon-Hodge, were all meant to position imperial hunters as heroes to a global audience that fantasized about African wildlife. Yet these colonial officers were aware of the illegality of their actions, which they documented only several years after leaving the colonial service, when they were not likely to be prosecuted for their deeds.⁶⁰ Some even believed that their big-game hunting did not have any significant negative impact on wildlife conservation as reflected in this statement attributed to the secretary to the government of northern Nigeria in 1907: "In my opinion, the amount of shots by the present small number of Government officials makes very little difference to the amount of game abounding; take for instance the country round Zungeru where the game is still swarming."[61] The secretary's statement may be correct, given that colonialism was just taking its root in the first decade of the twentieth century in northern Nigeria. The same could not be said, however, after decades of intensified colonial exploits.

One is fascinated by the contradictory manner in which colonial officers tried to justify their reckless shooting against the attractiveness of Africa's natural environment. For one thing, some colonial officers were aware of the division within the global big-game hunting community about "inhumane" or "atrocious" killing of wild animals. And they wanted their audiences to see big-game enthusiasts as people who also cared about or were at least aware of the negative consequences of indiscriminate shooting. This contradiction is apparent in Hastings's narrative. After admitting that "our gun and rifle gave us a goodly and varied bag: a fine waterbuck, killed drinking in the earliest light, kob antelope and reed buck and every sort of waterfowl, among them spur-wing geese and several kinds of duck and teal," he goes on to state that "careless or promiscuous shooting is both cruel and unsporting."[62] Similarly, after killing a bull, Oakley remarks: "But my heart was sick within me—I felt like a murderer. . . . I wonder what it is in our constitution: is it the struggle between the primitive instinct of hunting and the love for animals, a hallmark of civilization, that makes every Briton, if he allows himself to think, feel like this when he slays a wild creature."[63] But he follows this statement with another ambivalent representation of the exploitation of nature: "And yet at the next opportunity he [a Briton] is as keen as ever for the chase. It is the stalk, of course, that counts, and I suppose the climax—the shot, or better still the snap shot—is demanded as a proof to satisfy his ego. I was proud of my stalk, but I am not now proud of my slaughter."[64] In another portion of his book, he makes a startling disclosure of his contribution to the depletion of a wild animal: "I had not the least desire to be guilty of the crime of shooting the last hippo in the district in Yola, and I humbugged myself that I had only shot half-heartedly."[65] Fitz-Henry killed the last hippopotamus in his district, as his wife recounted. Her racist statement, that the locals "assembled and chattering like a jungle full of monkeys," similar to that of Hermon-Hodge, attempted to make a humanitarian act out of killing an exotic animal by describing the mood of the community that feasted on the large animals.[66]

The Nigerian Rifle Association and the Politics of Leisure Shooting

Rifle-range shooting was another European leisure activity in Nigeria. The first registered rifle club in Nigeria, the Lagos Rifle Club, was established in the 1880s by European expatriates, military officers, and colonial administrators in Lagos. The number of rifle clubs increased as colonialism was extended to the hinterland. Each rifle club, especially those in big cities and provincial capitals, had a shooting range measuring about two hundred to four hundred yards at which members met to socialize and share food and drinks with their families—while Nigerians watched with amazement. The rifle clubs that did not have a shooting range were occasionally permitted to use police and military facilities for target practice. As with other European-run recreation facilities across the country, membership in the rifle clubs was open only to Europeans—Africans were barred.

Shooting enthusiasts made use of newspapers to mobilize support for local rifle clubs. One advertisement for membership in a rifle club published in the January 30, 1909, issue of the *Lagos Weekly Record* painted the benefits of rifle shooting as going beyond the ability to hit targets and the appeal to the narrow social interest of a minority of Europeans, to the improvement of cognitive skill:

> The formation of a local Rifle Club means affordable opportunity to all who desire to avail it of learning how to use a rifle. That such knowledge will be useful need hardly be said, while it will mean creating something calculated to attract the attention and interest of our youth who are certainly in need of attraction of some sort which will tend to pin their interest. You cannot learn how to shoot straight unless you bend your attention on your shooting, and so the art may avail to improve the handicraftsman as well as the lawyer.[67]

The outbreak of World War I extended the mission of rifle clubs beyond their recreational importance. The government, in addition to allowing the clubs to maintain their core recreational mission, constituted the club in Lagos into a European local force called the Lagos Defence Force to protect the colony in the event of a German invasion.[68] Other activities promoting rifle shooting included publishing the outcome of rifle matches in the newspapers.[69]

The racial politics of the rifle clubs extended beyond the refusal to allow African membership; they were also manifest in the position that each

European nationality occupied within Nigerian colonial society. The public announcement of rifle shooting by the Kano Rifle Club in July 1939 was clear about the category of people invited: "All ladies and gentlemen of British nationality will be welcome."[70] To be sure, "British nationality" included only white Britons, not to those of other European background or black Britons. This is not surprising. Africanist studies have shown that terms like *Europeans* and *whites* in colonial context must be deployed with caution because nationality and gradation of whiteness shaped the ways in which Europeans saw and treated one another from one colonial post to another.[71] Europeans in Africa were therefore not a monolithic category. In various eras and under changing situations, such as during the world wars, the British Empire did define notions of European nationality to conform to the realities of global politics and colonial security. In addition, by the 1930s, the colonial government had begun to revise its vocabulary of racial othering by avoiding such racially definitive categories as "whites" to avoid backlash from the educated African elites (especially in places like Lagos), who used the print media to vocalize their agitation against racial inequality and the sites through which it manifested. The justification for racial discrimination in the admission to rifle clubs went beyond the established notions that whites were superior to Africans or other salient differences that were used to justify the color bar in recreation facilities. Rifles, as previously mentioned, were sophisticated firearms, which most Europeans believed were their exclusive preserve. If Africans were "irresponsible" with the "primitive" Dane gun, they would not do well with the rifle, in the view of the colonial establishment.

Rifle-range shooting did not become a potent domain of colonial politics of recreation and leisure until around 1916, when the Nigerian Rifle Association (NRA), the umbrella body of all rifle clubs in the country, was established. Article I of its constitution stated that the "objects of the Nigerian Rifle Association are the promotion and encouragement of Rifle Shooting throughout Nigeria." Although most of the big cities and provincial headquarters had civilian rifle ranges maintained by local rifle clubs, rifle shooting was not as popular as state-sanctioned "leisure and sports" such as polo, horse racing, tennis, cricket, and golf, which were integrated into mainstream colonial recreation and social functions. Affiliated with Britain's National Rifle Association, the constitution of the NRA allowed each club to maintain its autonomy in the areas of election of officers, collection of dues, shooting practice, and competitions.[72] However, clubs were required to pay an annual £5 affiliation fee to the NRA, which also coordinated lobbying and correspondence with regional and central governments, and international affiliations. By 1936, the rifle clubs in Lagos, Lokoja, Minna, Onitsha, Sokoto, Calabar, Abeokuta, Ibadan, Jos, and Kaduna, among others, were all dues-paying members of the NRA.

The status of rifle shooting in Nigeria remained ambivalent throughout the colonial period. On the one hand, it was "popular" in the sense that rifle clubs existed in most provincial capitals and cities; on the other hand, it was exclusive because only a minority group of shooting enthusiasts could participate. Indeed, big-game hunting was far more popular than rifle shooting, not only because it took place in the rural areas and involved the killing of large animals for meat, security, and trophy, but also because it did not, unlike rifle shooting, involve the payment of compulsory dues or adherence to rigid internationally endorsed safety regulations. Thus, the biggest challenge for rifle shooting was that it served a minority of upper-class European urban residents who had the money to buy rifles, to travel for local and international rifle shooting competitions, and to "waste" expensive ammunition shooting at targets. To many Europeans, target shooting, unlike hunting, held no obvious social or economic gain.

One might expect that financial resources for running rifle clubs would be forthcoming, giving that members were upper-class colonial officers and expatriates. However, that was not the case. Many members regularly refused or neglected to pay their dues. Dues were required not only for buying rifles for practice but also for paying for the construction and maintenance of shooting ranges and repairing and storing arms and ammunition in the government armory. But to the leading officers of the NRA, the best solution to the organization's financial problem was to encourage all Europeans in the country, regardless of social class or nationality, to join their local rifle club. Prior shooting experience was not required. Ownership of a rifle was not even necessary, as arms and ammunition were usually provided free of charge to newcomers who were later encouraged to become rifle owners. The more members the NRA had across the country, the easier it would be to convince the government to make it a "state leisure" activity and provide an annual subvention—similar to those granted to popular sporting activities like polo and tennis. "Application of grant by Government," according to a July 1936 NRA memorandum, "will be based upon replies indicating extent to which shooting is probable."[73] That year, the NRA through an intense lobbying effort secured a onetime government grant of £100 to purchase ten P.14's, a service rifle developed during the world war, and five hundred rounds of ammunition to be used in the 1937 Overseas .30-.30 Full Range Empire Postal Match and the West African Challenge Cup (WACC) competition.[74] If purchased by an individual, the total cost of one P.14 including import duties, license, and freight from England topped £50.[75] On many occasions, the army did loan firearms (.22 and .303 long rifles) to the clubs under the condition that they be withdrawn for inspection and maintenance every three months. Clubs were also required to sign a biannual agreement that no claim be made against the army "in respect of personal injuries to firer or other persons, or for any damage caused" when using loaned rifles.[76] Ammunition was not given free of charge—in October 1946, the army charged 20s. 6d. for one thousand rounds.

But in November 1946, the War Office discontinued this unusual arrangement, plausibly for security reasons.[77] Reacting to this news, the commander of the Northeastern Sub Area regretted that the decision of the War Office would "render the functioning of rifle clubs in Northern Nigeria extremely difficult." He asked rifle clubs to seek the help of the police and stated his willingness to loan out his .303 and .22 guns pending new orders from the Crown colonies. In addition, significant global developments affected the activities of the NRA—during the world wars, several rifle clubs across the country suspended their activities to yield to the government's call for the formation of local Europeans-only defense corps to defend the colony in the event of invasion by Nazi German forces.[78] Other challenges faced by the NRA went beyond the availability of rifles for shooting and the impact of global politics; they involved the maintenance of shooting facilities. Civilian shooting ranges were regularly abandoned, repurposed, or resited in response to safety concerns raised by administrators and the public. Abandoned ranges wasted choice land that, in the words of the district officer of Kano, "could be put into meaningful use."[79] Many rifle clubs became defunct when active members were posted to other locations.

Regardless of these challenges, rifle shooting in Nigeria did contribute to one core aspect of imperial politics—the creation of a community of colonial officers bound by a common "altruistic" purpose to help civilize the world. As in other forms of leisure activity, the coming together of colonial officials (both military and civilian) from the various British colonies for regional and international shooting competitions created sites through which colonial power was reinforced. Before the late 1920s, international shooting competitions were few. But in March 1928, after a year of intense debate, the NRA, through the efforts of its honorary secretary F. D. Evans, was able to convince Sir Graeme Thomson, the governor of Nigeria between 1925 and 1931, to create the WACC. Eight riflemen from the four British colonies in West Africa met yearly to compete for shooting in ranges between three hundred and six hundred yards.[80] The competition had a four-member organizing committee comprising two members from the armed forces, one representative each from the southern and northern police forces, and a representative of civilian rifle clubs. The NRA was convinced that the WACC would help in the recruitment of good riflemen who could represent Nigeria at the Bisley Championship, the most prestigious rifle shooting competition in the British Empire, held each year and organized by the National Rifle Association of the United Kingdom.[81] The Gold Coast won both the 1928 and 1929 meets—Nigeria, The Gambia, and Sierra Leone came in second, third, and fourth, respectively.[82] The WACC was popular, partly because it was less competitive, and because it was held in West Africa—thus it reduced the agony of long-distance travel. Representatives of each rifle club met in Lagos for the national championship to determine Nigeria's representative at the subcontinental championship.[83] Rifle clubs sent out information to all district officers and local branches about the dates and program to promote competitive shooting, and they tried to encourage amateurs. "Even a poor shot," the "Honorable Secretary" of the Lagos Rifle Club stated in affirmation, "has a very good chance of winning a few prizes."[84] The relative success of the WACC encouraged the NRA to press for more government support for Nigeria's increased participation at the Bisley Championship, which to many, including D. Dickinson, the secretary of the National Rifle Association, "was not good enough."[85]

The poor representation of Nigeria in the 1946 Bisley competition was visible enough to attract the attention of the secretary of state for the colonies, Arthur Creech Jones, who in July 1947 directed Nigerian administrators to initiate procedures to increase rifle shooting across the country. In response to this directive by his superior, the chief secretary to the government of Nigeria invited suggestions from all provincial and district officers about "desirable" and "practicable" ways to encourage rifle shooting.[86] More specifically, the chief secretary solicited his colleagues' opinions about passing a rifle ordinance (the so-called NRA ordinance), which the Gold Coast authorities used to institutionalize rifle shooting. The Gold Coast rifle ordinance was exactly what rifle-shooting enthusiasts in Nigeria had been clamoring for since the beginning of the 1900s—a legal arrangement that would guarantee the government's obligation and commitment to rifle shooting. In Lagos, the race course developed into the center of colonial spectacle, where Europeans of dissimilar nationalities and social classes met regularly for horse racing, among other sports; these meetings eventually were fused with regular activities such as the occasion of a change in political leadership, Empire Day, or the visit of important imperial authorities from abroad.

The proposed NRA ordinance seriously divided colonial officers. For one thing, many officers thought that rifle shooting was not a "safe," "useful," or "enjoyable" leisure that warranted the government's financial investment. In his response, the senior district officer of Ife Division expressed the belief that "shooting will appear to be admirable" but that government should support other sporting activities such as tennis and squash. His suggestion that the colonial government give grants to European social clubs that accepted African members other than the whites-only associations like the rifle clubs divided his contemporaries.[87] Yet he was not a lone voice in the debate over government support for the NRA. His superior, the acting resident of Oyo Province, also thought that the government should institutionalize rifle shooting only if it hoped to keep an auxiliary civilian European force in the event of war or serious internal trouble. "If however, the objects are social and the intention is to provide facilities for social intercourse and a healthy out-of-door activity," the government, according to him, should invest in other sports such as football (soccer) and cricket.[88]

The response of the assistant district officer of Ilesha Division is perhaps the most significant, for it delves into some of the widely held perceptions about the role of firearms in imperialism and racially discriminatory recreation in a profound and unusual manner. First, he queried the main goal of asking Nigeria to follow the Gold Coast model by attempting to evaluate the importance of rifle shooting from the perspectives of the military and public security. His antagonism against an NRA ordinance was based on a precedent—the government's unwise investment in the Supplementary Reserve (SR), a band of civilian European reserves established for the purpose of aiding the regular colonial army in the event of a Nazi invasion during World War II. Not only did he think the SR was "useless before the war"; he also believed it was "ignored during the war and is now moribund."

The officer did not condemn Europeans' use of rifles—in fact, he believed that all Europeans in Nigeria should be able to fire a rifle and that the government should make provisions for training. He was only against the government's institutionalization of the NRA through the passing of an ordinance and the encouraging of Africans, whom he thought were "often completely irresponsible in their methods of handling weapons," to receive government-sponsored training. He recommended that formal rifle shooting be restricted to the police and the military, and never be introduced to Africans, except those capable of being elevated to officer status in the event of another outbreak of global hostilities. Rifle use among Europeans, he submitted, should be restricted to self-defense against humans and animals. In sum, he did not think that an NRA ordinance "will be of any practical value."[89]

Even as administrators in Ife, Ilesha, and Oyo opposed the NRA ordinance, their counterparts in Ibadan and P. V. Main, the acting secretary of the Western Provinces, threw their weight behind it.[90] The district officer of Ibadan Division believed that the NRA ordinance "would be of the greatest value in stimulating" rifle shooting, and he also asked the government to support rifle clubs by loaning them arms at the early stage of their formation. To demonstrate the increasing popularity of rifle shooting among Europeans in Nigeria, he reported that the Osogbo branch of the Ibadan Rifle Club had recently completed a miniature range. He believed that the NRA and its affiliated rifle clubs could not survive without the government's financial support. He did, however, make a recommendation that could have appealed to the sentiment of the anti-NRA-ordinance camp—desegregating the NRA by extending membership to Africans. When the cloud of debate subsided, the central government abandoned the NRA ordinance and resorted to the old practice of providing discretionary financial help to rifle clubs. Not even the proposal that the government waive customs duties on rifles imported by the NRA received the government's blessing, for it would amount to a "hidden subsidy," decrease revenues from import duties, encourage abuse, and "might result in embarrassing requests from other social organisations."[91]

The political atmosphere of post–World War II Nigeria and the prevailing perception of the safety of rifle shooting, not lack of financial resources, were the two principal reasons the NRA ordinance did not become law. From all indications, rifle shooting was in competition with other state-sanctioned recreational sports whose facilities required constant maintenance. After World War II, Europeans-only clubs faced new opposition from the Nigerian nationalists who felt strongly that such clubs contravened the core principles of justice and equality of all humans—echoing the democratic rhetoric that the British had so recently used to galvanize support for the fight against Nazi Germany. Thus, promoting the NRA, which did not open its doors to Africans in the era of decolonization, appeared to be politically fraught to some administrators. In addition, the NRA debate took place during one of the worst eras of racial politics in Nigeria. In February 1947, Ivor Cummings, a black Briton and senior officer of the Colonial Office who was on an official visit to Nigeria, was denied lodging in the Bristol Hotel, a first-class hotel that enforced the color bar, even though the government had reserved a room for him. This development temporarily united the African nationalists, who came together under the umbrella of the United Front Committee to demand an end to all forms of racial discrimination.[92] The government made a public apology for the scandal and issued an official directive to its officers forbidding all forms of racial segregation and white privilege. Appropriately titled "Racial Discrimination," the circular, which was addressed to European officers, reiterated that racism was not an official policy of the government and demanded the elimination of "all possible grounds of suspicion for [racism]."[93] To show its seriousness to end the color bar, the government began the process of desegregating the Europeans-only residential quarters and social clubs. Thus, when the NRA ordinance proposal came up for deliberation in July 1947, it was behind the times, in that few colonial officers would any longer encourage government support for another social club that excluded Africans.

What is more, unlike other recreational sports (especially polo) that attracted the children and wives of European political officers and expatriates, the purported unsafe environment of the rifle range and its male-centeredness made it less attractive to a diverse group of Europeans and their families. Although the NRA was aware of the public's generally negative impression of rifle shooting and safety, not even its pamphlets and memorandums to political officers detailing safety measures could change the minds of most European residents. These safety measures included appointing a range officer, "who will be responsible for the conduct of shooting and all persons on the range shall be subject to his order." Another officer was entrusted with the issuing of ammunition, which was to be kept "under lock and key at all times." Only expert armorers were allowed to repair rifles for local and international competitions and target practice. To inform potential new members, the NRA published the minutes of its meetings in government publications and the local newspapers.

Rifle-range shooting was not the only form of recreational shooting practiced in Nigeria. Some Europeans, both members and nonmembers of rifle clubs, engaged in clay-pigeon shooting. Unlike rifle-range shooting, which involves firing at a still target, in clay-pigeon shooting, the shooter must aim at a flying object projected from the ground mostly by hand. It is like shooting at a flying bird. Clay-pigeon shooting, unlike rifle-range shooting, does not require a constructed or defined range and can be carried out in any open space. Most clay-pigeon shooters used a shotgun. By the early 1920s, the government was already concerned about the popularity of clay-pigeon shooting among Europeans, most of whom did the shooting in the back yard of their quarters, thus creating noise pollution for their fellow European neighbors and posing an apparent threat to public safety. In 1930, authorities in Lagos issued new guidelines preventing people from engaging in clay-pigeon shooting in residential areas. But this regulation was frequently violated. And in response to this contravention, the government then pushed to completely abolish the sport—a move that divided administrators.[94]

The case of G. Ronald Taylor, on the staff of Messrs. Green and Co., who sought the permission of the government of Lagos to use the old Polo Ground at the Ikoyi Club for clay-pigeon shooting in November 1930, can be used to illustrate the extent of disagreement among officials who held alternative views about the danger it posed.[95] Although Taylor indicated that the range of his shotgun would not exceed one hundred yards, administrators—such as the inspector general of police, the commissioner of lands, and the chief secretary to the government—all expressed deep concern about public safety and noise pollution.[96] The commissioner of lands believed the site was unsuitable because it was "frequented by the public." He asked Taylor to look for open stretches of land in the Victoria Beach area.[97] However, both the administrator of the colony and director of the Public Works Department not only minimized the impact of shooting on the community by stating that it would not cause considerable discomfort given that it would take place between 5 p.m. and 6 p.m.; they also argued that Taylor's proposal would help increase the recreational opportunities for European residents in the town.⁹⁸ After more than a month of internal administrative debates, the administrator of the colony granted Taylor the permission to carry out clay-pigeon shooting, provided the Ikoyi Club, which managed the space where the shooting would take place, agreed to allow him to use its facility.⁹⁹

Race and Gun Accidents

As previously noted, one of the core assumptions about firearms in Nigeria was that Africans were irresponsible handlers of these lethal weapons, which were vital European material achievements that demonstrated their scientific superiority over Africans. Therefore, gun accidents represented a sad but frequent occurrence that was one product of the exoticism of guns to Africans and of their lack of the intelligence, caution, and tact required to fire them. The following remarks, made in 1942 by the resident of Onitsha Province, are explicit on the intersection of race and the irresponsible handling of guns:

> Fatal accidents in the use of firearms are too frequent—and in every case which has been brought to my notice the licensee has been an African. It is obvious that the average African who uses firearms fails to exercise that degree of care which is customary with Europeans. It is an extreme rarity to hear of a European who has shot a man. A European will shoot a bird, say on the wing, and when he is certain that no one is in the line of fire or within the range spread of the pellets. If he fires at an animal he will fire only when the line of fire is clear and open and again when he is satisfied that there is no one within range. So many Africans behave differently. They will fire in a failing light, or even in the dark. They will fire when their vision is obscured or even because they think that they see something. All too often the "something" is a human being. They do not satisfy themselves that no one is within gunshot range.¹⁰⁰

The resident's assessment is wrong on several grounds. Indeed, documented accounts of hunting expeditions by Europeans clearly establish that anyone, regardless of race and social class, can commit hunting errors. Accidents were common among Nigerians largely because they were in the majority of firearms users. Indeed, a number of Nigerians, especially the professional hunters, were better marksmen than many Europeans who had never handled a firearm or who took to recreational shooting only upon arriving in Nigeria. Even official government documents reveal the prosecution of European residents for carelessness in the use of firearms. A detailed example is that of David Hunter, a thirty-four-year-old plate layer with the Nigerian Railway. On August 21, 1936, Hunter, who did not have a license to use a shotgun, shot twice at Buri, a forty-year-old woman, in Kukakwanche in Kano Province.[101] The first shot (estimated at about one hundred yards) hit and broke the big calabash that Buri was carrying on her head; the second made about sixteen pellet holes in her body, rendering her incapacitated for eighteen days. A day after the incident, Hunter sent his two African "boys," or assistants, and the community head to give Buri 10s. and phial and iodine. Two days later he sent bandages and lint. This case might have gone unnoticed by the colonial administration, but it did not. News spread around the community that Buri was shot by an intoxicated European. Local chiefs, who frowned on the use of alcohol in their Muslim community, used the opportunity to criticize the government for allowing the consumption of a beverage that was both un-Islamic and had caused injury to a local woman.

The chiefs' agitation against Hunter's conduct compelled the government to set up a commission of inquiry to investigate the incidence.[102] The core task of the commission, headed by Assistant District Officer J. M. Small-Wood, was to determine whether the accident was caused by Hunter's intoxication, not the thick vegetation, which Hunter claimed prevented him from effectively aiming at a guinea fowl, his main target. Eleven witnesses, including Buri, Hunter, his two African assistants, and local chiefs and residents, testified before the commission between September 30 and October 2, 1936. Aside from Hunter and his assistants, all witnesses expressed the belief that the vegetation in the area where the shooting took place was not overly tall or thick as to prevent visibility. The testimony by Buri and her friend Shatuwali, whom she was walking with when the incident took place, established that the shooting was premeditated: "I said to Shatuwali, 'Don't stop, don't let him take a photograph,' but Shatuwali said, 'Don't let him shoot at us.'"[103] When asked why he did not stop after firing the second shot to confirm if he hit his intended target, Hunter claimed that the trolley he was riding went on after the second shot and that the noise of the rail track prevented him from hearing Buri's agonized cry. He admitted taking some tea, not alcohol, in the house of a fellow European, who also loaned him the shotgun, with which he did the shooting.[104] Hunter's assistants testified that their boss was not intoxicated when the accident took place and that he did not know that he had shot a human until later in the evening of the shooting when a telegraph was sent to Hunter from the District Office.[105]

The outcome of the enquiry failed to establish the community's conviction that Hunter was under the influence of alcohol when the shooting took place. In his submission, Small-Wood cleared Hunter of intentionally shooting at Buri, claiming rather that "in the excitement of shooting" he did not take sufficient precaution to see that there was no one within range."[106] The inquiry, however, found him guilty of using a gun without a license and recommended that he be reprimanded for "negligence."[107] He was fined £1.10s.[108] The commission ruled that Buri was not entitled to further compensation other than the 10s. that Hunter previously gave her.

Hunter's case appears less serious when compared with several others across the country. During World War II, the intensification of military and European civilian shooting practice increased the number of gun accidents. People who lived near shooting ranges in Lagos and Ibadan were often afraid of moving around the neighborhood for fear of being hit by rifle bullets.[109] After a series of newspaper criticism, and to address the public anxiety of an impending external invasion by Nazi Germany, the government was compelled to publish public notices announcing the place and time when shooting practice would take place.[110] This decision was not satisfactory to the *West African Pilot*, for it failed to recognize the linguistic diversity of the population and, like most other government public notices, was not in tune with the living realities of the people—few of whom could read in English or buy the newspapers that announced the shooting practice. The press advised the government to adopt a method more suitable to the "targeted" audience—"a gong or bell, warning to them in a language they understand."[111]

Gun accidents also took place in situations of self-defense, or under the pretext thereof. One of the potent fears of colonial domination in Nigeria, as elsewhere in Africa, was that Nigerians would rise up against the foreigners in a bid to force them out of the colonies. Many cases of "insurgencies," such as the Egba uprising (Adubi War) in 1918, which claimed the lives of Europeans, only affirmed the well-established fear that the colony was a dangerous place to live.[112] The killing of Captain Moloney during public unrest in Keffi in 1902 remained a sad testimony to the precarious nature of imperial administration throughout the colonial period.[113] On June 16, 1929, M. Cadell, the district officer of Lafiaji, was shot and killed by his African servant, who committed suicide immediately after the incident.[114] A year later, Assistant District Officer C. M. Barlow was killed with a poisoned arrow by the Dimmuk people during an uprising.[115] Colonial officers, like their wives, experienced danger in their daily encounters with Nigerians. During their tour of the Ikom area in the Cross River region of southern Nigeria, Tom, Fitz-Henry's steward, hurriedly told his boss that he heard the local people remark that one of the European engineers would "make a very good chop [food]" because he was fat. In a show of imperial femininity, Mrs. Fitz-Henry, who was alone with Tom in their tent, because her husband and the "fat" engineer were out surveying the district, narrated her response to the rumored cannibalism: "I got up and went into the tent, and brought out the shotgun firing a shot into the air before propping it up against my chair. This may have been quite unnecessary but it gave Tom a lot of confidence and impressed the locals." Her additional remark "I was extremely glad when the two white men returned as dusk fell" indicates that she was truly scared by the rumor but found a temporary solace with her gun.[116]

Aside from the fear of popular unrest and cannibalism, European-armed self-defense was inevitable because Europeans were regular targets of armed robbers, who sought their exotic personal items. In his autobiography, Harold Smith, a colonial officer who served in Lagos in the mid-1950s, narrated that one of his neighbors at Ikoyi, a European, "swaggered" around with his loaded revolver, bragging that any "'wog' who broke into his house would get shot to little pieces." The following morning, the European woke up without his valuables, including clothes and the gun that he had placed under his pillow."[117] This observation by Smith, an unpopular colonial officer noted for contravening the government's order to manipulate popular elections during the final years of British rule in Nigeria, is not by any means an isolated case. Police reports noted that the homes of Europeans were regular targets for thieves looking for rifles, revolvers, and pistols—weapons that only a few Africans were allowed to own. Firearms trafficking in the European neighborhood was also common. On May 19, 1943, a police court in Ebute Metta sentenced Douglass Joseph, a steward of a European resident of Ikoyi, to eight months in prison for being in possession of the following items: a noiseless pistol weighing five pounds, nine and a half packets of ammunition, one tin of pistol oil, four tins of pistol grease, and five pistol parts. The *West African Pilot* reported that so scared were the spectators at the court that they "began to disappear" one after the other when the firearm was tendered as an exhibit. Joseph's accomplice, Gabriel Osapa, who was also sentenced to six months in prison, admitted stealing the gun from a ship at the Apapa wharf. The arrangement between the convicts was simple—Joseph, who was arrested at Ikoyi during a police patrol, was expected to return the gun to an agreed-on hidden location (a bush), after using it to rob his boss.[118]

Europeans were known to commit serious gun-related violence under the pretext of self-defense. In simple cases of altercation or disagreement, they sometimes used guns to threaten Nigerians. Cases in which law-abiding Nigerians were shot at—such as when M. Marsh, a railway inspector, fired at four African laborers for allegedly disturbing him while they were fetching water about a hundred yards away from his quarters—were rampant.[119] In February 1948, a Jos magistrate court sentenced John Ogle, a European mechanical inspector, to fifteen days in prison or a fine of £5 for intimidating A. M. Saad Zungur, a *West African Pilot* reporter, with a revolver for writing a story criticizing his handling of public works in Bauchi.[120] The laws preventing Africans from shooting in European residential areas were among the regulations aimed at protecting the European population from armed insurgency.[121]

Gun violence and threat did take place between Europeans, especially among the nonpolitical class or those not affiliated with the colonial administration. By 1947, the incidence of gun violence among Europeans of dissimilar nationality (mostly acting under the influence of alcohol) in the pubs and places of recreation that served sailors around the Apapa wharf was frequent enough to compel the port authorities to deliberate on regulations to prevent seamen from carrying firearms when they left their ship.[122] But the counterargument that foreign sailors needed their guns for protection in the dangerous red-light districts of Lagos seemed to be more valid than the threat of gun accidents. One case in the late 1940s provides a clearer insight into the circumstances under which gun violence between Europeans took place. After sharing drinks at the Irish House in Lagos on November 4, 1949, Philip Barlow, an employee with Messrs. Joe Allen Company, invited fellow European Roy John Ashbrooke to his house with the intent of selling him two guns for £85. But when Ashbrooke said he could buy only one of the guns and pay at a later date, a fight ensued. Barlow, who was said to be intoxicated, shot at Ashbrooke's car, breaking its headlight, as he drove away.[123] Barlow claimed to have shot in self-defense. A Lagos court found Barlow guilty of "carrying arms in the public in a way likely to cause terror" and sentenced him to two months in prison or a fine of £25.[124]

Few cases of shooting in self-defense came to the attention of the colonial administrators in Nigeria and London or of the leading African nationalists who possessed the network to expose the ills of colonial violence; fewer still were prosecuted because those involved were usually important colonial officers and expatriates. Zungur's and Barlow's cases were prosecuted because they involved a staff member of the *West African Pilot*, the best-selling newspaper of the period, and two Europeans. The alleged influence of alcohol in Hunter and Buri's case brought it to the attention of the government. But one case in Lagos in the 1950s made significant newspaper headlines and was debated in the Nigerian House of Representatives. This case was unique not only because it involved children but also because the perpetrator was a police officer, whom the public believed should have exercised significant caution and deployed sound judgment before shooting.[125] On May 2, 1954, two boys, Lamidu Omomeji (age nine) and Muyibu (seven), went into the compound of the assistant superintendent of police at Ikoyi to pick cashews. The boys' action was not out of the ordinary, even though it was by all indications a trespass, which carried some legal sanction. Both oral and written histories of colonial Lagos recount how young children usually flocked to the beautiful European quarters to gather fruit from the well-maintained trees.[126] Children lived with the risk of being shot by Europeans or bitten by their dogs. On seeing the boys, the officer fired his rifle, which hit Omomeji in his thigh. The badly injured and unconscious boy was taken to the Lagos general hospital, where the bullet was extracted.

This case did not go away. The press thought the police should prosecute the senior police officer for indiscriminate shooting.[127] At the July 1954 session of the House of Representatives, the Honorable Daniel Fafunmi of the Action Group moved for the house to query Attorney General Lionel Brett for negligence in handling of the incident which he described as "callous in the extreme" and an instance of "man's inhumanity to man." In his defense, Brett said that he thought the police officer's conduct was "extremely foolish" but that "prosecution was not always necessary in such cases." He took full responsibility for deciding that the case belonged to the class of "common assault, which could be dealt with departmentally." Brett's decision not to prosecute the senior police officer seemed prejudicial, given that even less fatal gun accident cases involving Nigerians received reprimand, ranging from fines and incarceration to the loss of guns and licenses.[128]

Conclusion

Firearms were one of the symbols of colonial domination in the Nigerian gun society. And the British colonialists knew this. During the first half of the twentieth century, the consolidation of colonialism went hand in hand with the introduction of new, and the transformation of old, ideas about firearms as a significant achievement of European civilization and domination. Imperial hunting was one of the sites through which the European notion of firearms as a symbol of colonial power was produced and reproduced. Directly and indirectly, imperial hunting helped sustain colonial service as a fulfilling career, despite its numerous challenges, and diversified the Nigerian gun society. But not all colonial officers were involved in big- and small-game hunting. Some did combine rifle-range shooting with hunting animals. Rifle clubs in big cities and administrative capitals served the needs of a minority of European military and civilian officers, who congregated on a regular basis to socialize amid shooting at targets. But rifle shooting was not as popular as state-sanctioned leisure activities such as polo, horse racing, and tennis. And from 1916 to the 1950s, the NRA lobbied the government to provide consistent financial support to rifle shooting. The debate over the institutionalization of rifle shooting as a "state leisure" witnessed the contest of notions of profitable versus unprofitable and legitimate versus illegitimate pastimes.

Notes

1. "Oyo ADO Shoots Himself in Office," *SND*, April 6, 1948; "ADO. Ends Own Life With Pistol," *Daily Service*, April 8, 1948.

2. Coverage in *WAP* included the following: "Police Believed to Be Still Investigating Death of Iseli," February 3, 1951; "'I Am Tired of Hanny and Sick of Weiss; They Will Kill Me': Inquest Is Told Wife of Dead Swiss Businessman Testifies," February 19, 1951; "Nigerian Wife of Ill-Fated Swiss Citizen Tells Story of £50 Cheque at the Coroner's Inquest," February 26, 1951; "'Don't Leave Me in This Country: I Have No Further Hope Here': Mrs Iseli Denies Making This Statement to Swiss Consul and Two Other Persons," March 5, 1951; "'My God If Theo Is Worried He Will Shoot Himself': Mrs Gaum Gartner Says This Statement Was Made by the Wife of the Dead Man," March 6, 1951; "Mrs Gaum Gartner Reveals the Scenes Leading to the Discovery of Iseli's Body," March 7, 1951; "Richard Weiss Tells Coroner of the Sum of £25,000 Sent Out from US to Iseli," March 9, 1951; "Muri Animashaun Tells Court of Iseli's Strange Statement: Swiss Businessman Is Alleged Having Said: 'One Day You Will Have to Miss Me,'" March 13, 1951; "Police Fail

to Produce Actual Photographs of Iseli's Body," March 14, 1951; "Coroner to Give Verdict on Iseli's Death This Morning," March 28, 1951; and "Coroner Says Theo Iseli Shot Himself Because He Was Worried by Financial Problems: Weiss and Hanny Could Not Have Killed Him," March 29, 1951.

3. "Mrs Gaum Gartner Reveals the Scenes."
4. "Don't Leave Me in This Country."
5. "Coroner to Give Verdict on Iseli's Death."
6. Useful comprehensive works on mental illness in colonial Nigeria include Heaton, *Black Skin, White Coats*; and Sadowsky, *Imperial Bedlam*.
7. Kirk-Greene, "Badge of Office," 178–210; Mangan, *Cultural Bond*; Haig, *Nigerian Sketches*, 33–36.
8. Brook, *One-Eyed Man Is King*, 85, 89, 91, 101, 111, 127, 140–45, 166; Atkinson, *African Life*, 82–87.
9. Brook, *One-Eyed Man Is King*, 127.
10. Martin, *Leisure and Society*, 154–97.
11. "Assistant District Officer of Ilesha to the Resident of Oyo Province," August 1, 1947, MLG 1467, NAI.
12. Woollacott, *Gender and Empire*; Midgley, *Gender and Imperialism*.
13. Kirk-Greene, *Britain's Imperial Administrators*; Kirk-Greene, *Glimpses of Empire*.
14. Kirk-Greene, "Badge of Office," 178–210; and Kirk-Greene, *Symbol of Authority*, 164–79.
15. Mackenzie, *Empire of Nature*, 7.
16. See the following works on eastern, central, and southern Africa: Marks, *Imperial Lion*; Ofcansky, *Paradise Lost*; Anderson and Grove, *Conservation in Africa*; Neumann, *Imposing Wilderness*; Storey, *Guns, Race, and Power*; Cannadine, *Ornamentalism*; Storey, "Big Cats and Imperialism"; Steinhart, *Black Poachers, White Hunters*; Beinart, "Empire, Hunting, and Ecological Change"; Beinart, "Men, Science, Travel and Nature"; Beinart and Coates, *Environment and History*; Sunseri, "Reinterpreting a Colonial Rebellion"; Davis, *Resurrecting the Granary of Rome*; Burton, *Two Trips to Gorilla Land*; Hulme and Youngs, *Cambridge Companion to Travel Writing*; Rich, "*Tata otangani oga njali biambie*."
17. Crocker, *Nigeria*, 111.
18. Niven, *Nigerian Kaleidoscope*, 34, 57–58; Crocker, *Nigeria*, 46, 52, 64, 101–2, 122; Hastings, *Nigerian Days*, 23–24, 38, 72–76, 80, 82, 86, 181–203; Smith, *Colonial Cadet in Nigeria*, 40, 52; Brook, *One-Eyed Man Is King*, 91, 117; White, *Dan Bana*, 14, 102; Langa Langa, *Up Against It in Nigeria*, 19–22, 44, 46, 91, 100, 107, 115, 119, 121–50; Fitz-Henry, *African Dust*, 20–21, 39, 42, 50; Rowling, *Nigerian Memories*, 28, 33, 61, 66; Russell, *Bush Life in Nigeria*, 35, 38, 85, 95–96; Allen, *Tales from the Dark Continent*, 75; Oakley, *Treks and Palavers*, 7–8, 22–23, 26, 29–30, 33–34, 37, 48–49, 59, 62, 64, 68–70, 89, 116-148; Kisch, *Letters and Sketches*, xii, 30, 38, 40, 50, 59, 63, 74, 76, 89–90, 94, 107–8, 137, 139–40, 149, 157–58; Kerslake, *Time and the Hour*, 55; Larymore, *Resident's Wife in Nigeria*, 9, 40, 41, 43, 53, 56, 79, 107, 129–31, 136, 137, 151, 171, 205, 217, 272, 280.
19. Larymore, *Resident's Wife in Nigeria*, 9, 40, 41, 43, 53, 56, 79, 107, 129–31, 136, 137, 151, 171, 205, 217, 272, 280.
20. Leith-Ross, *Stepping-Stones*, 1–78.
21. Fitz-Henry, *African Dust*, 20–21, 38–53. On women game hunters in southern Africa, see Thompsell, *Hunting Africa*, 101–33.

22. Callaway, *Gender, Culture, and Empire*; Woollacott, *Gender and the Empire*; Midgley, *Gender and Imperialism*; Clancy-Smith and Gouda, *Domesticating the Empire*.
23. Schneider, *Empire for the Masses*; Curtin, *Image of Africa*; Ramamurthy, *Imperial Persuaders*; Pratt, *Imperial Eyes*.
24. Harris, *Wild Sports of Southern Africa*; Pratt, *Imperial Eyes*.
25. Roosevelt, *African Game Trails*, 466–68.
26. Oakley, *Treks and Palavers*, 7–8.
27. Kisch, *Letters and Sketches*, xii.
28. Larymore, *Resident's Wife in Nigeria*, 150–51.
29. Oakley, *Treks and Palavers*, 49.
30. Hastings, *Nigerian Days*, 38.
31. Langa Langa, *Up against It in Nigeria*, 107; Larymore, *Resident's Wife in Nigeria*, 53.
32. Kerslake, *Time and the Hour*, 55.
33. Brook, *One-Eyed Man Is King*, 86.
34. Talbot, *Life in Southern Nigeria*, 95–96.
35. Crocker, *Nigeria*, 52, 64.
36. Kerslake, *Time and the Hour*, 56.
37. Langa Langa, *Up against It in Nigeria*, 44.
38. Ibid., 91.
39. Kisch, *Letters and Sketches*, 63.
40. Larymore, *Resident's Wife in Nigeria*, 272.
41. Crocker, *Nigeria*, 50.
42. Ibid., 160.
43. Langa Langa, *Up against It in Nigeria*, 19.
44. Niven, *Nigerian Kaleidoscope*, 35.
45. Smith, *Colonial Cadet in Nigeria*, 40.
46. Ibid., 52.
47. Oakley, *Treks and Palavers*, 136.
48. Hastings, *Nigerian Days*, 181.
49. Ibid., 202.
50. Ibid.
51. Kisch, *Letters and Sketches*, 155–56; Langa Langa, *Up against It in Nigeria*; Hastings, *Nigerian Days*, 181.
52. Hastings, *Nigerian Days*, 181–203; Langa Langa, *Up against It in Nigeria*, 53–65; Oakley, *Treks and Palaver*, 116–48.
53. Langa Langa, *Up against It in Nigeria*, 55–58.
54. Ibid., 56.
55. Ibid., 57.
56. Hastings, *Nigerian Days*, 190.
57. Ibid., 191.
58. Langa Langa, *Up against It in Nigeria*, 139.
59. Perham, *Lugard*, 182.
60. "Resident of Muri Province, to the Secretary to the Administration," July 25, 1907, Muri Prof., 2557/1907, NAK.
61. "Secretary to the Administration," July 28, 1907, Muri Prof., 2557/1907, NAK.

62. Hastings, *Nigerian Days*, 187.
63. Oakley, *Treks and Palavers*, 127–28.
64. Ibid., 128.
65. Ibid., 134.
66. Fitz-Henry, *African Dust*, 21.
67. "Weekly Notes," *LWR*, January 30, 1909.
68. "Artillery: Lagos Defence Force," *Nigerian Pioneer*, November 23, 1917.
69. From the *Nigerian Pioneer*: "Shooting," November 9, 1917; "Shooting," November 23, 1917; "Shooting Match: Lagos Rifle Club and H.M.S. Dwarf," June 30, 1922; and "Shooting Match: Lagos Rifle Club and H.M.S. Dwarf," July 7, 1922.
70. "Kano Rifle Club," July 24, 1939, Kano Prof., 43/1927, NAK.
71. Kennedy, *Islands of White*; Ranger, "White Presence and Power."
72. *Nigerian Rifle Association*.
73. "Nigerian Rifle Association," December 11, 1936, Ije Prof., 1368, NAI.
74. Ibid.
75. Ibid.
76. "Acting Secretary of the Western Province to the Resident of Oyo Province," September 18, 1946, Oyo Prof., 1, 1756, NAI.
77. "Commandant Nigeria Regiment to the Chief Commissioner, Western Province," November 11, 1946, Oyo Prof., 1, 1756, NAI.
78. "Resident of Kano Province to the Commandant, West Africa Command," June 12, 1946, Kano Prof., 43/1927, NAK.
79. "Kano Rifle Club," August 18, 1927, Kano Prof., 43/1927, NAK.
80. "West African Challenge Cup," October 16, 1927, Comcol, 459, NAI.
81. "Constitution of the West African Challenge Cup," 1928, Comcol, 459, NAI.
82. "West African Challenge Cup," December 19, 1928, Comcol, 459, NAI.
83. The activity of the Lagos Rifle Club was suspended during the WWII. "Lagos Rifle Club," *Daily Service*, September 17, 1946.
84. Honourable Secretary of the Lagos Rifle Club to the Resident of Oyo Province, February 6, 1925, Ije Prof., 1368, NAI.
85. "D. Dickinson to the Under Secretary of States," September 10, 1947, Bauchi Prof., 1049, NAK.
86. "Acting Chief Secretary to the General Officer Commanding," February 8, 1951, Bauchi Prof., 1049, NAK.
87. "Senior District Officer of Ife/Ilesha to the Resident of Oyo Province," July 28, 1947, MLG 1467, NAI.
88. "Acting Resident of Oyo Province to the Secretary of Western Province," August 11, 1947, MLG 1467, NAI.
89. "Assistant District Officer of Ilesha to the Resident of Oyo Province," August 1, 1947, MLG 1467, NAI.
90. "District Officer of Ibadan to the Resident of Oyo Province," July 25, 1947, Oyo Prof., 1756, NAI.
91. "Memorandum on the Proposed Rifle Shooting Ordinance," September 1, 1947, Oyo Prof., 1756, NAI.
92. See Aderinto, *When Sex Threatened the State*, chap. 1.
93. "Circular No. 25: Racial Discrimination," March 3, 1947, Comcol, 2900, NAI.

94. "Clay-Pigeon Shooting in Lagos," January 17, 1930, Comcol, 1123, NAI.

95. "G. Ronald Taylor to the Honourable the Administrator of the Colony," November 10, 1930, Comcol, 1123, NAI.

96. "Acting Commissioner of Police to the Administrator of Lagos," November 14, 1930, Comcol, 1123, NAI.

97. "Commissioner of Lands to the Administrator of Lagos," November 15, 1930, Comcol, 1123, NAI.

98. "Administrator of the Colony to the Chief Secretary to the Government," November 28, 1930, Comcol, 1123, NAI.

99. "Administrator of the Colony to G. Ronald Taylor," December 30, 1930, Comcol, 1123, NAI.

100. "Resident Explains Why He Revoked Enugu Arms Licenses," September 10, 1942; and "Resident Revokes Shot Gun Licenses in Enugu Urban Area," August 10, 1942—both in *WAP*.

101. "District Officer of Northern Division to the Resident of Kano Province," October 22, 1936, Kano Prof., 1833, NAK.

102. "An Enquiry Held at Kaugama, Northern Division, Kano Province, on September 30 1936 by Mr. J.M. Small-Wood," Kano Prof., 1833, NAK.

103. "Testimony Given by Buri," September 30, 1936, Kano Prof., 1833, NAK.

104. "Testimony Given by D. Hunter," October 2, 1936, Kano Prof., 1833, NAK.

105. "Testimony Given by John, Hunter's 'boy,'" October 2, 1936, Kano Prof., 1833, NAK.

106. "District Officer of Northern Division to the Resident of Kano Province," Kano Prof., 1833, NAK.

107. "Findings by Small-Wood," October 29, 1936, Kano Prof., 1833, NAK.

108. "District Officer of Northern Division to the Resident of Kano Province," December 22, 1936, Kano Prof., 1833, NAK.

109. "Victoria Beach Shooting Incident (Editorial)," *WAP*, July 22, 1941.

110. "Firing Practice Will Be Held 6 Hours Daily Till January 14," January 11, 1944; and "Guns Will Be Fired at Fire Command Today," May 18, 1945—both in *WAP*. "Gun-Fire Practice," *Daily Service*, August 14, 1944.

111. "Firing at Victoria Beach."

112. Hogan, *Cross and Scalpel*, 457–64.

113. Larymore, *Resident's Wife in Nigeria*, 54–55.

114. *Annual Report of the Police Department, Northern Provinces, for the year ended 31st December, 1926*.

115. *Annual Report of the Police Department, Nigeria for the Year 1930* (Lagos: Government Printer), 5.

116. Fitz-Henry, *African Dust*, 39–40.

117. Harry Smith, *Blue Collar Lawman*, http://www.biafraland.com/harold_smith/autobio.htm (accessed October 26, 2015).

118. "Man Is Jailed for Eight Months for Receiving a Stolen Pistol," *WAP*, May 20, 1943.

119. "European Rly. Permanent-way Inspector Alleged to Shoot African Labourers: RWU Demands a Thorough Investigation," *WAP*, November 30, 1945. See also "Gateman Is Alleged Shot by Foreman Who Succeeded in Blowing Off His Cap," November 1, 1944;

and "Joseph Younis Is Convicted for Possession of Firearms," July 7, 1944—both in *WAP*. Some cases also involved non-Europeans like Syrians, who regularly passed for "Europeans" in mainstream discourse of race. See, among others, from *SND*: "Women Shot on Arm at Oke Ado on Road near Ibadan Boys' High School," April 6, 1948; "Who Shot the Woman? (Editorial)" April 6, 1948; "Shooting at Oke Ado by Lawrence Makinde," April 8, 1948; "Reader Reveals Woman Shot at Oke Ado Is Muniratu Dada from Ilesha," April 12, 1948; "Syrian Is Arraigned on Revolver Charge," February 4, 1947; "'Ritz' Revolver Case Ends with £25 Fine," February 12, 1947.

120. See from *WAP*: "Hot Chase with a Revolver by Whiteman Reported," January 15, 1948; "Police Are Probing Alleged Gun Chase," January 23, 1948; "Alleged Revolver Chase of Mallam Saad Zungur Is Reported Taken to Court," January 24, 1948; "Revolver Chase Case Begins at Bauchi," January 27, 1948; "Judge Sends Revolver Suit to Magistrate Court," January 30, 1948; "Revolver Chase Case Fixed February Six," February 2, 1948; and "J. Ogle Is Fined £5 or 14 Days for Chasing with Revolver," February 17, 1948.

121. "African Hunter Is Said to Be Convicted in Circumstances Described as Puzzling," *WAP*, August 25, 1944.

122. "Sailor Is Said to Shoot and Wound during Quarrel," *WAP*, December 1, 1950.

123. "Court Hears Raising Story of Gun Shots in Firearms Deal," *WAP*, November 18, 1949.

124. "European Is Fined £5 in Gun Drama," *WAP*, December 23, 1949. In the *Daily Service*, see "Array of Lawyers Appear in European Shooting Case," November 18, 1949; "Lady in Shooting Case Testifies at Court," November 19, 1949; "Friend of Accused in Shooting Case Testifies," November 21, 1949; "Arms Expert Testifies in Shooting Case," November 23, 1949.

125. "Shooting Scandal by Franco Olugbake," *Daily Service*, August 4, 1954.

126. Williams, *Faces, Cases and Places*, 28–29.

127. "European Officer Shoots Boy, 9," *Daily Service*, July 30, 1954.

128. "Police Officer Acted Foolishly," *WAP*, August 21, 1954.

5

BREAD AND BULLET

Guns, Imperial Atrocity, and Public Disorder

In June 1951, police authorities in the northern Nigerian cities of Kano and Kaduna banned Hubert Ogunde's play *Bread and Bullet* for being seditious. Ogunde was also fined £6 for publicizing the play without government approval.[1] *Bread and Bullet* was about the (in)famous shooting and killing of twenty-one coal miners by the Nigeria Police Force (NPF) at the Iva Valley mine of the Enugu government colliery in November 1949. For the government, the play was a sad reminder of the horror of colonial domination in the era of increased agitation for self-determination. Acknowledging the volatility of the 1950s political scene, the government wanted to silence dissent period by preventing the artistic and dramatic reproduction of violence for public consumption. A published review of *Bread and Bullet* in the *Daily Service* described it as an "attempt to portray to the people what really happened at Enugu" and a "vivid and touching show." The audience at the premier staging of the play at the famous Lagos Glover Memorial Hall in April 1951, according to the review, "nodded their heads in sorrow" as Ogunde's troupe "demonstrated the actual killing with guns and revolvers." The review went on to describe the show as "exemplary" and a deep reflection of Ogunde's artistic maturity and ingenuity.[2] *Bread and Bullet* solidified Ogunde's status as the "Nigerian Shakespeare" who combined "talents with skill and wide imagination" in popularizing the richness of African culture that "hitherto could have remained underdeveloped." But aside from his artistic talent, Ogunde, the acclaimed father of contemporary Nigerian theater, was better qualified than most artists of the era to render a dramatic impression of the horror of gun cruelty—he was a constable (junior officer) in the NPF until his resignation in 1944. *Bread and Bullet* was just one of the many plays Ogunde wrote to highlight the ills perpetrated by the colonial government, which "considered his theatre as one of the most effective voices in the agitation for independence, and therefore sought to silence it."[3] His previous play *Strike and Hunger* (1945), described as "gate crashing," rendered an allegory of the inhuman treatment of the Nigerian labor force during the General Strike of 1945. Like *Bread and Bullet*, *Strike and Hunger* was also banned in some Nigerian cities.[4] *Tiger's Empire* (1946) and *Towards Liberty* (1947) sought to expose the "evil machination of colonial rule or to demand outright freedom" from British imperialism.[5]

Ogunde contested the northern authorities' decision to ban *Bread and Bullet*, describing as "untenable" the notion that it would cause civil unrest. For him, if the play did not cause any violence after it was staged in Enugu, where the shooting incident took place, and at Aba, Port Harcourt, and Onitsha, where riots broke out in connection with the horrific event, police authorities in Kano and Kaduna had "no justification whatsoever."[6] Moreover, he had successfully staged the play in other cities in the North such as Minna, Zaria, Funtua, Gusau, and Jos. Unfortunately, the police authorities could only stop Ogunde from showing his play—they could not prevent violence either among the people or against the government. Two years after his *Bread and Bullet* was banned in Kano, the city witnessed one of the worst interethnic assaults in colonial Nigerian history, when the indigenous Hausa population rose against the immigrants from the South in the wake of the controversy surrounding the suggestion by Anthony Enahoro in 1953 that Nigeria become an independent state in 1956.

Ogunde's *Bread and Bullet* exemplified the negative realities of the Nigerian gun society after World War II, one of the most violent eras in colonial Nigerian history, characterized by disorder under shifting circumstances. The title of the play is a brilliant metaphoric rendition of the experience of the Nigerian labor force, confronted with death (through a bullet) as they sought basic human need (food or bread). It rendered the stark reality of life and death that characterized colonial capitalist expropriation. One of the most popular myths about decolonization in Nigeria is that it was "peaceful." Those who subscribe to this fallacy, including Harold Smith, one of the last colonial officers to serve in Nigeria, who opined that "riots and rebellions hardly existed and no blood was shed in Nigeria in expelling the forces of imperialism," were thinking in comparative terms. They were comparing the independence movement in Nigeria with that in such countries as Algeria, Kenya, and Angola, where large-scale violence occurred. It is a truism that Nigeria, like Ghana, did not witness the level of violence that ushered in independence in Algeria and Kenya; however, the numerous inter- and intraethnic cruelties that arose from the introduction of internal self-rule from the early 1950s demand a careful deployment of the vocabulary of peace in describing the events leading to independence in 1960. The killing of Nigerians during tax riots and labor unrest across the country cannot be dissociated from the broader history of the circumstances that made independence a reality.[7]

In this chapter, I focus on the interconnections between firearms and public disorder in the relations between the colonial government and Nigerians, and among Nigerians. The deployment of superior firearms by the British was not only the most important reason Nigerian armed resistance to colonial conquest failed; it was also through sophisticated rifles, machine guns, and cannon that it was held together.[8] Guns also featured in the daily conflict among Nigerians of similar and dissimilar ethnicities for political control and access to economic resources. The imposition of colonial rule transformed preexisting conflicts, and introduced new ones among Nigeria's ethnic groups. Thus, none of the economic and political crises among Nigerian ethnic groups and subgroups can be understood in isolation from the significant changes wrought by colonialism. Colonial gun regulations, I argue, were successful only in ensuring that Nigerians did not have access to highly lethal arms that could undermine imperial expropriation; they were inadequate in ensuring peace and tranquility in local communities, especially in the South, where virtually everyone had a Dane gun.

The Nigeria Police Force and Colonial Security

What made colonialism a very violent episode in African history, as previously mentioned, was the deployment of guns of varying sophistication for sustaining it. Akinola Lasekan, a pioneering Nigerian cartoonist rendered an artistic impression of the relationship between the colonial government and Nigerians in one of his works published in June 1949. He depicted the British government (the official side), represented by gun-bearing men, confronting unarmed Nigerian politicians (unofficial side) and Nnamdi Azikiwe (armed with arrow and shield) during the period of decolonization, which was characterized by division among Nigerian leaders in the

Legislative Council, the judicial arm of the colonial state (figure 5.1).⁹ One of the best means of coming to terms with the character of colonial violence is to discuss the core features of the colonial security force: its strength, its main agenda, and its mode of operation. The British maintained two armed security apparatuses—namely, the West African Frontier Force (WAFF), later known as the Royal West African Frontier Force (RWAFF), which was largely used for imposing colonial rule and for prosecuting international conflicts like the world wars, and the NPF, which focused on day-to-day maintenance of law and order.[10] It was only in unusual uprisings—such as those at Iseyin-Okeiho (1916) and in the Abeokuta area (1918), both in the southwest, and the Women's War (1929) in the southeast—that the RWAFF was called in to assist the police. So ferocious were the first two cases that machine guns were deployed against fighters bearing Dane guns.

One of the shortcomings of existing works on police history, including Tekena Tamuno's foundational study, is their limited engagement with gun violence.[11] While not disputing the fact that the NPF carried out everyday crime-control activities, especially in big cities, I argue that the

Figure 5.1. Cartoon titled "Better to Die Honourably Fighting Alone Than Live Forever in an Enslaved State," by Akinola Lasekan, *West African Pilot*, June 17, 1949. Re-created for better reprint quality by Ganiyu Jimoh (Jimga).

police force, in Nigeria, as in other parts of the British African colonies, was established essentially to fight public unrest capable of undermining colonialism.[12] This core mission of the Lagos police—which was present at the beginning, in the mid-nineteenth century—did not change throughout the colonial period. Indeed, the diversification of the functions of the NPF from the 1920s—into firefighting, sanitation, traffic, and immigration control—did not supersede its primary role as upholder of public peace. These auxiliary functions of the police tended to swell the treasury of the colonial state through fines. When the police were not fighting to suppress uprisings, they were in the railway, ports, and provincial headquarters providing security to the economic infrastructure of imperialism and its colonial officers. In fact, the Native Authority Police Force (NAPF), used by the local chiefs for dues and tax collection, among other responsibilities, and whose officers were not allowed to possess and be trained to use firearms, was more effective in policing the community (especially in rural areas) than the NPF.[13]

The precarious peace maintained by the colonialists was guaranteed not only through the Nigerians' dread of the NPF rifles but also through their lack of access to arms and ammunition, which could have turned the tables against the colonialists. The Lee-Enfield rifle was the standard police and military rifle throughout the British Empire from the late decades of the 1800s to the 1950s (figure 5.2).[14] A magazine-fed, repeating bolt-action firearm, the Lee-Enfield rifle could fire up to ten rounds with a .303 cartridge. It possessed effective and maximum ranges of about five hundred and two thousand yards, respectively. The real strength of the NPF was not the size of its rank and file, but its effective use of the Lee-Enfield weapon. Before the outbreak of World War II, the strength of the rank and file of the NPF did not exceed four thousand in a country with more than twenty million inhabitants. As table 5.3 shows later in this chapter, Lagos, with a population of 126,000 in 1931, had the highest police-to-civilian ratio in the entire country because it was the capital of the colonial state and home to many European residents, businesses, and wealth.[15] The British did not increase the size of the NPF, not because it could not maintain a larger security force, but because it was afraid that the rank and file might turn against the colonial establishment. Hence, until the 1950s, no Nigerian was commissioned or allowed to lead the police during a crisis situation. What is more, the rank and file rarely carried firearms, except for riot control. This restricted access

Figure 5.2. The West African Frontier Force, ca. 1930s. Reproduced by the Courtesy of the National Archives Ibadan.

to firearms was meant to ensure that the police did not turn against the government.

While nationalist newspapers stereotyped Nigerian policemen as "dogs of the establishment," and "unintelligent" men incapable of controlling the wave of violent crime in the big cities, the British considered them effective in fulfilling their core mission to suppress riots. On a yearly basis, the African rank and file of the NPF took a shooting test called a musketry and rifle course to determine their shooting efficiency. In addition, regional shooting competitions were held to improve the shooting skills of the police. The outcomes of the annual musketry and rifle course, shown in tables 5.1 and 5.2, reveal some disparity in the results for the North and the South, which was attributable to the lack of common standards for evaluation. The 1931 annual report clearly states that the southern police rifle-shooting tests were more rigorous than those in the North—without explaining the basis for the dual standard.[16] Most of the firing was done at three hundred and four hundred yards, which were longer distances than would obtain in a typical conflict

Table 5.1. Annual musketry and rifle course results for the Northern Provinces

Year	Marksmen	First-class shots	Second-class shots	Third-class shots
1926	309	428	305	107
1927	346	487	251	79
1930	292	443	316	73
1931	344	437	281	82

Source: *Annual Report of the Nigeria Police Force* (Lagos: Government Printer, 1926–1931).

Table 5.2. Annual musketry and rifle course results for the Southern Provinces

Year	Marksmen	First-class shots	Second-class shots	Third-class shots
1926	23	235	463	503
1927	24	231	509	476
1929	49	391	677	550
1930	53	294	453	405
1931	71	342	591	454

Source: *Annual Report of the Nigeria Police Force* (Lagos: Government Printer, 1926–1931).

scenario. A rifle shot, regardless of how poorly aimed, in a typical riot scene was capable of hitting a human target and causing serious arm. The power of the rifle extended beyond its ability to fire lethal bullets. The bayonet attached to its muzzle ensured that a policeman could defend or attack in close hand-to-hand battle after expending all his bullets. Throughout the 1930s, 1940s, and 1950s, senior police officers expressed satisfaction with the quality of training of the NPF in handling the rifle and mastering riot drills.[17]

As the colonial state improved on the training of its security force, updating its firearms, and perfecting riot drills, the indigenous gun-making culture remained static. The most advanced firearms local gunsmiths produced in large quantity were the Dane guns. Indeed, there were more rifles (which were all imported) in circulation in southern Nigeria during the period of conquest in the late nineteenth century than after the imposition of colonial rule. Thus, by the 1910s, when the new gun culture described in chapter 2 had become firmly established, few Nigerians could claim to legally possess a functioning rifle and ammunition. The legality of guns reflected their technological capabilities. The wide disparity in performance between Dane guns and rifles largely explained why armed resistance to colonial rule could not succeed. Flintlock guns require frequent reloading and could fire only one shot at a time, and bad weather such as rain could inhibit successful firing because a damp flint and gunpowder were rendered useless. What is more, Dane guns could fire only at a relatively short distance with accuracy and maximum impact. There was also an international dimension to Nigeria's unequal access to firearms. Because the gunpowder used for firing Dane guns came from abroad, the government could easily control access and consequently affect the outcome of armed conflict. Nigerian colonial borders were not totally impervious—arms trafficking, as chapters 3 and 6 show, did take place across the borders. But border control was strong enough to prevent the importation of rifles and machine guns, among other classes of powerful weaponry.

The superiority of British rifles and machine guns over the indigenous arms was complemented by several other factors. To enhance the efficiency of violence, colonial officers, many of whom were ex-soldiers, would attack communities only at the height of their vulnerability, such as during the dry season, when visibility was high and firepower could have maximum efficiency. Geographical knowledge enhanced security decisions and intelligence gathering. After the imposition of colonial rule, colonial officers documented important information about geography, cultural attitudes, and precolonial military history, all of which were put to use in making decisions about crisis situations. Good judgment by colonial officers and sound military tactics played a crucial role in armed conflict. In one instance around the first decade of the twentieth century, A. C. Douglas wanted to arrest an Ibibio man accused of murder in Opobo. His twenty-five-man security force had ten rounds (each) of ammunition to confront an entire town armed with Dane guns. Instead of ordering his men to fire when community members prevented their kinsmen from being taken away, he retreated and returned some weeks later with ninety-five men and a Maxim gun, which (with availability of ammunition and enabling conditions) could fire up to a thousand rounds per minute.[18]

Moreover, the ethnic identity of policemen mobilized to quell an uprising was as important as the efficacy of their rifles. Right from the early years of colonial rule, officers followed Frederick Lugard's instruction that no member of a community should be allowed to participate in riot control in order not to undermine intelligence gathering. Successive administrators carried out this order to the letter.[19] Lagos newspapers reported that the policemen mobilized for removing the explosives at Enugu mines were northerners.[20] When renowned educationist Dr. Henry Carr complained about the overrepresentation of easterners in the NPF in Lagos at the Legislative Council in 1941, he probably did not know that it was in the best interest of the British to allow non-Yoruba to police the most important site of imperial power in West Africa. Carr believed that people who did not speak the language of the community could not do the job of policing effectively; to the government, however, quality policing was first and foremost a matter of loyalty to the state and ability to shoot a rifle.[21]

If some Nigerians, both during and after the colonial period, claimed to possess the power to cure or ward off shots from a Dane gun through magic or juju, few could claim to have a native remedy for rifle bullets. The survivors of an attack against the Eket's sacred grove of Edogbo Ukwa in 1902 were reported to have said, "The spirits of Grove or Tree are mighty for black men, but against white men's guns they are powerless to save."[22] In a strict technical sense, a shot from a Dane gun was less fatal at relatively long range partly because the bolts were not as lethal as a rifle bullet. Regardless, the main disadvantage of the Dane gun was not that it caused less havoc—a Dane gun shot from a good marksman could be more dangerous than a rifle shot from a less experienced shooter. Ian Brinkworth, a colonial officer, made the following remark about the lethality of Dane guns used by rioters in Burutu in 1947: "A few days later, the police arrived back nursing broken heads and wounds. I saw what a Dane gun could do and resolved then and there to make quite sure I got my shot in first if I were ever called upon to lead anti-riot troops."[23] Without the Maxim gun, the Iseyin-Okeiho (1916) and Adubi (1918) uprisings, where hundreds of hunters armed with Dane guns inflicted serious pain on both European officers and African police and soldiers, could have lasted longer.[24]

The reconfiguration of African indigenous military culture in the aftermath of the colonial conquest also explains the failure of "insurgency" during the first half of the twentieth century. The warrior and professional army class disappeared after the conquest. Nigerians could no longer wage "legitimate" and "conventional" war against their neighbors or prepare future generations in the art of warfare. In lieu of warfare, the disbanded precolonial armies and their successors turned to farming (especially in cash crops) and hunting with Dane guns. Professional hunting with Dane guns increased exponentially as the gunpowder trade and local manufacturing of gun stocks soared. The impact of the disappearance of Nigeria's indigenous war-making culture is evident in the manner in which the police were able to quell armed resistance. Those engaged in such resistance could only create massive unrest that jeopardized economic activities for a few days—they could not shut down the entire colonial state. The aftermath of each armed confrontation made future ones more difficult and unrealistic. Not only did most communities lose their brave fighters to police rifle fire or capital punishment; conflict areas were usually disarmed. Captain Ross, the resident of Oyo Province, gave the following order to his junior colleagues after the Iseyin-Okeiho uprising of 1916: "You should demand all guns and arrest all hunters and blacksmiths."[25] So indiscriminate were the arrests of people perceived to be involved in this uprising that a new temporary prison had to be built when the existing ones could not accommodate the detainees awaiting court trial (table 5.3).

As colonial rule progressed, so did the transformation of armed resistance. Knowing that they could not match the firepower of the NPF's rifles and machine guns, leaders of armed resistance to colonial rule used a combination of Dane guns, poisoned arrows, and landmines, which the British had outlawed. Lugard encouraged the importation of Dane guns because he thought it would discourage the use of poisoned weapons for hunting and, more important, for fighting against colonial rule. For Lugard, poisoned arrows were more lethal than firearms, especially the Dane guns. Incidents in the first decade of the twentieth century after he initiated this regulation and for several years after he left the colonial service proved him right. When the Mumuye people of Adamawa Province attempted to overturn colonial rule in early 1927, thirty-five rank-and-file police under the command of L. S. Ward were mobilized to impose order. The government lost four men to "poisoned devices and stalks."[26] Similarly, the Dimmuk people killed Assistant District Officer Barlow with a poisoned arrow during a riot in February 1930.[27]

Table 5.3. The strength of the Nigeria Police Force

Year	Northern Provinces	Southern Provinces	Lagos Colony	Total
1926	1,195	1,772	808	3,775
1927	1,195	2,113	676	3,984
1930	1,202	1,912	703	3,817
1931	1,144	1,938	712	3,794

Source: *Annual Report of the Nigeria Police Force* (Lagos: Government Printer, 1926–1931).

Yet it would be erroneous to conclude that the British in Nigeria, as in other parts of Africa, thought that the deployment of violence was the surest means of guaranteeing peace. For one thing, colonialism can maximize its economic goals only when conditions of limited armed confrontation with the colonized people prevail. Indeed, the institutionalization of the indirect rule system, the training of colonial officers in local languages and cultures, the creation of political alliances with local peoples, and the divide-and-rule strategy that pitched one ethnic group against the other were among the numerous steps put in place by colonial officers across the country to ensure that peace and tranquility reigned in their regions of political authority. Thus, the violent confrontations over such issues as payment of taxes and working conditions and disagreements over land and boundary delimitations were usually a product of the breakdown of "peaceful" negotiations.

It is naive to assume that colonial violence was without any check; in fact, international watchdogs and local nationalists deploying the language of "human rights" kept up demands for accountability in the handling of armed conflict. In response to the critics of colonial violence, the NPF, by the 1920s included a section in its annual report detailing how it handled the breakdown of law and order. This section contained information on the causes of conflicts as well as the number of police mobilized, casualty figures, duration of conflicts, and the manner in which they were handled by the force. Not surprisingly, official accounts of violent conflict tend to absolve the police of wrongdoing, even in cases when many civilian casualties occurred. For example, after stating that "the estimated casualties of the enemy were twelve killed by rifle fire," the 1927 NPF report on the Mumuye uprising states that the secretary of state for the colonies commended the police for the "patience and discretion with which they discharged a difficult and dangerous task."[28] In addition, only the colonial establishment accepts at face value the official claim that "the police behaved with great patience and fortitude during these operations and a pleasing feature was the absence of any serious complaints against them by the local inhabitants" when about 120 policemen were mobilized to quell a tax riot in which 237 people were arrested and charged in Warri Province in 1927.[29] The 1930 report stated that the "discipline of the police on patrol was excellent" during what appeared to be a revenge operation against the Dimmuk people who had killed Barlow during an uprising in February.[30] Moreover, after enumerating the activities of government security forces in maintaining public order in communities in Onitsha and Ogoja provinces, the 1931 report of the NPF exaggeratedly states that "the advent of the police had a quietening effect and it was unnecessary for them to use actual force in order to prevent further incidents."[31] The 1929 NPF report did not mention the actual casualties of the Women's War, even though it described it as a "novel and peculiar one" because it was executed predominantly by women.[32] Had a commission of inquiry not been put in place to investigate this sad event, historians might never have known that thirty-nine women died from gunshots, while another thirty-one were wounded by gunfire.[33]

In sum, the police presented inaccurate assessments of violence by reducing the figures of civilian casualties and downplaying the negative impact of their presence in communities. Moreover, by the 1920s, the NPF changed the vocabulary used for describing counterinsurgency or riots from terms like *expedition* (used during the early stages of colonial rule) to *escort* and *patrol* in order to minimize the level of militarism and the projected outcomes. *Patrol* and *escort* sound like conventional police duties, even though as many as nine hundred officers (as seen in the Enugu colliery shooting), armed with rifles, could be mobilized at any point in time for these police actions (see figure 5.2).

"An Error of Judgment": Firearms and the Enugu Colliery Shooting

Unbeknownst to many historians, the Enugu colliery shooting of 1949 was a turning point in the history of the British understanding of the connection between firearms and public disorder. A revisionist history of the violence as presented here is important not only for future works; it clearly reveals that we do not know as much as we should about some of the most popular events in Nigerian history. The conventional narratives of the Enugu colliery shooting have centered almost exclusively on labor agitation, colonial capitalist exploitation, and the radical mobilization for self-rule.[34] While the discourse of labor reforms remains valid, as Carolyn Brown among others have established, I argue that the relationship between firearms and colonial security was the most significant factor in the cause, course, and consequence of the shooting. The centrality of firearms to the story of the Enugu shooting goes beyond the obvious fact that twenty-one miners were gunned down with rifles and revolvers when the police were called in to remove explosives from the mine's magazines; it is because the massacre might not have taken place without the security report indicating that some "agitators with sinister forces" with "subversive purposes" were planning to "blow up Government offices and mercantile houses" with explosives used for mining operations.[35] In no period in Nigerian history was colonial intelligence more concerned about the use of explosives for violence against the state as in the events leading up to the shooting in November 1949. During the January 5, 1950, hearing of the Fitzgerald Commission, put in place to investigate the shooting, John Field, the senior security officer, whose job it was to "collate all security and intelligence reports," testified that the government decided to remove the explosives because a seditious pamphlet circulated in 1948, purportedly authored by the Zikist movement, asked people to "organise terrorist parties" and adopt a "positive action" and "militant attitude" needed to create "disturbances" in pursuit of immediate independence from Britain.[36] The Zikist movement also planned, according to Field, to blow up courts while people accused of sedition were being tried.

The Zikist movement was formed around February 1946 by the labor radicals in the National Council of Nigeria and the Cameroons (NCNC), who believed in a more proactive approach to independence. The movement's initial goal was to radicalize the NCNC from within. Later, the Zikists decided to form an independent body. Before the Enugu colliery shooting, the group was already giving the colonial government and its international supporters some sleepless nights. Such revolutionary calls for "dragging of the government down, and seizing power by force," attributed to the Zikist Ogedengbe Macaulay, and the admonition that "we have passed the age of petition. We have passed the age of resolution. We have passed the age of diplomacy. This is the age of action-plan, blunt and positive action," attributed to Zikist president-general Raji Abdallah, were strong enough to compel the government to round up leaders of the group, including Mokwugo Okoye, and try them for sedition.[37] In February 1950, the government went on to ban the group, calling it an "extremist" organization "dangerous to the good government of Nigeria."[38] What is more, the Zikists, composed predominantly of labor leaders, teachers, and civil servants, among others, constituted the largest owners of shotguns. The government feared that they would use their shotguns to create revolutionary chaos. The proclamation of the Zikist movement, as Hakeem Tijani has noted, was just one of the numerous steps taken by Britain to keep communist ideology away from Nigeria, as in its other colonies in Africa, during the Cold War.[39]

At Enugu, the relationship between the location of the explosives and labor activities was key. The Iva Valley mine and magazines possessed the largest quantity of mining explosives in any part of Nigeria. Coincidentally, the activities of the Zikist movement were confined largely to the South. The labor movement in the Middle Belt, another region that held large quantities of mining explosives, was not as radical as that of the South. Thus, it was not in the best interests of security chiefs to underestimate the danger events in the area posed to colonial stability; however, they also had to ensure that the explosives were removed "at all cost."[40] Moreover, the security report about the Zikist movement's plan to violently initiate independence was supported by concrete evidence. A few days before the shooting, thirty cases of explosives were stolen from the colliery's magazine (twelve were later recovered). There is no proof that the Zikists or their supporters stole the explosives in question. Others may have done so, for there was an underground market for explosives used for illegal mining across the country. Field also noted that some people were arrested with rifles and ammunition. Moreover, both Field and J. G. Pyke-Nott, the chief commissioner of the Eastern Provinces, and his council were convinced that some miners who were charged with caring for the explosives had been "radicalized" by the Zikists and were willing to render any help to the movement's agenda to bring down the colonial state.

From the foregoing, it is apparent that twenty-one miners would not have lost their lives if nine hundred policemen were not mobilized to remove the explosives in the mines.[41] The police who shot the miners were not called in to stop the ongoing work slowdown caused by the mining authorities' alleged withholding of £80,000 in allowance payments due to the workers—among other unresolved labor-related matters.[42] Neither were they there to prevent the breakdown of law and order. They were mobilized to help remove the explosives that security officers believed could be used against the government by the militant Zikist movement. Thus, the connection between firearms and colonial security, not any other factor, was the most important element in the Enugu colliery shooting.

Yet had the police not attempted to secure the help of the laborers to remove the explosives when they discovered that their men alone could not undertake the heavy lifting, the shooting might not have happened. The miners' refusal to help the police appeared legitimate—they thought the government wanted to shut down the mines, which would create a situation that would further impoverish them.⁴³ The police request also disrespected the prevailing protocol, power relations, and workplace regulations. Some of the miners' job descriptions did not include lifting loads. Senior Police Superintendent Frederick Strathern Philip, who ordered the shooting of the miners, was angered by the "hysterical state" of the Iva Valley, characterized by the miners' provocative "war dance . . . jumping up and down"—their "eyes were popping out of their heads and they were jerking their bodies in a dangerous mood."⁴⁴ As the investigation into the incident intensified in 1950, some of the claims published in the newspapers, such as that the shooting was premeditated and that the government had asked the doctors in Enugu clinics and hospitals to be on alert for casualties, were shown to be baseless.⁴⁵

The findings of the Fitzgerald Commission clearly support my position that firearms was the most important factor in the story of the shooting. After reviewing the evidence before it, which included testimony from an array of people directly involved in the fracas, the commission submitted that security chiefs (Field, Pyke-Nott, and others) committed "an error of judgement."⁴⁶ The security officers, according to the report, should have treated the agitation of the miners as an "industrial" dispute, not a political one. "The fact that those agitators stand poised ready to strike does not convert an industrial dispute into a political agitation," the report stated in its retracing of the origin of the crisis.⁴⁷ For the commission, Field's and Pyke-Nott's treatment of the industrial dispute as a political one "play[ed] right into the hands of the agitators." The most important element in the causes of the shooting, the Fitzgerald Commission submitted, was therefore the breakdown of security intelligence, a "misjudgment"—the inability of administrators to differentiate between an industrial and a political and security matter. The commission believed that the political situation in Nigeria had not reached the stage at which labor conflicts could metamorphose into massive political violence even though "evidence was in all conscience most grave, and if this underground activity cannot be held in check, it may well be that it would jeopardise public security."⁴⁸ Another portion of the report was more explicit about the grave error committed by administrators while justifying violence in the name of securing colonial order: "Again we reiterate that if there were any attempt on the part of subversive forces to obtain these explosives, and if there were any reasonable grounds to believe the miners were in league with those forces [the Zikist movement], resolute action was called for, and we should not hesitate to endorse an order that the attempt should be met by force, in which case the armed forces would not only be justified in shooting but it would be their duty to do so.... But there was no evidence on which he (Chief Commissioner) could assume that the miners were in league with those agitators."[49]

The Fitzgerald Commission, which included two British members, Chairman W. J. Fitzgerald and R. W. Williams, and two African members, S. Quashie-Idun and A. A. Ademola, was either ignorant of the security culture in the colony or refused to highlight the relationship between public unrest and politics to avoid backlash from the Nigerian nationalists and other critics of colonial rule.[50] The professional background of the commission's members qualified them to handle the legal component of the matter, but not the security or political ones. Fitzgerald was a former chief justice of the Palestine Mandate, while Ademola and Quashie-Idun were Supreme Court judges of their native countries of Nigeria and the Gold Coast, respectively. Williams was the legal adviser to the National Union of Mineworkers and representative of Wigan in the British House of Commons.[51] The secretary of state for the colonies and Governor Macpherson probably refused to appoint a colonial officer from either Nigeria or another British colony or a senior police officer with experience in handling unrest in order to allay the popular fear that the outcome of the enquiry would not favor the government. The presence of someone from the Nigerian miners' union on the commission could have helped answer the biggest questions that drove its work: Was the industrial dispute serious enough to lead to a breach of the peace, or were the miners planning to use the explosives to bring down the colonial state, as security reports affirmed?

The Fitzgerald Commission's affirmation that the "go-slow" strikes embarked upon by the miners were an "industrial" dispute that did not warrant a "political" action—that is, mobilizing the security force to remove the explosives that could be used to incite mass unrest—went contrary to the established colonialists' pattern of dealing with crises. Few colonial officers, including successive secretaries of state for the colonies, would agree with the Fitzgerald Commission that segregating "industrial" matters from "political" ones, especially after World War II, an era characterized by intense political tensions across the African continent, was possible. Throughout the history of European rule in Africa, politics and economics were not distinct—they were interrelated. Strikes, protests, and public disorder were all activities that the British viewed as having the capacity to undermine the smooth running of the colonial state and its economic infrastructure. When people embarked on a protest of a revolutionary nature, they targeted the political and economic infrastructure, such as the courts, businesses, and other strongholds of the hegemonic institution that undermined their livelihood. The security of life for their exploiters (the colonialists) meant little to them in their quest to correct the injustices of the past and the agonies of the present. In another vein, much of the violence that threatened the political order began as opposition to such economic policies as taxation. From the Adubi War in 1918 to the Women's War of 1929, one sees a close connection between economic and political issues. Nnamdi Azikiwe seemed to understand the true working of the colonial establishment better than the Fitzgerald Commission when he opined that "economic, social, and political forces" were all at play in the Enugu shooting.[52]

Related to this was how the colonial government dealt with the panic and constant volatility that was a part of colonial relations. The government did not have the luxury to commit prolonged hours to analysis of the security situation before mobilizing the police, which Ian Brinkworth, who served in southern Nigeria in the 1940s and 1950s, sarcastically described as the "dogs of the government."[53] Every situation of panic was met with the mobilization of the NPF and other resources needed to either prevent an impending danger or put an end to a small conflict before it grew into a larger one. Colonial officers worried over virtually everything concerning Nigerians—from the impact of traditional marriage culture on their "civilizing" mission to the incidence of venereal disease in the RWAFF. Anxiety had a hegemonic influence, shaping the tenor of colonial politics and tending to secure the allegiance of Africans. The more the colonialists worried, or appeared to be worried, about the progress of their civilizing mission, the more they appeared legitimate before their subjects.

Revisiting and rewriting the history of the Enugu colliery shooting goes beyond recognizing the central role of firearms and how anxiety over "terrorist" activities shaped the event. It also includes retracing the experience of the people who lived through it. The Fitzgerald Commission report downplayed the agonies of the miners, which were explicit in their testimonies, among those of other eyewitnesses to the shooting. After collecting all these testimonies, the commissioner refused to insert them into the final report because it was mainly concerned with the need to ensure that public disorder did not undermine imperialism. Thus, the vocabulary of human rights that shaped the ways critics of colonialism contested colonial violence was popular only in the media and in public protests—it did not reflect in the real workings of colonial administration.[54] By bringing the agonies of the miners who survived the horrific incident into the bigger story of colonial violence, the historian puts a human face on a truly colonial crime, which the British viewed primarily from the perspective of upholding public order. From the testimony of colliery blacksmith Emmanuel Okafor, who sustained six bullet wounds to the leg while trying to rescue a colleague shot in the chest, to that of driver Matthew Nwankwo Ajukwo, who shouted, "Do not shoot me!" when four police rifles were pointed at him, the true picture of colonial violence came to life in a clear manner.[55] "As the shots rang out, the workers ran helter-skelter, while those who were hit, screamed painfully," Lance Corporal Alexander Okolie stated during one of the sittings of the Fitzgerald Commission.[56] Other testimonies, especially those from police officers, tended to support the nationalist agitation that Police Superintendent Philip was a "racist rant." Police Constable Moses Ogbonnia and Okolie also testified to the commission that when one of the injured miners named Emmanuel cried, "I surrender, take me to the hospital," to Philip, he replied in an inhumane way, "I don't care."[57]

The Enugu colliery shooting revealed the extent to which the government was willing to go to defend its law enforcement officers. But for Nigerian politicians and nationalists, the incident presented them an opportunity to further lambast the British colonial government in their quest to secure independence for Nigeria.[58] Not only did they blame the government for minimizing the horror of the shooting by "trying to make a tragedy look like a comedy"; they also criticized the Colonial Office for placing "a premium on mediocrity" and called for the resignation of Sir John Macpherson, arguably the most unpopular British governor in Nigerian history, under whose watch "one of the bloodiest" episodes of that history took place.[59] The nationalists' critique of the Fitzgerald Commission report and the colonial administration in general were not without valid evidence. The report was biased in its depiction of the roles of Nigerians and Europeans in the shooting. While it used such adjectives as *dishonest, mischievous, inflammatory,* and *worthless* to describe the Nigerians involved, including Okwudi Ojiyi, a mine labor leader, it diplomatically used less-loaded terms like *misjudgment* for the Europeans' role.[60]

One of the fundamental missions of the aggrieved miners' most vocal counsel, Hezekiah Oladipo Davies, and the press during the hearings of the Fitzgerald Commission was to establish that the action of Philip and his men was a crime against humanity—"a dastardly action of wholesale massacre."[61] Davies, who studied under Harold Laski at the London School of Economics, reviewed the method of shooting and submitted "that there were no formalities, but only the idea to teach miners a lesson."[62] He wanted to prove that Philip "could have done his job without gun fire."[63] His evidence was convincing. The miners did not attack the police. The report of the medical examiner, Dr. Richard Akinwande Savage, on the wounded police officers revealed that their "minor" injuries were caused by "the splash from the bullet fired by the police," not from a Dane gun fired by the protesters.[64] This revelation countered the earlier claim of senior police and political officers that the miners shot at the police with a Dane gun. Hence the situation of the shooting was not typical of those where the government would legitimately authorize the use of deadly force to stop a crisis. Davies wanted to prove to the commission that Philip's action was motivated by racism and the colonialists' disregard for the lives of Africans. To further establish the inhumanity of the police conduct, he submitted that Superintendent J. B. G. Austin, one of the senior police officers present at the scene, was a "man very much addicted to the use of arms."[65]

For most nationalists and Nigerian politicians, the controversy over the shooting presented an opportunity to test the popularity of their cause. Indeed, it temporarily united the nationalists against their common enemy—the British government. But most important, it revealed the extent of the progress made for social justice. The nationalists believed that the injustice could be corrected only by securing punitive judgments—such as long-term imprisonment, dismissal from colonial service, forfeiture of pension and retirement benefits, and death sentences—for those involved, Africans and Europeans alike. "The officers responsible" for the shooting, Davies opined, "should be forced to bear the full consequences of the lives lost."[66] The "relatives of the dead men will be relieved," the *West African Pilot* submitted about the projected impact of justice for the shooting victims.[67] At a rally organized by the West African Students Union of Great Britain and Ireland at Trafalgar Square in London, on December 4, 1950, Azikiwe made the following remarks that resonated effectively with the position of people fighting for justice on behalf of the victims of the shooting: "It is for us, the living to show that their blood shall not have been shed in vain. . . . In this hour of national peril, Nigeria expects every patriot to stand firm in the cause of justice and righteousness."⁶⁸ In another powerful statement, delivered at an earlier gathering of leading nationalists at Lagos's Glover Memorial Hall in November 1949, Dr. Akinola Maja attempted to give a "pan-Nigerian" outlook on the violence to create a united front. He warned that "if a Nigerian can be shot for his legitimate demands, every other Nigerian is in danger."⁶⁹ As one might expect, the colonial government through its acting senior Crown counsel, Lionel Brett, vehemently defended the actions of its police officers, hacking on the fundamental philosophy of colonial police to secure public order. His statement that "vengeance for the dead was no justification for injustice to the living" introduced a moral language to discourse on colonial atrocity (figure 5.3).⁷⁰

For Nigerian nationalists, colonialism and violence were birds of a feather.⁷¹ Like other imagined outcomes of independence, the nationalists believed that self-rule would end police brutality. They believed that Nigerians in police uniform under an independent state would under no circumstances shoot at their fellow citizens. The connection between gun violence

Figure 5.3. Statue of the Enugu Colliery Shooting of 1949 at Enugu. Photograph by author, May 2015.

and foreign domination is explicit in the following statement by Mazi Mbonu Ojike at the public lecture organized in Lagos by the Elementary Rights Preservation Committee: "If those who govern a country are sons and daughters of that country, such government can never order its militia or police to shoot down members of the governed who dare to grumble in practical terms over any treatment which such members consider unjust."[72] Had Ojike not died in 1956, four years before the attainment of independence, he would have been disappointed by the spate of police and military atrocities against Nigerians in the postcolonial era. The brief transcript of his lecture, attended by about one thousand people at Glover Hall, was published with the headline "Ojike Foresees No Shooting by Police Were Nigeria Self-Governing" made a case for the preservation of the rights of Nigerians—a demand that colonial institutions rarely acknowledge as legitimate.

Beyond the Nigerian littoral, critics of colonial exploitation in Britain and in the global labor movement, especially those who subscribed to communist ideas, seized the opportunity to call for the uniting of all workers.[73] The *Daily Worker*, the official organ of the British Communist Party, reported that two hundred thousand miners in East Germany sympathized with their African comrades. The British government, reported another British newspaper, the *Daily Express*, banned the scheduled rally by West Indian workers in Guiana in solidarity with their Nigerian counterparts.[74] In one of its reports on the Enugu shooting, the *West African Pilot* attempted to depict the feeling of the people of the metropole in its attempt to demonstrate that the struggle to secure justice for victims transcended Nigeria: "The British public is also interested in the publication [Fitzgerald Commission report] as any one of them you mention the Enugu riot to, proudly dissociates himself or herself and calls it un-British."[75] However, the popularity of the incident in Britain was definitely an exaggeration; it went contrary to the well-acknowledged belief among top colonial officers like Secretary of State for the Colonies James Griffiths that "ignorance about the colonies in Britain is appalling."[76] Although few Britons on the streets of London were aware of the shooting, many middle-class educated people and the newspaper editors seemed to care about the atrocities committed by their government abroad. One *West African Pilot* news story claimed that all press outlets, with the exception of the *London Daily Mirror* (owners of the Lagos-based pro-government newspaper the *Nigerian Daily Times*), supported its call for justice for the miners.[77]

As Nigerians at home were protesting the shooting, their counterparts in the United Kingdom stormed the British Parliament, creating "a scene of angry voices" as they accosted the members of Parliament who were retreating from chambers, explaining what actually transpired at Enugu. Their demands that police never be allowed to carry firearms during riot control and that Nigerian and British labor leaders be represented in the proposed commission of inquiry (the Fitzgerald Commission) dovetailed with similar demands expressed across Africa and beyond.[78] The transcript of the House of Commons debate on both the Enugu massacre and another that preceded it (the Burutu shooting of 1947) reveals that the "progressive"-minded legislators in Britain were conscious of imperial atrocities and sought to hold both the secretary of state for the colonies and the officers on the ground accountable for them.[79] For one thing, the MPs did not trust these officers and their supporters in the House to give them accurate information about developments in the colonies. Their distrust of misinformation was justified when MP David Rees-Williams lied to the House that the miners attacked the police with spears and machetes and attempted to wrestle the explosives from them.[80] The Colonial Office did not yield to the advice of MP William Gallacher, a noted trade unionist, that the proposed Fitzgerald Commission include representatives of the Nigerian miners. Gallacher, a member of the British Communist Party was convinced that the aggrieved miners would not secure justice or have confidence in a commission on which they lacked representation.[81] For MP Thomas Driberg, the police should have used "humane methods," such as batons, which he described as "accepted colonial practice" in controlling demonstrators instead of shooting at them.[82] If the House debates revealed anything about imperial atrocities, it is that both British legislators and critics of imperialism did not have effective control over what the men on the front lines did in Nigeria, as elsewhere in Africa. Had the Colonial Office yielded to Gallacher's earlier advice, during the July 16, 1947, session of the House of Commons, that "never again will firearms be used on workers" who were demanding "decent condition[s]," the Enugu massacre might have been averted.[83]

Ethnic and Communal Clashes

The Enugu colliery shooting is one of the best-known episodes of colonial atrocity in Nigeria because the unarmed miners, who did not constitute an immediate threat to the infrastructure of colonialism or its agents, were killed in cold blood. Yet to see the severity of colonial gun violence mainly through the prism of that episode is to underestimate the full extent of death by the bullet in Nigeria's gun society. Before and after the Enugu colliery shooting, the RWAFF and NPF carried out countless indiscriminate shootings under the guise of quelling revolts and riots arising from unfavorable government economic and political policies, such as the imposition of new taxes. For instance, the Women's War of 1929 was more fatal than the Enugu colliery shooting in terms of casualties. This significant event transformed colonial perceptions of African women and laid the foundation for future anticolonial agitation. The politics of the Women's War might have taken on an entirely different dimension had it taken place in the aftermath of World War II, when the activities of the nationalists and their instruments (the newspapers) were at their peak. Yet the looting of a bank and a European business and the destruction of native courts seemed to justify the government's violent suppression and the shooting and killing of thirty-nine women, while another thirty-one were wounded by gunfire.[84] What we know about gun violence—its impact and intensity—is largely shaped by the circumstances and category of people involved and the time.

While gun violence between Nigerians and the colonial government tended to be well documented by nationalist newspapers (at least from the 1930s), incidents involving Nigerians fighting over land, boundaries, and chieftaincy titles received limited criticism by the press. Arguably, more Nigerians died from gun violence during inter- and intraethnic conflict than during protests against the government.[85] For one thing, there was an uncontrolled proliferation of Dane guns in rural communities where many of the communal clashes took place. If Dane guns were ineffective in prosecuting conflict between Nigerians and the colonialists, they proved lethal in inter- and intraethnic conflicts. The severity of gun violence in communal clashes varied widely—from the killing of "one Ibo man" with "a Dane gun" during a fight between the "indigenes" (Efik) and "foreigners" (Igbo) in Ikang, Calabar Province, in December 1949 to the massacre of three dozen people by a "gun bearing mob" during a land dispute in Jos.[86] In October 1936, a dispute over land in Awka Division left five people dead. This horrific development compelled the native authority to pass an order preventing people from carrying firearms in public places such as markets, courts, and public meetings, except for ceremonies such as funerals that were recognized by native law and custom.[87] So ferocious was the gun battle between the Awori and Egun in Badagry in 1953 that the governor of Nigeria issued an unusual proclamation to ban the carrying of firearms in the coastal community nearby Lagos.[88]

The spate of communal conflicts between the 1940s and 1960 counters the often-repeated claim that colonialism was able to maintain "peace" among the hundreds of Nigerian ethno-cultural cleavages. A news report with the headline "Tivs and Udan District in Gun Battle" described the use of "native guns" in the violent communal clash between the Tiv of Mbaduku, among other villages, and the Udam of Ogoja Province.[89] In 1954 in the northeast, the Maiduguri town council and Bornu Division outer council made a "revolutionary change" to established customs by outlawing the carrying of all types of arms (guns, knives worn as bracelets, hilted swords in girdles, bows and arrows) in public because of the "various unlawful killings for which the province [Bornu] has become notorious."[90] Similarly, from the early 1900s, the established convention among some Igbo communities that firearms should not be used in communal conflicts was regularly being broken by the people, who acknowledged its effectiveness in internal strife. In one instance, conflict among several quarters in the town of Awka over infringement and appropriation of proprietary blacksmith rights lasted for several months without any "restraint from using guns" and left several men dead "outright."[91]

In central Nigeria, the age-old conflict between agriculturist and nomadic communities took a more violent turn when firearms were added to the list of assault weapons. Here, the ongoing struggle to protect economic assets—crops of agriculturists and cattle of nomads—consistently pitted dissimilar ethnic groups against one another. In his report on the communal clashes among some communities in eastern Jos Province in 1941, the resident officer noted that each group of nomads carried Dane guns, which they used for protecting their animals from farm and landowners who set traps and land mines. He argued that the increasing demand for gunpowder in some parts of the province was directly linked to the increase in popularity of Dane guns among the nomads.[92] Similarly, a coroner's inquest reported that eight of the ten people who died after a major conflict between nomads and agriculturists in late 1941 were shot with Dane guns. In southwestern Nigeria, the emergence of cocoa plantations from the late nineteenth century not only introduced new regimes of land ownership, which contravened "traditional" customary practices, but also fueled the possession of firearms for self-defense against dangerous animals during the opening up of dense uncultivated forest for planting and for guarding against theft of the cocoa crop. But more worrisome was the protracted conflict over district and provincial boundaries. In no part of southwestern Nigeria did this become more serious than in the Ibadan and Ijebu areas. Land conflict near the provincial boundaries, where many of the plantations were located, became severe because cocoa was a permanent crop that yielded considerable revenues. In the 1940s, cocoa plantation owners acquired guns, which they used regularly in the endless struggle over ownership. Groups of gun-bearing hooligans working with rich plantation owners raided cocoa farms.[93]

Few critics of colonialism kept tabs of incidents of intra-Nigerian gun violence, in part because they took place in remote parts of the country, and in part because their consequences had only a limited impact on the broader politics of imperial justice and decolonization. They did have an economic impact, however, because unrest destabilized the smooth running of the districts where the violence took place. Hence, the brutal killing of an undocumented number of Nigerians by the NPF during communal clashes went largely unnoticed. Therefore, it is difficult to establish a distinction between "native-versus-government" violence and "native-versus-native." Indeed, much of the conflict among Nigerians over chieftaincy titles and land and boundary delimitation was a product of the colonial government's indiscriminate policies in key sectors of the colonial economy, such as the cash-crop agriculture. For instance, boundary disputes in most parts of southwestern Nigeria were due to the rise of cocoa wealth that fueled the imperial treasury.[94]

One of the least appreciated consequences of the Enugu shooting was that it led to increased surveillance of the nationalists concerning similar events across the country, with the purpose of understanding the legitimacy of police killings. Instead of just reporting inter- and intraethnic violence as a result of disagreements over land and chieftaincy titles, the newspapers became more assertive in attempting to understand the rationale for police shootings during incidents of public disorder, regardless of the circumstances or the atmosphere of the particular scene.[95] Akinola Lasekan, the pioneering Nigerian cartoonist, made an artistic contribution to the struggle for justice, depicting colonial administrators asking for more armies and bombs instead of political self-determination at an international meeting on the future of European empire in Africa (figure 5.4). The change in the nationalists' attitudes toward shooting in communal clashes was reflected in an editorial in the *West African Pilot* about the killing of three Nigerians by the NPF during a land dispute in the remote village of Ngoshe in northeastern Nigeria in 1950. Aside from calling for an investigation by "independent unofficial persons or group of persons" into the shooting, the editorial asserted that the fact that the senior police officer who ordered the shooting was the only "credible" source of information about the tragedy clearly revealed the difficulty of tracking the intensity of police brutality.[96] Similarly, when police fired twenty-seven shots by order of the resident of Ondo during a boundary dispute between Ondo and Idanre people in January 1952, the *West African Pilot* editorialized that the "killing of Nigerians has got to stop," criticizing the police for being "tactless" in handling what it called "delicate disputes." The coroner's inquest into the shooting deaths revealed that six people died from police gunshots.[97] But the racial dimension the editorial introduced connected gun violence to the well-established notion in nationalist circles that white political and security officers were trigger-happy men whose low temperament was informed by their assumption of racial superiority over Nigerians. Yet intra-Nigerian conflicts rarely received the urgent attention of the colonial government. Many "minor" communal clashes were brought under control by local chiefs and settled in accordance with prevailing custom. Unless he suspected a gross injustice, the district officer rarely mobilized the NPF to quell any conflict not directed against the government. Unfortunately, colonial officers were regularly accused of partiality and of promoting violence by one group against another. After thirty-nine people were reportedly killed when a Kalabari canoe "fully armed and manned" opened fire at Okrika fishermen in August 1950, ethnic unions on both sides blamed District Officer W. H. Newington for his partiality.[98]

For the colonial government, shooting was the last resort when use of the baton and nonviolent intervention failed. But more important, it was necessary to shoot when the crowd turned against the police and colonial officers for alleged improper handling of communal conflicts—such as taking sides. Shooting in self-defense was hard to fault, especially when high-ranking political officers were involved.[99] The fact that special commissions of inquiry or coroner's inquests were instituted to investigate "minor" shooting incidents during communal clashes undermines the extent to which police claims of shooting in self-defense was illegitimate. The coroner's inquest absolved the police in the killing of six people during the land dispute between the Idanre and Ondo when it ruled that the victims were "killed

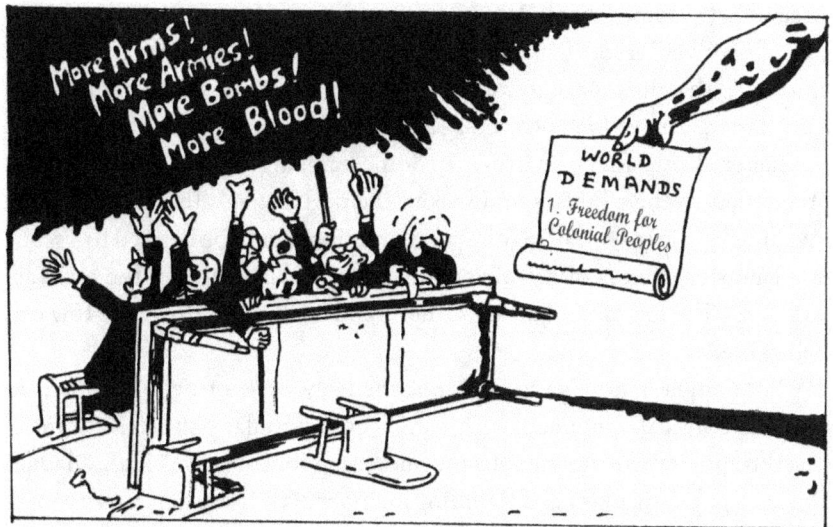

Figure 5.4. Cartoon titled "Not on the Agenda," by Akinola Lasekan, *West African Pilot*, April 11, 1951. Re-created for better reprint quality by Ganiyu Jimoh (Jimga).

in self-defence."[100] In another case, the police fired three shots at three hundred armed rioters who attacked the district officer and a community leader over the introduction of new taxes in Karim Lamido, the headquarters of the Wurkum District of Muri Emirate in Adamawa. One of the "ringleaders" died from a gunshot, and several others sustained injuries.[101]

"Davies Came with a Gun": Party Politics and Political Violence in the Era of Decolonization

The violence following the introduction of regionalism and internal self-rule from the early 1950s not only laid the foundation of postcolonial political problems; it also clearly shows that the British colonial government alone could not be blamed for indiscriminate killing of Nigerians. Guns played a significant role in domestic and national party politics, which was the main catalyst for much of the public disorder in the last decade of colonial rule. Party loyalists and hooligans used guns to intimidate opponents during campaigns and elections. The sight and sound of a gun was far more terrifying that other dangerous weapons such as machetes, stones, and broken bottles used for political violence. The title of a *West African Pilot* front-page news story on events preceding the election for the Western House of

Assembly (in Idowa, Ijebu Province) in 1956 read: "Campaign Takes a New Turn: Revolver Fired." The story goes on to render a firsthand account of the efficacy of the gunshot that was fired: "Whoever remains at that meeting is a dead man. Then someone fired a revolver and the crowd that gathered . . . ran helter-skelter for their lives. . . . Some campaigners ran into the bush, others fled to their houses and locked themselves up." The actions of the invading hooligans following the pandemonium could be likened to a scene in a gangster movie, with which many Nigerian urbanites of the era were familiar: "The terrorists quickly jumped into a van and drove off towards Ijebu Ode."[102]

Yet nameless hooligans were not the only class of people known to threaten political opponents with guns—even popular politicians were accused of publicly using guns to intimidate opponents. Hezekiah Oladipo Davies, a popular lawyer and founding member of the Nigerian Youth Movement, was reported to have fired a gun into the air during the 1953 riot in Oyo. During the conference of the Northern Peoples' Congress (NPC) held in Jos in April 1954, a member of the Northern House of Assembly representing Bornu pulled out a shotgun. The following report about the atmosphere following the action by the gunman, described as a Kanuri-born politician who "played the rancher from Texas" at the "sensational conference," reveals the efficacy of guns in unleashing political chaos: "The gun was not loaded, so they say. But no one waited to examine it. No one would have waited."[103] These examples were by no means isolated events—firearms and party politics went hand in hand. In one episode, a political thug broke into the home of Prince Adeyinka Oyekan, an Action Group supporter (who would later become the king of Lagos in 1965), with a loaded revolver in 1951; in another, a police report stating that hired assassins "armed with guns" were planning to kill Adegoke Adelabu (aka the Lion of the West), a frontline Ibadan politician and vocal critic of the ruling AG, in 1956. In addition, elaborate violent riots were incited by local political parties to create a breakdown of law and order, and embarrass the ruling party.[104] Apparently informed by the well-publicized threat to Adelabu's life, a young male admirer, M. Jaji, a student at Kaduna Medical Auxiliary School, wrote a letter dated August 1, 1957, promising to help the politician with a native bulletproof vest: "Arrange with a simple honest man and come to me," Jaji affirmed. "I will send you One Thing that can Protect you against Any Metal Made Weapons! Just Dash I Repeat Medicine for Knive-Arrow-Cutlass-dane or every Metal

Guns it will BREAK before the Person Using it will come within a reach or even when he intended to do befor Hand [sic]!!"[105] In 1958, Adelabu died in an auto accident purportedly staged by his political enemy; it was initially rumored that he was killed by an assassin's bullet. If Jaji's letter and other evidence suggest anything, it is that the road to independence in Nigeria was paved with violence.

There was a stark contrast in the manner in which the nationalists and politicians, through their newspapers, addressed partisan gun violence. Although they tended to blame the police for extrajudicial killings during riots and strikes directed against the government, the language of reporting political violence placed the responsibility of loss of life on the opposition party rather than on the NPF or the colonial government. In one example, the *West African Pilot*, the official organ of Azikiwe's National Council of Nigeria and the Cameroons (NCNC), reported a gun duel between supporters of the Northern Elements Progressive Union (NEPU) and the NPC ruling party, led by Premier Ahmadu Bello, in March 1956. The NCNC entered into an alliance with the NEPU in the early 1950s. About fifteen people fell victim to gunshots by the police during the violence, which Bello described as "cowardly" and "disgraceful" acts. He considered the 141 people convicted for riotous acts lucky to have escaped death at the hands of the police. Bello's comments in 1956 about the use of children (between the ages of eight and fourteen) in local political violence at the meeting of the Northern House of Chiefs resonate strongly in light of similar events in postcolonial Nigeria: "Last month, the Government held a press release condemning the growing tendency in the region to exploit young children for political ends.... No government in the world can tolerate the grave social danger of young children growing up in a generation of irresponsible hooligans" (by which he meant the NEPU). He then went on to state the responsibility of the government and adults toward minors in the drive toward decolonization and nation building: "Innocent children should be protected from mental and physical contamination and the adult and women must always teach children the virtues of good citizenship, honesty, obedience and respect for their elders."[106]

Two cases—namely, the Kano riot of 1953 and the Oyo riot of 1954—can be examined to further explicate the intersection of gun violence and decolonization.[107] Had Anthony Enahoro anticipated the violence that would follow his motion for "Self-government for Nigeria in 1956" during the March

31, 1953, sitting of the Nigerian House of Representatives, he probably would have kept mute at a gathering of elite Nigerians, the majority of whom were educated in letters but not in the theory and practicality of modern democracy with which they were experimenting. The northern leaders perceived the call for independence in 1956 as an attempt by southerners, who had the lead in virtually all areas of modern politics, education, and economy, to dominate the North. While history books have highlighted how the tour of northern cities by the coalition of Action Group and NCNC leaders aimed at canvassing for independence in 1956 created a tense political atmosphere that degenerated into the infamous Kano riot, what is largely unknown is that the riot involved the first major deployment of firearms in ethnic-party violence in Nigeria. Official reports put the casualties at 277, of which 36 were deaths (15 northerners and 21 southerners).[108]

The government's official report, published in such newspapers as the *West African Pilot* and the *Daily Service*, cataloged about eighty injured victims of the Kano riot, including useful information such as name, age, ethnicity, occupation, and address. But more important, it revealed the nature and location of each victim's injury.[109] About twenty of the eighty injured victims sustained gunshot wounds.[110] This information comes from only one hospital (Kano City Hospital) on May 20; it excludes victims in other hospitals, those who sought private treatment, and several others who were fatally wounded. One worrisome aspect of the use of firearms in the Kano riot was the use of shotguns, the firearm of educated Nigerians. As we saw in chapter 2, the government granted the "enlightened" population of northern Nigeria the right to use shotguns mainly for self-defense against armed robbers and for hunting. The government did not anticipate the use of the weapon in a massive riot, which took place mainly in the area inhabited by southern "foreigners."

In his broadcast to the country after the smoke of the violence had cleared, Governor John Macpherson, apparently speaking to the critics of the empire at home and abroad, bragged about the effectiveness of his government in restoring peace using the regular police force, not the army—even though the latter was on standby.[111] He warned against the situation that caused the violence in the first place—"the danger of exciting public opinion and inflaming passion" arising from the contest over the date for independence. While blaming the nationalist leaders for spreading rumors that escalated the violence, he expressed satisfaction that the 450 policemen mobilized to quell the riot "worked tirelessly and with admirable coolness and restraint," and did not kill anyone, even though the rioters "used Dane guns against the police."[112] For Macpherson and his security chiefs, this was a great improvement in peacekeeping, as compared to the infamous 1949 Enugu shooting tragedy.

Nationalists and Nigerian politicians did not agree with the interpretation of the government and the "ultra conservative elements" in the metropole as to the causes of the violence and the assessment of its handling.[113] In an editorial response to Macpherson's broadcast, the *Daily Service* critiqued the government's labeling of the violence as "intra-tribal" and blamed Lagos for not dispatching police to stop the violence until the situation had become bad. In the view of the editorial, which clearly represented the outlook of the southern nationalists, the British government deliberately allowed the violence to degenerate in order to extend British rule and label the nationalists as people incapable of presiding over a multiethnic independent nation-state.[114] As Macpherson was busy addressing the nation in the radio broadcast, his superior, Minister of State for Colonial Affairs Henry Hopkinson, described the riot as a "savage outbreak" and "useless violence" while being grilled by the House of Commons about the government's handling of the crisis, with a particular focus on police conduct. Hopkinson informed the House that "some of the rioters were equipped with firearms."[115] To the British government, the Kano riot was a Nigerian affair—a matter of violence inflicted on Nigerians by Nigerians. The government wanted to distance itself from it, even though the foundation for such violence was laid by British colonial divide-and-rule policies.

The Kano riot was not the only occasion where the use of guns dictated the pattern of partisan violence during the era of decolonization. A year after the Kano riot, another major riot broke out in the South. While the main belligerents of the Kano riot were the southern immigrants and their northern hosts, the Oyo riot of 1954 was an intraethnic conflict with roots in diverse political ideologies and the uneasy relationship between traditional political institutions, which the British colonialists reinforced under indirect rule, and modern democratic practices that came through the introduction of regionalism in the early 1950s. But the riot in Oyo, like the one in Kano, was a violent episode associated with the struggle for political dominance as the British began gradually to lower the Union Jack over the colony. From the early 1950s, administrative reforms at local government level across Nigeria introduced new conflict between and among different classes of elites, political parties, and the colonial government. Local government reforms by the Action Group, the ruling political party in the Western Region, drastically curtailed the power of the *Alaafin* (King) Adeniran Adeyemi II who had previously amassed enormous political and economic resources under the indirect rule system that flourished until the early 1950s. The new reforms prevented Adeyemi from collecting taxes, introduced new levies, and elected councilors, who vied for political power with the king. In response to these unfavorable actions of the ruling party, the king entered into an alliance with the NCNC, the opposition party in the Western Region. The uneasy situation between the Action Group and Adeyemi led to serious violence, culminating in the exile of Adeyemi in 1954.[116]

The published transcript of the commission of inquiry into the Oyo riot, led by Richard D. Lloyd, provides vivid insight into how firearms shaped the tenor of the conflict. The investigative commission revealed that the violence started because some people shot sporadically at their enemies. According to the Lloyd Commission, the Oyo Southern District Council made a "fantastic allegation" against the Egbe Omo Oyo Parapo for shooting sporadically for eight hours during the period of the violence. The gunshots were "meant to kill all the Councillors."[117] Not only were prominent politicians like Davies accused of causing the riot because of "rashness" and of leading thugs with a gun in hand; the Action Group was said to have cultivated a tradition of tying a cock (the symbol of the NCNC) to a tree and shooting at it during every meeting to terrorize opponents and compel members to be loyal to its cause. The newspapers' sensationalizing of the testimony given before the Lloyd Commission—headlines blared: "Davies Came with a Gun and Then They Attacked," "There Were Guns and Cutlasses," "AG Ties Cock to Tree and Shoots at It during Political Meetings"— fed into the prevailing culture of highlighting the role of firearms amid the incessant strife.[118] During the October 21, 1954, sitting of the Lloyd Commission, lawyer Andrew Thomas was said to have fired three shots at one Laniregun, the deputy organizing secretary of the Oyo Action Group and a member of the Oyo Divisional Council, who lived about fifty yards away, when he came to attack Thomas's family. Before the riot broke out, Lagunna, one of the anti-*Alaafin* (king) chiefs, claimed that farmers had prepared a sacrifice consisting of "guns, cutlasses, hoes, rats and maize" as a symbol of their revolt against rent payments and dissatisfaction against the *Alaafin*.[119]

Conclusion

In writing guns into colonial Nigeria's gun society, this chapter focuses on the sites and circumstances that brought the British and Nigerians into conflict with each other. It revisits notable events such as the Enugu colliery shooting, repositioning firearms as the most important factor leading to the tragedy. It has demonstrated that the training of the colonial security force in the use of rifles and other superior firearms that Nigerians did not possess was largely responsible for the failure of the armed anticolonial movement. The use of guns in intraethnic conflicts and partisan political disputes laid the foundation for much of the violence in the postcolonial era. Obviously, the British alone cannot be blamed for gun cruelty in Nigeria. The leading politicians and nationalists introduced a brand of bitter ethnic politics promoted violently with guns.

Notes

1. "Hubert Ogunde Says Banning of Play Unjustified," *Daily Service*, June 28, 1951; "Hubert Ogunde's Play Is Said to Be Seditious," *Daily Service*, May 11, 1951; "Hubert Ogunde Regards the Ban on Play Strange Issue," *WAP*, June 25, 1951; "Police Wants Boy Paster of 'Bread & Bullet' Posters," *WAP*, May, 22, 1951.

2. "Enugu Tragedy Recalled on the Stage," *Daily Service*, April 21, 1951.

3. Clark, *Hubert Ogunde*, xi–xii.

4. "P.R.O Version of Ban by Police at Jos on Staging of Native Play Is Proved Baseless," October 29, 1946; "Hubert Ogunde Vindicates Us (Editorial)," October 30, 1946—both in *WAP*.

5. Clark, *Hubert Ogunde*, 83; "Ogunde's Plays May Be Filmed," *Daily Service*, August 14, 1951.

6. "Ogunde Says Banning of Play Unjustified"; in *WAP*, see "One Man Killed in Port Harcourt Riots," November 26, 1949; and "Rioting in Port Harcourt," November 26, 1949.

7. Harry Smith, *Blue Collar Lawman*, http://www.biafraland.com/harold_smith/autobio.htm (accessed October 26).

8. Falola, *Colonialism and Violence in Nigeria*; Tamuno, *Police in Modern Nigeria*, 217–48.

9. Akinola Lasekan, "Better to Die Honourably Fighting Alone Than Live Forever in an Enslaved State," *WAP*, June 17, 1949.

10. For the history of the army, see Ubah, *Colonial Army and Society*; Killingray, "Maintenance of Law and Order"; and Ukpabi, *Origin of the Nigerian Army*.

11. Tamuno, *Police in Modern Nigeria*.

12. Stapleton, *African Police and Soldiers*.

13. For more on the native authority police, see Rotimi, *Police in a Federal State*.
14. Markham, *Guns of the Empire*, 110–12.
15. Mabogunje, *Urbanization in Nigeria*, 257.
16. *Annual Report of the Police Department for the Year 1931*, 4.
17. See the various annual reports of the police listed in the bibliography.
18. Talbot, *Life in Southern Nigeria*, 296.
19. Lugard, *Political Memoranda*, 250.
20. "Northern Policemen Did Enugu Shooting," *WAP*, December 21, 1949.
21. "Leg. Co. Adjourns Sin Die," *NDT* 16, 1941.
22. Talbot, *Life in Southern Nigeria*, 112.
23. Brook, *One-Eyed Man Is King*, 91.
24. From *Nigerian Pioneer*: "Murder of a European," July 12, 1918; "Surrendering of Arms and Ammunitions," July 12, 1918; and "Egba Affairs," August 2, 1918.
25. Quoted in Atanda, "Iseyin-Okeiho Rising of 1916," 512.
26. Ibid.
27. *Annual Report of the Police Department, Nigeria, for the Year 1930*, 5.
28. *Annual Report of the Police Department: Northern Provinces, for the Year 1927*, 5.
29. Ibid., 9.
30. *Annual Report of the Police Department, Nigeria, for the Year 1930*, 5.
31. *Annual Report of the Police Department for the Year 1931*, 5–6.
32. *Annual Report of the Police Department: Colony and the Southern Provinces, for the Year 1929*, 10.
33. Matera, Bastian, and Kent, *Women's War of 1929*, 3.
34. Olusanya, "Zikist Movement"; Sklar, *Nigerian Political Parties*; Iweriebor, *Radical Politics in Nigeria*; Brown, *"We Were All Slaves"*; Akpala, "Enugu Colliery Shooting"; Ajayi, "Politicisation of Trade Unionism"; Olorunfemi and Adesina, "Labour Unions"; Tijani, *Britain, Leftist Nationalists*; Adebiyi, "Radical Nationalism."
35. "Security Officer Alleges Plan to Blow Up Government in East," *WAP*, January 6, 1950.
36. Ibid.
37. Adebiyi, "Radical Nationalism," 221–22.
38. "Unlawful Society," *Nigerian Gazette*, April 13, 1950.
39. Tijani, *Britain, Leftist Nationalists*.
40. *Report of the Commission of Enquiry*, 39.
41. Ibid., 35.
42. Ibid., 39.
43. "Police Officer at Enugu Shooting Tells His Story," *WAP*, December 21, 1949.
44. *Report of the Commission of Enquiry*, 39.
45. "Did Dr. Savage Give Stand-By Order before or after Shooting?" *WAP*, January 6, 1950.
46. "Police Officer Who Ordered First Enugu Shooting Was Guilty of Misjudgment," *WAP*, June 10, 1950.
47. *Report of the Commission of Enquiry*, 34.
48. Ibid., 34.
49. Ibid., 35–36.
50. Ibid., 49.

51. Brown, "We Were All Slaves," 315.

52. "Enugu Blood Bath by Zik," May 22, 1950; "Freedom Fight in Africa by Zik," *WAP*, January 19, 1950—both in *WAP*. For the labor union's interpretation of the origins of the violence, see "Railwaymen Speak before Fitzgerald Commission," January 4, 1950; "Railwaymen Speak before Fitzgerald Commission (2)," January 5, 1950—both in *WAP*.

53. Brook, *One-Eyed Man Is King*, 91.

54. Ibhawoh, *Imperialism and Human Rights*.

55. From *WAP*: "Blacksmith Shows Inquiry His Wounds," January 6, 1950; "Colliery Blacksmith Gets Six Gunshot Wounds," January 6, 1950; "Four Police Rifles Face Curious Driver," January 6, 1950; and "Three Miners Explain How the Explosives Affair Led to Shots," January 4, 1950.

56. "Two Policemen Who Saw Enugu Shooting Speak," *WAP*, January 4, 1950.

57. Ibid.

58. From *WAP*: "Enugu Report Is Said to Attack Present Regime," May 17, 1950; "Fitzgerald's Recipe for Freedom (Editorial)," June 12, 1950; "Advice to Sir John and His Advisers," June 14, 1950; "Nigerians in London React to the Report on Enugu Massacre," June 15, 1950; "Only Self-Govt. Now Will Prevent More Shooting Incidents," June 17, 1950; "National Day of Mourning," June 17, 1950; "Tide of Freedom," June 17, 1950; "Brutal Exploitation of All Nigeria Must End," January 24, 1950; "Enugu Shooting Inquiry Report Is Completed, "January 6, 1950; "Nigeria: A Police State?" April 28, 1950; and "Against Police Imperialism," May 3, 1950.

59. From *WAP*: "Commission Attempted to Cover the Uncoverable: Mbadiwe Says," June 20, 1950; "Macpherson, Foot and Co. Must Go!" June 13, 1950; "Nigerian Labour Congress Sees Enugu Shooting as Preconceived," June 20, 1950; "Press Freedom in the Colonies," July 1, 1950; "On the Enugu Massacre," July 5, 1950; "Delay of the Enugu Report," May 3, 1950.

60. "Sir John Macpherson's Regime Is on Fire!" *WAP*, June 12, 1950.

61. "National Body to Probe Recent Enugu Shooting," November 23, 1949; "Enugu Butcher Must Be Tried," June 12, 1950—both in *WAP*.

62. "Govt. Officials' Evidence Was Highly Exaggerated," *WAP*, January 7, 1950.

63. From *WAP*: "Police Superintendent Could Have Done His Job without Gun Fire," June 13, 1950; "H. O. Davies Objects to Devised Evidence," January 6, 1950; "Davies Wants Three Europeans to Talk," January 1, 1950; "M.P. Defends Police Chief Who Ordered Enugu Shooting but Official Insists He Is to Blame," July 20, 1950.

64. "Doctor Says Men Were Shot by Police Rifles, Not Guns," *Daily Service*, December 19, 1949; "Police Had Trivial Injuries from Their Own Bullets," *WAP*, December 19, 1949.

65. "Guilty Men of the Enugu Kill Must Be Punished," *WAP*, January 9, 1950.

66. Ibid.

67. "Enugu Report: Police Officer Shot Miners and He Is to Be Sacked," *WAP*, June 14, 1950.

68. "Enugu Blood Bath by Zik," *WAP*, May 23, 1950.

69. "World Inquiry Wanted to Probe Enugu Massacre," *WAP*, November 24, 1949.

70. "Policemen Acted in Good Faith, Defends Crown Counsel Brett," *WAP*, January 9, 1950.

71. "Northern Policemen Did Enugu Shooting."

72. "Ojike Foresees No Shooting by Police Were Nigeria Self-Governing," *WAP*, July 8, 1947.
73. "United Nations Told of Enugu Incident," *Daily Service*, November 28, 1949.
74. "Troops from U.K. Will Be Flown to West Africa," *WAP*, November 28, 1949.
75. "Governor Macpherson Said to Urge Rejection of Enugu Riot Report," *WAP*, May 19, 1950.
76. "Britain's Appalling Ignorance about the Colonies Revealed," *WAP*, May 19, 1950.
77. "Chief Commissioner and Philip to Be Sacked," *WAP*, June 13, 1950.
78. "Police Ought No More to Carry Arms on Duty," *WAP*, December 2, 1949.
79. Strike, Nigeria (Disorder) House of Commons Sitting, July 16, 1947, vol. 440, cc. 385–87, http://hansard.millbanksystems.com/commons/1947/jul/16/strike-nigeria-disorder (accessed June 1, 2015); "Enugu Colliery, Nigeria (Disturbances), House of Commons, November 1949, vol. 470, cc. 359-62, 359, http://hansard.millbanksystems.com/commons/1949/nov/23/enugu-colliery-nigeria-disturbance (accessed June 2, 2015). From *WAP*: "TUC Says Strike in Burutu UAC Continues in Spite of Police Fire," June 26, 1947; "Official Version of Shooting Is Desired," August 12, 1947; and "Adedoyin Recalls Loco Tear Gas over Motion to Probe into Burutu Shooting," March 9, 1948.
80. Mr. Rees-William, in "Enugu Colliery, Nigeria (Disturbances)."
81. Mr. Gallacher, in "Enugu Colliery, Nigeria (Disturbances)."
82. Mr. Driberg, in "Enugu Colliery, Nigeria (Disturbances)."
83. Strike, Nigeria (Disorder) House of Commons Sitting; "MPs Nettled at Shooting of Burutu UAC Workers," *WAP*, July 21, 1947.
84. Matera, Bastian, and Kent, *Women's War of 1929*, 3.
85. From *WAP*: "Chief Commissioner Advises Ilesha People on Grievances," April 16, 1941; "Ataoja of Oshogbo and Chief Quarrel at Council Meeting," June 5, 1941; "Trouble in Oshogbo," June 5, 1941; "Ilesha Riot," June 20, 1941; "Members of Ilesha National Council Refuse Compensation," October 10, 1941; "Aggressive Tribalism," December 9, 1941; "Crowd of Women and Children Attack Palace of Awujale of Ijebu," July 20, 1942; "Trial of Ijebu Ode Rioters Begins before Large Crowd," August 15, 1942; "3 Alleged Killed and Sixty Injured in Serious Clash," January 6, 1948; "Tivs and Udan District in Gun Battle," June 3, 1950; "Several People Are Sentenced to Prison Following Disturbance," February 13, 1951; "Kalabari Cry Down Newington's Handling of Tribal Skirmishes," August 17, 1950; "Rioting in Igbirra Did Not Just Crop Up Spontaneously," September 20, 1951; "Another Shooting Incident by Mallam H. R. Abdallah," September 22, 1951; "1 Person Killed in Oke Odo Disorder," November 22, 1952; "Tension at Isale Eko (Editorial)," November 24, 1952; "Oke Ode Disturbances (Editorial)," December 6, 1952; "Reign of Terror by E. E. Adeniyi," December 12, 1952; "Another Sad Day! (Editorial)," June 4, 1953; "Badagry Riot (Editorial)," July 17, 1953; "Police Open Fire on Mob at Akuna," March 2, 1954; "Two Persons Killed in Riot," July 26, 1954; "Riot Not Caused by Evacuation of Some Landowners: Official," August 27, 1954; and "Ogbomoso Riot: 40 Persons Nabbed," February 3, 1955. See also from the *Daily Service*: "Hundreds of Houses Burnt and Several Persons Killed in Clash over Boundary," March 13, 1952; "Hausa Leaders Charged Following Disturbances," April 27, 1953; "Street Demonstration Features Coronation Day," June 3, 1953; "Arms Freely Used in Chieftaincy Clash," September 1, 1953; "Clans Clash on Merger Proposals," May 19, 1954; "Riot Beaks Out in East," October 15, 1954; and "Women Lead Riot in Bende," January 10, 1955.
86. "Efik Versus Ibo Riot: One Ibo Killed," *WAP*, December 19, 1949.

87. "District Officer of Awka to the Resident of Onitsha," November 24, 1936, AW 763, NAE.
88. "Carrying of Firearms Declared Illegal in Badagry," *Daily Service*, April 24, 1953.
89. "Tivs and Udan District in Gun Battle"; "Gaskiya Tafi Kwabo Narrates Incident Leading to Makurdi Riot: 13 Rioters Die," *WAP*, June 17, 1947.
90. "Carrying of Arms in Bornu Forbidden," *Daily Service*, July 16, 1954.
91. Basden, *Niger Ibos*, 379.
92. "Control of Cattle," February 20, 1941, Jos Prof., 2193, NAK.
93. Aderinto, "Where Is the Boundary?"; Aderinto, *"Ijebu a b'eyan . . . ?"*
94. Aderinto, "Where Is the Boundary?"
95. "Tiv and Udan District in Gun Battle"; "Northern Villages Quarrel into a Pitched Battle," *WAP*, May 15, 1950.
96. "Ngoshe-Veledva Shooting," *WAP*, May 17, 1950.
97. "Coroner Says Police Killed Six Idanres in Self-Defence," *WAP*, February 18, 1951.
98. "Kalabaris Cry Down Newington's Handling of Tribal Skirmishes," August 17, 1950; "Twenty-Three Okrika Men Killed in Clash with Armed Kalabari," August 12, 1950—both in *WAP*.
99. "Riot Not Caused by Evacuation of Some Landowners."
100. "Coroner Says Police Killed Six Idanres."
101. "Hausa Leaders Charged."
102. "Campaign Takes a New Turn: Revolver Fired," *WAP*, May 15, 1956.
103. "Malam Pulls-Out Shotgun at NPC Meeting," *Daily Service*, April 30, 1954.
104. "Armed Youth Breaks into the Compound of Prince Oyekan," January 23, 1951; "Assassination of Adelabu Allegedly Planned in Ibadan," April 19, 1956—both in *WAP*.
105. M. Jaji to Adelabu, August 1, 1957, quoted in Post and Jenkins, *Price of Liberty*, 405.
106. "Sardauna Speaks on Kano Riot," *WAP*, March 31, 1956.
107. See Vaughan, *Nigerian Chiefs*, 69–95; and Coleman, *Nigeria*, 396–408.
108. Coleman, *Nigeria*, 400.
109. "Official Casualty List on Kano Riot," *Daily Service*, May 25, 1953; "Casualty List Published," *WAP*, May 23, 1953.
110. "Press Release," May 28, 1953, Oyo Prof., 6056, NAI.
111. "Text of Broadcast by H. E. the Governor (Sir John Macpherson, G.C.M.G.) on the Nigerian Broadcasting Service on the 20th May, 1953," Oyo Prof., 6056, NAI.
112. Ibid.
113. "Inter-Tribal War They Call It!," May 27, 1953; "Kano Riot," May 19, 1953—both in *Daily Service*.
114. "Kano Riots," *Daily Service*, May 19, 1953.
115. Nigeria (Kano Riots) House of Commons Debate, May 20, 1953, vol. 515, cc. 2082–85.
116. Vaughan, *Nigerian Chiefs*, 88–95.
117. "Oyo Inquiry Report," *WAP*, June 9, 1955.
118. "There Were Guns and Cutlasses," *Daily Service*, October 10, 1954; "Davies Came with a Gun and Then They Attacked," *Daily Service*, October 22, 1954; "AG Ties Cock to Tree and Shoots at It during Political Meetings," *WAP*, October 23, 1954.
119. "There Were Guns and Cutlasses."

6

A FEARFUL WEAPON

Violent Crime and Gun Accidents in Everyday Nigeria

> A stage has been reached where we feel the use of firearms in certain provincial areas should be partially restricted by the Native Authorities, if the citizens of this country would continue to enjoy life, unhaunted by the spectre of insecurity. Early this week, we published the doleful news of the untimely death of a damsel at Okigwi whose life has been cut away by those who mistook her for a thief. And even before this, we had published several other items bearing on where one person or another had been mistaken for a game and shot dead.
>
> —"These Gun Shot Accidents!" *Eastern Nigeria Guardian*, May 7, 1948

"Darkness was around the corner, and the burial was near. Guns fired the last salute and the cannon rent the sky."[1] Chinua Achebe used these statements in his classic *Things Fall Apart* to describe the frenzied atmosphere at the closing of the funeral ceremony of Chief Ezeudu, the oldest man and one of the most decorated chiefs in the village of Umuofia. The events following this carnival-like scene were a calamity. Okonkwo, the main character of the novel, accidentally kills a sixteen-year-old teenager and son of the deceased during the sporadic shooting that was characteristic of numerous ceremonies and rites in Igboland, as elsewhere in Nigeria. The circumstances leading to the gun accident in *Things Fall Apart* adequately mirror the realities of the time. Big and strong men like Okonkwo who had never fired a shot decided to extend the sphere of their superior masculinity to the use of firearms. But Chief Ezeudu's funeral accident was not the first time Okonkwo would be involved in an incident of gun violence. He nearly killed Ekwefi, his second wife, in an episode that would have been ruled a homicide. During the preparation for the New Yam Festival, an important ceremony in the community that pays homage to Ani, the goddess of earth and fertility, an angry Okonkwo beats Ekwefi for the flimsiest of reasons. He decides to quench his anger by going out hunting with his "old rusty" gun, which he had never used. When he asks Ikemefuna, a member of his household, to fetch him his gun, the annoyed Ekwefi ridicules her husband's prowess and his impotent gun, murmuring something like "guns that never shot" audibly enough that Okonkwo hears her.[2] In escalating anger, Okonkwo runs into the house, picks up the loaded gun, and fires it at Ekwefi to prove that his gun could indeed fire a shot. The shot misses its target—the "shaken and frightened" Ekwefi, lucky to be alive. But Okonkwo's life trajectory does not remain the same after the funeral accident—a good portion of *Things Fall Apart* dwells on the implications of his action. To millions of readers across the world, Achebe's description of gun violence was merely a fiction; but to the peoples of colonial Nigeria, it represented a tragic reality of their gun society. Achebe's rendition of the relationship between masculinity and gun violence epitomizes how literary production can train a bright light on historical actuality.

Seeing the danger of firearms mainly from the perspective of public disorder and the violent relations between Nigerians and the British, and among Nigerians of similar and dissimilar ethnicities, as demonstrated in the preceding chapter, underestimates the core role that lethal weapons played in the everyday construction of fear. In this chapter, I take the narratives of gun violence from the big issues of maintenance of colonial order to a more micro level and focus on a grassroots discourse of gun accidents during hunting and ceremonial shooting and in armed robbery. The frequency with which cases of gun accidents appear in court records, oral histories, and newspaper accounts in the 1940s and 1950s shows that they were ubiquitous. It is by appraising the people's encounter with guns on a daily basis that we can come to terms with the institutionalization of firearms in a colonial gun society. And if the British conceived of this as a product of Nigerians' irresponsible use of firearms, the people interpreted it beyond the narrow confines of the abuse of weapons. Gun accidents were coded in spiritual and religious terms and tended to reflect the people's worldview of the challenges of living and dying.

Armed Robbery in Colonial Nigeria

Conventional history of Nigeria attributes the rise in incidence of armed robbery to the proliferation of firearms following the Nigerian Civil War (1967–1970). However, research has shown that this is historically inaccurate. In fact, the incidence of robbery with guns increased after each world war. Thus, the post-1970 development did not occur without precedent. Indeed, before the imposition of colonialism, thieves and bandits, working under the command of powerful oligarchies and warlords, used Dane guns for terrorizing communities and caravan routes.[3] The relationship between firearms and armed robbery mirrored the significant transformation of the core structure of colonial society. Armed robbery took on a new dimension with the introduction of colonial currency, meaning that stolen items could be transformed into wealth or used to meet daily financial needs. The intensification of the activities of international trading companies like the UAC and John Holt, and establishments such as banks, post offices, and the government's treasury, which held large sum of cash, indirectly fueled the activities of men of the underworld. Indeed, the government and private businesses put measures in place in an effort to stay a step ahead of the thieves. In the 1930s, thieves would shoot at a bank vault if heavy tools like sledgehammers proved ineffective. One of the most audacious daylight bank robberies in colonial Nigeria took place in Kaduna in 1942. At about 10 a.m. on May 12, a group of "daredevil" robbers, numbering fifteen, attacked the branch of the Bank of British West Africa. They first ignited two large cases of gunpowder and fired about ten gunshots into the sky to disperse the workers before carting away more than £2,000 meant for the payment of staff salaries of the departments of education and public works, which had been brought to the vault a day earlier.

The geography of violent crime and the types of firearms used mirrored the unequal distribution of political and economic capital across the country. While in the rural communities home invasions with Dane guns were popular, in the cities, especially Lagos, banks, post offices, and large European businesses were the target of armed robbers using arms of precision such as pistols, revolvers, and rifles.[4] A *Daily Service* crime report in November 1946 established that "a special gang of burglars" operating in major commercial centers and cities "are all fully armed with revolvers." So nefarious was their activities that night watchmen, who used single-shot

Dane guns "are giving up their jobs *en masse*. They seem to have preferred unemployment to serious threat to their lives from revolver shot" the report suggested.[5] The variety of firearms used for robbery operations was an indication that the urban proliferation of arms of precision was attributable to the large number of educated elites, security outfits, commercial firms, and ports. Dane guns were more likely to be used for robberies in the rural communities because they were the primary firearms for hunting. Robbery operations in the cities required sophisticated arms, easy to conceal and capable of firing multiple shots, because the security situation was tighter than in the rural areas where the main aim of using a Dane gun was to scare people with its loud report. In Lagos, thieves targeted the homes of Europeans and senior police officers and administrators precisely for their rifles and pistols. The intrepidity of Lagosian thieves seemed not to have any bound as the public, the police, and even military armories were looted for guns. In April 1947, three men—Jeremiah Ayepe, Thompson Omieke (both burglary ex-convicts), and Benson Fedefele—were arraigned in a Lagos magistrate court for breaking into a police station armory and stealing ten out of the twelve police rifles in stock.[6] The accused sold each stolen rifle for £4 in Warri Province.[7] City thieves not only knew how to steal firearms; they could also assemble and maintain them.

Much of the armed robbery in rural communities went unchecked because the crimes were perpetrated far from the main center of political authority and because much of the gun violence had no direct or obvious impact on the colonial treasury because they were mostly home invasions. So virulent were the activities of thieves in the villages around Ogbomoso that the chiefs, in a protest letter to the government, claimed that their town was "being slowly but surely ruined." The petitions concerning burglaries are replete with thought-provoking adjectives that establish the agonies that communities were going through. While Councilor Ladapo Ogunleye described the thieves ravaging Owo as "unsympathetic hands," other petitioners pleaded to be saved from the "ceaseless molestation," "ravages of these turbulent individuals," and "uninvited marauders" who "rendered our lives and properties imperiled."[8] Official records, like the following extracts from the 1939 annual report of the NPF, are explicit about the modus operandi of armed gangs and confirm the well-acknowledged efficacy of firearms in robbery operations: "Gangs of men armed with Dane guns and cutlasses raided lonely villages, firing their guns as they approached. The frightened inhabitants ran into the bush and any who remained were either severely beaten or, as happened in some cases, killed. The village was then ransacked and property stolen."[9] In another incident, a gang of Hausa robbers hired one Adam Ibadan, a Yoruba man, to scream "Ole" (thieves), amidst the release of gunshots, before attacking a village near Osogbo in 1942. "This psychological trick," confessed Adam Ibadan during the court trial, was "intended to create a state of pandemonium" in the village.[10] In the community of foreigners (Sabon Gari) in Zaria, armed robbers provided advance warning of an attack to residents and demanded between £15 and £20 in order not to raid the community.[11]

But the geography of armed robbery and firearms went beyond the fluid dichotomy of urban and rural violence. The incidence of highway and transborder robbery increased as the British built more facilities to aid the rapid movement of people and goods, and thereby expand capitalist enterprise. In June 1954, a gang of highway robbers operating on the Enugu–Nsukka road fired at the tire of a car carrying John Holt director A. Baun, bringing the vehicle to a halt. They then removed £2,000—money meant for the payment of the company's local produce buyers.[12] A month earlier, the company's location in Umuahia lost £10,000 to armed robbers.[13] Similarly, the press reported that the police were "completely baffled" and "bewildered" by the mode of operation of the "seasoned crooks" who specialized in robbing passenger lorries along the Ikorodu–Lagos road. The Ikorodu-Lagos gang on two separate operations robbed lorry passengers of more than £300, overpowering their victims with guns and using women pretending to be prospective passengers as bait to stop and rob moving vehicles.[14] Another passenger lorry coming from Ilorin was waylaid and robbed. This time, the robbers pretended to be in need of gasoline on the roadside in order to bring the lorry to a halt.[15]

Some highway robbers operated in police uniforms. Sources are not explicit about whether the uniforms were genuine or fake. But during the colonial period, there was an underground market for official uniforms of law-enforcement agencies and other social clubs, such as the Boy Scouts and Girl Guides. In April 1955, police arrested a gang of seven highway robbers (Patrick Ekong, Victor Ukandu, Alhaji Garuba, Israel Nwobi, James Okolo, Clinton Onwuka, and Sunday Akpan) along the Aba–Oron highway, all dressed in police uniform.[16] In addition, car theft at gunpoint increased as the popularity of automobiles soared among the emergent Nigerian middle class, which included teachers, clerks, journalists, and bookkeepers. Nigerian armed robbers of the 1940s and 1950s used stolen vehicles to facilitate their activities—some of which were then sold on the underground market for used cars and car parts. Not even government and military vehicles were safe from the marauders of colonial Nigeria. On April 25, 1947, two armed robbers were arraigned for stealing a military lorry at gunpoint in front of a police station in Mushin, Lagos. The published transcript of the court proceedings stated that one of the robbers "pulled out his revolver and ordered the corporal and the station orderly to hold up their hands or he would shoot them."[17]

Another major feature of violent crime in Nigeria was transborder smuggling, which further exposed the artificiality of colonial boundaries created in the second half of the nineteenth century. One main incentive for smuggling was the difference in economic and tariff policies of the European colonies (French and German) in the southern fringes of the Nigerian littoral. Essential items were smuggled into Nigeria because they could be purchased more cheaply in the neighboring countries or to avoid paying excise duties on the goods. Customs officers were unable to check the activities of "some well-off personalities who have formed themselves into a well-articulated syndicate of smugglers." When in November 1950 a "lorry load" of police raided the Aba home of Willy Njaka, described as a rich and popular smuggler, they recovered contraband ranging from revolvers to Spanish brandy and "dangerous" drugs purportedly imported from the Spanish colony of Fernando Pó.[18] The activities of the smugglers, according to a commentator in the *Daily Service*, were capable of inflicting "economic disaster" and "social bankruptcy" on eastern Nigeria in particular and the entire country in general.[19]

Transborder smuggling was problematic not just because smugglers used firearms to prevent the police and rivals from seizing their goods, or because the border towns of Idiroko and Meko were literally reduced to a war zone during an exchange of fire between the customs service and smugglers. The "unrestricted and unknown" quantity of arms and ammunition smuggled into the country from neighboring French and Spanish territories created significant panic among security operatives. As early as 1905, a police report established that a "large quantity of guns, gin and tobacco" was smuggled across the French Dahomey border. Not even the deployment of about fifty soldiers of the West African Frontier Force could check smuggling.[20] Arms trafficking increased unabated over the decades. The consequences of illegal arms smuggling, according to a newspaper crime report of 1955, "are foreseeable and too numerous to mention."[21] Although the newspaper did report the remarkable activities of customs policemen, which included an episode in which one officer gallantly and independently resisted attack from smugglers, shooting three in the process—for the public, the corruption within the rank and file of the police was the main reason smuggling remained profitable and unabated.[22] The solution to smuggling, described by the press as "one of the greatest public enemies in this country today," was a complete "purge" of the rank and file of the NPF and customs and excise departments.[23] In 1955, the government hired five anti-smuggling European officers and bought a naval ship, the *Challenger*, to reinforce its border patrol.[24]

The published biographies of popular armed robbers of the 1950s render insights into the professionalization of banditry, the manner of criminal operations, and, more important, the role of firearms in criminal exploits. One of Nigeria's best-known robbers of the 1950s was Asuquo, who led a gang of about a hundred thieves drawn from six districts in Calabar Province. He specialized in highway robbery and hired assassination. Described as a "muscular and hefty giant of a man" and the "most dangerous, ingenious, black-eyed rogue that has ever infested" the province, Asuquo and his gang shot and killed policemen on a regular basis. After several failed attempts, a force of more than one hundred armed policemen, led by Senior Police Superintendent S. C. Smith, successfully attacked the gang's jungle hideout in May 1955. Asuquo turned himself in a week after the police raid. Recovered from his group were twenty shotguns, one rifle, six pistols, fifty-one Dane guns, £1,000, 150 pounds of gunpowder, and local charms, or juju. The *Daily Service* described its report on Asuquo as the "greatest crime story of the year."[25] Not all the notorious criminals of colonial Nigeria confined their activities to certain regions of the country. The activities of transborder criminals further established the porosity of colonial boundaries. After allegedly shooting and killing twelve soldiers during an attempt to arrest him in 1955, Musa Gonimi, a notorious Chadian transborder criminal, fled to Nigeria, where he remained at large. The French authorities promised a reward of £50 for information that could lead to his arrest. Gonimi was eventually apprehended by the NAPF in July 1957 in a village between Kukawa and Gajiram in the Borno Province of Nigeria.[26]

The monetization of the colonial economy or introduction of a cash economy is inadequate for explaining the transformation of armed robbery in colonial Nigeria. Among other well-acknowledged motivations for armed robbery were poverty, unemployment, and mass socioeconomic marginalization.[27] The sporadic colonial economy, characterized by depressed conditions and unstable prices for cash crops and solid minerals used for running the colonial state, manifested in the creation of a pool of unemployed people (mostly in the cities) who lived on the proceeds from criminal behavior and the underground economy. In the early 1920s, about twenty thousand unemployed people registered with the government labor department in Lagos, which had a population of about one hundred thousand.[28] The government itself attributed the increasing crime rate to a postwar structural crisis. In 1946, the annual police report drew a direct correlation between armed robbery and the war just concluded: "It is almost axiomatic that an increase in crime follows every war. After being discharged from the Army many men, with little or no education are not prepared to return to life on the farm, and settle in the towns where it is nearly impossible to provide them with work."[29] Of the 247,077 unemployed Nigerians in 1948, ex-servicemen accounted for 27,432.[30] The importance of the relationship between crime and the postwar situation went beyond the obvious criminalization of men who had risked their lives for the British Empire but were betrayed by the colonial government, which refused to fulfill its demobilization promises.[31] The proliferation of and illicit trafficking in firearms after 1945 were attributed to a lack of proper reintegration of the soldiers to civilian life. Ex-servicemen were accused of roaming their communities with their service rifles and personal guns, which they used for extortion and all sorts of violent crimes.[32] The government's attribution of the increase in the crime rate to the broader postwar condition was a deliberate attempt to deflect blame for poor policing from the inept NPF.

The alleged involvement of the ex-servicemen in armed robbery and gun-running criminalized their identity and reduced government and public sympathy for them. Their well-documented violence against the civilian population tended to tarnish the legitimate role they had played in defending the British Empire against the Nazis.[33] In 1950, a "lorry load" of police laid a four-day siege against the house of World War II veteran Chinkwe Ohaja at Umuakwu Nsulu, in search of a machine gun and a Bren gun (a light semi- or fully automatic machine gun) he allegedly stole from the government armory while he was being demobilized. The search party recovered a Bren gun, a revolver, and a Dane gun.[34] Sources did not reveal the model of the Bren gun recovered from Ohaja. But the British MK-I Bren model, which used a top-mounted 30-round magazine, could theoretically discharge between 480 and 540 rounds per minute.[35] Ohaja remained at large until he was arrested on January 8, 1953.[36]

Moreover, the Nigerian state was underpoliced. The centrally controlled NPF that came into existence in the second half of the nineteenth century was originally established essentially to protect the colonial masters and the economic and political infrastructure of domination. Effective public policing in Nigeria, as elsewhere in British Africa, was measured largely by the ability of security forces to curtail social unrest capable of causing the breakdown of law and order and undermining colonialism. Ironically, many of the violent crimes in Nigeria (such as robbery and assault) were directed at ordinary people, not against the government, which had strong police protection. The numerical weakness of the NPF and the NAPF clearly revealed the crisis of policing the colonial state. Osogbo Division, with an estimated population of 362,000 in the early 1930s, had fewer than fifty NAPF officers.[37] About eighteen thousand rank and file of the NPF policed a country with an estimated population of fifty million in 1965–66.[38]

The NAPF, which was closer to the people, was used mainly for protecting the local chiefs and enforcing tax and sanitary laws. During the period of decolonization and internal government in the 1950s, political parties and emergent leaders used the NAPF for terrorizing opponents in the bitter struggle for power.[39] To worsen the situation, the officers of the NAPF were neither trained nor allowed to carry firearms because of the fear by the British that the chiefs could constitute them into a militia force to fight the government. Rather, they were permitted to use truncheons.[40] Even the rank and file of the NPF rarely carried guns while on patrol—only senior European police and customs officers carried revolvers and pistols while on duty. It was during the period of rioting and social unrest that the police and other security agents used firearms in a much pronounced matter. Also, day and night police patrols were not conducted in tandem with the realities of criminal activities of the time. In the 1940s it was only in big cities that police patrolled at night with conventional patrol vans.[41] In most parts of Nigeria, both the NPF and the NAPF patrolled on bicycles. Very few used motorcycles. In addition, crime control method was as elitist as the fundamental principle of colonial policing. In October 1947, the NPF established an emergency telephone line (666) and an information room to wirelessly coordinate intelligence in Lagos. "It will speed up the investigation of crime and give the public a much better service than at present exists," Police Commissioner T. B. W Finlay boasted at a press conference to unveil the new scheme.[42] But very few Lagosians had access to a telephone; fewer were willing to pay to use the few public telephones stationed at major business districts and segregated African and European neighborhoods to report crime.[43]

The government's decision not to arm its police with guns endangered the lives of policemen in big cities where thieves and smugglers used revolvers, pistols, and rifles during daylight robberies. The sight of policemen running away from gun-bearing thieves was a regular occurrence in the 1940s. So low was the public's confidence in the NPF that some critics recommended the use of ex-servicemen, who, it was believed, as a result of their military training, would be better suited for handling the deplorable security situation.[44] Yet not all policemen ran away in the face of apparent danger to their lives. On November 21, 1946, at about 3:35 a.m., four plainclothes detectives of the NPF stopped three "suspicious characters" during a patrol in Palm Church Street, Lagos. While two of the suspects took to their heels, the third, named Bisiriyu Omolade, fired a German automatic pistol at Sergeant Igbinosu Evboma, one of the undercover policemen, who gallantly overpowered his assailant using his baton. Omolade was arrested and taken to the police station. At the station, the police discovered that Evboma might have been killed had it not been for the jamming of two live rounds in the breech of Omolade's pistol. Evboma was awarded the King's Medal for Gallantry for his heroic exploit.[45] Omolade was found guilty of attempted murder, being armed with the "intent to break and enter a dwelling house," and unlawfully possessing firearms and ammunition. He was sentenced to six months in prison or a £200 fine.[46] Omolade's sentence was consistent with most others—the average length of incarceration for armed robbery was one year. But stiffer punishment was given if the robbery led to loss of life, as in the case of Mallam Adam, Danjijiri, and Momoh Moriah, who attacked a village near Oshogbo killing one person with their revolver. On December 2, 1942, after a trial that lasted four days, Justice C. C. Francis sentenced the three men to death by hanging. Not even their legal representation by Andrew O. Thomas, Esq., could save them from capital punishment.[47]

But for the critics of poor policing in Nigeria, Evboma's story was just an exception, not the rule. Criticism of police ineptitude published in the leading newspapers identified the intersection of race and social class in the protection of lives and property. Reporting also touched on the lack of both intelligence gathering and well-trained educated Nigerians on the police force.[48] A *West African Pilot* editorial on police ineptitude pointed out that there was "no fairplay" in the distribution of policemen in Nigerian cities; that every European quarter had a police guard, while a community with five hundred or six hundred people was underpoliced and left "absolutely to the mercy" of armed robbers.[49] The following extract from another editorial, "Crime Wave in Lagos," seems to capture the tensions under which several Nigerian communities lived in the early 1950s:

> Unsafe to leave one's window open; unsafe to move at night; unsafe to leave small children about; unsafe to be born under impecunious circumstances! In other words, society in many Nigerian cities is rapidly developing the symptoms of modernity—of crime waves, of hooliganism, of mystery murders, of born but abandoned babies, etc. If that is what modernity brings, what a price to pay! And how grudgingly we must pay it! Grudgingly indeed, for none of all of the social welfare benefits of Western civilization can compensate for the social chaos now coming over us.[50]

THE POLITICS OF PRIVATIZATION OF SECURITY

The realities of the time led to the reintroduction of the hunter guard system, or the privatization of community policing, from the 1930s.[51] Essentially, groups of professional hunters patrolled their community in rotation. To be sure, before the imposition of colonial rule, hunters and warriors did police communities from incessant raids by slavers and thieves. But after the imposition of colonial rule, the government banned the activities of hunter guards, putting in place a police system that was loyal to its agenda.[52] The colonial government's disposition toward the reintroduction of hunter guards, which most communities believed would help "retard the progress of these pests, and thus make life worth living," varied markedly.[53] While some thought that hunter guards would complement the work of the regular police force, others believed they were simply indispensable in the wake of the unprecedented crime wave, especially in the suburbs. "Peace and good order," said the assistant district officer of Osogbo, cannot be achieved without the help of the hunters. He considered the use of hunters for policing Osogbo town and its villages "as a satisfactory arrangement."[54] The Osogbo hunters not only arrested a gang of robbers specializing in looting European businesses in the town; they recovered arms including ten pounds of gunpowder, eight Dane guns, and two shotguns from them.[55]

In Ogbomoso, a drop in the rate of burglary was recorded when hunters were mobilized to police the town. "We are perfectly satisfied thus far with the arrangement," the chiefs of Ogbomoso submitted about the efficacy of the hunter guards in 1940.[56] In Ondo, the division officer described the hunter guards, most of whom were Igbos from eastern Nigeria, as "reasonably efficient, but inclined to slack" if not well monitored. He noted that burglaries "are practically unknown" since they began to operate. Another unexpected impact of the hunter patrols included a drop in nightlife, especially entertainment, which the government frowned on, and a consequent reduction in the consumption of kerosene for lighting.[57] The hunters' success in helping to check thieves owed to a number of overlapping factors, which both the chiefs and the government recognized in varying proportion. To the chiefs, the marauding thieves could be stopped only by hunters who possessed indigenous medicine (*juju*). Both the government and the chiefs agreed that the hunters were good marksmen. Shooting, according to the secretary to the government, was the "prime occupation" of the hunters, unlike the officers of the NAPF who were not allowed to carry firearms. In addition, the hunter guards stood a better chance of catching robbers because they knew the terrain of the community they policed well. The statement of the acting district officer of Ibadan summed up the realities of the era, the role of hunter guards in traditional Nigerian society, and the government's failed responsibility in protecting the lives of its subjects: "The use of hunters as night guards is rooted in native law and custom and I doubt if we could stop it even if we wanted to. *Nor from a practical point of view do I think it desirable to stop it as it is financially impossible to afford adequate police protection to every village.*"[58] By the early 1940s, hunter guards had become an established form of public policing in most communities in southern and northern Nigeria. The government's approval of hunters to police Calabar in 1952 even made the news as a sign of an effective response to the deplorable security situation in that town.[59]

But three main issues problematized the use of hunters for guarding communities. First, they were private individuals, not directly employed by the state, assuming the responsibility of the government to secure lives and property. Some colonial officers clung to the view that public safety was a fundamental responsibility of the government. To allow private "untrained," "illiterate" citizens unfamiliar with legal issues to assume this role was to abdicate a central power of government. The government's biggest challenge was therefore to mold the thinking of the hunters in conformity with legalities concerning public policing and self-defense, and to confine their role to aiding in the maintenance of law and order. The difficulty inherent in this situation is more explicit in another candid submission of the assistant district officer of Ibadan Division:

> I think that the right approach in these cases is to say that there is no objection to the use of hunters as night guards as long as it is realized that they are not a constituted force and have no greater legal power to the ordinary civilian. They should be warned that if anyone is wounded or killed by the use of firearms while a felony is being committed the hunter concerned will not escape the penalty of the law unless it can be shown in court that the use of armed force was justifiable in the circumstances and that in practice it is very difficult to satisfy the courts on this point.[60]

Second, the government was unwilling to pay the hunters for their "job." Although all parties involved agreed that hunters could not be paid like NAPF or NPF officers, they still thought that the hunters must be compensated for their time and service, since they lost income when they patrolled the town instead of hunting animals in the forest. The hunters were also reluctant to bear the cost of gunpowder used for firing their Dane guns. But for the government, putting the hunters on the payroll could motivate them to establish a union and demand better conditions of work—a situation that city administrators were already facing among ex-servicemen, who were used as private guards by the government and private trading firms. In July 1947, some ex-servicemen, under the umbrella of the Night Watchmen's Union, mounted a protest demanding better work conditions from the government. The commissioner of the colony exaggeratedly described the gathering of the gun-bearing guards "as a reminder of the horror of the last war" and worried that the government must address the "mental terror" that ex-servicemen created with their guns. "How can the policemen secure peace, if they [the ex-servicemen] begin to shoot at the crowd?" the commissioner wondered in his correspondence to the governor of Nigeria about the security of the veterans' protest.[61] In its editorial about a riot by ex-servicemen in Umuahia in October 1950 (in which one person was seen brandishing a revolver), the *West African Pilot* presented the paradox of a colonial army and the welfare of demobilized men:

We do not justify rioting. But nevertheless, when you put a man in uniform, put a gun in his hand, teach him how to kill in the name of preserving democracy in a lost world and pin medals on his breast for services rendered, but fail to find him a means of livelihood in the aftermath of war, what happens? Will he fold his arms and patiently await the problem to solve itself? Or will he not use the only means at his disposal to make his unhappiness felt.[62]

But the government's fear that the hunter guards would demand more rights if officially recognized went beyond mere speculation. In May 1947, one thousand hunters in Osogbo, organized as the Union of Hunters, petitioned the government to increase the allowance of 2d. they received. What appeared worrisome to the district officer of Osogbo was the tone of the letter and the hunters' internalization of their significant role within the society. By emphasizing their importance in helping to ward off burglars and "evil spirits, wild bears, maniacs etc.," the hunters appeared to be arrogating more power to themselves. They even threatened to "cease watching and guarding" the town if the native authority did not meet their demands for better pay.[63] The most difficult situation for the government was therefore how to allow the hunters to operate within some constraints, yet without being recognized as government employees entitled to better pay and benefits. The practice in most parts of southern Nigeria was to impose an "informal" and involuntary levy to pay for the service of the hunters. The more the government disconnected itself from financial matters, the more it retained its power to punish misconduct and abuse of power delegated to the hunters.

Third and most important, the government expressed its reluctance to allow the hunters actually to carry firearms by issuing "a no gun on patrol" policy.[64] This policy was unacceptable to the hunters. The government's reservation was based on the assumption that the hunters would abuse their authority by shooting indiscriminately and engaging in extrajudicial killings. While affirming that the hunters' presence would help mitigate violent crime, the resident of Oyo Province warned them to "realise that if they shoot burglars or others in the supposed protection of property they will be arrested and tried for murder or manslaughter as the case may be."[65] But the resident was not merely attempting to mold his personal belief into official colonial policy. Rather, the following section of the criminal code on self-defense clearly limited the rights of people to protect their property: "It is lawful for any person who is in peaceful possession of any moveable property, and for any person acting by his authority, to use such force as is reasonably necessary in order to resist the taking of such property, provided that he does not do harm to the trespasser."[66] The "no gun on patrol" directive exposed the hunters to the danger of being shot by thieves, who were equally aware of the directive that hunters should patrol unarmed.[67]

But incidents of abuse by the hunter guards justified the government's stance that they should not carry firearms.[68] In three different cases during the nights of October 26 and 27, 1940, the hunter guards in Ogbomoso shot at three people in "self-defense." The casualties of the events included one Ogundare Ajao, who was severely wounded by two gunshots while searching for his lost horse. Two others died.[69] The hunters involved were later arrested and tried. One was convicted for manslaughter and sentenced to nine months in prison; a second was convicted for unlawfully wounding and sentenced to one month; the third was acquitted on grounds of self-defense.[70] Cases of this nature created tension between district officers and local chiefs, who were often accused of not taming the excesses of the hunters. Reacting to this particular case, the *Soun* of Ogbomoso reminded the district officer of a recent robbery during which thieves cut off the breast of a woman and at "three different occasions shot at those who tried to foil them from carrying out their wicked design."[71] He pointed out that the hunters needed to be armed for self-defense and that the "no gun on patrol" policy was unacceptable to them. Sensing the possibility that the government might outlaw the hunter guards, he accepted full responsibility for their misdeeds, while assuring his district officer of compliance with their unpopular order.[72]

Aside from unlawful killings, the hunters were frequently accused of using their position to terrorize their perceived enemies under the guise of policing the community. In his petition to the district officer of Osogbo, one Labanji pleaded with the government to stop hunter guards "armed with guns" from threatening his life. He did not want to be "killed for nothing for I have many enemies among them."[73] In addition, a newspaper report about hunter guards in Olorunsogo, with the headline "Village Is Harassed by Night Hunters," labeled the guards "terrorists" and an "organised armed gang" who "go out by night, armed with machetes, dane-guns, and clubs spiked with six-inch nails." The alleged leader of this group was a bus station tout.[74] Other problems of using night guards bordered on fraudulent financial practices. In Badagry, for instance, a writer (A. I. Balogun) decried that the annual payment of 6s. levied on each household, for the maintenance of night guards generated an annual total of £1,600, a sum far above the £250 required. He suspected fraud by the town council and advocated that the citizens themselves, not designated night guards, should "sacrifice" their time by guarding their community.[75]

Therefore, the biggest challenge of using hunters to police communities was reconciling their unjust violence against innocent victims with their useful role of fighting crime.[76] It would appear that most communities saw the excesses of the hunters as an inevitable evil they had to put up with as they weighed the available options for their security needs. Prevailing approaches included constant oversight of the power given to the night guards, in response to the evolving security situation. After supporting the institutionalization of a night-guard system (the Ashogbon Police Force) in Lagos in 1941 because of the increase in crime attributable to the wartime emergency, the government was forced to outlaw the system in 1946 following complaints about the force's excessive and criminal activities, which included impersonating the NPF, extortion, illegal arrest and detention, and extrajudicial killings.[77]

The case of Ikorodu in 1955 can help explain this contradictory situation that the use of hunter guards created. A wave of armed robbery swept through the ancient border town when the government disbanded the hunter guards after they shot and killed one Bolaji Kasali. A front-page report in the *Daily Service* stated that armed robbers attacked thirty houses and removed property estimated at £700 in just one week. The story gave further insight into the mode of operation of the armed bandits: "On getting into the rooms of their victims, [the robbers] warned the inmates to choose between their lives and their property. All the people had to do was to allow the burglars to have their way in order to save their lives." So pronounced were the activities of the robbers that "no body considered this township a safe place to live. . . . Nobody comes out after 8 p.m. Otherwise the night marauders might kill him."[78] A public protest of about five hundred people was organized to call the attention of the government to the security situation in a town that had only twelve policemen. Only three were on night duty. The situation had not changed four months after the *Daily Service* crime report was published. This prompted a powerful editorial, titled "A Grave Menace," decrying the "reign of terror" as "disgraceful" and "dreadful" and demanding that the government reinforce peace and security in the town that had been rendered desolate by armed robbers.[79]

Rather than helping reduce gun violence, the policy of "no gun on patrol" created a serious legal tussle. Not only did it discourage hunters from guarding communities because of the incessant charges of criminal liability brought against them; it appeared to have empowered the thieves, whose activities grew more threatening. In one instance, the chiefs of Ikoyi in a petition attributed the escalation of armed robbery in their community to the banning of hunters from patrolling at night following a shooting incident.[80] By the late 1940s, the government in the Western Provinces revised its policy on hunter guards. Of the new rules, the most cogent was allowing the use of firearms. Hunters were officially permitted to use firearms only in self-defense. They were admonished not to use a gun "against a suspected person merely because he runs away and does not answer a challenge."[81] The policy eliminated the use of uniforms—approved by some native authorities in Ondo Province—to further emphasize the hunters' unofficial status as security agents. To prevent extrajudicial killings, hunters had to take suspects directly to the police station, not to the head of the community or chiefs, as was their usual practice.[82]

The "no gun on patrol" regulation seemed to have been put in place to protect colonial officers, not Nigerian citizens. Homicide caused by indiscriminate use of firearms during patrols was not considered as critical a matter by the colonial administration as the killing of its officers, who feared the conglomeration of gun-bearing hunters for any purpose. The government worried that enemies of the state, especially some dissident chiefs, could use the hunter guards to undermine the peace. In the view of some officers, the patrolling of hunters in the dark hours of the night tended to militarize the community—a situation that could easily degenerate into violence during important periods such as tax collection season or the settlement of land, boundary, and chieftaincy disputes.

Gun Accidents and Everyday Fears

Colonial newspapers, official government documents, and court records provide vivid insight into the circumstances under which gun accidents took place.[83] These circumstances ranged from reckless handling of firearms during ceremonies and hunting to everyday encounters with lethal weapons. The *Nigerian Pioneer* newspaper sympathized with the "parties concerned" in the death of a boy steward of a European staff member of John Holt named Caddock, who was killed while trying to hand a revolver over to his master in Itori in December 1914. Critical of the horror of the event but trying to be objective, the newspaper reported that available evidence suggested an accident, not a willful killing.[84] Even the courtroom, the citadel of colonial legal power, was not immune to gun accidents; in April 1942, a Calabar court messenger mistakenly pulled the trigger of a gun during a cross-examination.[85] The identities of people involved in gun accidents also varied widely—from experienced gun bearers like hunters to novices like another African steward of a European who in early 1942 unknowingly pulled the trigger of his master's double-barreled gun while loading it into a taxi, killing the driver in the process.[86]

Gun accidents seemed inevitable—a firearm, like any other mechanical tool, could malfunction. But many an accident (especially among educated elites who owned shotguns) happened because an owner was not required to know how to use the lethal weapon before obtaining a license and buying it. Even Dane guns, whose use was regulated by a number of complex social customs related to age, social status, and initiation into the hunter guild, were often misused. Dane guns were particularly prone to abuse by individuals and families trying to impress their community with the loudest noise during a ceremony or festival. Eyewitness accounts attributed gun accidents during ceremonial shootings to excessive loading of gunpowder in a quest to produce the loudest sound possible. The heavy charge of the powder was capable of bursting the barrels and wreaking havoc among shooters and spectators alike.[87] In other instances, as P. Amaury Talbot demonstrates in his description of gun firing during the New Yam Festival among the Efik, gun accidents took place because of alcohol consumption by the firers.[88] The harm caused by gun accidents varied from minor injuries to serious ones, even death. Ian Brinkworth described the fatal capacity of the Dane gun, which did not require a license to bear by 1948, in his usual sarcastic manner: "Owners of Dane guns frequently blew their own heads off, a regrettable occurrence which often happened when the lethal weapons were being fired in salute to a distinguished visitor.... No license was needed to decapitate yourself with a Dane gun."[89]

Except in a few cases, such as that of a mentally ill man who killed his "promising young" son in Umuahia in 1941, sources provide limited information about the true mental status of the health of gun assailants.[90] Indeed, the criminal justice system rarely took into cognizance the mental state of people accused of murder or manslaughter. But published accounts of gun violence attributed to mental illness of African soldiers reveals some of the least appreciated aspects of colonial military service and the experience of men who helped the British to maintain colonial rule. These sources suggest that mental illness among African solders was tied directly to the problem of racism and the poor welfare of these soldiers during service and after demobilization.⁹¹ And this problem was as old as the history of the colonial military force. In a particular case recorded in Zungeru around 1903, an African soldier being punished for "insolence" and "insubordination" escaped the guardroom with a rifle and ran to the parade ground "shrieking vengeance on all 'Batures' (Englishmen) calling on them to come and be shot." One of the soldier's shots pierced the door of the military base clinic. This "nasty occurrence" ended with "much relief" when the "unfortunate lunatic" was killed.⁹² Historians may never know the circumstances leading to this event, not only because it took place during the early years of the establishment of colonial rule in northern Nigeria, but also because the only documented evidence comes from Constance Larymore, a British wife of a district officer, whose narrative clearly favored the colonial establishment while demonizing the sick soldier.⁹³

However, two cases in the 1940s that took place in Lagos were recorded by both the government and nationalist newspapers and tried in a civilian court. The first involved Kofi Dagarti, a thirty-year-old Gold Coast national attached to the Yaba (Lagos) military base of the Nigerian Regiment of the RWAFF. Dagarti alleged that his superior, white officer Captain Eric Weller, aside from refusing to pay Dagarti's wife's allowances in the Gold Coast, inflicted severe punishment on him.⁹⁴ On April 14, 1945, Dagarti—described as a fair-complexioned man, five feet eight inches tall—escaped from the guardroom, took a rifle and fifty rounds of ammunition, and shot two people (one military, one civilian) while running amok looking for Weller to avenge his poor treatment. He fled the military base, roamed the streets, and intimidated people with his rifle. He remained at large until April 20, 1945, when three plainclothes detectives from the Criminal Investigation Department of the NPF arrested him at Iganmu-Apapa, several miles away from the Yaba military base, by disguising themselves as a palm-wine sellers. The tense atmosphere cooled off, and the print media, fervently critical of the NPF, showered an unusual accolade on the CID for exemplifying "courage and boldness."⁹⁵ Not even the legal representation by F. R. A. Williams, a renowned nationalist and lawyer, could save Dagarti from capital punishment. Published proceedings of the case and Williams's request that the court establish a distinction between accidental and intentional shooting, as well as his contention that Dagarti was "extremely provoked" by Weller, reveal the story of a mentally disturbed man, failed by the military he had served.[96]

The second incident further establishes the need for historians to invest scholarly energy in the untold hardships of men of the colonial military force. On November 10, 1944, Private Aston Iwolabo, after enduring "mock insult" from his African and European colleagues and superiors, dressed up in his military gear, obtained a rifle from the base armory, and killed four comrades. After the mass killing, he "discharged the last bullet in the sky and saluted the flag," and proceeded to the camp commandant to turn himself in.[97] Although the court acknowledged the "technical difficulties" of the Iwolabo case, he was, like Dagarti, sentenced to death by hanging. The government did not conduct a careful medical investigation into the mental state of these two convicts. It seemed the civilian court was more interested in preventing future "insubordination" that could jeopardize the security of the colony during World War II than in critically addressing the mental status and other motivations behind the soldiers' ordeals.

Not all cases of gun violence (including those related to mental illness) were easy to define as criminal acts, given conflicting evidence, or the lack thereof. For one thing, multiple interpretations of causation related to gun violence often conflict with the validity of claims made by eyewitnesses. This is particularly true in the case of suicide. In March 1954, the resident of Irolu town (near Shagamu) found the lifeless body of twenty-eight-year-old Bukola Oshuntade, a hunter and farmer, whose wife had just delivered a child, with gunshot wounds to his head. The community ruled Oshuntade's death as suicide, probably because he was known to be mentally ill and ashamed of the stigma associated with mental illness. The hunters' guild proceeded to conduct sacrifices to cleanse the community to prevent a reoccurrence and to appease the gods and goddesses—suicide in most Nigerian communities was considered taboo. The police thought it was murder and proceeded to conduct an investigation using undercover policemen.[98] In another case in 1949, the resident of Osogbo did not think that Raliatu, a thirty-five-year-old woman, committed suicide, unlike Oshuntade. Rather, a witness, her husband (Lamidi Amao), alleged that her son, eight-year-old Busari, accidentally shot her while she was cracking palm kernel. Amao was the owner of the Dane gun with which Raliatu was shot. But the police disagreed with the popular narrative of an accidental discharge, arguing that the boy "could not stretch the gun alleged shot by him," and went on to order an autopsy.[99]

Gun accidents, regardless of the circumstances under which they took place, were treated as criminal offenses, with attendant imprisonment and fines, and capital punishment if a victim was killed. When cases of firearms accidents came up for trial, the prosecution and judge attempted to evaluate the extent to which a gun user was reckless in handling the lethal weapon, the situation of the incident, the state of mind of the accused, and the charges filed by the police on behalf of the victims of the shooting.[100] When Tiamiyu Adeshina's Dane gun accidentally fell from his hand and fired while he tried to collect a cup of wine, causing serious injury to Joseph Oyeboke's toes in Igbobi in 1954, the court sentenced Adeshina to one month in prison or a fine of £2. He was made to pay a restitution of £1 to Oyeboke. Adeshina's punishment would have been heavier but for his hiring of a lawyer (J. A. Olaloye), given that the accident took place within the circumstances of a likely intoxication.[101] Similarly, Judge Evelyn Brown of Yaba magistrate court sentenced twenty-five-year-old Titus Akanbi to six months in prison for firing a loaded toy pistol at twelve-year-old Mushudi Sunmola, causing serious injury to the boy's left eye on New Year's Eve, 1954. Opinion was divided among colonial officers over the extent to which toy guns should be permitted.[102] The age of the accused did shape outcomes of legal judgments on gun accidents. In April 1953, a Benin court presided over by Magistrate J. S. Sowemimo sentenced fifteen-year-old Romanus Akwatu to six strokes of the cane for firing a pistol that wounded a child. Sowemimo would have received a prison sentence if he were sixteen, the age at which someone could stand criminal trial. The gun was confiscated.[103] On rare occasions, a person who committed a gun accident did not wait for prosecution. For example, Abdu Aska, a cook of a European development officer at Gusau, allegedly under the influence of alcohol, shot and killed his best friend, Ibrahim Sokoto, with his master's double-barreled gun. When a crowd who heard the gunshot assembled at the scene, Aska ran in and "blasted his own skull with a shot from the gun."[104]

The most documented and perhaps most common type of gun accident took place during hunting. Incidence tended to be high during the rainy season when the vegetation, which impedes visibility, was high and during group hunting. Hunting expeditions conducted at night in the thick dense forest were risky, so also the ones carried out around farmland during the day because of human movement and activity. Yet for professional local hunters, accidents were not merely a result of the failure to take adequate precaution before firing or bad weather or seasonal vegetation changes. Indeed, like most types of misfortune or bad luck, many people believed they were caused by supernatural evil forces—a product of the anger of the gods, such as Ogun, the Yoruba god of iron, hunting, and warfare.[105] After accidentally killing Ogunyale while hunting at Ogbomoso in June 1944, Omoyooye was reported to be "sobbing profusely and challenging the god of iron demanding what he had done to incur his displeasure" before shooting and killing himself.[106] People could incur the wrath of the gods and goddesses for many reasons. In some instances, hunters who refused to make the required sacrifice to the gods of iron or hunting, or to other deities associated with their families and clans, would be bewitched to make mistakes during hunting. In other instances, betrayals within the hunters' guild, according to a widely shared worldview, also led to accidents during hunting. Important life events of hunters, such as having children, getting married, and building a new home, were all connected with spirituality, which had the power both to enhance hunting expeditions or to lead to accidents.[107]

What is more, animals in the worldview of most people, were not mere mammals. Rather, they possessed powers capable of leading a hunter, if not well fortified with juju, to make shooting mistakes.[108] As we saw in chapter 2, professional indigenous hunters believed that marksmanship was not the only important factor in a successful hunting expedition. Hunters were expected to know the praise names and poems of animals, when and where to shoot at them, and the sacrifices to be performed before or after killing them.[109] Some animals were protected by customary laws—they could not be killed or eaten.[110] Thus, the indigenous ecology and cosmology fused with complex cultural norms about nature conservation that most professional hunters still respect today. Up to the 1930s, anyone who killed a python among the Enugu-Aka of Ache and the Aboovia of Awgu was required to perform a formal burial arranged by a priest. The dead python was placed in a grave with a chicken and gunpowder. The gunpowder was then fired, just as was done during the burial rites for a human.[111] Among the Isu-Ochi, a hunter who accidentally killed a leopard would forfeit his gun to the priest after performing a formal burial for the carcass.[112] Moreover, the forest was not just the abode of game animals—it was also home to countless spirits capable of causing havoc for any hunter not well fortified with juju. Attached to the butt of Dane guns and to the hunter's other gear were numerous good-luck and danger-evading charms.

Anthropological surveys and oral histories are replete with useful information about the connections between animal totems and hunting.[113] Among the Ekoi, for instance, all humans have an animal totem (the most popular of which were the elephant, leopard, and buffalo) capable of transforming into an animal at will. It was an abomination for hunters to kill animals of their own affinity. Some with greater supernatural power frequently transformed into animals to unleash terror on the community or their enemies. When the gods and human enemies wanted to punish a hunter, they turned his killed game into a human and invited the community to witness his ordeal. One day around the late 1910s, a new colonial officer in Oban District of the Ekoi people killed a buffalo that unfortunately was the totem of the community leader Awaw Anjanna. The totem buffalo was shot as it was drinking water in the stream near the officer's station. The wounded buffalo escaped into the forest and died two days later. About an hour before the buffalo's carcass was discovered, Awaw Anjanna was found dead in his hut.[114]

Colonial legal experts and police rarely acknowledged the customary interpretation of gun violence—even though they knew it was a vital part of indigenous cosmology.[115] Hunting accidents in criminal proceedings were shaped by the extent to which the culprits should be blamed for carelessness. If there was no counterclaim of murder or attempted murder from the family of the victim, the court usually proclaimed hunting accidents as manslaughter or attempted manslaughter. Punishment for most manslaughter cases ranged from one to twelve months in prison and a fine of £10. Yet hunting accidents became a criminal issue only if the case was reported to the government. In most cases, communities tended not to report cases to the government, if they were convinced that it was an accident. This is evident in the case of one Suberu Adesope, who accidentally shot and killed his cousin Ajibola while hunting in Saki in April 1948. Adesope reported the case to the family, but news reached the police as the community tried to bury the corpse "privately."

Few people involved in gun accidents hired lawyers, not only because their charges were high, but also because the few practicing lawyers confined their activities to the big cities. However, Adesope, who pleaded not guilty of murder, hired the famous Obafemi Awolowo to defend him at his trial.[116] Adesope was unlucky that the accident took place in Saki, a relatively large town not too far from Ibadan, where Awolowo's office was located. Many a hunting accident in a smaller community went unreported, because hunters knew it would involve a criminal charge in a colonial court, which they did not trust to deliver a right judgment. Rather, the hunters' guild, priest, and community leaders evaluated the circumstances involved using traditional methods of detecting crimes, including the swearing of an oath by the perpetrator, and then proceeded to perform sacrifices to prevent the reoccurrence of such a bad situation. If the killing was deliberate, the killer died mysteriously after taking the oath. If the killer was innocent, rituals were performed to reintegrate him back into the community.[117]

Aside from imprisonment, people convicted of the improper use of firearms lost their gun and license. Very few people contested this ruling. But in one unusual case, the complex interpretation of firearms law and punishment for infringement brought legal and political officers into conflict over a government officer. Oran Bayer, a police officer, accidentally killed a man with his personal shotgun while hunting deer in Gboko Division of Benue Province in 1940.[118] He was charged for manslaughter and sentenced to one month in prison. The presiding judge, Justice N. J. Brookes, ordered the seizure of Bayer's gun until he completed his prison sentence. The outcome of this case was based on the nature of the accident and Bayer's reaction to it. First, the medical examiner's report revealed that the victim was hit not by Bayer's bullet, but by a ricochet, which the court believed "in ordinary circumstances would not have proved fatal."[119] Second, Bayer came to the aid of the victim after the accident and ensured that he received prompt medical attention, transferring him from the poorly equipped local clinic to a regional hospital and footing the medical bill.

But D. M. H. Beck, the resident of Benue Province, was not satisfied with Brookes's ruling on Bayer's case. He accused Brookes of dealing with the case "leniently" and "deliberately" awarding a light sentence so that Bayer, a long-serving police officer, might not lose his pension.[120] But the political officers did not have the power to override the decision of a court; rather, after complying with the ruling that Bayer should have his gun returned to him, the district officer confiscated the gun eleven days later citing a section of the arms ordinance that empowered a colonial administrator, being the firearms-license-issuing authority, to revoke a gun license and then confiscate a gun.¹²¹ For Beck, the manslaughter charge was a different matter from the contravention of the arms ordinance, which empowered the political officer to revoke an arms license in the interest of public safety. The case not only created administrative controversy among the highest-ranking political and legal officers in northern Nigeria and Lagos; it further exposed some of the obvious limitations of arms regulations, which occasionally gave administrative officers more power than legal officers had in the administration of justice. When the legal and administrative tussle subsided, the chief secretary to the government upheld the decision of his junior officer that Bayer lose his gun and license.¹²²

Regardless of the circumstances under which gun accidents took place, both the colonial government and Nigerians believed that the incidence was too high and that something should be done to redress the situation. As we shall see in the next chapter, while the government worried about homicide, it was more concerned with the use of firearms to undermine public peace. For some Nigerian newspapers, gun deaths deprived the society of taxpayers capable of contributing to the development of the society. This is best reflected in an editorial in the *Eastern Nigeria Guardian*, part of which is reprinted as this chapter's epigraph. The editorial's engagement with conditions under which gun accidents took place complicated the solution and its impact on the society:

> In taking up these incidents, we are not unmindful of the fact that there are accidents which are unavoidable. We believe also that a man can't simply be carrying his gun about with a view to killing without cause. And we concede furthermore, that those who are responsible for these accidents might be people of unquestionable character. But none will disagree that by taking the good intentions of everybody for granted, and leaving these tragedies to be repeating themselves without a check, we may wake up one morning to discover that potential taxpayers and citizens of grand destinies had been snatched away from us through what we call accidents. This issue is not yet one which we can place in the hand of the government. Our native authorities can use their initiatives by exercising a limited control. We demand it.¹²³

Closely related to gun accidents is killing in self-defense. As in other classes of gun violence, killing in self-defense was a criminal matter if reported to the government. It posed difficulties for the police because, to get a court conviction, the prosecution had to establish the extent to which the murder was not premeditated. Most killings in self-defense tried by the courts took place during communal conflicts. Ideally, people arrested after a major riot that claimed lives would be charged with murder, which charge could be converted to manslaughter or disorderly conduct if the defense, aided by eyewitnesses, was able to prove that the death occurred under a chaotic situation or was not premeditated. The standard practice of the era was that a person accused or convicted of killing in self-defense, regardless of the circumstances under which it happened, lost his or her gun and license. But one case stands out. In October 1946, Frank Krumfor and his wife were embroiled in a domestic conflict in Brass. When Deinkoru Ekuneze, his nephew, intervened to resolve the conflict, Krumfor threw a spear at him. In self-defense Ekuneze shot and killed Krumfor and fled the scene. He was later arrested and charged with murder. In his judgment, Supreme Court judge C. N. S. Pollard, after "weighing the evidence of both the prosecution and the defence," ruled that Ekuneze killed Krumfor in self-defense. "Certainly you have to return the gun to the owner who was quite justified in using it," Pollard declared, when the police inquired about the fate of Ekuneze's gun. Even Ekuneze was surprised that his case went against the grain: "[He] was stupefied when ordered to leave the dock as he was not sure that he had been let off."[124]

Conclusion

Gun violence and accidents are the obvious negative consequences of the colonial Nigerian gun society. Not everyone would use a gun as a productive tool, such as for hunting and ceremonial shooting; many deployed it to unleash terror on fellow citizens and businesses, robbing them of their property. Armed robbery did not take place in isolation of other component of Nigerian society—its transformation was direct consequence of the firm establishment of colonial capitalism and a cash economy. As the spate of robberies intensified, Nigerians adopted means of dealing with the criminal acts. The debate over the use of hunter guards for policing communities challenged some of the dominant notions about colonial police. Moreover, gun accidents during ceremonial shooting and hunting were among the misfortunes of life in colonial Nigeria. Their increase and severity were tied directly to the institutionalization of guns for myriad economic, social, and cultural purposes. But the indigenous interpretations of the causes of gun accidents were not always in agreement with the colonialists' views because each group understood the physical and symbolic attributes of guns differently.

Notes

1. Achebe, *Things Fall Apart*, 124.
2. Ibid., 38–39.
3. Falola, "Brigandage and Piracy."
4. From *WAP*: "11 Men Face Charge of Armed Burglary and Theft," March 16, 1942; "Unlawful Possession Lands Man in Gaol," September 27, 1946; and "Judgement Given in Revolver Charge," December 23, 1946.
5. "Robbers Order Constable and Alhaji to 'Hands Up': Sensational Revolver Incident at Offin Road," *Daily Service*, November 9, 1946.
6. "Ten Rifles Disappeared out of Twelve after Store Raid," *WAP*, April 11, 1947.
7. "Six Witnesses Give Evidence in Epe Police Armoury Theft Case," *Daily Service*, April 11, 1947.
8. "Extract from the Minutes of the Owo Town Council Meeting Held on Saturday, the 30th May 1953," Owo Div. 22, NAI; "Ojo Onidimo Village Hunters to the Olubadan and Council," September 17, 1948, Ibadan Div. 1714, NAI; "Messrs. Adeyemo the Bale to the Ibadan Native Authority," August 24, 1953.
9. Tamuno, *Peace and Violence in Nigeria*, 81. See also Falola, "Theft in Colonial Southwestern Nigeria," 10.
10. "Three Burglars Will Be Hanged."
11. "Zaria Community Forms League against Gang of Terrorist," *WAP*, November 10, 1950.
12. "Highway Robbery at Enugu," June 2, 1954, OW.435/14, NAE.
13. "£2000 Removed after Shots," *Daily Service*, June 29, 1954.
14. "Crime Wave Hits Lagos," *Daily Service*, October 16, 1954.
15. "Armed Gangs Attacked Lorry," *Daily Service*, October 7, 1955.
16. "Police Nab Seven Aba Highway Men," *WAP*, April 28, 1955.
17. "Armed Bandits Loot Lorry from Police," *WAP*, April 28, 1947; "Two Armed Lorry Thieves Still at Large," *Daily Service*, April 29, 1947.
18. "Rich Trader Weeps after Discovery of Guns in Room," *WAP*, November 22, 1950.
19. "Battle Declared: Police vs. Smugglers," *Daily Service*, May 17, 1955.
20. Tamuno, *Police in Modern Nigeria*, 42–43.
21. "Battle Declared."
22. "Preventive Police Is Alleged to Have Shot Smugglers Fatally," *WAP*, December 1, 1942.
23. "Are Policemen Aiding Smuggling?" *Daily Service*, May 12, 1955; "Smuggling Menace in the East," *WAP*, July 22, 1954.
24. "Smuggling Rings in Nigeria," *Daily Service*, April 28, 1955. From *WAP*: "Seven Days in Jail for Smugglers," July 24, 1954; and "Man Shot Dead by Illicit Gin Dealers," July 5, 1954.
25. "Police Raid Robbers' Jungle," *Daily Service*, May 18, 1955.
26. *Nigerian Citizen*, July 24, 1957.
27. For the Ibadan and Lagos story, see Fourchard, "Urban Poverty, Urban Crime."
28. Mabogunje, *Urbanization in Nigeria*, 257.
29. Tamuno, *Peace and Violence*, 80.
30. Mabogunje, *Urbanization in Nigeria*, 261.
31. Olusanya, "Role of Ex-Servicemen."

32. Tamuno, *Peace and Violence*, 80.

33. "Our Soldiers and Discipline," *WAP*, August 29, 1941; from *Daily Service*: "Soldier Charged with Manslaughter Is Released on Bail," June 3, 1943; "Our Ex-Servicemen," January 6, 1947; "Ex-Serviceman Convicted for Murder of 30-Year-Old Man," February 17, 1947; "Ex-Soldier Kills Wife and Hangs Himself," February 8, 1947; and "15 Soldiers Are Convicted for Malicious Damage, Rioting, Affray and Assault," December 14, 1944.

34. "Police Find Revolver and Bren Gun in Ex-Servicemen's Home," *WAP*, September 4, 1950.

35. Markham, *Guns of the Empire*, 148–49; Grant, *Bren Gun*, 13.

36. "Veteran Is Arrested on Bren Gun Charge," *WAP*, January 9, 1953.

37. "Assistant District Officer of Northern District of Oshogbo to the District Officer of Ibadan," February 25, 1935, Oshun Division, 24/1, NAI.

38. Tamuno, *Police in Modern Nigeria*, 298–303.

39. Rotimi, *Police in a Federal State*, 160–168.

40. Ibid., 117–21.

41. From *Daily Service*: "Police Force and Policy," May 8, 1948; and "Police Recruiting and Training Must Be Revolutionised by H. O. Davies," September 22, 1948.

42. "Police Plans Information Room to Wave Off Crimes More Efficiently," *Daily Service*, October 24, 1947.

43. From *Daily Service*: "Ring 666," November 18, 1947; and "666: More Public Telephones Wanted," November 22, 1948.

44. "Minutes of the Meeting of the Oba and the Chiefs with the Commissioner of the Colony Held at Iga Idunganran on Tuesday the 12th of November 1946," Comcol, 1257, NAI.

45. Tamuno, *Police in Modern Nigeria*, 201. From *WAP*: "Man Is Jailed for Eight Months for Receiving a Stolen Pistol," May 20, 1943; "Gang of Burglars Tracked by Police," May 11, 1950; and "Apapa Burglars Ring Broken by Police," May 12, 1950.

46. "Man Held for Firing at Police Constable," November 23, 1946; "Revolver Case Ends," November 26, 1946—both in *WAP*.

47. "Three Burglars Will Be Hanged for Murdering Youngman," *WAP*, December 3, 1942.

48. From *WAP*: "Code of Conduct for the Policemen," April 2, 1954; "Helping the Police," February 25, 1954; "Preventive Police at Idiroko," June 5, 1951; "Thieves in Jos," December 28, 1953; "Inadequate Police Patrols for Yaba," November 14, 1953; and "Crime Wave—Challenge to Police," February 15, 1955.

49. "Helping the Police."

50. "Crime Wave in Lagos," *WAP*, November 25, 1952.

51. See application to employ hunter guards written by communities in southwestern Nigeria in the following files from NAI: "Hunter Guards," Oyo Prof., 2465; "Hunters-Use of as Night Guards," Ibadan Div. 1714; "Night Guards Bye Laws," Owo Div. 22; "Night Guides Bye Laws," Ondo Prof., 3271; "Night Guards," AG.350; "Hunter Guards," Oshun Div. 24/vol. 1.

52. For more on the vigilantes, especially after 1960, see Fourchard, "New Name for Old Practice."

53. "Chief Akintola, the Bada Olubadan, to the District Officer of Ibadan Division," August 30, 1948, Ibadan Div. 1714, NAI.

54. "Assistant District Officer of Northern District of Oshogbo to the District Officer of Ibadan," February 25, 1935, Oshun Division, 24/1, NAI.
55. Ibid.
56. "Bale of Ogbomoso to the District Officer of Oshogbo Division," October 15, 1940, Oshun Division, 24/1, NAI.
57. "District Officer of Ondo Division to the District Office of Owo Division," November 3, 1953, Owo Div. 22, NAI.
58. "Acting District Officer of Ibadan Division to the Resident of Oyo Province," October 11, 1948, Ibadan Div. 1714, NAI, emphasis added.
59. "Government Okays Society of Hunters," *WAP*, June 21, 1952.
60. "Acting District Officer of Ibadan Division to the Resident of Oyo Province," October 11, 1948, Ibadan Div. 1714, NAI.
61. "Protest by Ex-Servicemen in Lagos," July 20, 1947, Comcol 5/S.15, NAI.
62. "Ex-Soldiers Revolt against Tax," *WAP*, October 27, 1950.
63. "Union of Hunters to the District Officer of Ibadan Northern District, Oshogbo," May 13, 1947, Oshun Division, 24/1, NAI.
64. "District Officer of Ibadan to the Assistant District Officer of Northern District," February 28, 1935, Oshun Division, 24/1, NAI.
65. "Resident of Oyo Province to the Assistant District Officer of Northern Province, Oshogbo," September 6, 1939, Oshun Division, 24/1, NAI.
66. Ibid.
67. "Night Burglars Kill Coco Co. Sentinel," *WAP*, January 16, 1953.
68. "Condemned Night Guard Wins Appeal," *Daily Service*, April 14, 1943.
69. "District Officer of Ibadan Northern District to the Senior District Officer of Ibadan," December 13, 1940, Oshun Division, 24/1, NAI.
70. "District Officer, Ibadan Northern District, to the Honourable, the Senior Resident of Oyo Province," March 29, 1941, Oshun Division, 24/1, NAI.
71. "Bale of Ogbomoso to the District Officer," December 10, 1940, Oshun Division, 24/1, NAI.
72. Ibid.
73. "Labanji to the District Officer of Osogbo," June 2, 1938, Oshun Division, 24/1, NAI.
74. "Village Is Harassed by Night Hunters," *WAP*, December 12, 1952.
75. "Night Guards," *WAP*, June 29, 1954. "Night-Watchmen," *Daily Service*, July 18, 1945.
76. "Night Hunters by Councillor L. A. Oluwo," *WAP*, January 7, 1953; "Watchman Apprehends Three Night Burglars at Ereko," *Daily Service*, August 13, 1948.
77. "Ashogbon Police: Statement of Commissioner of the Colony," August 19, 1946; "End of Case against 'Ashogbon Police': First and Third Accused Found Guilty and Sentenced," September 24, 1946—both from *NDT*. "Allen Says Only Nigeria Police Is Genuine," *Daily Comet*, August 19, 1946; "Ashogbon Police Force Is Virtually Disbanded: Colony Commissioner Says They Have No Authority to Arrest," *Daily Service*, August 19, 1946; "Public Now Warned about Mock 'Police," *WAP*, August 19, 1946.
78. "Ikorodu Now Den of Rogues," *Daily Service*, June 4, 1955.
79. "Grave Menace," *Daily Service*, October 3, 1955.
80. "Olukoyi and Chiefs to the Olubadan in Council," May 9, 1949, Ibadan Div. 1714, NAI.

81. "Acting Resident of Oyo Province to the District Officer of Ibadan Division," October 2, 1948, Ibadan Div. 1714, NAI.

82. Ibid.

83. See from *END*: "Man Shoots Colleague in Mistake for Animal," April 17, 1941; "Mr. E. Igwe Is Killed by Friend While Hunting," July 21, 1941; "Illicit Gun Monger Is Fined £10 or 6 Months," October 31, 1941; "Hunter Shoots Man to Death," July 3, 1943; "Man Fired Gun Shots at His Wife Mistaking Her for Nocturnal Evil Doer," October 30, 1944; "Horse Boy Is Blown Up by Detective Gun," April 17, 1945; "Pandemonium Reigns and Cowards Flee as Gun Is Fired in the Open Court," November 3, 1945; "Hunter Accidentally Shoots His Friend and Attempts to End His Own Life," November 19, 1945; "Promising Youth Is Shot Dead by Insane Father with Gun Picked from a Hunter," March 1, 1946; "Hunter Mistakes Woman for Animal and Shoots," July 2, 1946; and "Man Who Shot His Nephew Is Justified by Court and Given Back His Gun," October, 31, 1946. See from *SND*: "Hausaman Shot by an Unknown Person," April 24, 1946; "Bullet Kills Young Boy," November 6, 1947; "Hunter Shoots at Man," March 13, 1948; and "Hunter Shoots and Kills Woman," May 6, 1948. From *WAP*: "14-Year-Old Student Is Shot Dead by Hunter," October 9, 1942; "Hunter Is Alleged to Have Shot Fisherman during a Scuffle," November 26, 1942; "Koko," June 15, 1943; "Oshogbo," November 8, 1943; "Canoe Men on Their Way to Onitsha Are Found Murdered," May 23, 1945; "Oshogbo," June 16, 1945; "Girl of 18 Is Alleged Killed by a Hunter," April 24, 1947; "Man Shot Down Dead on 'Oke-Okpe' Stage," January 22, 1947; "Chief Balogun of Ira Dies from Gun Shot," January 29, 1947; "Ogwashi-Uku," August 22, 1950; "Boy Gets Lashes for Shooting Child," April 27, 1953; "Gun Fires at Man as It Falls Down," February 4, 1954; "Man Is Found Shot Dead while Hunting," March 20, 1954; "Hunter Shot Dead by Fellow Hunter," March 25, 1954; "Toy Pistol Gets Him Six Months," January 4, 1955; and "Guard Dies from Own Bullet," December 1, 1955. From *Daily Service*: "Hunter Has Narrow Escape from Gun Shot," August 15, 1949; "Woman Alleged Shot Dead by Her 8-Year-Old Son," October 29, 1949; "Gun Wounds Man Who Fires It," April 11, 1950; "Man Mistaken for Animal and Shot Dead," June 7, 1950; "Inexperienced Hand Pulls the Trigger and Kills 18-Year-Old Girl," November 11, 1951; and "Is It Murder or Suicide?" March 5, 1954. From *Nigerian Pioneer*: "A Sad Case of Man-slaughter," December 26, 1924; "A Stupid Joke," February 13, 1925; "Unlawful Possession of Cartridges," February 5, 1926; and "Attempted Murder," February 12, 1926.

84. From *Nigerian Pioneer*: "Itori Shooting Fatality," December 31, 1914; and "Two Serious Accidents," November 24, 1922.

85. "Pandemonium Reigns and Cowards Flee"; "Man Is Shot Dead while Taking Bath at Night," *WAP*, April 10, 1942.

86. "Gun Accident in Mr. Biney's Yard Ends Life of Taxi Driver," *WAP*, February 21, 1942.

87. Oral interview with Mr. Manare Adegboyega Rasheed at Mamu on May 27, 2015.

88. Talbot, *Life in Southern Nigeria*, 266.

89. Brook, *One-Eyed Man Is King*, 86.

90. "Promising Youth Is Shot Dead."

91. Matthews made just one reference to the mental health of demobilized soldiers; see Matthews, "Clock Towers for the Colonized," 269.

92. Larymore, *Resident's Wife in Nigeria*, 107.

93. Ibid., 107.

94. "Middle-Aged Soldier Is Still at Large with Rifle and 59 Rounds of Ammunition," *WAP*, April 17, 1945. Another soldier, Danga Perri, committed suicide after shooting at many people at Obalende in Lagos. "Soldier Runs Amuck and Starts Shooting at Obalende," *Daily Service*, November 25, 1948.

95. "Soldier Bandit Is Captured at Iganmu Village with 31 Rounds of Bullets," *WAP*, April 20, 1945; "Soldier Who Ran Amuck Is Captured," April 21, 1945; "Solider Shoots European and African Comrades Dead and Runs into Bush at Yaba," April 16, 1945—both in *Daily Service*.

96. From *WAP*: "Soldier Kofi Dagarti Faces Murder Charge," April 23, 1945; "Preliminary Investigation Opens in Alleged Murder Charge against Soldier Kofi Dagarti," April 30, 1945; "Judge and Jury Hear Evidence of Seven Witnesses in the Dagarti Shooting Case," June 9, 1945; and "Yaba Killer Kofi Dagarti Will Face the Gallows for the Murder of Fellow Soldier," June 22, 1945.

97. "Young Soldier Is Found Guilty of Murdering Three Comrades," December 7, 1944; "Soldier Charged with Murder of 4 Comrades Is Condemned to Gallows," December 7, 1944—both in *Daily Service*.

98. "Is It Murder of Suicide?"

99. "Woman Alleged Shot Dead."

100. From *Daily Service*: "Sensational Revolver Shot Drama," July 6, 1943; "Six Men Are Sentenced to Death for the Murder of One Belo Akande," August 14, 1944; and "Unknown Hunter Shoots and Kills Two Men," August 16, 1944.

101. "Gun Fires at Man."

102. "Toy Pistol Gets Him Six Months."

103. "Boy Gets Lashes for Shooting Child."

104. "Hausa Cook Shoots His Own Friend," *WAP*, November 14, 1950; "Hunter Who Shot Friend Committed Suicide to Avoid Murder Charge," *Daily Service*, June 15, 1944.

105. Talbot, *People of Southern Nigeria*, 9:913–16.

106. "Hunter Who Shot Friend."

107. Oral interview with Mr. Aransi Yusuf at Akanran on May 30, 2015.

108. Meek, *Law and Authority*, 55.

109. Talbot, *Tribes of the Niger Delta*, 323–25.

110. Ibid., 254–55.

111. Meek, *Law and Authority*, 258.

112. Ibid., 254.

113. Talbot, *Life in Southern Nigeria*, 96–106.

114. Talbot, *Shadow of the Bush*, 86.

115. Hives and Lumley, *Ju-ju and Justice in Nigeria*.

116. "Hunter Shoots and Kills Woman," *SND*, May 6, 1948.

117. Oral interview with Mr. Akanji Olayiwola at Akanran on May 30, 2015.

118. "Oran Bayer to the District Officer of Gboko," July 18, 1940, SNP 23610/S.967, NAK.

119. "W. M. McCreery to the Registrar of Kaduna High Court," April 8, 1940, SNP 23610/S.967, NAK.

120. "D. M. H. Beck, the Resident of Benue Province, to the Secretary of Northern Provinces," August 5, 1940, SNP 23610/S.967, NAK.

121. "Secretary of Northern Provinces to the Chief Secretary to the Government," August 21, 1940, SNP 23610/S.967, NAK.

122. "Chief Secretary to the Government to the Secretary of the Northern Provinces," September 2, 1940, SNP 23610/S.967, NAK.

123. "These Gun Shot Accidents!," *ENG*, May 7, 1948.

124. "Man Who Shot His Nephew Is Justified."

7

"YOU ARE TO BE ROBBED OF YOUR GUNS"

Firearms Regulation and the Politics of Rights and Privilege

> Dane guns are the local equivalent of the gentleman's sword in the Middle Ages or the spear in Bornu. The country will be better without them, for it is not I suggest in the main a question of men who like the European sportsman keeps his gun to shoot game or burglars but of people who habitually go about armed, hence quarrels, fights, and trouble of various sort.
>
> —H. R. Palmer, acting lieutenant governor of the Northern Provinces, May 9, 1921[1]

> I have no doubt, in my mind, that the effective registration of existing Dane guns in Nigeria is impracticable, and it does not appear to be desirable to enact legislation which cannot be enforced, apart altogether from the possibility that grave unrest among the native population may be caused by pursuing a course of action which is not demanded by any circumstances which now exist or are likely to exist in Nigeria.
>
> —Donald Cameron, acting governor of Nigeria, 1921[2]

"We repeat, we are not in Europe but in Africa," a *Nigerian Pioneer* editorial emphasized as it criticized the government for its ineptitude toward firearms control following the shooting of the lawyer Moronfolu Abayomi at the court premises of Tinubu Square in Lagos on August 25, 1923.[3] The practice of comparing Nigeria with Europe featured prominently in the print media and popular rhetoric of colonial modernity. While Europe remained the yardstick for measuring the progress of Africa, it was also the reference point for any misfortune that local critics believed was characteristic of their model or idealized modern society. But beyond the politics of comparative modernities, Abayomi's murder shocked the Lagos elite community, not only because it took place at the court premises, the citadel of colonial judicial power, but also because of the unusual motivation for the crime. Duro Delphonso, a popular Lagos entrepreneur from a "good and respected family," while being led to the prison following his conviction for committing arson on his home and business in order to defraud his insurance company, shot Abayomi with a revolver, then immediately shot himself with the same gun—the coroner's inquest on the incident established.[4] While Abayomi died from excess bleeding from his bullet-damaged lungs while being transported to the hospital, Delphonso was hospitalized, refused to accept treatment for his wounds, and died on August 31.[5] The motivation for the shooting was obvious to the people involved—Abayomi had presented evidence leading to Delphonso's sentencing. *Eleti Ofe*, a Lagos bilingual newspaper described the shooting as "unparalleled in the annals of Lagos" and rightly predicted that "it will be difficult to obliterate it from the pages of history."[6]

Delphonso's ordeal did not end with this murder-suicide.[7] When the Salvation Army decided to conduct his burial rites, after his church (the Wesleyan Olowogbowo) had turned its back on his corpse, the *Nigerian Pioneer* wrote another editorial reinforcing a Yoruba custom that a person who commits suicide must be buried far from the community—in the bush to forestall a reoccurrence.[8] Yet the *Nigerian Pioneer*'s critique of Delphonso's burial arrangement appeared to be in contrast with the mood of his friends and admirers. At least ten thousand people, reported the *Eleti Ofe*, witnessed Delphonso's burial procession, amid cameras of varying sizes, "a pomp befitting the funeral of a Caesar, a Lincoln or a Garibaldi," and the enchantment of the performance of Lagos Eyo masquerades.[9] Nicknamed "Alapafon" (the unrepentant murderer), by the *Eleti Ofe*, Delphonso not only committed suicide but also murdered a member of one of colonial Nigeria's most powerful families; hence he did not deserve a respectable burial—the *Nigerian Pioneer*, the mouthpiece of a section of the divided Lagos elite community contended. Abayomi was the son-in-law of Sir Kitoyi Ajasa, the first Nigerian to receive British knighthood and a pioneer in the legal profession. Labeled by adversaries such as nationalist Herbert Macaulay as a British "collaborator" for his pro-government stance on many political issues, Ajasa, the proprietor of the conservative *Nigerian Pioneer*, was the true model of a colonial educated elite whom the British sought for Nigeria—imperial subjects raised in "Yoruba aristocratic tradition and of a Victorianism."[10] Abayomi's marriage to Oyinkan, Ajasa's daughter, was barely three months old when the incident happened. Seven years after the death of her first husband, Oyinkan remarried, this time to the physician Kofoworola Abayomi. The new couple would later become popular politicians, helping to shape the contours of nationalism and gendered politics of colonial Nigeria.[11]

If Abayomi's murder divided the Lagos elite community, it disturbed the basic assumption about elites' access to arms of precision—only the "illiterate" Dane-gun users in the villages would commit gun violence. It was inconceivable in the 1920s that an elite like Delphonso would commit a homicide with a gun. Moreover, Delphonso did not have a license to bear the revolver he used for committing the suicide-murder. Yet this case, like many others discussed in the preceding chapter, could lead one to conclude that the British government did not seriously deliberate on the need to revise its firearms laws. Conversely, the liberalization of nonprohibited firearms came through a series of policies and laws aimed at regulating gun use across time, region, social class, and situations. But the colonial Nigerian gun society was a paradox. On the one hand, trade in firearms including gunpowder helped the colonial treasury through taxes and permit fees paid by users and trading firms. On the other hand, gun violence, regardless of its intensity and the people involved, represented just one consequence of the consolidation of a gun society. Gun-control debates thus involved maintaining a difficult balance between economic considerations and the dangers that firearms posed to public order. The most important debate about Dane guns, in particular, revolved around the failure of the government to implement compulsory registration and to have reliable data about the number of guns in circulation. Although serious political unrest by rural communities bearing Dane guns did disrupt the peace, the British remained firm about the efficacy of their superior machine guns to uphold order. Much of the antipathy by some colonial officers toward the use of firearms, regardless of type, was informed by the assumption that Nigerians could not be responsible with firearms.

If the political, ethnic, and religio-cultural diversity of Nigeria shaped the spread and popularity of firearms of different types, it also informed the debates and policies on regulation. Thus, while the regulation of Dane guns, the most popular firearms in the country, occupied the attention of southern administrators, that of shotguns, pistols, revolvers, and rifles dictated the tempo of gun politics in the North. Yet there were more arms of precision in the South than in the North. But southern administrators paid limited attention to the regulation of arms of precision until the early 1950s because of the assumption that the educated and traditional elites posed a limited threat to public peace compared to the "illiterates" who used Dane guns. Northern administrators, more than their southern counterparts, believed that Nigerians in their jurisdictions could not be trusted to make wise use of shotguns, among other classes of firearms.

Let us examine the regional disparity and changing phases of firearms regulation politics between 1900 and 1960. First, we will focus on the control of Dane guns in southern Nigeria until 1948, when the government declassified them nationwide—thus lifting the requirement that Nigerians register or renew the license for any Dane gun. Next, we will devote specific attention to the control of arms of precision in northern Nigeria. Then we will engage how the Enugu colliery shooting sparked a new wave of gun law reforms throughout the last decade of colonial rule in Nigeria.

Debating Dane Guns in Southern Nigeria

By the third decade of the twentieth century, the number of Dane guns in circulation and the socioeconomic significance of this class of firearms were so visible as to prevent the reversal of gun liberalization, as some colonial officers advised. The government's projection that the Dane gun would bring in significant revenue through the payment of annual license fees did not pan out. Few people close to government offices renewed their licenses to avoid arrest, prosecution, or loss of their guns. Blacksmiths across the country produced Dane guns in contravention of the firearms law, while the big trading companies (UAC, CFAO, and John Holt) sold thousands to people who did not have a license to bear firearms. The companies were far more proactive in enforcing the regulation on the sale of shotguns, pistols, revolvers, and rifles than on Dane guns, which brought them significant profits because of their popularity.

Much of the debate about control of Dane guns in the early 1920s centered on the enforcement of compulsory registration and annual licensing. Two contrasting scenarios emerged. While registration would significantly increase government revenue, especially in southern Nigeria, where an estimated five hundred thousand Dane guns were believed to be in circulation, it might provoke armed resistance against the government. Governor Hugh Clifford, unlike many of his subordinates, was not willing to enforce compulsory registration of Dane guns, which he believed "would cause discontent, hardship, and unrest." He admitted that Dane guns and gunpowder "are necessities for the rural population."[12] Realizing that relations between Nigerians and the colonial government would deteriorate in the advent of forced registration, the resident of Benin Province suggested that the native authorities and chiefs, who were closer to the people than any colonial officer, could help with the exercise. But gun control was a significant security issue, which most colonial officers did not want to delegate to the chiefs. Not only could the chiefs turn against the government; they could also be in danger for serving as the puppets of the British. "Criminal prosecution for breach of the law would also be extremely difficult to carry out," the resident of Benin submitted, on possible unrest following any attempt to enforce compulsory registration using the native authority.[13]

For the lieutenant governor of the Southern Provinces, using the native authority to register the guns would present other problems such as "extortion" by the chiefs and "blackmail" by the people. His conclusion was based on the everyday crisis of administering justice in the native courts, where chiefs were often accused of extortion in influencing the course of justice. He believed that firearms registration must proceed by first "gaining the confidence of the natives" and convincing them they would not be targets of confiscation. The secretary of the Southern Provinces spoke from experience—previous attempts at registering Dane guns in Abeokuta and Oyo provinces were "practically a failure." He went on to tie the troubles involved with registration of Dane guns to the familiar practice of grouping Africans into different levels in the ladder of civilization: he insisted that if it was hard to register arms in Abeokuta and Oyo, even with the help of the chiefs, it would be harder still to conduct the exercise among the peoples of eastern and central provinces, whom he classified as "less sophisticated." Like his colleagues, he believed that compulsory registration would cause "serious trouble all over the country" and create opportunity for critics of colonial rule to allege, "You are to be robbed of your guns."[14] The resident of Ogoja viewed the proposed project from a purely administrative perspective. For him, registration of an estimated ten thousand firearms in his area of jurisdiction would "occupy a very large portion" of a district officer's time.[15]

The comments of H. R. Palmer, the acting lieutenant governor of the Northern Provinces, echoed the position of most northern officers, who more than their southern counterparts abhorred the use of firearms by locals in their region. Their position was informed largely by race—that is, by the notion that firearms (regardless of type) as one of the symbols of European racial superiority must never be in the hands of Nigerians. Moreover, they assumed the so-called martial race of northern Nigerians was more violent than southerners. Unlike his southern counterparts, who highlighted the significance of hunting to people's livelihood, the lieutenant governor of the Northern Provinces thought that the use of Dane guns for "hunting, defence, etc. is unimportant," and a stricter control of firearms would only have adverse effects on the culture of firing guns during festivals, which be believed was "unnecessary in a peaceful and settled country." He recommended that the government should make buying of Dane guns "extremely difficult," that only important chiefs should be allowed to use firearms for "ceremonial purposes and festivals," and that customs duties on Dane guns should be "very high."[16]

The resident of Warri Province, another anti–Dane gun advocate, argued that contrary to the well-received knowledge that Dane guns were important necessities for the livelihood of hunters and farmers, they were used mainly in interethnic conflict. He believed that the government would be able to manage the foreseeable crises emanating from complete prohibition and that effective registration of Dane guns was possible if government officials could take the time to oversee it. Regardless of the incentives provided for registration, the resident affirmed, the government should not expect all gun owners or even half of them to register their guns. The benefits of prohibition, he wrote convincingly, would justify the loss of government revenue derived from import duties and other levies imposed on traders and importers. The last of his overlapping recommendations was for the restriction of the gunpowder trade. He believed that the use of Dane guns would decrease and that people would return to using poisoned arrows (which he considered less dangerous than Dane guns), if an import restriction was imposed on gunpowder. If Nigerians could survive during the acute shortage of gunpowder during World War I, they would do well without it in peacetime, he submitted. Deliberation over changing the core philosophy of Dane gun possession as a right also sufficed. The sponsor of this idea, the resident of Ogoja Province, wanted the government to treat the "primitive" flintlock like the shotgun, the possession of which was counted a privilege associated with social class.[17]

Not all colonial officers believed that Africans were irresponsible handlers of firearms, or that the negative consequences of gun use should drive prohibition. One of the few dissenting voices of the period was that of the resident of Calabar Province. He agreed with his colleagues and superiors that it would be difficult to enforce compulsory registration of arms, and that the army, not the regular police, might be needed for the purpose. But unlike his colleagues who tried to delegitimize the importance of firearms, or view them mainly from the perspective of colonial security and order, the resident believed that farmers needed protection from dangerous animals such as leopards and bush cows. He said the only "misuse" of Dane guns he had observed in his twenty-two years of service in the region were accidental shootings by hunters "due to carelessness in firing before clearly sighting animals." He viewed Dane guns as "harmless," "except in close quarters [range]," and believed that the number of gun accidents that claimed lives was "small."[18] Another dissenting voice came from the resident of Onitsha, a province with an estimated population of two million. He believed that "thousands of Dane guns are in the hands of peaceful people" who use their guns mainly for "protection, sports, and hunting for livelihood."[19] But his main concern was that the prohibition of Dane guns could compel Nigerians to return to poisoned arrows, which most colonial officers, including Lugard, believed were more dangerous than the flintlock guns. The resident was speaking from experience—he was involved in two expeditions during the conquest of the Igarra region and saw the devastation caused by poisoned arrows.[20] Regardless of the diversity of opinion about the registration of Dane guns in the 1920s, colonial officers seemed to agree that force would be counterproductive and that the government must exercise "extreme diplomacy" in dealing with the matter.[21]

Throughout the 1920s and 1930s, Dane gun laws continued to be haphazardly enforced, based on the popularity of the firearms and the pattern of relations between administrators and the communities under their watch. Few colonial officers policed the blacksmiths who made and repaired guns. However, Nigerians who committed accidents or homicide with their guns would lose them. The total prohibition of Dane guns in an entire community was a measure temporarily imposed after incidents of major unrest against the government. When the situation returned to normal, people were free to continue to use their guns. People whose guns were confiscated by the government could get a local blacksmith to make another one for them or buy one from the European firms.

The last major attempt to overhaul the Dane gun culture came in 1942, when Attorney General H. C. F. Cox put before the Legislative Council a bill that would grant free permit to every owner of a firearm who was "considered [a] proper person." But such persons would have to obtain a license to use the firearm. For the first time in the history of firearms regulation politics in Nigeria, the government tried to differentiate between a "license" and a "permit"—terms that had historically been used interchangeably. The bill established a confusing difference between gun rights—that is, a "license" to bear firearms—and a "permit," or the need to have one. In the past, the permit or license gave an individual the right to use a gun. Cox believed his proposed amendment to the arms ordinance would help solve the long-standing problem—"to ascertain exactly where and in whose custody" guns were.[22] The novelty of this idea was defeated by the equally long-standing consideration of the impact any radical change in Dane gun culture could have on relations between the government and Nigerians. The end to the debate over the Dane gun came in 1948 when an amendment to the arms ordinance removed it from the class of nonprohibited firearms that required either license or permit.

Northern Nigeria and the Arms of Precision

The difference between northern and southern Nigeria, as scholars have firmly established, transcends the diversity of geography, topography, and weather in the two regions. Cultural, political, and religious disparity shaped by the precolonial history of state- and empire-building were not only visible; they informed many of the administrative politics of the colonial government. Historians are familiar with how the separate evolution of northern and southern Nigeria crystalized into the crises of the independence movement in the 1950s and nation-building challenges since independence.[23] But they are largely unaware that the British administration of gun control laws was also shaped by the cultural and political differences between the North and the South. When Lugard, among the early colonial administrators, allowed educated Nigerians to own rifles, shotguns, pistols, and revolvers, the so-called arms of precision, it was the southerners who took advantage of his policy. The idea of a shotgun as a marker of class distinction was entrenched mainly in the South. Few northern traditional elites had shotguns or pistols; firearms (of all types) were more common among southerners, whom the British believed were more "enlightened" because of their positive reception to Western education. Southern administrators did not begin to take the regulation of shotguns, rifles, and pistols seriously until after the Enugu colliery shooting, which revolutionized the politics of gun control.

By the second decade of the twentieth century, the unprecedented movement to the Northern Provinces of southerners (owing largely to the railway), who went to take up jobs in the government establishment as clerks, teachers, and railway workers, diversified the "indigenous" population in the North. Southern immigrants not only brought their Bibles and practices such as alcohol consumption considered "unholy" by the Muslim northerners; they also came with their guns. In places like Zungeru, Zaria, and Kaduna, according to a 1912 report, southern immigrants were allowing their "illiterate" northern hosts to use their shotguns.[24] The government could not monitor the shotguns in circulation because many owners either did not have licenses or did not renew them on a yearly basis. This new development compelled northern administrators to review their gun laws. Existing firearms law applied to residents of the region defined as "natives" of northern Nigeria. But the new southern immigrants did not qualify to be defined as "native" of northern Nigeria. Thus, the government could not legally revoke their licenses or confiscate their guns.

Hence, an amendment to northern Nigeria's Firearms and Ammunition Proclamation of 1910 redefined the term *native* to include anyone from "tropical Africa which shall mean and include all that part of the African continent lying between 20th degree N. Latitude and the 22nd degree S. Latitude." It prohibited the possession of shotguns, rifles, and pistols, among other types of arms of precision, by the natives, which now included the southerners who had brought their arms with them from the South or bought them from trading companies operating in the North. They were required to submit their firearms to any political or law-enforcement officer, or return them to the seller for reimbursement.[25] The new amendment, however, provided concessions related to social class, meant to please the traditional elites: first-, second-, and third-grade traditional chiefs, with the approval of the governor, would be allowed to bear a shotgun.[26] A public notice on this new regulation clearly introduced racial bias—"only persons of European descent would be given a permit to bear a rifle."[27]

But this double standard differentiating between native Africans and "persons of European descent" came with occasional problems, and enforcement was far from perfect. In a number of cases, people who did not properly fit the category of "persons of European descent" attempted to manipulate their identity to satisfy the government requirement. In June 1925, F. Stuart Campbell, who had lived in Kano for twenty-four years, serving for ten years as a railway station master, applied for permission to bear a rifle for his planned trip across the Sahara. Records are not explicit about Campbell's actual racial identity—he was variously described as "admittedly descended from African stock" and as having "ancestors [who] have lived in Canada for several generations."[28] Campbell was probably of mixed racial descent. His case raised an important point because he claimed he was not a native, even though he had lived in northern Nigeria for more than two decades, but a Canadian national and British subject.[29] Because he was not European, or a person of "European descent," he was not qualified to bear a rifle. The station magistrate ruled that he was a native but recommended that he be licensed to bear a rifle because he was well known in the community.[30] The Campbell case was not by any means an isolated one. The colonial government's confusing racial classifications, based on numerous, sometimes conflicting, sociopolitical and economic purposes, regularly led to disputes. On several occasions, residents of Lebanese descent, among other non-Europeans in Nigeria, were classified as "nonnatives" even though they were born and raised in the country.

The 1910 amendment to the firearms ordinance did not produce the anticipated result of helping to monitor the amount of arms of precision in circulation. Rather, it drove possession of arms underground. Several northerners and southerners, including people classified as "educated," continued to keep their guns. A fair system (similar to that which obtained in the South) that allowed "responsible natives" to have guns appeared more like a first step toward controlling access to all guns. The 1921 amendment gave the following groups and individuals the opportunity to have guns: (1) government employees with fifteen years in service; (2) chiefs, "whose good behavior and loyalty to Government have been proved by fairly long acquaintance"; and (3) employees of notable private firms with long years of service who were recommended by their employers. Members of those categories would lose their gun license if they were dismissed or left the service of their employers. Chiefs would lose their license in the event of conflict with the government.³¹ Although this new regulation mirrored what obtained in the South, it varied in some respects. For instance, the number of years in government service was not a requirement to bear arms of precision in the South until the mid-1950s. By the late 1920s, however, the criterion of length of years in northern government service was removed, providing all civil servants instant access to shotguns. This new regulation did produce some anticipated results. The acting resident of Ilorin Province withdrew the shotgun license of Usumanu, the emir (chief) of Pategi, when he was deposed in January 1931 for stealing public funds, practicing pawnship, imposing double taxes on his people, and concealing population figures, which were utilized in determining taxation.³² The emir, ruled the acting resident of Ilorin Province, "is not now a proper person to have a gun."³³

Contemporaneously, a gun-license quota based on the discretion of each resident officer came into vogue from the late 1920s and remained one of the distinctive features of arms regulation in the North.³⁴ The gun-license quota was based on the number of applications received, the level of "advancement of the applicant," and his community's loyalty to the government. The following gun quota in Zaria Province will suffice the politics of gun regulation: 147 (1930), 162 (1931), 142 (1932), 158 (1933), 142 (1934).³⁵ But the gun quota did lead to a buildup of arms over time. Between 1930 and 1934, 751 new arms of precision were registered in Zaria Province alone. Most of these licenses, which were not renewed on a yearly basis, went to two main cities, Zaria and Kaduna.³⁶

While refusal to register or renew a gun license was attributed largely to people's deliberate decision to break the law, in other instances, it was the result of ignorance of arms laws. The case of one J. B. Sagoe, a twenty-nine-year veteran of the Royal West African Frontier Force who renewed his personal shotgun uninterruptedly for ten years (between 1923 and 1932) can be used to further explain the problems of interpreting gun laws. In 1933, he was fined £10 and lost his shotgun license because he did not renew it for the year 1933. Sagoe claimed that he did not know he needed to renew his license because the gun was damaged and he did not use it throughout the year. Sagoe's final submission in his protest letter revealed not only the important role of guns in people's daily lives but also how some Nigerians interpreted criminal liability for an item they cherished so much: "Your Honour is doubtless aware what sport one gets in the use of a gun and how deplorable it would be for the owner to be deprived of being allowed to be in possession on account of a first offence."[37] Sagoe's plea for the reinstatement of his license did not sway the decision of the station magistrate of Kaduna, who ruled that "there are many more worthy applicants" for shotguns.[38]

European residents in northern Nigeria also shared in the blame for disobeying gun regulations. The European population in the North increased as the railway and mining sectors developed in response to the intensification of transport facilities needed to move Nigeria's solid minerals, among other items of world capitalist trade, to the coast of southern Nigeria. The foreign trading companies, which were operating in the North even before the twentieth century, expanded their businesses, bringing in many Europeans. The inspector general of police of northern Nigeria argued that the possession of a group gun license by European residents and illegal transfers of arms were the "two points which make it difficult to correctly check" arms trafficking. The law on the issuing of "group licences" was not clear to most administrators for a long time—many thought that one license was good for all arms.[39] But the law stipulated that each gun had to have a separate license. The practice of issuing group gun licenses not only prevented the government from monitoring the number of guns in possession of an individual; it deprived it of the revenue that would have accrued from additional annual gun permits.[40] Yet the government held that it was its responsibility to educate people about "one permit, one gun" and that many "honourable gentlemen" would not mind obtaining licenses for all their guns, if they knew "group licenses" were illegal.[41]

Another problem was the illegal transfer of arms between Europeans and Africans. On the minefield in Jos, for instance, the chief inspector of mines reported that a large number of Europeans who went on leave and did not return left or "transferred" their rifles, revolvers, and pistols to their African friends, employees, or "boys."[42] But another European expatriate, the chief veterinary officer, tried to allay the fear of illegal possession of these arms of precision. He argued that many of the abandoned guns in the hands of "ignorant" persons were "useless" because of lack of ammunition.[43]

Yet the problem of illegal transfer of arms was not just between Europeans and so-called irresponsible Africans. It also took place among Europeans. In one case, a European named Clarson was in possession of a revolver belonging to another European who went on leave around 1926 but never returned.⁴⁴ Cases of this nature came up regularly in the police records. The inspector general of police in northern Nigeria painted this picture of the circumstances under which such transfers happened in an October 1930 correspondence:

> Example 1: A brings three weapons into Nigeria at say Sokoto obtains three licences to bear arms, later he goes to Kano where he buys a gun and obtains a licence to bear it. This making four licences in all. Before leaving Nigeria he clears his arms at Ilorin, where he states he has only two weapons and produces his licences to bear them. The official there has no means of knowing that this is incorrect and issues a clearance certificate. It is only some considerable time later, when the copy of this certificate reaches the Central Register, that it is discovered that two weapons have not been accounted for.
> Example 2: B applied for clearance certificate at Ilorin before leaving Nigeria. He produces licence to bear four guns. Two of which he states he is taking out of the country and two he has left in charge of C at Jos. There is nothing to show the issuing officer that B's statement is correct. He may have disposed of them illegally or again he may have handed them to C as he states, but in this case there is nothing to prevent C illegally disposing of the weapons and denying that B ever gave them to him.⁴⁵

The boldest step to control the proliferation of arms of precision in northern Nigeria was taken in 1933 with the inauguration of a committee comprising the controller of customs, resident officers, and a government law officer. The committee was charged with the responsibility to consider "the adequacy of the present regulations in preventing arms of precision from getting into the hands of natives who are ignorant and irresponsible or into the hands of any person likely to use them for a nefarious purpose."⁴⁶ The findings of the committee did not contradict what top colonial officers already knew—many northerners held guns illegally. It affirmed that after initial registration, the government failed to follow up on yearly renewals, and to monitor the movement or transfer of arms from one person to another. The most important aspect of the committee's recommendations was the creation of a "Central Registry" for arms and ammunition brought into northern Nigeria and their subsequent history, which included transfer, export, and so on. Each province, the committee recommended, most have its own registry for arms of precision. The committee advised that all arms be kept in the provinces where they were licensed, to help keep track of guns within the region and from the South.⁴⁷ The last major recommendation was that the police, not political officers (that is, district or resident officers), should be responsible for issuing gun licenses. Other recommendations included (1) annual publication of the firearms laws, which "are not sufficiently well known to the public at large"; (2) abolition of gun transfer and public armory charges, to encourage people to report changes of ownership and to store their arms with the government whenever they left their location, a measure expected to improve people's confidence in the administration of gun laws; and (3) government registration of all unlicensed arms "without query" or punishment, to encourage gun owners who may "have been too lazy or careless" to renew their licenses.[48]

Administrators' reactions to the firearms committee's recommendations varied. For some, unanswered questions, such as the location of the proposed arms registry, were obvious. The resident of Plateau Province suggested the registry should be domiciled with the controller of customs, the office that granted import licenses for all guns brought into the country.[49] However, this would both additionally burden one of the busiest offices in the nation and remove the power to regulate arms from political officers closer to the people. Even the suggestion that each province should have a single arms-licensing office was problematic. If it was hard for district officers, who were closer to the people, to enforce registration and annual licensing of arms, it would definitely be harder to centralize arms control in the provincial headquarters. The suggestion that all gun owners be summoned to a public meeting on a yearly basis, at which all transactions, including the payment of annual licenses and settlement of gun transfers would take place, was unpopular: it was feasible only in small communities, and such an occasion would surely lead to riotous situations. Having a lot of gun bearers in one location could threaten public security.[50]

Another recommendation that all newcomers to any northern province, whether for a long or a short stay, first report to the resident of the province to declare his arms, was opposed for sounding more like a limit on the movement of people than of arms.[51] The 1933 committee thereby did more to expose the loopholes in firearms regulation than to solve the problems of proliferation of guns. Advocates of stricter gun control did not get what they wanted—a complete overhaul of the arms ordinance that would further restrict northern Nigerians' access to guns. Although administrators tried to draw a connection between the proliferation of guns and violent crime, the uneven distribution of crime across northern Nigeria made it difficult to justify the regulating firearms because of criminality.[52]

Throughout the 1930s, each resident and district officer addressed access to guns based on the circumstances unique to his station and the people involved. In the 1940s, international developments such as World War II provided further justification for stronger gun control. Worried about the impact of wartime mobilization, which intensified the government's expropriation of the country's human and material resources, the administrators stopped issuing new licenses, but they renewed existing ones and approved arms transfers between Africans who already had permission to bear arms.[53] This policy was relaxed when the war came to an end in 1945. The 1947 arms regulation that stopped private persons (regardless of race, class, or position) from directly ordering their shotgun cartridges from abroad, but required they be bought from local trading companies, appeared to be influenced more by economic than by security concerns.[54] This decision was not popular among colonial administrators and African elites, whom it affected most. Their criticism was legitimate from an opportunity-cost perspective. John Holt was selling one hundred rounds of shotgun cartridges for £4. 2s. 0d. If imported directly from Europe, the same item would cost about £1. 17s. 6d., customs duties included.[55] In all, although northern administrators paid more attention to the proliferation of arms of precision, none of their policies and regulations helped. Rather, illegal possession of guns intensified as new rules surfaced.

Gun Control in the Era of Decolonization

Much of the debate over arms of precision focused on northern Nigeria; southern administrators felt less threatened by the shotguns in the hands of the middle- and upper-class educated Nigerians. Cases like that of Abayomi were not only treated as exceptions; they had limited impact on colonial rule because they were not directed against the government.[56] However, the assumption that the educated group would not use their guns to undermine colonial peace did not last till the end of colonial rule in 1960, as the security implications of the Enugu colliery shooting led to a major transformation of the arms of precision laws. Indeed, the Fitzgerald Commission's strong conclusion that the labor agitation that led to the shooting of the twenty-one miners at Enugu was an industrial issue without political implications and incapable of undermining the peace of the state remained valid only to its members, all of whom were legal, not political, experts. For the colonial state, the shooting and its aftermath revealed the extent to which it had underestimated radicals among the labor movement, who were Zikists—members of a group whose message of militant nationalism appealed to the sentiments of the owners of arms of precision.

Government officials suspected a popular uprising against European residents might follow upon the Enugu shooting; just as the news that troops would be flown in from the United Kingdom suggested a lack of confidence in the local security force to forestall the impending violence.[57] "Would an explosion of violence follow?" Ian Brinkworth recalled the fear that gripped the colonial service as he worried about the safety of his wife and little children. To demonstrate the government's ability to control the impending unrest, Brinkworth's boss asked him to evacuate his family to Asaba, which was guaranteed to have better protection should post-Enugu rioting spread from the east across the river Niger to the western part of the country. Instead of attacking European residents, rioters looted foreign businesses, and a long chain of public disorder ensued, along with further casualties.[58] All told, Nigerian-British relations suffered irreparable damage as a result of the massacre.

In the aftermath of the Enugu colliery shooting, the colonial government commenced an overhaul of its laws on arms of precision with a January 1950 memo by the chief secretary to the government of Nigeria regretting the "considerable laxity" in firearms control. The senior administrative officer noted that the "accurate" registration of arms "is a matter of the greatest importance," and called for "strictest scrutiny" in licensing starting from January 1950.[59] Much of the problem of gun control was attributed to a lack of enforcement of licensing and annual registration. Indeed, the so-called important people who had arms of precisions were doing what the "illiterate" holders of Dane guns were criminally accused of—refusing to register or renew their firearms licenses. A new course of action created the Central Arms Registry, the first integrated national record of arms of precision in the entire country, domiciled with the Criminal Investigation Department of the NPF in Lagos. The chief secretary to the government, in a statement on this new initiative, was explicit about the issues at stake: "I am to emphasise that for reasons of security it is regarded as absolutely vital at this present juncture that *all* arms of precision should be registered and that accurate details of each weapon should be available."[60]

All political officers were expected to submit, on a monthly basis, data showing the names and address of gun owners, their occupation, race or nationality, and the type, manufacturer, and license number of their guns (figure 7.1). A public announcement for the registration of all unregistered arms was issued. But the police and district officers were directed to exercise "leniency" in dealing with those who willingly come out to register their arms, since the motive of the project was not to punish defaulters, but to monitor the guns in circulation.[61] The new gun-registration drive produced varying results across the country. By October 1955, the inspector general of police, R. J. P. Mclaughan, concluded that the system "has not proved altogether satisfactory."[62] A change therefore seemed inevitable. One important element was the manner of communicating gun data between the political officers across the country and the CID. Instead of allowing political officers to send the monthly returns of licensed arms directly to the CID, the new procedure stipulated that they must first be submitted by political officers to the superintendent of police in their respective provinces, who then forwarded them to the CID.[63] Intensification of border security to check the importa-

OWNER'S NAME	DEPARTMENT OR OCCUPATION	NATIONALITY	TYPE OF ARM	BORE	MAKER'S NAME	MAKER'S NUMBER	LICENCE NUMBER	DATE LICENSED
Mr. C.S.M.Davidson	P.W.D.,Ibadan	European	Pistol	.410	Smooth	2441	207961	8.1.51
" C.S.M. Davidson	- do -	- do -	Auto.Pistol	.45	Colt	1630902	207963	8.1.51
" - do -	- do -	- do -	Savage Rifle	.22	Savage St.Etienne/France	(No Number) 270370	207962	8.1.51
Chief E.A. Adeyemi	C.F.A.O.,Ibadan	African	D.B. Shot Gun	12			207964	9.1.51
Mr. Julius A.Adebayo	7,Ajasa St.,Lagos	- do -	D.B. Shot Gun	12	Greifalt & Co mit	28769	207965	9.1.51
" S.A. Bashorun	Barclays Bank,Ibn.	- do -	D.B. Shot Gun	12	Army & Navy	59350	207966	9.1.51
" Moses Oye	Orela's Crt.,Okotedo	- do -	D.B. Shot Gun	12	Francisae Iyarmes	28498	207967	9.1.51
" J.B. Adesanya	Nig.Railway,Ibadan	- do -	D.B. Shot Gun	12	Wamber Arms Coy.	133955	207968	9.1.51
" E. Adeyinka	- do -	- do -	D.B. Shot Gun	.12	Clarough & Johnstone	12809	207969	9.1.51
" D.R.Rosewear	Forest Dept.,Ibn.	European	Rifle	.22	B. S. A.	5794	207970	9.1.51
" - do -	- do -	- do -	S.B.Smoothbore Collector's gun	.410	Foreign Make	N11	207971	9.1.51
" K.R.Mac.Donald	- do -	- do -	D.B. Shot Gun	12	Ferguson	87826	207972	9.1.51
" - do -	- do -	- do -	D.B. Shot Gun	450	N11	2536	207973	9.1.51
" S.L. Dairo	Kobomoje Smp.Ibn.	African	D.B. Shot Gun	16	Roburst	97178	207974	9.1.51
" Saleh Saimon	Ogbomosho	Lebanese	Rifle	12	Macsme Model B	72141	207976	10.1.51
" David S. Moukarim	The Box Store Ibn., Kaduna	- do -	Long "	22	Minghester Repeater U.S.A.	5437	207977	10.1.51
" C.S. Moukarim	The Rex Cinema,L	- do -	D.B. Shot Gun	12	Fox Sterling Work U. A.	123024	207978	10.1.51
" A.S. Moukarim	P.O.Box 108,Ibn.	- do -	Auto Pistol	8.82	Lugard	M/N5119D	207979	10.1.51
" Sheriff Shaer	Lebanon St.,Ibn.	- do -	D.B. Shot Gun	12	Belgium	871374	207980	10.1.51
" R.S. Moukarim	- do -	- do -	P.M.Auto Pistol	9m/m	Parager Oberndov Carloxfalrik L	47266	207981	10.1.51

Figure 7.1. Sample of a gun register, 1951. Ibadan Div. 844, NAI.

tion of unauthorized arms continued and received a greater boost. Cargo going into Nigeria received more attention than ever before. Enhanced border control did produce the anticipated result. In August 1950, a Briton Richard Hamid, the managing director of UK-based Luxham Import and Export Company, was fined £900 for wrongfully declaring "steel tubing" allegedly used for making guns as "cycle accessories" in their consignment to their Nigerian business partner, Adetola and Ladipo Brothers, based in Lagos.[64]

Another gun regulation passed in the post-Enugu climate was the gradual removal and denial of gun import licenses to Nigerian traders. The government's position was that firearms imported by Nigerians could be used by "terrorists" for local violence. Moreover, private armories belonging to both the big European trading companies and smaller ones operated by Nigerians could potentially be robbed for arms. To reduce the number of private armories, the government simply began to decline permission to sell guns sought by Nigerian importers. But this policy did not go unchallenged. The case of E. I. Okoroigbo of Enugu reveals the extent to which administrators were willing to sacrifice economic gain for security concerns. In June 1951, Okoroigbo, a former agent of John Holt, who had apparently done some research on firearms importation approached his local authority, P. F. Grant, for the permission to import shotguns from Belgium.[65] Grant directed Okoroigbo to the controller of customs, who granted import licenses and tried to discourage him that "the turn-over of the business would inevitably be very small."[66] Instead of yielding to Grant's unsolicited counsel, Okoroigbo went ahead to obtain the permit to import firearms from the controller of customs.[67] However, he was denied the license to sell the guns in Enugu on the grounds that the small quantity of firearms he wanted to import did not justify having a private armory in the administrative capital of the Eastern Provinces.[68] In his last correspondence, which seemed to put the conflict to rest, Okoroigbo accused the government of denying him a license in order to safeguard the economic interests of European businesses trading in guns.[69] Although the government did discriminate against Africans in the granting of licenses for popular goods in order to protect the economic interests of big foreign firms, Okoroigbo's case had more to do with the fragility of the peace in the time immediately after the Enugu colliery shooting than with economic sabotage. The riots in some parts of the southeast had created significant unrest, and to allow Okoroigbo to sell shotguns in Enugu in 1951 appeared unwise from a security perspective.

The conditions in which people could lose their arms of precision or be denied licenses before 1950 were rare. But they became more frequent in the 1950s.[70] Gun owners who were associated with conflicts, regardless of the intensity and circumstances, regularly lost their firearms to the government. In one case, a district officer in Ilorin Province refused to renew the license of Augustine Obianwu Ugochukwu, a locomotive engine driver, because of his alleged involvement in a local dispute—even though he did not shoot anyone with his gun.[71] In his protest letter challenging the government's decision, Ugochukwu reinforced his socioeconomic status claiming that he paid the highest income tax in the Jebba Locomotive Shed of the Nigerian Railway Corporation. "It is all the more heart-rending," Ugochukwu petitioned, "when it is realised that those who are junior to me both in rank and length of service are allowed to fill up fresh forms for possession of shotguns." He highlighted his good conduct by self-identifying as a mentee of psychologist G. A. Dudley, who gave him "personalized coaching" on how "to be cool and tolerant in all aspects of human relationship."[72] Aware of the government's growing antipathy toward gun violence, Ugochukwu pointed out that he used his gun mainly for sport and did not belong to any political party accused of causing unrest.[73] His protest letters did not change the government's position, and his gun was later confiscated and deposited in the government armory.[74] Another case of gun-license denial involving an important king who was directly involved in party politics during the era of decolonization is worth narrating. In July 1953, the *Olowo* (king) Olagbegi II of Owo was compelled to deposit his revolver, which he had inherited from his late father, with his district officer at the height of an interparty and chieftaincy dispute in his town.[75] His application for a license to use the gun was later denied.[76] When the pressure to grant the king's request from the lieutenant governor of the Western Region, among other high-ranking Nigerian politicians, intensified in early 1954, the government gave two excuses claiming that Olagbegi was not "accustomed to handling a revolver" and did not justify his reason to want to possess an "arm of this nature."[77]

The government also began to enforce the violation of the gun-transfer regulation, which most people took for granted. Before the early 1950s, the underground gun market deprived the government of the 5s. fee required for completing a gun transfer.[78] People who wanted to follow the rules could not trace the history of their guns in the absence of the original gun license required for a proper transfer transaction. The matter of inherited guns was even more complex. When Olumuyiwa Ayobade of Owo Division died in 1950, he left three firearms (valued at more than £60), which his successors fought one another to inherit. The government was drawn into the family's crisis when it received multiple applications from members of the deceased's family asking for the transfer of the firearms. Similarly, when Bello Akanle II, the *Onirun* (king) of Irun in Akoko Division died, his successors applied to the district officer for transfer of the gun, which apparently had led to a family wrangling.[79] But unknown to the people involved in these two cases, they were legally obligated to deposit the firearms in the public warehouse, until a legal transfer was completed by an applicant who was also expected to have a license to bear arms.[80] But aside from the attempt to circumvent the law, cultural and financial factors inhibited the proper transfer of inherited guns. In some cultures, the estate of a deceased person cannot be properly inherited until several months or years after death.[81] Few people would pay 6d. per week to keep the firearm of someone deceased in a public warehouse while they followed inheritance customs.[82] Yet the government reserved the power to auction or destroy a firearm kept in the public armory if the owner was up to six months in arrears for storage fees.[83]

As decolonization intensified in the 1950s, so did violence across ethnicities, regions, and political ideologies. In 1953, the artificiality of the Nigerian state, characterized by the separate evolution of the North and South, manifested in the Kano riot. Victims of that horrific event included those who were mauled or injured by a variety of guns, including shotguns, that the British believed would only be used for hunting and self-defense against animals.[84] For the government, the Kano riot validated the need to intensify the security apparatus of the colony. If Nigerians could kill each other just because of disagreement over the termination of colonial rule, they would not hesitate to attack the Europeans responsible for their lack of independence, the government concluded. Hence, racial tensions that peaked following the Enugu shooting resurfaced. In central Nigeria, the *West African Pilot* reported, European residents were forming a local militia or "gun club" to defend their community against possible attack by Nigerians.[85] During a confrontation that could have degenerated into a race riot on June 29, 1953, two European men named Russley and Whitely, armed with automatic pistols, went to the African Club in Jos, firing shots into the air and wounding the club president, P. A. Yagba, while reportedly screaming, "We have been warned to go about armed against you Africans." After leading the police in a car chase, the gunmen were arrested and arraigned before a magistrate court.[86]

Inspired by the Kano riot of 1953 and its aftermath, the colonial administration passed another amendment to the arms ordinance in 1954 that gradually began to remove the power vested in political officers (i.e., district and provincial officers) to grant gun licenses and renewals. The new policy centralized arms licensing, entrusting a senior police officer in each province with the task.[87] Gun possession was a security matter that the government thought should be handled by the police, not the political officer. Yet a district officer was closer to the people under his jurisdiction than a superintendent of police who only became publicly visible during uprisings or disturbances. In several provinces, the district and resident officers continued to handle the administration of firearms law through the end of the colonial period.

But the most radical gun regulation of the 1950s was passed in 1956, when income and employment became the criteria for granting a license. As previously discussed, nearly all classes of "educated" Nigerians, from doctors to third-grade clerks, had guns, especially in the South. The 1956 amendment gave the following four classes of people (in the order of importance) eligibility to possess arms: (1) members of the armed forces and police, with the rank of a sergeant and above who had been consistently employed for fifteen years and were recommended by a lieutenant colonel or officer of higher rank (for the military) and the commissioner of police for member of the NPF; (2) government officers with annual taxable income of £600 or higher (a category that included very few Nigerians; as the provincial adviser of Ibadan advised his junior staff, "You and I know how scandalously few persons there are in Ibadan who pay tax on income of £600 and over");[88] (3) government workers with an annual income of £350 who had been employed for twenty years in government service and were recommended by their head of department; and (4) "Members of the public whose age and status, or record of long and loyal service in a responsible position, place them on par with persons" in the first three categories. After fulfilling these requirements, applicants also had to meet other conditions that did not exist before 1956:

1. He is fit and proper person to possess a shotgun
2. He is competent to use a shotgun

3. He is sufficiently intelligent to be safe with shotgun
4. He has adequate facilities for the safekeeping of the shotgun and has the means and authority to deny its use to unauthorised persons
5. He has *"positive need"* of a shotgun. Examples of "positive need" are: substantial business, to safeguard large sum in transit. Professional hunter. Sportsman, for bonafide game shooting. Farmer, for protection of crops against wild animals in areas where substantial crop damage is being caused by wild animals.

Restricting the demography of holders of gun licenses only reflected the relationship between social class and loyalty to the government; it did not associate different categories of guns with the havoc they were capable of causing (figure 7.2). The new regulation prevented civilians from possessing pistols, revolvers, and rifles. They could only have a shotgun. No one, regardless of class and income, could possess a 9 mm rifle. Only members of a rifle club (who were all Europeans) and the security forces could have a .303 caliber rifle, which had to be stored in a public warehouse. Each administrative unit throughout the country was given the freedom to decide its gun-license quota on the basis of the number of firearms users in its jurisdiction. In Ibadan Province, the resident did not approve more than thirty applications within six months. Applications in Oshun Division were limited to fifteen.[89] The gun-license quota was a tactical maneuver to remove guns from circulation (with limited outcry)—people whose annual registration was denied automatically lost their guns to the government.[90]

As revolutionary as the 1956 gun-control reforms were, they increased the work of the colonial administrators. Yet the government did not want to delegate the job of gun licensing to Nigerian staff for the fear of undermining the security of the project. Some gun-license applicants thus waited for months or even years without any response from the authorities.[91] So high was the volume of correspondence that the government adopted a generic letter of denial that read thus: "I have the honour to refer to your application of the [date inserted] and regret to say that I am unable to grant your permission to bear firearms."[92] This outright rejection, according to the resident of Ibadan Province, was meant "to save work."[93] Justification for denial was rarely given. But internal correspondence among colonial officers does reveal that some applicants were denied a license because the licensing of-

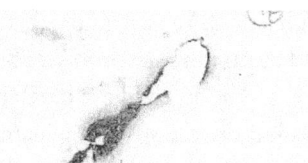

Figure 7.2. Sample of a gun license, 1937. Comcol 1, 5/S.16, NAI.

ficer was not convinced that they had a "legitimate" need to bear arms or "facility for safe custody" of their arms.[94]

The barrage of new gun regulations did not go over well with many gun owners. Indeed, the reactions of Nigerians who believed they were eligible to bear arms, having passed income and "behavioral" eligibility standards, show how gun owners internalized gun possession as a right, not just a privilege. One detailed reaction to license denial came from I. O. Bosede of Akure. Unlike several people who begged the district officer for a reconsideration of their denial, Bosede criticized the government for not making its new regulations known to the public through a press release and gazette notice. "Merely giving a reply to an applicant that no more permits are being issued," Bosede complained, "will not satisfy anybody and I am particularly not satisfied. . . . And I shall not be satisfied until I see it legislated that permit to bear arms should not be issued to anyone qualified for it."[95] Another petition, from a Muslim cleric, Chief Imam B. O. Olufowoshe, lamented, "There is nobody who had been privileged for this permit in my town. . . . Why?"[96]

While petition writing remained the conventional method through which Nigerians contested their "right" to bear arms, some gun owners were willing to take their fight to another level—seeking the help of lawyers. The use of lawyers to fight denial of gun licenses predated the 1950s. For instance, in 1937, Sokoto resident J. O. Ajaegbu, a John Holt clerk, hired a Lagos-based law firm, Alakija & Alakija Barrister at Law, to challenge the government's refusal to grant him a license to bear arms because his length of service with his employer was not long enough.[97] In addition, the activities of European law firms such as John C. Hughes of Kano and Michael Holden of Jos appeared in legal battles over arms possession in the 1940s.[98] But in the second half of the 1950s, lawyers' interventions increased as the government's aggressive gun-control agenda intensified. Most of the people who hired lawyers to write petitions for them had strong cases and political visibility. In one case in 1957, retired civil servant A. Akinajo hired Akinloye & Gomes Solicitors based in Ibadan to contest the confiscation of his .404 caliber rifle by the police.[99] It would appear that the district officer made an administrative error when he granted the permission to import the arm, because civilians by 1956 were not permitted to have such weapons.[100] After two months of correspondence and legal tussle, the acting deputy governor instructed the police to return Akinajo's £50 rifle.[101]

People who employed lawyers stood a better chance of arguing their case successfully with the government. But few people would write petitions, and fewer still would hire lawyers—not necessarily because they lacked the resources or did not know their rights, but because they did not want to attract the government's attention. An underground market for fake gun licenses arose in response to the government's stern policy.[102] A 1956 report demonstrated that gun importers worked with a group of forgers to issue fake licenses.[103] While some gun owners were aware of this fraudulent arrangement, others were not. In March 1953, James Aijiabhu, a lumber contractor based in Owo who described himself as "a novice about the bearing of arms" approached a friend about the procedure for obtaining a shotgun license. Two months later he obtained, through two Nigerian staff (J. Adeleye and Rufus Jemigbe) of the resident and district office, a fake permit to use a double-barrelled shotgun. But when Aijiabhu went directly to the government's office to renew the license in 1954, the district officer confiscated his weapon and went on to prosecute the staff members.[104] Had Aijiabhu refused to renew his license, like most gun owners, he might never have known he was in possession of a fake license.[105] But his case did not end with the conviction of the forgers. Instead of being issued a new genuine gun license, the district officer of Owo advised Aijiabhu to sell the gun to someone with a legitimate license. He refused and continued to plead for a gun license for another two years while paying the cost of storing his shotgun in a government warehouse (which ran up to £3) and going there "at interval to clean and oil the gun."[106]

Many gun owners simply refused to apply for a license or a renewal, knowing that denial would automatically lead to confiscation of their guns. In Oyo District in 1957, seventy-four gun owners did not renew their license for the year. Opinions among administrators were divided over the best means of dealing with this situation. Should the government continue to register defaulters who willingly applied for renewal of licenses after several years? From an economic point of view, some administrators in the North continued to renew licenses provided the owner was willing to pay a fine and the accumulated cost of the default years. In the South, especially the southwestern part of the country, administrators believed defaulters should be punished. "The intervening years does not condone the illegal acts of possessing the weapon unlicensed during that time," the acting divisional adviser of Oyo Division declared. He directed his staff to compel defaulters to provide "a good reason" for contravening the law before renewing their licenses.[107] He went on to raise an important factor—that change of address was partly responsible for nonrenewal of licenses. However, new legislation would be required to implement a requirement that every gun owner must update his residential information with the government.[108] This additional requirement was never implemented during the colonial era.

Conclusion

Gun liberalization did not mean that the colonial government no longer debated responsible use of firearms. As in other gun societies across the world, in Nigeria debate over firearms regulation was based on both the utility of guns and the impact of strict regulation on the fundamental assumptions that underlay gun use. Much of the debate over gun use also reflected the established notions among the colonialists that Africans could not be trusted with firearms because they were racially inferior and inherently irresponsible. It was also informed by the difference between Dane guns and arms of precision. The foundation on which gun liberalization was based was revenue centered—that is, revenue from gun licenses suffered a serious setback when Nigerians refused to pay fees for gun licenses. The lack of payment meant that the government could not monitor the number of Dane guns in circulation. By 1948, the government finally removed the Dane gun from the list of nonprohibited guns that required a license to use. Conversely, the intensification of efforts to control shotguns, among other arms of precision, was one consequence of the Enugu colliery shooting. From the early 1950s, the government began to pass a series of regulations that largely removed shotguns from circulation through compulsory annual registration.

Notes

1. "Memo on Arms Control by H. R. Palmer," May 9, 1921, CSO 26/03620, NAI.
2. "Memorandum on Arms Control by Donald Cameron, Acting Governor of Nigeria," March 1921, CSO 26/03620, NAI.
3. "Unlawful Possession of Firearms," September 21, 1923; "Possession of Firearms," December 14, 1923—both in *Nigerian Pioneer*.
4. "Coroner's Inquest," *Nigerian Pioneer*, September, 7, 1923. "Itopase Iku Loya Abayomi ni Ile Ejo Kekere," *Eleti Ofe*, September 5, 1923.
5. "Iku ati Sisin Duro Delphonso," *Eleti Ofe*, September 5, 1923.
6. From *Eleti Ofe*: "Lawyer Abayomi Was Shot Dead," August 29, 1923; Scrutator, "Revolver Shooting Sensation: A Plea for Justice," August 29, 1923.
7. "Tragedy in Tinubu Square," *Nigerian Pioneer*, September 14, 1923.
8. "Salvation Army and the Burial of Delphonso," *Nigerian Pioneer*, October 5, 1923.
9. From *Eleti Ofe*: "Miscellany," September 5, 1923; "Delphonso's Funeral," September 5, 1923; "Duro Delphonso (Alapafon) Fere Gba Aburo: Afi Olodumare Ti O Nbe Fo," September 12, 1923; and "Awon Loya Wa: Iku Loya Abayomi Fa Oro Jade," September 12, 1923.
10. Leith-Ross, *Stepping-Stones*, 86.

11. Aderinto, *When Sex Threatened the State*, chap. 1; Cole, *Modern and Traditional Elites*.
12. "Memorandum on Arms Control by Donald Cameron."
13. "Resident of Benin Province to the Secretary of the Southern Provinces," May 6, 1920, CSO 26/03620, NAI.
14. "Memorandum on Arms Control, NAI."
15. "R. H. J. Sasse, Acting Divisional Officer of Ogoja Division, to the Resident of Ogoja Province," December 24, 1919, CSO 26/03620, NAI.
16. "Memorandum on Arms Control," NAI.
17. "Resident of Ogoja Province to the Secretary of the Southern Provinces," May 12, 1920, CSO 26/03620, NAI.
18. NAI, CSO 26/03620, "Resident Officer of Calabar Province to the Secretary of the Southern Provinces," May 6, 1920.
19. "Resident of Onitsha Province to the Secretary of the Southern Provinces," May 4, 1920, CSO 26/03620, NAI.
20. Ibid.
21. "Acting Divisional Officer to Resident of Ogoja Province," January 10, 1920, CSO 26/03620, NAI.
22. "Arms Ordinance, by the Honourable, the Attorney-General, Monday 7th September, 1942," in *Nigeria: Legislative Council Debates*, 43.
23. Ikime, *In Search of Nigerians*.
24. "Acting Resident of Central Province to the Assistant Commissioner of Police of Naraguta," February 23, 1912, SNP 370/1910, NAK.
25. "Chief Secretary to the Government to the Resident of Naraguta Province," November 15, 1911, SNP 370/1910, NAK.
26. *Firearms and Ammunition Proclamation 9 of 1910 Schedule, Chapter 32* (Government Printer, Northern Nigeria), 48.
27. Gazette No. 3 of 1912 (T. B. Macaulay, Government Printer, Northern Nigeria), 60.
28. "Station Magistrate to the Senior Resident of Kano Province," June 8, 1925, Kano Prof., 76/1925, NAK.
29. "F. Stuart Campbell to the Station Magistrate of Kano," June 6, 1925, Kano Prof., 76/1925, NAK.
30. "Station Magistrate to the Senior Resident of Kano Province," June 8, 1925, Kano Prof., 76/1925, NAK.
31. "Secretary of Northern Province to Residents and Heads of Northern Provinces Department," October 20, 1921, SNP 17/1, 10260, NAK.
32. "Acting Resident of Ilorin Province to the Secretary of Northern Provinces," November 4, 1934, SNP 17/1, 10260, NAK.
33. "Acting Resident of Ilorin Province to the Secretary of the Northern Provinces," September 22, 1934, SNP 17/1, 10260, NAK.
34. "Northern Provinces Office Guide," 1930, SNP 17/1, 10260, vol. 3, NAK.
35. "Resident of Zaria to the Secretary of the Northern Provinces," May 21, 1935, SNP 17/1, 10260, vol. 13, NAK.
36. "Acting Resident of Benue Province to the Secretary of the Northern Provinces," August 15, 1935, SNP 17/1, 10260, vol. 13, NAK.

37. "J. B. Sagoe to the Chief Commissioner of the Northern Province," December 7, 1933, SNP 17/1, 10260, NAK.
38. "Station Magistrate of Kaduna to the Resident of Zaria Division," December 14, 1933, SNP 17/1, 10260, NAK.
39. "Acting Chief Secretary to the Government to the Resident of Naraguta Province," August 4, 1912, SNP 370/1910, NAK.
40. "Solicitor General to the Secretary of the Northern Provinces," September 6, 1935, SNP 370/1910, vol. 13, NAK.
41. "Gun Licences," SNP 2527/1921, NAK.
42. "Acting Chief Inspector of Mines to the Inspector General of Police," June 27, 1933, SNP 13619, NAK.
43. "Chief Veterinary Officer to the Inspector General of Police," June 16, 1933, SNP 13619, NAK.
44. "Acting Station Magistrate to the Resident of Plateau State," October 16, 1930, SNP 370/1910, NAK.
45. Ibid.
46. "Resident of Plateau Province to the Secretary of the Northern Provinces," March 24, 1993, SNP 13619, NAK.
47. "Resident of Benue Province to the Inspector-General of Police," June 15, 1933, SNP 13619, NAK.
48. "Resident of Kano Province to the Inspector-General of Police," June 20, 1933, SNP 13619, NAK.
49. "Resident of Plateau to the Inspector-General of Police," June 20, 1933, SNP 13619, NAK.
50. Ibid.
51. "Resident of Bauchi Province to the Inspector-General of Police," July 28, 1933, SNP 13619, NAK.
52. "Secretary of the Northern Provinces to the Residents of the Northern Provinces," December 8, 1937, BAU Prof., 1283, NAK.
53. "Resident of Kano Province to the Local Authority," September 9, 1941, Kano Prof., 302, vol. 12, NAK.
54. "Notice: Importation of Ammunition," *Daily Service*, March 10, 1947.
55. "Resident of Ogoja Province to the Secretary of Eastern Provinces," July 9, 1947, CSEP/85/8651, NAE.
56. From *Daily Service*: £5 For Possession of Live Ammunition," August 15, 1947; and "Man Fined £50 for Unlawful Possession of Arms," February 26, 1948.
57. "Troops from U.K. Will Be Flown to West Africa," *WAP*, November 28, 1949.
58. From *Daily Service*: "Looters in Aba are Penalised," December 9, 1949; "H.E. Imposes Press Censorship and Curfew in Eastern Provinces," November 28, 1949; and "Police Opens Fire on Onitsha Crowd," November 28, 1949.
59. "Chief Secretary to the Government to the Secretary of Northern, Western, and Eastern Provinces," November 25, 1949, Iba Div. 1/1, 65/1, NAI.
60. "Chief Secretary to the Government to the Secretary of Northern, Western, and Eastern Provinces," March 9, 1950, Iba Div. 1/1, 65/1, NAI.
61. "Chief Secretary to the Government to the Secretary of Northern, Western, and Eastern Provinces," November 25, 1949.

62. "Force Order: Registration and Licensing of Firearms by Inspector General R. J. P. Mclaughlan," October 1, 1955, Oshogbo Div., 157/4, NAI.
63. Ibid.
64. "U.K. Firm Fined for Exporting Gun Materials To Nigeria," *WAP*, August 17, 1950.
65. "E. I. D. Okoroigbo to the Local Authority," June 18, 1951; and "District Officer of Onitsha to the Resident of Onitsha Province," June 20, 1951—both in ONDIST, 20/1/1907, NAE.
66. "Local Authority P. F. Grant to Mr. E. I. Okoroigbo," July 23, 1951, ONDIST, 20/1/1907, NAE.
67. "Resident of Onitsha Province to Mr. E. I. D. Okoroigbo," August 18, 1951, ONDIST, 20/1/1907, NAE.
68. "Local Authority P. F. Grant to Mr. E. I. D. Okoroigbo," July 2, 1951, ONDIST, 20/1/1907, NAE.
69. "E. I. D. Okoroigbo to the Local Authority, Enugu," July 17, 1951, ONDIST, 20/1/1907, NAE.
70. "John Soke to the District Officer of Ondo Division," November 15, 1954, Ondo Prof., 51D, vol. 3, NAI.
71. "Resident of Ilorin Province to Mr. A. O. Ugochukwu," March 12, 1957, Comcol, 29, NAI.
72. "A. O. Ugochukwu to the Resident of Ilorin Province," April 25, 1957, Comcol, 29, NAI.
73. "Augustine Obianwu to the Chief Administrative Officer," April 5, 1958, Comcol, 29, NAI.
74. "A. O. Ugochukwu to the Resident of Ilorin Province," October 13, 1957, Comcol, 29, NAI.
75. "Olowo of Owo to the Divisional Officer," July 8, 1953, Owo Div. 64, vol. 1, NAI. For more on the Owo dispute, see, Albert, "From 'Owo Crisis.'"
76. "District Officer of Owo to the Senior Resident of Ondo Province," July 10, 1953, Owo Div. 64, vol. 1, NAI.
77. "Civil Secretary of Western Region to the Olowo of Owo," February 12, 1954, Ondo Prof., 1/1, 216A, vol. 1, NAI.
78. "R. F. Goldie to the Divisional Adviser of Oshun Division," May 18, 1956, Osun Div. 157, vol. 11, NAI.
79. "Akoko Federal Native Authority to the District Officer of Owo," June 22, 1953, Owo Div. 64, vol. 1, NAI.
80. "D. N. Mordi to the District Officer of Kano," June 23, 1956, Kano Prof., 302/S1, NAK.
81. Talbot, *Peoples of Southern Nigeria*, vol.3.
82. "James Ashaolu to the District Officer of Ondo," January 19, 1955, Ondo Div. 1/1, 51, vol. 6, NAI.
83. "Recent Amendment to Arms Ordinance Will Sanction Sale of Unclaimed Arms," *WAP*, April 29, 1944.
84. Brook, *One-Eyed Man Is King*, 165.
85. "Gun Club Is Reported Formed at Jos," *WAP*, June 30, 1953.
86. Ibid.

87. "Deputy Governor of Western Region to the Residents of Abeokuta, Ibadan, Ijebu, Benin, Ondo, Oyo, and Delta Provinces," October 8, 1954, Ondo Div. 1/1, 51, vol. 6, NAI.

88. "Provincial Adviser of Ibadan Province to the Senior Divisional Adviser of Ibadan Division," July 27, 1956, Oshogbo Div. 51, NAI.

89. "Resident of Ibadan Province to the Senior District Officer of Ibadan and the District Officer of Oshun Division," May 19, 1953, Oshun Div. 1/1, 1571/1, vol. 2, NAI.

90. "African Timber and Plywood Limited," March 7, 1957, Ondo Div. 1/1 51, vol. 10, NAI.

91. "A. W. Badaru to the Resident of Kano," June 28, 1955, Kano Prof., 302, NAK.

92. "Acting Administrator of the Colony to Mr. G. A. Oyerinde," September 29, 1954, Ike Div. 3 (2nd Accession), NAI.

93. "Resident of Ibadan Province to the Senior District Officer of Ibadan and the District Officer of Oshun Division," August 12, 1954, Oshun Div. 1/1, 1571/1, vol. 2, NAI.

94. "Office of the Officer in Charge of the Nigeria Police," May 30, 1957, Ilesa Div. 1/1 57, NAI.

95. "I. O. Bosede to the District Officer of Ondo Division," March 30, 1954, Ondo Div. 1/1, 51, vol. 6, NAI.

96. "Chief B. O. Olufowoshe to the District Officer of Owo District," June 1, 1954, Ondo Prof., 1/1, 216A, vol. 1, NAI.

97. "Resident of Sokoto Province to the Secretary of the Northern Province: Petition by Mr. J. O. Alaegbu," September 13, 1937, Kano Prof., 302, vol. 17, NAK.

98. "Michael Holden (Solicitor and Barrister) to the Local Authority, Kano," Received April 8, 1946, Kano Prof., 302, vol. 17, NAK.

99. "Akinloye & Gomes to the Governor of Western Region," July 17, 1957, Oshun Div. 157/5, NAI.

100. "Local Government Adviser of Oshun Division to Messrs Akinloye and Gomes," July 25, 1957, Oshun Div. 157/5, NAI.

101. "Acting Deputy Governor of Western Region to Messrs Akinloye and Gomes," September 28, 1957, Oshun Div. 157/5, NAI.

102. "Police Report of Fake License in the Possessing of Some People," June 11, 1955, Ondo Prof., 1/1, 216A, vol. 2, NAI.

103. "Olowo of Owo to the Divisional Adviser of Owo," July 27, 1956, Ondo Prof., 1/1, 216A, vol. 2, NAI.

104. "James A. Aijiabhu to the District Officer of Owo," November 29, 1954, Ondo Prof., 1/1, 216A, vol. 2, NAI.

105. "James A. Aijiabhu to the Resident of Ondo Province," January 3, 1956, Ondo Prof., 1/1, 216A, vol. 2, NAI.

106. "James Aijiabhu to the Registrar of Magistrate Court of Akure," February 13, 1956, Owo Div. 64/1, vol. 2, NAI.

107. "Circular: Renewal of Firearms Licences," February 13, 1957, Ilesa Div. 1.1, 57, NAI.

108. Ibid.

EPILOGUE
Guns and the Crisis of Development in Postcolonial Nigeria

The caption of a *Nigerian Observer* photo of two boys dressed in military gear and holding toy guns at a children's Christmas party in Benin City in December 1972 reads in part: "Children live in a world of their own and since the menace of the 'gbomogbomos' [kidnappers] who says children have not become security conscious."[1] This picture and caption do more to paint the image of a militarized postcolonial state and its attendant insecurity than to capture the true role of children in crime fighting (figure EPI.1).[2] Of greater importance is that the image fed public opinion that both adults and children were exposed to dangers. While adults were the main victims of armed robbery, which assumed a new dimension following the Nigerian Civil War (1967–70), minors suffered from the menace of child kidnappers.[3] There was no time in Nigeria's history that children were totally immune to abductors; but the petro-naira economy of the 1970s fueled ritual moneymaking, among other diabolic means, for which kidnapped children were supposedly used.[4] The representation of guns, crime, and insecurity in the print media, popular music (like Ayinla Omowura's commentary on child kidnapping), famous stage plays and literature, and other creative works in the 1970s further imprinted violence in the consciousness of millions of Nigerians.[5]

The causes of insecurity, one of the most potent manifestations of underdevelopment in postcolonial Nigeria, are easy to itemize. Failures of leadership and political and economic marginalization of much of the population gave birth to a teeming demographic of unemployed, miseducated young people capable of diverting their energies to activities that fulfilled

Figure EPI.1. Nigerian children with toy machine guns at a Christmas party in Benin City, December 1972. *Nigerian Observer,* January 3, 1973.

their immediate financial needs. Porous borders and the corruption of security agencies and traditional customs granted Nigerians illegal access to prohibited firearms to jeopardize the peace. Local blacksmiths took advantage of poor policing to perfect the making of prohibited firearms (especially handguns), which, though inadequate for confronting the state, could effectively unleash terror on unarmed Nigerians. Indeed, postcolonial gun regulations removed arms of precision only from people who owned them legally—armed robbers and terrorists, among other criminals, had near-unlimited illegal access to firearms far more sophisticated than pistols, revolvers, shotguns, and common rifles. The gun has remained the primary symbol of postcolonial political order, as it was in the colonial era. For it was through arms that military dictators and many civilian leaders came to power and maintained their illegitimate rule.

The proliferation of guns in postcolonial Nigeria, as elsewhere in Africa, can also be explained in terms of the changes in the physical and political geography of the world following the collapse of European imperialism after World War II. In the first half of the twentieth century, European nations respected mutual agreements about the international sale of prohibited firearms to their colonies. But after granting independence to their former colonies, they flooded the continent with weapons of war in the global struggle against Soviet influence, supporting one armed group against another during civil wars and other Cold War–inspired conflicts. Lack of proper disarmament and demobilization after each major domestic conflict meant that firearms remained in circulation decades after wars and were recycled for use in subsequent strife. Thus, firearms used to prosecute the civil wars in Liberia and Sierra Leone easily made it to Nigeria through elaborate trafficking networks, coordinated by notorious cartels and corrupt law-enforcement officers close to the main levers of political power. Trafficked war weapons, including assault rifles, such as Kalashnikovs (especially AK-47 varieties) and the newer Chinese-made Norinco Type 56s, light machine guns (e.g., Norinco Type 80s), rockets, tanks, ground-to-air missiles, and even fighting jets have been used by nonstate actors and groups across Africa to prosecute secessionist and terrorist agendas.[6] All together, the illegal firearms circulating in postcolonial Nigeria include those leased and/or sold by corrupt government or security personnel; those from past or ongoing conflicts in neighboring countries; those illegally imported into the country by importers with the aid of corrupt law-enforcement officers; and those from past armed conflicts, such as civil wars and insurgencies within Nigeria. This epilogue places the story of guns in postindependence Nigeria at the center of the crisis of nation building and underdevelopment. I briefly review the core developments from the 1960s that have shaped the possession of guns and the main individuals involved.

Gun Regulation in Postcolonial Nigeria

The argument that a gun society existed in colonial Nigeria as espoused in the preceding chapters is difficult to sustain in the postcolonial period as a result of the reconfiguration of access to firearms and notable structural transformations. The postcolonial leaders who inherited power from the British completed the process of removing legal possession of arms of precision from Nigerians, by first entrusting the power to grant gun licenses only to the executive, the head of state or president of Nigeria, "acting in his discretion."[7] The centralization of gun licensing was meant to frustrate the majority of Nigerians. But citizens who are close to the power structure in Abuja are still able to receive and renew licenses for arms of precision. When Abdul-Azeez Arisekola Alao, a popular Ibadan millionaire and loyalist of the dictatorial government of General Sani Abacha, was attacked by the students of the University of Ibadan in November 1998, four handguns were recovered from his entourage.[8] The guns disappeared into the mob and were never recovered. Fear increased that the guns would end up in the hands of student cultists who unleashed violence on the university community, as plainclothes security personnel infiltrated the student population looking for the culprits of Alao's attack.[9]

Public opinion was not sympathetic to Alao, who narrowly escaped lynching—for the people, his unruly treatment was justified on the grounds of his support for a cruel regime. But what primarily caught the attention of the public and the press was the fact that he owned four guns for personal protection—a privilege to which only a few Nigerians were entitled. When the public outcry about his alleged illegal possession of firearms intensified, Alao published copies of his gun license in the newspapers. This act of disclosure opened the eyes of many Nigerians to social privilege as it related to firearms, for very few citizens had ever seen a gun license. Nigerians of the 1930s, 1940s, and 1950s would not have reacted the way their 1990s brethren did on seeing the published gun license, for such permits were common in their day. Thus, the postcolonial state streamlined its definition of an "elite" for the purpose of gun bearing to only a minority of highly important personalities like Alao and top military officers. The status of the Dane gun remains the same—it is not a prohibited firearm, and Nigerians do not need a license to own and use one.

Other imponderable structural, economic, social, and cultural transformations since the 1960s have undermined the gun society that flourished in Nigeria in the 1920s, 1930s, and 1940s. Unprecedented "modernization" and the expansion of both Christianity and Islam have undermined traditional culture and religion, the crucial sites of ritualized and ceremonial shooting. The unprecedented urbanization and massive rural-to-urban migration has depopulated many rural communities, the main domain of the daily manifestation of traditional culture that upheld the colonial gun society. Ceremonies such as Empire Day and other commemorations that placed shooting at the center of imperial spectacle have been replaced by events such as Children's Day that rarely feature shooting. Except in military-related events like Armed Forces Remembrance Day and the burial of soldiers, ceremonial shooting connected to the main structure of political power has virtually disappeared. Gun noise is no longer essential to Nigerian life, as it used to be under colonial rule.

The huge increase in the population of Nigeria, from 55 million in 1963 to more than 150 million in the second decade of the twenty-first century, has had a devastating effect on the country's forest resources, such as game animals.[10] Except in a few government forest and game reserves, wildlife has virtually disappeared, reducing the significance of professional hunting and decreasing the use of Dane guns. Corruption of forest guards has led to unlawful killing of the few wild animals left.[11] The intensification of rural poverty in the wake of postcolonial economic crises and bad leadership has meant that fewer people engage in the forms of hunting that supported the gun society. With the depletion of the forest, many former hunters and farmers have moved to the city to engage in more "profitable" crafts or businesses, or to find work as laborers in construction. Many have become professional guards, securing the homes of rich people and businesses in the city. Their marksmanship and charms (*juju*) are relevant credentials, which make them in demand in the crime-ridden cities (figure EPI.2).

Although many communities depended on hunters for their basic meat supply in the colonial period, the depletion of the forest of such bushmeat, such as antelope and grasscutters, as well as the intensification of the cattle trade between north and south and the importation of processed turkey and chicken, now limit these traditional food sources to a less important place in the daily diet. The oral history I collected from Mamu and Alatamun villages in Oyo and Osun states in the summer of 2015 indicates that big bushmeat is not only becoming a rarer and smaller part of people's diets because of ecological change and deforestation; also, the meat of the few animals hunters do kill is more expensive than cattle meat, which is also more readily available. Today, bushmeats are considered delicacies, sold to "big" or "rich" people traveling across the highways that connect the evaporating rural communities with the big cities. So small are the bush animals like grasscutter that hunters dare not shoot at them at a close range, to prevent complete decapitation. Trapping with wires and cages is becoming increasingly dominant as a hunting practice, thus reducing further the use of guns. Worse yet, it is not unusual for village hunters of over twenty years' experience to have never sited a buffalo, to say nothing of a leopard.[12]

Figure EPI.2. The author with a locally made shotgun (with luck and protective charms on gun butt) during fieldwork at Alatamun village, Oyo State, June 2015. Photograph by Adeyemi Afolabi.

The cocoa plantation economy that drove the acquisition of guns for defense against animals and intruders has been overtaken by the oil economy. Improvement in road networks and transportation facilities mean that fewer people rely on firearms for protection from wild animals than they did with the constant trekking in the dense forest of the 1930s and 1940s. The limited use of Dane guns has also choked the international trade in gunpowder. Today, most hunters make their own gunpowder by mixing charcoal with sulfur, which is readily available in public markets, unlike in the colonial period. Hunters have continued to rely on blacksmiths for the shots or bullets they need.[13]

The Metamorphosis of Armed Robbery and Violent Crime after Independence

Contrary to popular belief, the rise in incidence of armed robbery in Nigeria did not begin in the post–Civil War era (after 1970). But, like other forms of criminality, the transformation of armed robbery beginning in the 1960s reflected a significant change in the core elements of Nigerian society. Nigeria inherited from the British a policing system that focused heavily on the exercise of political authority by the rulers. This was evident in the 1960s, Nigeria's bloodiest decade. Military coups took place in quick succession, centralizing and monopolizing the security state apparatus, and helping the elites to take and hold power. The leaders of the fragile independent state were concerned more with forcibly holding the disunited country together than with focusing on core elements of nation building such as the provision of education and welfare services to directly benefit millions of Nigerians. The quest for centralized power left the society to fend for itself; as a result, self-help criminality flourished as vast numbers of Nigerians were politically and economically marginalized. Corruption of law-enforcement and customs officers, among other classes of people whose work is central to public security, has its roots firmly in the colonial state, but the postcolonial political leadership has proved ineffective and reckless in monitoring the activities of its officers.[14]

The philosophy and mode of policing adopted by the NPF could not match the sophistication of Nigerian thieves of the 1960s and 1970s. In this period, the legacy of colonialism continued to haunt the NPF, whose firearms training was directed mainly toward confronting popular armed conflict against the state, not the demands of daily or regular policing of the streets and communities. It was common for NPF officers to police communities without their rifles in the 1960s and 1970s; the few policemen with rifles lacked ammunition to use them. Corrupt policemen even loaned their rifles to thieves, who not only mastered their use but also utilized gun noise to terrify and subdue communities. But unlike their colonial counterparts, who rarely shot their victims, the brutality of postcolonial armed robbers was not matched by their predecessors. The distinctive feature of armed robbery in the postindependence period was the increasing use of weapons of war, submachine guns, and rifles, and incessant police and civilian casualties. This is why many people assume that the "beginning" of armed robbery dates to the post–Civil War era, which was characterized by the proliferation of firearms.[15]

The identity and methods of operation of thieves like Isola Oyenusi who gained notoriety in the 1960s had a strong influence on future generations of armed robbers in the country. Born in 1945, the self-styled "Dr. Oyenusi" started his criminal career in 1965; he was arrested and sentenced to two years in prison when his gang attacked and stole £1,400 from a Lagos store the same year. After completing his prison sentence in 1967, his gang of four carted away £14,000 from a branch of Standard Bank of West Africa (now First Bank of Nigeria) and snatched a Peugeot for another robbery operation in which he was arrested for the second time. He was again sentenced to imprisonment. Oyenusi did not complete his sentence; he escaped to lead another operation in the faraway northern town of Maiduguri. Aside from robbing banks, Oyenusi's gang targeted vehicles carrying workers' salaries, killing people and police in the process. In November 1967, his gang waylaid a vehicle carrying cash by firing their rifles repeatedly from an abandoned car stationed at the Onigbogbo end of Ikorodu Road in Lagos. A chase by military personnel who heard gunshots led to Oyenusi's third arrest. He received a twenty-five-year sentence—among the longest of the era. Shortly afterward, he made his second prison break from the Kirikiri Maximum Security Prison in Lagos. In his last major operation in March 1971, Oyenusi, armed with a submachine gun and fifty rounds of ammunition, killed a police escort and removed £10,000 from the West Africa Household Utilities Manufacturing Company.[16] He was later caught, convicted, and killed by firing squad on September 8, 1971.[17]

Oyenusi's place in Nigerian crime and firearms history transcends his use of machine guns and killing of police. He and his fellow armed robbers of the era, such as Mighty Joe (Isiaka Busari), forced the state to revise its laws on armed robbery. During the colonial period, armed robbers were sentenced to death by hanging only if their operation resulted in a human fatality. They were mostly sentenced to short prison terms, as little as a few months or up to five years. One of the problems of the colonial prison system identified in a 1944 report by Alexander Paterson was the high rate of prisoner turnover. Short sentences, Peterson contended, did not serve as a deterrent and tended to populate the prison with inmates who felt comfortable living off the government.[18] The postcolonial state's attitude toward prison sentences for serious offences was a radical change from that of its predecessor. The first amendment to armed robbery law after independence, Decree 2: The Suppression of Armed Robbery Decree of 1967, allowed for a maximum of a life sentence for armed robbery convicts. But upon realizing that thieves could break out of jail, and acknowledging the increasing civilian and police casualties, the military government of General Yakubu Gowon promulgated Decree No. 47 (Robbery and Firearms—Special Provisions) of 1970 and set up the Armed Robbery and Firearms Tribunal (ARFT) to prosecute accused persons.[19]

The procedure and rules of the ARFT mirrored the militarized mentality of the Nigerian state during and after the Civil War. Its judgments could not be overturned by another court; only state military governors had the power to overrule them.[20] Although firearms were generally considered the most lethal weapon in the robber's arsenal, thieves caught with such offensive arms as bow and arrow, machete, cutlass, or spear were brought before the tribunal. This was the case of twenty-three-year-old Boniface Opurum, sentenced to death by firing squad for hitting Omada Osayi (who survived the attack) with a machete and a stick at Eyaen, near Benin City, in September 1970.[21] Unlike in the colonial period, when convicts received a death sentence only if their activities led to the loss of life, the ARFT pronounced a death sentences regardless of whether a fatality occurred. Condemned convicts were publicly executed by a firing squad. In Lagos, executions took place on a preannounced date at the popular Bar Beach amid a large crowd that assembled to witness the death of outlaws. Newspaper stories with such headlines as "As Mighty Bullets Silence 'Mighty Joe'" and pictures of convicts tied to a raised stalk, voicing their last words, added unpleasant color to the spectacle of public violence characteristic of military-era Nigeria.[22] Fifty thousand people, according to the *Nigerian Tribune*, witnessed the killing of Dr. Oyenusi and seven other condemned robbers in Lagos on September 8, 1971.[23] Another fifteen thousand, reported the *Nigerian Observer*, watched ex-federal soldiers Clement Olorungbamigbe and Ilesanmi Ojo die by firing squad at Akure in March 1972.[24] Between 1970 and 1976, more than four hundred armed robbers met this fate.[25] For the military government, armed robbers were competing with the state in the deployment of arms; its response thus mirrored a conventional military approach to armed conflict, utilizing maximum violence.

The government's projection that capital punishment would help stop the increasing wave of robberies did not materialize. Protests against the "uncivilized" and "undemocratic" manner of the firing squad and of prosecutions compelled the new civilian government of Shehu Shagari to overturn the ARFT in 1979. Prosecution of accused persons thus reverted to the regular civilian courts, which could impose capital punishment by hanging, but not by firing squad. When the military took over again in 1984, the ARFT and firing squads resumed operation.[26]

While punitive approaches to armed robbery varied across time, the failure to adequately address the main reasons that it flourished became more obvious. More and more rifles were falling into the hands of Nigerians who felt marginalized in a society where much of the massive income from oil revenue was being stolen or misappropriated by the ruling elites. The statistics of recorded robbery in the 1970s stood in stark contrast with those in the 1980s. Whereas 12,150 and 105,857 cases of armed robbery were recorded in 1970 and 1976, respectively, 271,240 and 311,961 cases came to the government's attention in 1982 and 1983, respectively.[27] Not even the N83 million budgeted for fighting crime in 1981 succeeded in abating the activities of armed robbers.[28] Much of this money, if not stolen by politicians and administrators, was not used appropriately to intensify policing through training and the provision of quality firearms to the police. Hopes for a greater future for Nigeria when the military government of Muhammadu Buhari toppled the highly corrupt and negligent civilian administration led by Shagari in December 1983 were short lived. Buhari's regime, which was already showing signs of respectability in the fight against corrupt practices, was removed in a "bloodless" coup less than two years after coming to power. General Babangida, who would become known as one of Africa's most notorious dictators, assumed office in August 1985 but lacked the legitimacy and discipline to combat armed robbery. Babangida's government reinstated punitive measures such as public execution of armed robbers. He also refused to address the problem of crime at the source through a systemic transformation of the society by massive investment in education, social service, and a concerted war against corruption. The era of the petro-naira in the 1970s would give way to a decline in revenues from oil and a serious economic crisis that led to the introduction of the structural adjustment program (SAP). This internationally imposed fiscal policy was popularly viewed as the equivalent of administering poison to a dying economy.[29]

A review of the biography of Lawrence Anini (aka "The Law"), among other notable armed robbers of the 1980s, is helpful in coming to terms with the realities of violent crime in Nigeria. Born in 1960, Anini gained fame for his mastery of the rifle and the legendary mythic power that rendered him invisible to law-enforcement officers. In the print media, sensationalized headlines such as "Anini: Jack the Ripper," "Anini: A Robin Hood in Benin," and "Armed Robbers Get More Bloody" spread his notoriety across the country and beyond, intensifying Nigerians' sense of powerlessness. What made Anini's activities especially brutal was not just that he killed and raped his victims but that he mauled policemen. Not even the popular belief that he was a "revolutionary class fighter" helping redistribute wealth by stealing from the rich and giving to the poor satisfactorily explains the terror he unleashed on residents and businesses in Bendel, Anambra, and Ondo states, where the government was forced to impose a dusk-to-dawn curfew. Following the prosecution and killing of two members of his gang of twenty-one by the government in October 1986, Anini vowed to kill a hundred policemen, fifty each for his fallen comrades. In the process he allegedly killed nine officers in six months, mostly in cold blood and without provocation.[30] The military government, which staked its legitimacy on the use of maximum violence, was embarrassed that it could not deploy its "superior" power to challenge the armed bandits. The government was clearly embarrassed by the popular saying that of the nineteen states in the country, Anini possessed three (Ondo, Anambra, and Bendel). In a national broadcast on October 1, 1986, General Babangida announced the reorganization of the NPF, to create new directorates at the national headquarters and seven area commands. Recognizing the already-established knowledge that Anini and his gang had infiltrated police intelligence, the new NPF reorganization transferred eighty senior police officers from Benin, bringing in new officers from the north of the country.[31] Eventually, on December 3, 1986, Anini was captured in a private residence in Benin City with eight "girlfriends." He and three of his associates were sentenced to death and executed in March 1987. His main police informant and arms supplier, Police Chief Superintendent George Iyamu, was also executed.[32]

The killing of Anini brought only temporary relief to the residents of Benin City, his main area of operation, and to police officers. But it did not change the core crisis of leadership and underdevelopment that made firearms available to people who used them for illegal purposes. The economic crisis of the 1980s roared heavily into the 1990s. The military government of General Abacha, like his predecessor's, focused on preserving its own power, thereby neglecting the needs of the populace. AK-47s, among other assault rifles from the years of civil war in Liberia (1989–97) and Sierra Leone (1991–2002), became more popular in perpetrating armed robbery than ever before. And thieves constantly tried to outdo their predecessors. The popular outlaw Olusegun Adeshina Kuye became a household name in the 1990s. His alias "Rambo" evoked the mental image of Sylvester Stallone (from the popular *Rambo* films) dressed in a bandolier, rapid-firing firearms ablaze, the epitome of superior gun masculinity capable of unleashing untold violence.

The approach to combating armed robbery in the 1990s intensified the militarization of the country. Each state established a combined police and military security outfit that patrolled communities, often unleashing violence on innocent citizens and carrying out extrajudicial killings. As in previous decades, the threat of capital punishment (by firing squad) did not deter the criminals. Nigerian customs, intelligence, and police remained corrupt as the government paid lip service to protecting the lives and property of the citizenry. The proliferation of guns, both homemade and imported, and their regular use by criminals outpaced the efforts of police. Not even the numerous vigilante bands, community policing groups, ethnic militias, and other concerned citizens could curb armed robbery.[33] Members of these groups, like the police, ended up killing more citizens than criminals. And like the police, they often were directly involved in the crimes they professed to be fighting.

The patterns of the 1990s held true into the new millennium. The promise of a better life for Nigerians that followed the reintroduction of democratic rule in 1999 did not materialize. Corruption in various shapes and forms has reached all-time high. As in previous decades, the NPF has continued to serve the elites and the power structure, leaving the populace unprotected. According to Parry Osayande, the chair of the Police Service Commission, of the 330,000 policemen and policewomen in Nigeria in 2011, 100,000 were attached to politicians, elites, and their foreign collaborators, leaving the rest to secure a country of more than 150 million people.[34] Kidnappings for ransom, in addition to armed robbery, have transformed public criminality. Criminals soon discovered that they could make more money through kidnapping while avoiding the inherent risks of armed robbery. Kidnapping has reconfigured both the victimology of crime and criminal outcomes. Many of the victims of armed robbery or home invasion were "ordinary" Nigerians whose neighborhoods were underpoliced as well as big business and banks, whose money was usually insured; but victims of the new wave of kidnapping are rich citizens and professionals who could be compelled to pay a steep ransom. The limited risk to the perpetrators involved in attempted kidnapping and the proliferation of cell phones by which to conduct transactions have broadened the geography of criminal exploit and diversified the identity of the people involved. Amateur criminals, including university graduates, have been known to seize prominent people, demanding as much as N360,000,000 ($1 million), a sum that most professional armed robbers, using advanced war rifles, would not make even if they broke into a bank vault. Except in cases involving influential Nigerians close to the federal government—such as Chief Olu Falae, a former presidential candidate, in 2015—most victims of kidnapping paid the ransom or died in captivity.[35] Few Nigerian kidnappers have ever been prosecuted.

Kidnapping for ransom has opened up the debate, in print and social media, about armed self-defense and the liberalization of nonprohibited firearms like pistols.[36] The manner in which abductions are conducted, mostly by first-time criminals, has convinced some critics of poor policing that armed self-defense would be effective. "In view of psychological fear factor among criminals or vandals, liberal gun ownership will curb criminality among hoodlums," stated the president of the Nigerian Medical Association, Dr. Osahon Enabulele, echoing the sentiment of some of the association's members at the height of the abduction of doctors in 2012.[37] But the most pertinent factor concerning the liberalization of pistols for self-defense is the illegal diversion of guns for criminal activities. Because the procedure for obtaining a license to use a handgun is so difficult, only military chiefs and top politicians can secure the necessary presidential approval. Most Nigerians are not aware that they could use a Dane gun for personal protection. But one problem with the use of Dane guns is that they are made by blacksmiths, most of whom did not have a license to make them. Except in criminal cases, the government has historically overlooked the activities of blacksmiths who supplied Dane guns to hunters. Their work was illegal but tolerated.

Public Unrest, Civil War, and Terrorism

The intensity of violence during the colonial era is no match for that of the postcolonial era. Indeed, no scholar of Nigeria can say in firm terms how many instances of public unrest and how many casualties have occurred since the Union Jack was lowered in 1960. What is certain is that conflict across ethnicity, religion, political party, and region over secession, control of economic resources, and religious purity have assumed dangerous dimensions. The causes of public disorder are legion, but the failure of political leadership at all levels of the society is the most important. Failed political leadership manifests in the varied crises of nation building, including, but not limited to corruption, economic and political marginalization, poverty, abuse of human rights, and inequality. Yet the end product of these crises is often armed conflict and violence, featuring firearms.[38] There are two complementary dimensions of the intersection of firearms and armed conflict—proliferation of war weapons and disarmament. Let us take a closer look at each.

When the Nigerian army was indigenized and transformed from a colonial security force to an independent armed force in 1960, many of its firearms were appropriate only for dealing with domestic conflict. This prompted the government's establishment of the Defence Industries Corporation of Nigeria (DICN) to produce arms for the country. Yet the quantity and quality of weapons produced by the DICN were inadequate to prosecute the war against the secessionist forces, which took a decisive turn on August 17, 1967, when the Biafran Army, under the command of Colonel Chukwuemeka Ojukwu, invaded Ore, 135 miles from Lagos, the nation's capital. The Nigerian and Biafran armies accumulated large stocks of weapons from "friendly" nations from Europe and other parts of the world. When the Biafrans' newly acquired B-26 bomber flew to demonstrate its might, to the bewilderment of the Nigerian army, General Gowon turned to the Soviet Union to acquire twelve reconditioned MiG-17 fighters and another twelve trainers—he had been turned down by Britain, which claimed that such weaponry was too sophisticated for Nigeria. This singular act brought the Nigerian Air Force, established in 1964, into a combat-ready status. The federal blockade of supplies and restriction of its finances led the Biafran army, through the innovation of scientists and engineers, to produce firearms locally. Among their newly invented arms was the popular Ojukwu bucket, or *Ogbunigwe* (meaning "mass killer"), which was made in different sizes and shapes for use as hand grenades, rocket-propelled and ground-to-air missiles, or land mines. Ojukwu's men also built five MFI-9Bs, nicknamed "Biafra babies."[39] By the time the last shot in the Civil War was fired in January 1970, about a million Nigerians had lost their lives in the thirty-month-long carnage, made possible by the advancement and maximum deployment of technologies of violence.

The indisputable importance and centrality of the Nigerian Civil War to the unity of the state obscured several other minor and major armed conflicts across the country between 1967 and 1970. One such conflict was the Agbekoya ("farmers renounce suffering") "revolt" in Nigeria's Western State between September 1968 and July 1969.[40] This conflict was rooted in the economic crises following the drop in global cocoa prices and devastating impact of the swollen-shoot disease that afflicted cocoa, the main cash crop produced in the rural communities in the 1950s. Officers of the government's produce board were also accused of shorting the farmers in the grading and pricing of cocoa. When the government imposed new taxes, hunters, farmers, artisans, and other citizens were deeply affected. They took up arms against the state, killing security officers and attacking the Ibadan prison to set free their incarcerated comrades. At least one notable chief, the king named Olajide Olayode of Ogbomoso, was among the civilian casualties.[41]

Although scholars refer to the event a "peasant revolt," the people involved called it the Agbekoya War.[42] The difference between a revolt or riot and a war transcends mere terminology; the choice of one term over the other is loaded with political meaning that gauges the legitimacy and projected outcome of events as understood by the different actors and major players. For the Agbekoya, the struggle was a legitimate one to fight injustice; to the government, it was a riot, an act of insubordination against its authority. The Agbekoya conflict resembled the pattern of resistance to colonial rule, in which rural communities mobilized and armed themselves with Dane guns in a manner that plainly mirrored precolonial warfare, as executed by warlords who held allegiance to a military hierarchy rooted in ancestral history. But it was a much bigger campaign and better coordinated than those during the colonial era in that many communities were involved in a well-articulated common cause. Indeed, it was the most elaborate and longest tax "riot" in Nigerian history. What started as resistance to the military government's draconian policy assumed new forms and an expanded mission across communities and shaped intergroup relations in unpredictable ways. Several theories have been advanced for why the rebellion lasted a year, despite the superior firepower of the state. One explanation is that the government was reluctant to divert resources from the more critical Civil War to a domestic crisis. However, the "rebels" attributed their success to the efficacy of their Dane guns, their hardworking blacksmiths who produced firearms in large number to meet wartime demand, the effectiveness of their juju, and the quality of the leadership provided by Tafa Adeoye and Folarin Idowu, among others (figure EPI.3).[43]

Figure EPI.3. Agbekoya fighters, Akanran, 1968. Reproduced by the Courtesy of the National Archives, Ibadan.

The foundation of the politicization of religion in postcolonial Nigeria was laid during the colonial era when the British adopted a divide-and-rule policy. But from the 1980s, religious politics became more visible, fueling an ethno-religious crisis that featured the use of both imported and locally made firearms. The transformation in the use of guns in ethno-religious and communal conflicts mirrored the increasing access and advancement in firearms technology and the goals of the groups involved.[44] The Maitatsine Islamic fanatics attacked the government's troops with Dane guns in the early 1980s, not unlike the Boko Haram terrorists of the twenty-first century who have launched successful onslaughts on the federal army using state-of-the-art weapons, claiming about twenty thousand lives as of 2016.[45] The Boko Haram insurgency has produced some of the highest casualties in Nigerian history since the Civil War in part because of the use of conventional military tactics and sophisticated arms, but also because of the deployment of suicide bombers and improvised explosive devices (IEDs). The administration of President Muhammadu Buhari, who succeeded Dr. Goodluck Jonathan in May 2015, has exposed one of the main reasons Boko Haram could not be checked for more than five years—corruption of security chiefs and diversion to election campaigns of funds meant for arms procurement.[46]

The second element of the intersection of firearms and violent conflict is sometimes termed *disarmament*. Africanist scholars have established that the politics of disarmament, including demobilization, and reconstruction after each armed conflict significantly shape the dynamics of future crises.[47] This is particularly the case in Nigeria, where postconflict disarmament, reconstruction, and transitional justice have been poorly conducted. Many firearms used for prosecuting the Civil War were not recovered through a coordinated, state-sponsored disarmament project. Fearing persecution, few ex-Biafran soldiers would abide by the Firearms Prohibition Order of 1970 requiring that they surrender their arms within fourteen days. Most of the ex-Biafran soldiers were therefore not rehabilitated or reabsorbed into the Nigerian army. Olukunle Ojeleye observes in *The Politics of Post-War Demobilisation and Reintegration in Nigeria* that "it remains unknown how many weapons were turned in and in what condition."[48]

The widespread assertion in the 1970s and 1980s that the unemployed soldiers turned to armed robbery because "the practice of violence already cultivated during the war years stayed" with them and that their "minds had become somehow diseased through exposure to the sordid realities of war" reflected the public's beliefs about the identity of the armed robbers. Another notion that the ex-soldiers adopted "the tactics and strategies" learned in the army and through watching foreign war films in their criminal exploits fed the popular imagination of robbery operations that mimicked a wartime situation.[49] But the identities of the people convicted for robbery were diverse—some were even college students and serving police officers.[50] With the notable exception of the ex-federal soldiers Bashiru Fatola, Sunday Ohifueme Omokhudu, Olorungbamigbe, and Ojo, most of the popular armed robbers of the 1970s and 1980s were not ex-soldiers.[51]

Yet this does not negate the obvious fact that one direct consequence of the proliferation of weapons after 1970 was the unprecedented escalation of armed robbery across the country. On March 14, 1971, the *Daily Times* published an open letter and photo of an ex-Biafran soldier, First Lieutenant Stanislaus Muoghalu, who threatened to become a highway robber if the government did not give him a business loan of £5,000.[52] Muoghalu's story mirrors the experience of thousands of demobilized federal and Biafran soldiers—he failed in the two businesses he set up after demobilization because of lack of government financial support. "The stage has been reached where I vehemently refuse to be insulted, embarrassed or humiliated anymore by any object by man called money," Muoghalu concluded. If the public read Muoghalu's letter with amazement and a dose of entertainment, the NPF seemed worried. On March 22, the *Daily Times* reported that Muoghalu was invited by the police to speak with them about his threat.[53]

Similarly, between 1999 and 2014, the government conducted a number of disarmament programs as part of the peace settlement with Niger Delta militants. But like in previous episodes, corruption and lack of trust meant that most of the weapons retrieved from fighters later returned to them. Indeed, the speed with which armed groups have been able to rearm following the breakdown of a peace agreement suggests that a true disarmament did not happen in the first place.[54] As in the case of the Civil War, guns recovered from armed groups in one part of the country soon found their way to another region or abroad: what is true about the Civil War and the militants of the Niger Delta is correct in the case of other conflicts across the country.

This short epilogue has focused on the transformation of gun control in postcolonial Nigeria, with particular emphasis on the incidence of violence and illegal possession of arms. The assumption that the legal possession of firearms would lead to escalation of violence has no historical basis in Nigeria. In fact, more Nigerians legally owned various classes of nonprohibited guns (both legally and illegally) in the colonial era than in any other period of Nigerian history. Yet the ferocity of gun violence in colonial Nigeria was less than what obtained after the demise of imperial rule. The reason for this is not hard to see. The main success of colonial firearms regulation was the ability to prevent most Nigerians from having access to truly lethal arms (e.g., rifles, submachine guns, dangerous explosives) that could undermine imperial rule and public peace. Conversely, the virulence of armed conflict in postcolonial Nigeria is attributable in part to the failure of leaders to effectively police the country's international borders and control access to weapons of war by criminals, terrorists, and other people who pose a threat to political stability. In a broader context, the story of gun violence after independence cannot be dissociated from the crisis of development and nation building.

Notes

1. "Wonderful Kiddies!" *Nigerian Observer*, January 3, 1973.
2. For the representation of children in colonial Nigerian newspapers, see Aderinto, "Researching Colonial Childhoods."

3. "Baby's Body in a Briefcase," *Daily Times*, January 30, 1971; "Kidnap Suspect Nabbed in Jos," *Nigerian Observer*, January 1, 1972; and from the *Nigerian Tribune*, "Police Wade into Mystery of Missing Boy," July 3, 1971; "Baby's Body Found in Dust Bin," August 9, 1971; and "Bodies of Two Kids Exhumed," October 21, 1971.

4. Aderinto and Osifodunrin, "500 Children Are Missing in Lagos," 97–121.

5. Omowura, *Challenge Cup*; Barber, "Popular Reactions to the Petro-Naira"; Ogbobine, *Armed Robbery in Nigeria*; Idowu, *Armed Robbery in Nigeria*; Ukadike, *Black African Cinema*, 161–62.

6. UNODC, *Transnational Organized Crime*, 33.

7. "Firearms Act: Chapter 146, Law of the Federal Republic of Nigeria, 1990," http://www.nigeria-law.org/Firearms%20Act.htm (accessed January 23, 2016).

8. From the *Nigerian Tribune*: "Abubakar's UI Visit after the 'War,'" November 24, 1998; "'Why We Attacked Arisekola,'" November 21, 1998; and "Day of Rage at UI," November 22, 1998.

9. "Arisekola's Guns with UI Cultist?" *Nigerian Tribune*, November 29, 1998.

10. Aluko, "How Many Nigerians?," 374.

11. "I Killed Four Elephants in a Week," *Daily Times*, February 28, 1971.

12. Oral interview with Mr. Ademola Adekesin at Akanran on May 28, 2015.

13. Oral interview with Mr. Fehintola Olorode at Akanran on May 28, 2015.

14. Aderinto, "Sorrow, Tears, and Blood."

15. See the following *Daily Times* articles: "Director Shot in Daylight Robbery at Ilupeju Estate, £37,000 Snatched," January 2, 1971; "Three to Die for Armed Robbery," January 5, 1971; "Court Told How Armed Men Shot a Farmer," January 11, 1971; "Poor Joseph after a Gang Opened Fire," January 18, 1971; "Seven Executed for Armed Robbery," January 29, 1971; "High Rate of Robbery Deplored," January 30, 1971; "Tribunal Condemns Four to Death," February 1, 1971; "Three Men to Die for Armed Robbery," February 14, 1971; "Man Arrested for Keeping Arms," February 15, 1971; "Night-Guard Shot Dead in Raid by Robbers," February 17, 1971; "Robbery Tribunal in Kwara Soon," February 24, 1971; "Six Night-Guards on Murder Charge to Wait Till March," February 26, 1971; "Taxi Driver Shot Dead in 3 a.m. Attack by Gangster," March 1, 1971; "Man, Wife Shot in Bed by Bandits," March 5, 1971; and "Tailor Shot Dead in 3 a.m. Attack," March 19, 1971. In the *Nigerian Observer*, see "Man Shot Dead by Armed Robbers in Dawn Raid," January 18, 1972; "College Student to Face Firing Squad," February 8, 1972; "It's Firing Squad for Two Armed Robbers," February 18, 1972; "Oyenusi's Man to Die for Armed Robbery," March 16, 1972; "Ten Men to Face the Firing Squad in Kwara," October 6, 1972; "Five Bandits Executed in Calabar," October 18, 1972; "Two Robbers to Face Firing Squad," December 13, 1972.

16. "How £10,000 Booty Was Shared," *Nigerian Tribune*, August 14, 1971.

17. "'Dr' Oyenusi in Last Minute Drama," *Nigerian Tribune*, September 9, 1971; "Oyenusi Smiles to His Death," *Daily Times*, September 9, 1971.

18. "Crime and Its Treatment in the Colony and Protectorate, 1944," Oyo Prof., 4113, NAI.

19. Dambazau, *Law and Criminality in Nigeria*, 85.

20. Ibid.

21. "Tapper to Die for Highway Robbery," *Daily Times*, January 13, 1971.

22. "As Mighty Bullets Silence 'Mighty Joe' It Is . . . ," *Daily Times*, June 2, 1973.

23. "Three Collapse at Execution," *Nigerian Tribune*, September 9, 1971; "Seven Executed for Armed Robbery," *Daily Times*, January 29, 1971.

24. "15,000 Watched Two Robbers Die at Akure," March 21, 1972.
25. Ekpenyong, "Social Inequalities," 23.
26. Dambazau, *Law and Criminality in Nigeria*, 84.
27. Ekpenyong, "Social Inequalities," 23.
28. Barber, "Popular Reactions to the Petro-Naira," 437.
29. Okome, *Sapped Democracy*.
30. Marenin, "Anini Saga," 259–81.
31. Ekpenyong, "Social Inequalities," 24.
32. Marenin, "Anini Saga," 259–81.
33. Pratten, "Introduction," 1–15.
34. "100,000 Police Officers Carry Handbags for Wives of Moneybags and Politicians," *Nigeria Police Watch*, October 19, 2011, http://www.nigeriapolicewatch.com/2011/10/100000-police-officers-carry-handbags-for-wives-of-moneybags-and-politicians/ (accessed July 2, 2015).
35. "How I Was Abducted by Olu Falae," *Premium Times*, September 28, 2015, http://www.premiumtimesng.com/news/headlines/190728-how-i-was-abducted-tortured-released-olu-falae.html (accessed January 24, 2016).
36. "Should Private Guns Be Allowed in Nigeria?" *Nairaland*, September 29, 2009, http://www.nairaland.com/330436/should-private-guns-allowed-nigeria (accessed March 20, 2016); "Should Nigerians Be Allowed to Have a License to Own Guns/Firearms?" *Nairaland*, July 1, 2010, http://www.nairaland.com/472282/should-nigerians-allowed-license-own (accessed March 20, 2016).
37. "We Need Private Guns: Members of Nigeria Medical Association Tell FG," *Daily Post*, September 6, 2012, http://dailypost.ng/2012/09/06/we-need-private-guns-members-nigeria-medical-association-tell-fg/ (accessed January 24, 2016).
38. Aderinto, "Yakubu Gowon."
39. Stremlau, *International Politics*; Umoh, "Making of Arms," 339–58.
40. Adeniran, "Dynamics of Peasant Revolt," 363–75.
41. Ibid.
42. Ibid.
43. Beer, *Politics of Peasant Groups*.
44. John et al., "Gun Violence in Nigeria"; Bienen, "Criminal Homicide in Western Nigeria."
45. Isichei, "Maitatsine Risings in Nigeria"; Pérouse de Montclos, *Boko Haram*.
46. "$2.1bn Arms Probe: Ex-DMI, General Wiwa Arrested," *Vanguard*, February 16, 2016 http://www.vanguardngr.com/2016/02/2-1bn-arms-probe-ex-dmi-gen-wiwa-arrested/ (accessed March 3, 2016).
47. Ojeleye, *Politics of Post-War Demobilisation*, 109–36.
48. Ibid., 118.
49. Idowu, *Armed Robbery in Nigeria*, 14–15; Ogbobine, *Armed Robbery in Nigeria*, 16–32.
50. From the *Nigerian Observer*: "College Student To Face Firing Squad," February 8, 1972; and "Two Police Officers Looted £19,000 Court Told," March 20, 1971. From the *Nigerian Tribune*: "Two Top Cops in Court Today," July 7, 1971; "Three Cops, Five Others Held," July 30, 1971.

51. "Soldier, Trader to Die for Robbery," *Nigerian Observer*, December 22, 1972; "Army Officers Sentenced to Death by Tribunal," *Daily Times*, January 7, 1971.

52. "I Am Going to Turn to Highway Robber If I Fail to Get £5000 Loan," *Daily Times*, March 14, 1971.

53. "Man Invited by Police over Threat to 'Turn to Robber,'" *Daily Times*, March 22, 1971.

54. Hazen and Horner, *Small Arms, Armed Violence*, 94–106.

BIBLIOGRAPHY

ARCHIVES

National Archives of the United Kingdom
Colonial Office (CO), 583/159/8

National Archives Ibadan
Abeokuta Provincial Office, 2nd Accession 1–9
Ado Ekiti Divisional Office Papers 1–5
Chief Secretary's Office Records 1–122
Commissioner of the Colony Office, Lagos 1–15
Criminal Record Books, 1910–1955, 1
Ekiti Divisional Office Papers 1–5
Ibadan Provincial Office Papers 1–4
Ife Divisional Office Papers 1/1
Ijebu Provincial Office Papers 1–10
Ondo Divisional Office Papers 1–5
Ondo Provincial Office Paper, 2nd Accession
Osun Divisional Office Papers
Owo Divisional Office Papers 1–9
Oyo Provincial Office Papers 1

National Archives Enugu
Aba District Office Papers 1–22
Calabar Provincial Office Papers 1–54
Obubra District Office Papers 1–15
Ogoni District Office Papers 1–3

Onitsha Provincial Office Papers
Orlu Provincial Office Papers
Owerri Provincial Office Papers

National Archives Kaduna

Bauchi Provincial Papers
Ilorin Provincial Papers
Jos Provincial Office Papers
Kano Local Authority Papers
Kano Provincial Office Papers 4/6
Katsina Provincial Office Papers "Federal"
Makurdi Provincial Office Papers 31–51
Minna Provincial Office Papers "State" 7/1–8/1
Secretariat of Northern Provinces Papers 1–17
Sokoto Provincial Office Papers
Yola Provincial Office Papers
Zaria Provincial Office Papers

NEWSPAPERS

Daily Service, 1940–50
Daily Times, 1970–90
Eastern Nigeria Guardian, 1941–50
Lagos Weekly Record, 1900–1910
Nigerian Daily Times, 1970–87
Nigerian Observer, 1970–75
Nigerian Pioneer, 1920–24
Nigerian Spokesman, 1945–55
Nigerian Tribune, 1990–2000
Southern Nigeria Defender, 1940–50
West African Pilot, 1938–60

CD

Ayinla Omowura and His Apala Group. *Challenge Cup*. Ivory Music. 1975. CD.

PUBLISHED PRIMARY DOCUMENTS

Annual Report on the Police Department: Colony and the Southern Provinces for the Year 1929. Lagos: Government Printer, 1929.
Annual Report on the Police Department for the Year 1931. Lagos: Government Printer, 1931.

Annual Report on the Police Department: Nigeria for the Year 1930. Lagos: Government Printer, 1930.
Annual Report on the Police Department: Northern Provinces for the Year 1927. Lagos: Government Printer, 1927.
Arms Ordinance (Chapter 132 of 1933). In *The Annual Volumes of the Laws of Nigeria Containing All Legislation Enacted during the Year 1933.* Lagos: Government Printer, 1934.
Blue Book. Lagos: Government Printer, 1930–50.
Debates in the Legislative Council of Nigeria, 1942. Lagos: Government Printer, 1942.
Enquiry into the Disorders in the Eastern Provinces of Nigeria: Proceedings of the Commission 2 vols. London: His Majesty's Stationery Office, 1950.
Nigeria: Legislative Council Debates. Lagos: Government Printer, 1942.
Nigerian Rifle Association: Constitution and Rules. Lagos: Daily Times, 1930.
Regulations Made under the Arms Ordinance 1917. In *The Annual Volumes of the Laws of Nigeria Containing All Legislation Enacted during the Year 1917.* Lagos: Government Printer, 1918.
Report of the Commission of Enquiry into the Disorders in the Eastern Provinces of Nigeria, November 1949. London: Colonial Office, 1950.
The Wild Animals Preservation Ordinance. In *The Annual Volumes of the Laws of Nigeria Containing All Legislation Enacted during the Year 1935.* Lagos: Government Printer, 1936.

BOOKS, ARTICLES, AND DISSERTATIONS

Achebe, Chinua. *Things Fall Apart.* New York: Anchor Books, 1994.
Adas, Michael. *Machines as the Measure of Men: Science, Technology, and Ideologies of Western Dominance.* Ithaca: Cornell University Press, 1989.
Adebiyi, Nike L. Edun. "Radical Nationalism in British West Africa, 1945–1960." PhD diss., University of Michigan, 2008.
Adeleye, R. A. *Power and Diplomacy in Northern Nigeria, 1804–1906: The Sokoto Caliphate and Its Enemies.* New York: Humanities Press, 1971.
Adeniran, Tunde. "The Dynamics of Peasant Revolt: A Conceptual Analysis of the Agbekoya Parapo Uprising in the Western State of Nigeria." *Journal of Black Studies* 4, no. 4 (1974): 363–75.
Aderinto, Saheed. "Discrimination in an Urban Setting: The Experience of Ijebu Settlers in Colonial Ibadan, 1893–1960." In *Inter-group Relations in Nigeria during the 19th & 20th Centuries,* edited by Olayemi Akinwumi, Okpeh O. Okpeh Jr., and Gwamna D. Je'adayibe, 356–86. Makurdi: Aboki Publishers, 2006.
———. "Ijebu a b'eyan . . . ?" ("Ijebu or a Human Being . . . ?"): Nineteenth Century Origin of Discrimination against Ijebu Strangers in colonial Ibadan, Nigeria." In *Minorities and the State in Africa,* edited by Chima J. Korieh and Michael Mbanaso, 143–68. Amherst: Cambria Press, 2010.

———. "European Invasion and African Resistance." In *Africa and the Wider World*, edited by Hakeem Ibikunle Tijani, Tiffany Jones, and Raphael Njoku, 247–61. Boston: Pearson, 2010.

———. "Researching Colonial Childhoods: Images and Representations of Children in Nigerian Newspaper Press, 1925–1950." *History in Africa: A Journal of Method* 39 (2012): 241–66.

———. "'Sorrow, Tears, and Blood': Fela Anikulapo Kuti and Protest in Nigeria." In *The Routledge History of Social Protest in Popular Music*, edited by Jonathan C. Friedman, 319–30. New York: Routledge, 2013.

———. "Where Is the Boundary? Cocoa Conflict, Land Tenure, and Politics in Western Nigeria." *Journal of Social History* 47, no. 1 (2013): 176–95.

———. "Isaac Fadoyebo at the Battle of Nyron: African Voices from the First and Second World Wars, c. 1914–1945." In *African Voices of the Global Past: 1500 to the Present*, edited by Trevor Getz, 107–38. Boulder: Westview Press, 2014.

———. "Yakubu Gowon: The Challenge of Nation Building." In *Nigerian Political Leaders: Visions, Actions, and Legacies*, edited by Apollos O. Nwauwa and Julius O. Adekunle, 230–48. Glassboro: Goldline & Jacobs Publishing 2015.

———. *When Sex Threatened the State: Illicit Sexuality, Nationalism, and Politics in Colonial Nigeria, 1900–1958*. Urbana: University of Illinois Press, 2015.

Aderinto, Saheed, and Paul Osifodunrin. "'500 Children Are Missing in Lagos': Child Kidnapping and Public Anxiety in Colonial Nigeria." In *Children and Childhood in Colonial Nigerian Histories*, edited by Saheed Aderinto, 97–121. New York: Palgrave Macmillan, 2015.

Adesina, Olutayo Charles. "The Colonial State's Wartime Emergency Regulations and the Development of the Nigerian Entrepreneurial Class, 1939–1945." *Ibadan Journal of Humanistic Studies* 7 (1997): 67–76.

———. "Modern Agriculture in Nigeria: A Historical Exegesis." *Benin Journal of Historical Studies* 4, nos. 1–2 (2002–4): 59–80.

Afigbo, A. E. *The Warrant Chiefs: Indirect Rule in Southeastern Nigeria, 1891–1929*. London: Longman, 1972.

———. "Patterns of the Igbo Resistance to British Conquest." *Tarikh* 4, no. 3 (1973): 14–23.

Ahire, Philip Terdoo. *Imperial Policing: The Emergence and Role of the Police in Colonial Nigeria, 1860–1960*. Buckingham: Open University Press, 1991.

Ajayi, J. F. Ade, and Robert Smith. *Yoruba Warfare in the Nineteenth Century*. Cambridge: Cambridge University Press, 1964.

Ajayi, Rotimi. "The Politicisation of Trade Unionism: The Case of Labour/NCNC Alliance in Nigeria, 1940–1960." *Ufahamu: A Journal of African Studies* 27, nos. 1–2 (1999): 48–62.

Ajuwon, Bade. "Ogun's Iremoje: A Philosophy of Living and Dying." In *Africa's Ogun: Old World and New*, edited by Sandra T. Barnes, 173–98. Bloomington: Indiana University Press, 1989.

Akintoye, S. A. *Revolution and Power Politics in Yorubaland, 1840–1893: Ibadan Expansion and the Rise of Ekitiparapo.* New York: Humanities Press, 1971.

Akpala, Agwu. "The Background of the Enugu Colliery Shooting Incident in 1949." *Journal of the Historical Society of Nigeria* 3, no. 2 (1965): 335–63.

Akyeampong, Emmanuel. *Drink, Power, and Cultural Change: A Social History of Alcohol in Ghana, c. 1800 to Recent Times.* Portsmouth: Heinemann, 1996.

Albert, Isaac Olawale. "From 'Owo Crisis' to 'Dogon Dispute': Lessons in the Politicization of Chieftaincy Disputes in Nigeria and Ghana." *Roundtable* 97, no. 394 (2008): 47–60.

Allen, Charles, ed. *Tales from the Dark Continent.* New York: St. Martin's Press, 1979.

Aluko, S. A. "How Many Nigerians? An Analysis of Nigeria's Census Problems, 1901–1963." *Journal of Modern African Studies* 3, no. 3 (1965): 371–92.

Anderson, D., and R. Grove, eds. *Conservation in Africa: Peoples, Policies and Practice.* Cambridge: Cambridge University Press, 1987.

Appadurai, Arjun, ed. *The Social Life of Things: Commodities in Cultural Perspective.* Cambridge: Cambridge University Press, 1986.

Apter, Andrew. "On Imperial Spectacle: The Dialectics of Seeing in Colonial Nigeria." *Comparative Studies in Society and History* 44, no. 3 (2002): 564–96.

Atanda, J. A. "The Iseyin-Okeiho Rising of 1916: An Example of Socio-Political Conflict in Colonial Nigeria." *Journal of the Historical Society of Nigeria* 4, no. 4 (1969): 497–514.

Atilade, E. A. *Iwe Oriki Awon Orile Yoruba.* Lagos: New Nigeria Press, 1963.

Atkinson, M. C. *An African Life: Tales of a Colonial Officer.* London: Radcliffe, 1992.

Atmore, Anthony, and Peter Sanders. "Sotho Arms and Ammunition in the Nineteenth Century." *Journal of African History* 12, no. 4 (1971): 534–44.

Atmore, Anthony, J. M. Chirenje, and S. I. Mudenge. "Firearms in South Central Africa." *Journal of African History* 12, no. 4 (1971): 545–56.

Awe, Bolanle. "Notes on Oriki and Warfare in Yorubaland." In *Yoruba Oral Tradition*, edited by Wande Abimbola, 267–92. Ile-Ife: University of Ife Press, 1975.

Babalola, Adeboye. "A Portrait of Ogun as Reflected in Ijala Chants." In *Africa's Ogun: Old World and New*, edited by Sandra T. Barnes, 147–72. Bloomington: Indiana University Press, 1989.

Barber, Karin. "Popular Reactions to the Petro-Naira." *Journal of Modern African Studies* 20, no. 3 (1982): 431–50.

Barnes, Andrew E. *Making Headway: The Introduction of Western Civilization in Colonial Northern Nigeria.* Rochester: University of Rochester Press, 2009.

Barnes, Sandra, ed. *Africa's Ogun: Old World and New.* Bloomington: Indiana University Press, 1989.

Barth, Henry. *Travels and Discoveries in North and Central Africa.* 3 vols. New York: Drallop Publishing, 1890.

Basden, G. T. *Niger Ibos.* London: Frank Cass, 1938.

Beer, Christopher. *The Politics of Peasant Groups in Western Nigeria.* Ibadan: Ibadan University Press, 1976.

Beinart, William. "Empire, Hunting, and Ecological Change in Southern and Central Africa." *Past and Present* 128, no. 1 (1990): 162–86.

———. "Men, Science, Travel and Nature in the Eighteenth and Nineteenth-Century Cape." *Journal of Southern African Studies* 24, no. 4 (1998): 775–99.

Berg, Gerald M. "The Sacred Musket: Tactics, Technology, and Power in Eighteenth-Century Madagascar." *Comparative Studies in Society and History* 27, no. 2 (1985): 261–79.

Bienen, Leigh. "Criminal Homicide in Western Nigeria, 1966–1972." *Journal of African Law* 18, no. 1 (1974): 57–78.

Bohannan, Paul. *Justice and Judgement among the Tiv*. Prospect Heights: Waveland Press, 1957.

Bradlow, E. "The Significance of Arms and Ammunitions on the Cape's Northern Frontier at the Turn of the 18th Century." *Historia* 26, no. 1 (1981): 59–68.

Brook, Ian (Ian Brinkworth). *The One-Eyed Man Is King*. New York: Putnam's Sons, 1966.

Brown, Carolyn A. *"We Were All Slaves": African Miners, Culture, and Resistance at the Enugu Government Colliery*. Portsmouth: Heinemann, 2003.

Burke, Timothy. *Lifebuoy Men, Lux Women: Commodification, Consumption, and Cleanliness in Modern Zimbabwe*. Durham: Duke University Press, 1996.

Burns, Alan. *Colonial Civil Servant*. London: George Allen & Unwin, 1949.

Burton, Richard. *Two Trips to Gorilla Land and the Cataracts of the Congo*. Vol. 1. London: Sampson, Low, Marston, Low, and Searle, 1876.

Byfield, Judith A. *The Bluest Hands: A Social and Economic History of Women Dyers in Abeokuta (Nigeria), 1890–1940*. Portsmouth: Heinemann, 2002.

———. "Feeding the Troops: Abeokuta (Nigeria) and World War II." *African Economic History* 35 (2007): 77–87.

———. "Women, Rice, and War: Political and Economic Crisis in Wartime Abeokuta (Nigeria)." In *Africa and World War II*, edited by Judith A. Byfield, Carolyn A. Brown, Timothy Parsons, and Ahmad Alawad Sikainga, 147–65. Cambridge: Cambridge University Press, 2015.

Callaway, Helen. *Gender, Culture, and Empire: European Women in Colonial Nigeria*. Urbana: University of Illinois Press, 1987.

Cannadine, David. *Ornamentalism: How the British Saw Their Empire*. Oxford: Oxford University Press, 2001.

Caulk, R. A. "Firearms and Princely Power in Ethiopia in the Nineteenth Century." *Journal of African History* 13, no. 4 (1972): 609–30.

Chew, Emrys. *Arming the Periphery: The Arms Trade in the Indian Ocean during the Age of Global Empire*. New York: Palgrave Macmillan, 2012.

Chuku, Gloria. "'Crack Kernels, Crack Hitler': Export Production Drive and Igbo Women during the Second World War." In *Gendering the African Diaspora: Women, Culture, and Historical Change in the Caribbean and Nigerian Hinterland*, edited by Judith Byfield, LaRay Denzer, and Anthea Morrison, 219–44. Bloomington: Indiana University Press, 2010.

Clancy-Smith, Julia, and Frances Gouda, eds. *Domesticating the Empire: Race, Gender, and Family Life in French and Dutch Colonialism*. Charlottesville: University of Virginia Press, 1998.
Clark, Ebun. *Hubert Ogunde: The Making of Nigerian Theatre*. Oxford: Oxford University Press, 1979.
Cole, Patrick. *Modern and Traditional Elites in the Politics of Lagos*. Cambridge: Cambridge University Press, 1975.
Collingham, Lizzie. *The Taste of War: World War II and the Battle for Food*. New York: Penguin Press, 2012.
Comaroff, Jean, and John Comaroff. "Goodly Beasts, Beastly Goods: Cattle and Commodities in a South African Context." *American Ethnologist* 17, no. 2 (1990): 195–216.
Corbin, Alain. *Village Bells: Sound and Meaning in the Nineteenth-Century French Countryside*. New York: Columbia University Press, 1998.
Crocker, W. R. *Nigeria: A Critique of British Colonial Administration*. London: George Allen & Unwin, 1936.
Crummey, Donald, ed. *Banditry, Rebellion, and Social Protest in Africa*. London: James Currey, 1986.
Curtin, Philip. *The Image of Africa: British Ideas and Action, 1780–1850*. Madison: University of Wisconsin Press, 1964.
———, ed. *Africa Remembered: Narratives by West Africans from the Era of the Slave Trade*. Prospect Heights: Waveland Press, 1967.
———. *Economic Change in Precolonial Africa: Senegambia in the Era of the Slave Trade*. Madison: University of Wisconsin Press, 1975.
Dambazau, A. B. *Law and Criminality in Nigeria*. Ibadan: Ibadan University Press, 1994.
Davis, Diana. *Resurrecting the Granary of Rome: Environmental History and French Colonial Expansion in North Africa*. Athens: Ohio University Press, 2007.
Dewey, Clive, and A. G. Hopkins, eds. *The Imperial Impact: Studies in the Economic History of Africa and India*. London: Athlone Press, 1978.
Dibwe dia Mwembu, Donatien. "The Role of Firearms in the Songye Region, 1869–1960." In *The Objects of Life in Central Africa: The History of Consumption and Social Change, 1840–1980*, edited by Robert Ross, Marja Hinfelaar, and Iva Pesa, 41–64. Leiden: Brill, 2013.
Dike, K. O. *Trade and Politics in the Niger Delta, 1830–1885*. Oxford: Clarendon Press, 1956.
Dike, K. O., and Felicia Ekejiuba. *The Aro of South-eastern Nigeria, 1650–1980*. Ibadan: Ibadan University Press, 1990.
Dusgate, Richard H. *The Conquest of Northern Nigeria*. London: Frank Cass, 1985.
Echenberg, Myron J. "Late Nineteenth-Century Military Technology in Upper Volta." *Journal of African History* 12, no. 2 (1971): 241–54.
Egharevba, Jacob. *A Short History of Benin*. Ibadan: Ibadan University Press, 1960.

Ekpenyong, Stephen. "Social Inequalities, Collusion, and Armed Robbery in Nigerian Cities." *British Journal of Criminology* 29, no. 1 (1989): 21–34.

Eltis, David. *The Rise of African Slavery in the Americas*. Cambridge: Cambridge University Press, 2000.

Falola, Toyin. "Brigandage and Piracy in 19th Century Yorubaland." *Journal of the Historical Society of Nigeria* 23, nos. 1–2 (1985–86): 83–106.

———. "Cassava Starch for Export in Nigeria during the Second World War." *African Economic History* 18 (1989): 73–98.

———. "'Salt Is Gold': The Management of Salt Scarcity in Nigeria during World War II." *Canadian Journal of African Studies* 26, no. 3 (1992): 412–36.

———. "Theft in Colonial Southwestern Nigeria." *Africa: Rivista trimstrale di studie e documentazione dell'Istituto Italo-Africano*, Year L–N, no. 1 (March 1995): 1–24.

———. *Colonialism and Violence in Nigeria*. Bloomington: Indiana University Press, 2009.

Falola, Toyin, and Akanmu Adebayo. *Culture, Politics, and Money among the Yoruba*. New Brunswick, NJ: Transaction Publishers, 1999.

Fanon, Frantz. *Black Skin, White Masks*. Translated from the French by Charles Lam Markmann. New York: Grove Press, 1967.

Fisher, Humphrey J., and Virginia Rowland. "Firearms in the Central Sudan." *Journal of African History* 12, no. 2 (1971): 215–39.

Fitz-Henry, Lassie. *African Dust*. London: Macmillan, 1959.

Fourchard, Laurent. "Urban Poverty, Urban Crime, and Crime Control: The Lagos and Ibadan Cases, 1929–1945." In *African Urban Spaces in Historical Perspective*, edited by Steven J. Salm and Toyin Falola, 287–316. Rochester: University of Rochester Press, 2005.

———. "A New Name for an Old Practice: Vigilantes in South-Western Nigeria." *Africa: The Journal of the International African Institute* 78, no. 1 (2008): 16–40.

Freund, Bill. *Capital and Labour in the Nigerian Tin Mines*. London: Longman, 1981.

Gemery, Henry A., and Jan S. Hogendorn, eds. *The Uncommon Market: Essays in the Economic History of the Atlantic Slave Trade*. New York: Academic Press, 1975.

———. "Technological Change, Slavery, and the Slave Trade." In *The Imperial Impact: Studies in the Economic History of Africa and India*, edited by Clive Dewey and A. G. Hopkins, 243–58. London: Athlone Press, 1978.

Gilman, Sander L. *Difference and Pathology: Stereotypes of Sexuality, Race, and Madness*. Ithaca: Cornell University Press, 1985.

Goody, Jack. *Technology, Tradition and the State in Africa*. Cambridge: Cambridge University Press, 1980.

Grant, Neil. *The Bren Gun*. Oxford: Osprey Publishing, 2013.

Gray, Richard. "Portuguese Musketeers on the Zambezi." *Journal of African History* 12, no. 4 (1971): 531–33.

Guy, J. J. "A Note on Firearms in the Zulu Kingdom with Special Reference to the Anglo-Zulu War, 1879." *Journal of African History* 12, no. 4 (1971): 557–70.

Hahn, Hans Peter. *Consumption in Africa: Anthropological Approaches.* Berlin: Lit Verlag, 2008.

Hahn, Hans Peter, and Hadas Weiss, eds. *Mobility, Meaning and the Transformation of Things: Shifting Contexts of Material Culture through Time and Space.* Oxford: Oxbow Books, 2013.

Haig, E. F. G. *Nigerian Sketches.* London: George Allen & Unwin, 1931.

Harris, William Cornwallis. *The Wild Sports of Southern Africa.* Cape Town: C. Struik, 1963.

Hasting, A. C. G. *Nigerian Days.* London: John Lane, 1925.

Hawkey, Arthur. *The Amazing Hiram Maxim: An Intimate Biography.* Stroud: Spellmount, 2001.

Hazen, Jennifer, and Jonas Horner. *Small Arms, Armed Violence, and Insecurity in Nigeria: The Niger Delta in Perspective.* Geneva: Graduate Institute of International Studies, 2007.

Heap, Simon. "'A Bottle of Gin Is Dangled before the Nose of the Natives': The Economic Uses of Imported Liquor in Southern Nigeria, 1860–1920." *African Economic History* 33 (2005): 69–85.

Heaton, Mathew M. *Black Skin, White Coats: Nigerian Psychiatrists, Decolonization, and the Globalization of Psychiatry.* Athens: Ohio University Press, 2013.

Hendy, David. *Noise: A Human History of Sound and Listening.* London: Profile Books, 2013.

Hives, Frank, and Gascoine Lumley. *Ju-ju and Justice in Nigeria.* London: John Lane, 1930.

Hogan, Edmund M. *Cross and Scalpel: Jean-Marie Coquard among the Egba of Yorubaland.* Ibadan: NEBN Publishers, 2012.

Hopkins, A. G. *An Economic History of West Africa.* New York: Columbia University Press, 1973.

Hulme, Peter, and Tim Youngs, eds. *The Cambridge Companion to Travel Writing.* Cambridge: Cambridge University Press, 2002.

Hutchinson, Sharon E. *Nuer Dilemmas: Coping with Money, War, and the State.* Berkeley: University of California Press, 1996.

Ibhawoh, Bonny. *Imperialism and Human Rights: Colonial Discourse of Rights and Liberties in African History.* Albany: State University of New York Press, 2007.

Idowu, Sina. *Armed Robbery in Nigeria.* Lagos: Jacob and Johnson Books, 1980.

Ikime, Obaro. *The Fall of Nigeria: The British Conquest.* London: Heinemann, 1977.

———. *In Search of Nigerians: Changing Patterns of Inter-Group Relations in an Evolving Nation State.* Lagos: Impact Publishers, 1985.

Inikori, J. E. "The Import of Firearms into West Africa, 1750–1807: A Quantitative Analysis." *Journal of African History* 18, no. 3 (1977): 339–68.

———. *Africans and the Industrial Revolution in England: A Study in International Trade and Economic Development.* Cambridge: Cambridge University Press, 2002.

Inikori, J. E., and Stanley L. Engerman, eds. *The Atlantic Slave Trade: Effects on Economies, Societies, and Peoples in Africa, the Americas, and Europe.* Durham: Duke University Press, 1992.

Isichei, Elizabeth. *A History of the Igbo People.* New York: St. Martin's Press, 1976.

———. "The Maitatsine Risings in Nigeria, 1980–1985: A Revolt of the Disinherited." *Journal of Religion in Africa* 17, no. 3 (1987): 194–208.

Iweriebor, Ehiedu E. G. *Radical Politics in Nigeria, 1945–1950: The Significance of the Zikist Movement.* Zaria: Ahmadu Bello University Press, 1996.

Jackson, Robert. "The Twenty Years War: Invasion and Resistance in Southeastern Nigeria, 1900–1919." PhD diss., Harvard University, 1975.

Jhally, Sut. *The Codes of Advertising: Fetishism and the Political Economy of Meaning in the Consumer Society.* New York: Routledge, 1990.

John, Ime A., Aminu Z. Mohammed, Andrew D. Pinto, and Celestine A. Nkanta. "Gun Violence in Nigeria: A Focus on Ethno-Religious Conflict in Kano." *Journal of Public Health Policy* 28, no. 4 (2007): 420–31.

Johnson, Cheryl. "Female Leadership during the Colonial Period: Madam Alimotu Pelewura and the Lagos Market Women." *Tarikh* 7, no. 1 (1980): 1–10.

Jones, Karen, Giacomo Macola, and David Welch. *A Cultural History of Firearms in the Age of Empire.* Surrey: Ashgate 2013.

Kea, R. A. "Firearms and Warfare on the Gold and Slave Coasts from the Sixteenth to the Nineteenth Centuries." *Journal of African History* 12, no. 2 (1971): 185–213.

Kennedy, Dane. *Islands of White: Settler Society and Culture in Kenya and Southern Rhodesia, 1890–1939.* Durham: Duke University Press, 1987.

Kerslake, R. T. *Time and the Hour: Nigeria, East Africa and the Second World War.* London: Radcliffe Press, 1997.

Killingray, David. "The Maintenance of Law and Order in British Colonial Africa." *African Affairs* 85, no. 340 (1986): 411–37.

Kirk-Greene, Anthony. "Badge of Office: Sport and His Excellency in the British Empire." In *The Cultural Bond: Sport, Empire, Society*, edited by J. A. Mangan, 178–210. London: Frank Cass, 1992.

———. *Britain's Imperial Administrators, 1858–1966.* Oxford: Macmillan, 2000.

———. *Glimpses of Empire: A Corona Anthology.* London: I. B. Tauris, 2001.

———. *Symbol of Authority: The British District Officer in Africa.* London: I. B. Tauris, 2006.

Kisch, Martin. *Letters and Sketches from Northern Nigeria.* London: Chatto & Windus, 1910.

Kopytoff, Igor. "The Cultural Biography of Things: Commoditization as Process." In *The Social Life of Things: Commodities in Cultural Perspective*, edited by Arjun Appadurai, 64–91. Cambridge: Cambridge University Press, 1986.

Lander, Richard. *Records of Captain Clapperton's Last Expedition to Africa.* 2 vols. London: Henry Colburn and Richard Bentley, 1830.

Langa, Langa (H. B. Hermon-Hodge). *Up against It in Nigeria.* London: George Allen & Unwin, 1922.

Larkin, Brian. *Signal and Noise: Media, Infrastructure, and Urban Culture in Nigeria*. Durham: Duke University Press, 2008.
Larymore, Constance. *A Resident's Wife in Nigeria*. London: George Routledge, 1908.
Last, Murray. *The Sokoto Caliphate*. New York: Humanities Press, 1967.
Law, Robin. "Horses, Firearms and Political Power in Pre-Colonial West Africa." *Past and Present* 72 (1976): 112–32.
Legassick, Martin. "Firearms, Horses, and Samorian Army Organisation, 1870–1898." *Journal of African History* 7, no. 1 (1966): 95–115.
Leith-Ross, Sylvia. *Stepping-Stones: Memoirs of Colonial Nigeria, 1907–1960*. London: Peter Owens, 1983.
Leonard, Arthur Glyn. *The Lower Niger and Its Tribes*. New York: Macmillan, 1906.
Lloyd, P. C. "Osifekunde of Ijebu." In *Africa Remembered: Narratives by West Africans from the Era of the Slave Trade*, edited by P. D. Curtin, 217–88. Prospect Heights: Waveland Press, 1967.
Lofkrantz, Jennifer, and Olatunji Ojo. "Slavery, Freedom, and Failed Ransom Negotiations in West Africa, 1730–1900." *Journal of African History* 53, no. 1 (2012): 25–44.
Lugard, Frederick. *Political Memoranda*. London: Frank Cass, 1970.
Mabogunje, Akin L. *Urbanization in Nigeria*. London: University of London Press, 1968.
Mackenzie, John M. *The Empire of Nature: Hunting, Conservation, and British Imperialism*. Manchester: Manchester University Press, 1988.
Macola, Giacomo. *The Gun in Central Africa: A History of Technology and Politics*. Athens: Ohio University Press, 2016.
Mamdani, Mahmood. *Citizen and Subject: Contemporary Africa and the Legacy of Late Colonialism*. Princeton: Princeton University Press, 1996.
Mangan, J. A. *The Cultural Bond: Sport, Empire, Society*. London: Frank Cass, 1992.
Mann, Kristin, and Richard L. Roberts, eds. *Law in Colonial Africa*. Portsmouth: Heinemann, 1991.
Marenin, Otwin. "The Anini Saga: Armed Robbery and the Reproduction of Ideology in Nigeria." *Journal of Modern African Studies* 25, no. 2 (1987): 259–81.
Markham, George. *Guns of the Empire: The Firearms of the British Soldier, 1837–1987*. New York: Arms and Armour Press, 1990.
Marks, Stuart. *The Imperial Lion: Human Dimensions of Wildlife Management in Central Africa*. Boulder: Westview Press, 1983.
Marks, Shula, and Anthony Atmore. "Firearms in Southern Africa: A Survey." *Journal of African History* 12, no. 4 (1971): 517–30.
Martin, Phyllis M. *Leisure and Society in Colonial Brazzaville*. Cambridge: Cambridge University Press, 1995.
Matthews, James K. "Clock Towers for the Colonized: Demobilization of the Nigerian Military and the Readjustment of Its Veterans to Civilian Life, 1918–1925." *International Journal of African Historical Studies* 14, no. 2 (1981): 254–71.

Mavhunga, Clapperton Chakanetsa. *Transient Workplaces: Technologies of Everyday Innovation in Zimbabwe*. Cambridge: Massachusetts Institute of Technology Press, 2014.

McCracken, Grant. *Culture and Consumption: New Approaches to the Symbolic Character of Consumer Goods and Activities*. Bloomington: Indiana University Press, 1990.

Meek, C. K. *Law and Authority in a Nigerian Tribe: A Study in Indirect Rule*. London: Oxford University Press, 1937.

Metcalf, George. "A Microcosm of Why Africans Sold Slaves: Akan Consumption Patterns in the 1770s." *Journal of African History* 28, no. 3 (1987): 377–94.

Midgley, Claire, ed. *Gender and Imperialism*. Manchester: Manchester University Press, 1998.

Miers, Sue. "Notes on the Arms Trade and Government Policy in Southern Africa between 1870 and 1890." *Journal of African History* 12, no. 4 (1971): 571–77.

Milne, Malcolm. *No Telephone to Heaven: From Apex to Nadir—Colonial Service in Nigeria, Aden, the Cameroons, and the Gold Coast, 1938–1961*. Lancaster: Meon Hill Press, 1999.

Mkutu, Kennedy Agade. *Guns and Governance in the Rift Valley: Pastoralist Conflict and Small Arms*. Oxford: James Currey, 2008.

Montclos, Marc-Antoine. *Boko Haram: Islamism, Politics, Security, and the State in Nigeria*. Leiden: African Studies Centre, 2014.

Muffett, D. J. M. *Empire Builder Extraordinary Sir George Goldie: His Philosophy of Government and Empire*. Douglas: Shearwater Press, 1978.

Nassau, Robert. *In an Elephant Corral, and Other Tales of West African Experiences*. New York: Negro University Press, 1969.

Neumann, Roderick. *Imposing Wilderness: Struggles over Livelihood and Nature Preservation in Africa*. Berkeley: University of California Press, 1998.

Niven, Rex. *Nigerian Kaleidoscope: Memoirs of a Colonial Servant*. London: C. Hurst & Company, 1982.

Njoku, O. N. "Export Production Drive in Nigeria during the Second World War." *Transafrican Journal of History* 10 (1981): 11–27.

Oakley, Richard. *Treks and Palavers*. London: Seeley, Service & Co., 1938.

Ochonu, Moses. *Colonialism by Proxy: Hausa Imperial Agents and Middle Belt Consciousness in Nigeria*. Bloomington: Indiana University Press, 2014.

Ofcansky, Thomas. *Paradise Lost: A History of Game Conservation in East Africa*. Morgantown: West Virginia University Press, 2002.

Ogbobine, R. A. I. *Armed Robbery in Nigeria: Causes and Prevention*. Warri: Rufbine Book Center, 1982.

Ohadike, Don. *The Ekumeku Movement: Western Igbo Resistance to the British Conquest of Nigeria, 1883–1914*. Athens: Ohio University Press, 1991.

Ojeleye, Olukunle. *The Politics of Post-War Demobilization and Reintegration in Nigeria*. Farnham: Ashgate, 2010.

Okome, Mojubaolu Olufunke. *A Sapped Democracy: The Political Economy of the Structural Adjustment Program and the Political Transition in Nigeria, 1983–1993.* Lanham: University Press of America, 1998.

Olorunfemi. A., and Olutayo Charles Adesina. "Labour Unions and the Decolonisation Process in Nigeria, 1940–1960." *Ilorin Journal of History* 1, no. 1 (2003): 9–18.

Olukoju, Ayodeji. "Prohibition and Paternalism: The State and the Clandestine Liquor Traffic in Northern Nigeria, c. 1898–1918." *International Journal of African Historical Studies* 24, no. 2 (1991): 349–68.

———. "Rotgut and Revenue: Fiscal Aspects of the Liquor Trade in Southern Nigeria, 1890–1919." *Itinerario: European Journal of Overseas History* 21, no. 2 (1997): 66–81.

———. "Government, the Business Community, and Quality Control Schemes in the Agricultural Export Trade of Nigeria, 1889–1929." *African Economic History* 26 (1998): 99–118.

———. "Confronting the Combines: Producers' and Traders' Militancy in Western Nigeria, 1934–1939." *Nordic Journal of African Studies* 9, no. 1 (2000): 49–69.

———. "The United Kingdom and the Political Economy of the Global Oils and Fats Business in the 1930s." *Journal of Global History* 4, no. 1 (2009): 105–25.

Olusanya, G. O. "The Zikist Movement: A Study in Political Radicalism, 1946–50." *Journal of Modern African Studies* 4, no. 3 (1966): 323–33.

———. "The Role of Ex-Servicemen in Nigerian Politics." *Journal of Modern African Studies* 6, no. 2 (1968): 221–32.

Osadolor, Osarhieme Benson. "The Military System of Benin Kingdom, 1440–1897." PhD diss., University of Hamburg, 2001.

Osifodunrin, Paul. *Armed Robbery in Post-Colonial Lagos, 1960–2007.* Osogbo: UNIOSUN College of Humanities and Culture Monograph, 2010.

Ottenberg, Simon. *Boyhood Rituals in an African Society: An Interpretation.* Seattle: University of Washington Press, 1989.

Oyemakinde, Wale. "The Pullen Marketing Scheme: A Trial in Food Price Control in Nigeria, 1941–1947." *Journal of the Historical Society of Nigeria* 6, no. 4 (1973): 413–23.

Parsons, Timothy. *The African Rank-and-File: Social Implications of Colonial Military Service in the King's African Rifles, 1902–1964.* Portsmouth: Heinemann, 1999.

Perham, Margery. *Lugard: The Years of Authority, 1898–1945.* London: Collins, 1960.

Post, Kenneth W. J., and George D. Jenkins. *The Price of Liberty: Personality and Politics in Colonial Nigeria.* Cambridge: Cambridge University Press, 1973.

Pratt, Mary Louise. *Imperial Eyes: Travel Writing and Transculturation.* New York: Routledge, 1992.

Pratten, David. "Introduction: The Politics of Protection: Perspectives on Vigilantism in Nigeria." *Africa: The Journal of the International African Institute* 78, no. 1 (2008): 1–15.

Prestholdt, Jeremy. *Domesticating the World: African Consumerism and the Genealogies of Globalization*. Berkeley: University of California Press, 2008.

Preteceille, Edmond, and Jean-Pierre Terrail. *Capitalism, Consumption, and Needs*. Oxford: Basil Blackwell, 1985.

Ramamurthy, Anandi. *Imperial Persuaders: Images of Africa and Asia in British Advertising*. Manchester: Manchester University Press, 2003.

Ranger, Terence. "White Presence and Power in Africa." *Journal of African History* 20, no. 4 (1979): 463–69.

Rich, Jeremy. "'Tata otangani oga njali, mbiambie!': Hunting and Colonialism in Southern Gabon, ca. 1890–1940." *Journal of Colonialism and Colonial History* 10, no. 3 (2009). doi: 10.1353/cch.0.0085.

Richards, Thomas. *The Commodity Culture of Victorian England: Advertising and Spectacle, 1851–1914*. Stanford: Stanford University Press, 1990.

Richards, W. A. "The Import of Firearms into West Africa in the Eighteenth Century." *Journal of African History* 21, no. 1 (1980): 43–59.

Richardson, David. "West African Consumption Patterns and Their Influence on the Eighteenth-Century English Slave Trade." In *The Uncommon Market: Essays in the Economic History of the Atlantic Slave Trade*, edited by Henry A. Gemery and Jan S. Hogendorn, 303–30. New York: Academic Press, 1975.

Rodney, Walter. *How Europe Underdeveloped Africa*. Washington, DC: Howard University Press, 1981.

Roosevelt, Theodore. *African Game Trails: An Account of the African Wanderings of an American Hunter-Naturalist*. London: John Murray, 1910.

Ross, Robert, Marja Hinfelaar, and Iva Pesa. Ed. *The Objects of Life in Central Africa: The History of Consumption and Social Change, 1840–1980*. Leiden: Brill, 2013.

Rotimi, Kemi. *The Police in a Federal State: The Nigerian Experience*. Ibadan: College Press, 2001.

Rowling, Noel. *Nigerian Memories*. Devon: Merlin Books, 1982.

Russell, Elnor. *Bush Life in Nigeria*. Self-published, 1978.

Ryder, A. F. C. *Benin and the Europeans, 1485–1897*. New York: Humanities Press, 1969.

Sadowsky, Jonathan. *Imperial Bedlam: Institutions of Madness in Colonial Southwest Nigeria*. Berkeley: University of California Press, 1999.

Schneider, William H. *An Empire for the Masses: The French Popular Image of Africa, 1870–1900*. Westport: Greenwood Press, 1982.

Sklar, Richard L. *Nigerian Political Parties: Power in an Emergent African Nation*. Princeton: Princeton University Press, 1963.

Smaldone, Joseph P. *Warfare in the Sokoto Caliphate: Historical and Sociological Perspectives*. Cambridge: Cambridge University Press, 1977.

Smith, John. *Colonial Cadet in Nigeria*. Durham: Duke University Press, 1968.

Smith, Robert S. "The Canoe in West African History." *Journal of African History* 11, no. 4 (1970): 515–33.

———. *Warfare and Diplomacy in Pre-colonial West Africa*. Madison: University of Wisconsin Press, 1989.

Stapleton, Timothy. *African Police and Soldiers in Colonial Zimbabwe, 1923–1980*. Rochester: University of Rochester Press, 2011.

Steinhart, Edward. *Black Poachers, White Hunters: A Social History of Hunting in Colonial Kenya*. Athens: Ohio University Press, 2006.

Storey, William K. "Big Cats and Imperialism: Lion and Tiger Hunting in Kenya and Northern India, 1898–1930." *Journal of World History* 2, no. 2 (1991): 135–73.

———. *Guns, Race, and Power in Colonial South Africa*. Cambridge: Cambridge University Press, 2008.

Stremlau, John J. *The International Politics of the Nigerian Civil War, 1967–1970*. Princeton: Princeton University Press, 1977.

Sunseri, Thaddeus. "Reinterpreting a Colonial Rebellion: Forestry and Social Control in German East Africa, 1874–1915." *Environmental History* 8, no. 3 (2003): 430–51.

Talbot, P. Amaury. *In the Shadow of the Bush*. New York: George H. Doran, 1912.

———. *Woman's Mysteries of a Primitive People: The Ibibio of Southern Nigeria*. London: Cassell, 1915.

———. *Life in Southern Nigeria: The Magic, Beliefs and Customs of the Ibibio Tribe*. London: Macmillan, 1923.

———. *Tribes of the Niger Delta: Their Religions and Customs*. London: Frank Cass, 1932.

———. *The Peoples of Southern Nigeria*. 4 vols. London: Frank Cass, 1969.

Tamuno, T. N. *The Police in Modern Nigeria, 1861–1965: Origins, Development, and Role*. Ibadan: Ibadan University Press, 1970.

———. *The Evolution of the Nigerian State: The Southern Phase, 1898–1914*. New York: Humanities Press, 1972.

———. *Peace and Violence in Nigeria: Conflict-Resolution in Society and the State*. Ibadan: Panel on Nigeria since Independence History Project, 1991.

Taussig, Michael. *The Devil and Commodity Fetishism in South America*. Chapel Hill: University of North Carolina Press, 1980.

Temple, O. *Tribes, Provinces, Emirates and States of the Northern Provinces of Nigeria*. Cape Town: Argus, 1919.

Thomas, Martin. *Violence and Colonial Order: Police, Workers, and Protest in the European Colonial Empires, 1918–1940*. Cambridge: Cambridge University Press, 2012.

Thomas, Nicholas. *Entangled Objects: Exchange, Material Culture and Colonialism in the Pacific*. Cambridge: Harvard University Press, 1991.

Thompsell, Angela. *Hunting Africa: British Sport, African Knowledge and the Nature of Empire*. New York: Palgrave Macmillan, 2015.

Thornton, John K. *Warfare in Atlantic Africa, 1500–1800*. New York: Routledge, 1999.

Tijani, Hakeem Ibikunle. *Britain, Leftist Nationalists, and the Transfer of Power in Nigeria, 1945–1965*. New York: Routledge, 2005.

Tylden, Geoffrey. "The Shoulder Firearms in South Africa, 1652–1952." *African Notes and News* 12 (1957): 204–6.
Ubah, C. N. *Colonial Army and Society in Northern Nigeria*. Kaduna: Baraka Press, 1998.
Ukadike, Nwachukwu Frank. *Black African Cinema*. Berkeley: University of California Press, 1994.
Ukpabi, Sam. *The Origin of the Nigerian Army: A History of the West African Frontier Force, 1897–1914*. Zaria: Gaskiya Corp., 1987.
Umoh, Ubong Essien. "The Making of Arms in Civil War Biafra, 1967–1970." *Calabar Historical Journal* 5, nos. 1–2 (2011): 339–58.
United Nations Office on Drugs and Crime. *Transnational Organized Crime in West Africa: A Threat Assessment*. Vienna: UNODC, 2013.
van den Bersselaar, Dmitri. *The King of Drinks: Schnapps Gin from Modernity to Tradition*. Leiden: Brill, 2007.
Vandervort, Bruce. *Wars of Imperial Conquest in Africa, 1830–1914*. Bloomington: Indiana University Press, 1998.
Vaughan, Megan. *Curing Their Ills: Colonial Power and African Illness*. Cambridge: Polity Press, 1991.
Vaughan, Olufemi. *Nigerian Chiefs: Traditional Power in Modern Politics, 1890s–1990s*. Rochester: University of Rochester Press, 2000.
von Hellermann, Pauline, and Uyilawa Usuanlele. "The Owner of the Land: The Benin Obas and Colonial Forest Reservation in the Benin Division, Southern Nigeria." *Journal of African History* 50, no. 2 (2009): 223–46.
Watson, Ruth. *"Civil Disorder Is the Disease of Ibadan": Chieftaincy & Civic Culture In a Yoruba City*. Athens: Ohio University Press, 2003.
White, Gavin. "Firearms in Africa: An Introduction." *Journal of African History* 12, no. 2 (1971): 173–84.
White, Stanhope. *Dan Bana: The Memoirs of a Nigerian Official*. New York: James H. Heineman, 1966.
Williams, Fatayi. *Faces, Cases and Place: Memoirs by Fatayi Williams, Nigerian Jurist*. London: Butterworths, 1983.
Woollacott, Angela. *Gender and Empire*. New York: Palgrave Press, 2006.
Wright, Fergus Chalmers. *African Consumers in Nyasaland and Tanganyika*. London: HMSO, 1955.

INDEX

Abacha, Sani, 258, 265
Abayomi, Moronfolu, 225–27, 239
Abdallah, Raji, 167
Abeokuta, 35–36, 65, 105, 136, 158, 229
Abeokuta Local Merchants Committee, 105
abolitionism, 41
Achebe, Chinua, 84, 193–94
Action Group, 148, 182, 184, 186
Adamawa Province, 164
Adelabu, Adegoke, 182–83
Adeoye, Tafa, 269
Adeshina, Olusegun (Shina Rambo), 265
Adubi War, 145, 163, 171
advertisement, 13–14, 75, 121, 134
Agbekoya uprising, 269–70
Ago-Iwoye, 105
agriculture, 10, 70, 108, 179
agriculturist, 178
Ajasa, Kitoyi, 226–27
Akpa, 37
Alakija, A. A., 80, 248
Alao, Abdul-Azeez Arisekola, 257–58
ammunition, 1–3, 5, 18, 31, 35–36, 38–40, 49–50, 55, 58, 81, 93–94, 131, 136–37, 141, 146, 159, 161–62, 168, 198, 202, 211, 233, 236–37, 261–62
ancestor, 11–12, 234
ancestress, xiii
Anglican missionaries, 35
animal, xi, 22, 43, 57, 61–62, 64–66, 67–71, 74, 122, 124, 126–29, 131–33, 136–40, 143, 149, 178–79, 205, 213–14, 244, 246, 259–60

Anini, Lawrence, 264–65
antelope, 8, 119, 129, 133, 259
Arab, 29
archeology, 46
Aredi, 105
armed robbery, 20, 24, 59, 194–97, 200, 202, 208–9, 218, 255, 260–66, 271
Armed Robbery and Firearms Tribunal, 262
Armistice Day, 86
armory, 49, 136, 196, 201, 212, 238, 242–44
arms registry, 13, 20, 74, 77, 238, 240
Aro expedition, 50
Arondizuogu, 38, 89
Ashogbon Police Force, 208
assassin, 120, 182–83, 199
Association of West African Merchants, 101–2, 105, 108–10
Atlantic ocean, 6, 29–30, 32, 39, 42
autobiography, 112, 146
Awolowo, Obafemi, 85, 216
Axis powers, 101
Ayetoro, 98, 102
Azikiwe, Nnamdi, 85, 157, 171, 173, 183

Babangida, Ibrahim, 264–65
Badagry, 96, 99, 178
bank, 2, 8, 104, 120, 177, 195, 198, 262, 266–67
Bank of British West Africa, 195
bankruptcy, 104, 198
Barbot, John, 29–30, 32
Barth, Henry, 29, 40–41, 51

Basden, G. T., 66
Bassey, Ekpenyong Ita Hogan, 1–3, 8, 12
Bauchi, 127, 129, 147
Bayer, Oran, 216–17
Bello, Ahmadu, 183
Benin City, 71, 255–56, 263, 265
Benin Kingdom, 30–32, 34, 37, 69, 213, 229
Biafra, 77, 271
Biafran army, 268
biography, 46, 132, 264
bird, 55, 65, 68, 128, 130, 142–43, 174
Birmingham Small Arms Company, 127, 131
Bisley Championship, 138
black market, 3, 102, 105, 113
blacksmith, 3, 11, 21, 36–37, 60, 63, 73, 113, 164, 172, 178, 228, 231–32, 256, 260, 267, 269
blunderbuss, 37, 42
boar, 31
Boko Haram, 270
Bonny, 33–34, 39
bookkeeper, 55, 72, 198
border, 12, 25, 81, 100, 162, 198–99, 208, 241, 256, 272
Borgu, 127
Bornu, 29, 39–41, 70, 95, 127, 132, 178, 182, 225
Boston, 36
bow and arrow, 30, 32–33, 35, 44, 58–59, 61–62, 66, 124, 128, 145, 157, 164, 178, 182, 230–31, 263
boys, 43, 64–65, 82, 144, 148, 209, 213, 236, 255
Boy Scouts, 197
Brazil, 42
Bread and Bullet (play by Hubert Ogunde), 155–57
Bren gun, 200–201
Brinkworth, William Ian, 56, 63, 65, 121, 128, 163, 171, 210, 240
British Parliament, 18, 176
Brussels Conference, 49, 55
buffalo, 48, 64, 78, 215, 259
Buhari, Muhammadu, 264, 270
bullet, 5, 35, 36–38, 43–44, 46, 58, 63, 78, 130–31, 145, 148, 155–57, 161, 163, 172–73, 177, 182–83, 185, 212, 216, 226, 266
burglary, 195–96, 204, 206, 208, 225
burial rite, 45, 83–84, 214, 226
Burutu, 96–97, 99
Burutu shooting, 176
Busari, Isiaka (Mighty Joe), 262
bush meat, 65

Calabar, x, 1–2, 33, 37, 62, 98, 104, 109, 136, 204, 210, 231
Calabar Shot Gun and Licence Holder Union, 81
calabash, 44, 144
Cameron, Donald, 225
Cameroons, 33, 106, 107
Canada, 121, 234
cannon, 15, 31, 39, 42–43, 46, 49, 57, 85–86, 157, 193
canoe, 3, 39, 180
capitalism, 10–11, 218
carbine, 49
Carr, Henry, 163
cars, 13, 72, 85, 198
cartridge, 3, 5, 30, 37, 58, 72, 78, 81–82, 128, 159, 239
cash crops, 10, 62, 67, 93, 104, 163, 179, 200, 269
cash economy, 24, 66, 200
cassava, 67
cavalry, 40
Central Africa, 6–7, 123
ceremonial salute, 14, 33
ceremonial shooting, 8, 14–15, 21–22, 24, 33, 38, 44–45, 51, 62, 82–83, 85, 87, 95, 194, 210, 218, 258
ceremonies, 8, 14–15, 24, 44–45, 48, 57, 82, 84–86, 93, 177, 193, 209, 258
Challenger, 199
chassepots, 38
Chief Secretary to the Government, 142, 217, 240
Christianity, 258
Church Missionary Society, 34, 78
citizenship, 3, 183
civilization, 17–18, 41, 123, 133, 149, 203, 229
Clapperton, Hugh, 29, 40
clay-pigeon shooting, 142–43
clerk, 55–56, 72, 77, 80, 198, 233, 245, 248
Clifford, Hugh, 59, 95, 100, 228
climate, 121, 242
cloth, 32, 44, 106, 146, 202, 211, 258
cocoa, 62, 67, 70, 78, 93, 104–5, 178–79, 260, 269
colonial officer, 9, 19–20, 56, 58–61, 65–66, 81, 83, 86, 102, 111–13, 121, 123–25, 127–30, 132–33, 136– 37, 139, 141, 146, 148–49, 156, 159, 162–63, 165, 170–71, 175, 180, 204, 209, 213, 215, 227–29, 231, 237
commodity, xii, 2, 4–5, 10–14, 22, 56, 93, 101
conflict, 4, 15, 16, 18–19, 23, 25, 29, 34–35, 38, 46, 49, 65, 67, 69–71, 74, 79, 105, 157–58, 160, 162, 164–65, 169, 171, 177–80, 185–87, 212, 216, 218, 230, 234, 242–43, 257, 261, 263, 267–72
consumption, 6, 9–10, 12–14, 22, 87, 100, 107, 109, 128, 144, 155, 204, 210, 233
controller of customs, 74, 97, 100–101, 237–38, 242
coroner's inquest, 21, 109, 120, 178, 180, 226
corruption, 25, 106, 199, 256, 259, 261, 264, 266, 268, 270, 272

court, 1–2, 20–21, 25, 40, 63, 72, 80, 83, 99, 104, 146–47, 149, 164, 167, 170–71, 177, 194, 196–98, 205, 209–13, 215–18, 225–26, 229, 245, 263
cowries, 34, 44
cricket, 135, 139
crime, 24, 56, 58, 71, 106, 133, 158, 160, 172–73, 193, 195–96, 198, 200–203, 206, 208, 216, 226, 238–39, 255, 259–60, 262, 264, 266
Criminal Investigation Department, 211, 240
criminals, 2, 199, 256, 266–67, 272
Crocker, W. R., 128–29
Cross River, 70, 84, 102, 106–7, 146
cruelty to animals, 74
Cummings, Ivor, 141
currency, 195
custom, 69, 178, 210, 244, 256
customs department, 20, 74, 81, 97, 99–101, 140, 198–99, 242, 266
customs duties, 230, 238
customs officer, 1–2, 198, 201, 237–38, 261, 266

Dada, L. A., 80
Dagarti, Kofi, 221–22
Dahomey, 36, 100, 198
Daily Express, 175
Daily Service, 21, 67, 86, 105, 155, 184–85, 195, 198–99, 208
Daily Times, 78, 175, 271–72
Dane gun: in accident, 213, 215; in armed conflict, 18, 35, 37, 57–59, 157–58, 161–64, 173, 177–78, 185, 195; in ceremonial shooting, 14, 44, 83, 85–86, 201; in crime, 195–96, 199, 201, 204–5, 207; as economic exchange, 71–72; and gunpowder, 36, 93–117, 205; in hunting, 61–71, 124–25, 128, 130, 135; local production of, 42, 161; in the precolonial era, 29–51; regulation of, 3, 10, 13, 19, 24–25, 49, 55, 57–60, 225–39, 258–60, 267, 269–70; in slave trade and slavery, 33–35; social class, 56, 73–75, 78
Davies, Hezekiah Oladipo, 173, 181–82, 186
decolonization, 19, 23, 74, 79–80, 85, 141, 156–57, 179, 181, 183, 185, 201, 239, 243–44
deer, 66, 216
Defence Industries Corporation of Nigeria, 268
deforestation, 65, 259
Degema Division, 107
Delphonso, Duro, 226–27
Dempster, Elder, 1, 98
detonators, 111–13
disarmament, 57–60, 257, 268, 271–72
dog, 62, 65, 128, 148, 160, 171
Driberg, Thomas, 176

drum, 15, 44–46, 84
Dutch, 31–32, 121
dynamite, 19, 110, 112–13

East Africa, 126
Eastern Nigeria Guardian, 21, 105, 193, 217
Eastern Provinces, 82, 103–4, 107, 109, 168, 242
Ebute Metta, 146
ecology, 62, 66, 70, 130, 214
educated Nigerians, 10, 13, 17, 42, 55–56, 72–73, 75, 85, 123, 135, 175, 184, 196, 203, 210, 226, 228, 232, 234, 239, 245, 255
Efik secret cult, 84
Ejigbo, 60
Eket, 42, 59, 71, 163
Ekiti, 37
Ekitiparapo, 37, 44, 57
Ekoi, 43, 215
Ekwefi, 194
electronics, 13
elephant, 48, 63, 64, 66–70, 78, 126, 129, 131–32, 215
Eleti Ofe, 226
Emergency Powers Defense Acts, 108, 110
Empire Day, 86, 139, 158
Enahoro, Anthony, 156, 183
Ene, Okon, 1
entrepreneur, 2, 43, 72, 226
Enugu, 10, 20, 85, 111, 155–56, 163, 168–69
Enugu colliery shooting, 16, 18, 23, 25, 77–79, 166–77, 187, 228, 233, 239–40, 242, 250
environment, 3, 14, 22, 38–39, 56, 61, 64, 70–71, 81, 121–22, 125, 127, 130–31, 133, 141
ethnicity, 7, 38, 55, 87, 184, 267
ethno-religious crises, 25, 270
Europe, 6, 12, 30, 32–35, 40, 45, 50, 94, 120, 225, 239, 268
European, 3, 5–7, 10–11, 13–20, 22–23, 30–35, 37–51, 57, 62, 68, 71–72, 78–83, 98–99, 106, 119–49, 163, 170, 172–73, 177, 179, 195–96, 198–99, 201–4, 209–10, 212–13, 225, 230, 232–34, 236, 240, 242, 244, 246, 248, 256
expatriates, 121–22, 134, 136, 141, 148
explosion, 96, 98–99, 112, 240
explosives, 3, 5, 19, 22–23, 57, 96–99, 110–13, 163, 166–70, 176, 272
exports, 10, 32, 34, 67, 70, 237, 242
ex-servicemen, 200, 202, 205
extrajudicial killing, 24, 183, 206, 208–9, 266

Fafunmi, Daniel, 148
family, x, 2, 82, 85, 112, 186, 215, 226, 240, 244

farmers, 62, 93, 104–6, 186, 212, 230–31, 246, 259, 269
Fernando Pó, 198
Field, John, 167–69
fines, 100, 148, 159, 213
Firearms Prohibition Order, 271
firearms registration, 83, 299
firefighting, 159
firing squad, 262–63, 266
Fitzgerald Commission, 167, 169–73, 175–76, 239
Fitz-Henry, Lassie, 125, 133, 146
forest, 43, 62, 64–65, 67–68, 70, 72, 101, 129, 205, 214–15, 259, 260
forest guards, 55, 72, 259
France, 15
funeral rite, 3, 83–84

Gambia, 138
game reserve, 259
Gardner, Bam, 5, 120
Gatling gun, 5, 49–50
gelatin, 110–13
gelignite, 110–11
gender, 15, 44, 69, 227
General Strike of 1945, 16
girl, 64, 84, 120
Girl Guides, 197
globalization, 2, 12, 30, 66
Glover Memorial Hall, 155, 174
Gold Coast, 138–39, 170, 211
Gombe, 127
Gongola river, 128, 131
Gowon, Yakubu, 262, 268
grasscutter, 65, 124, 259
guinea fowl, 124, 128, 144
gun: gun licenses, 60, 72, 81, 95, 236, 238, 245–46, 248, 250, 257; gun noise and sound, 14–15, 24, 82, 259, 261; liberalization of, 19, 24; registry of, 241; regulation of, 4, 7–8, 20, 25, 59, 68, 74, 79, 87, 157, 235–36, 241–42, 245, 247, 256–57
gunpowder: in hunting, 63, 66, 73, 124; importation of, 3, 13, 32, 34, 50, 58, 60; political economy of, 93–113; use in Dane gun, 14–15, 36, 44, 73, 78, 82–86, 162, 178, 210, 260; in warfare and violence, 31, 37, 46, 49, 195, 199, 205, 230
gunshot, 14–15, 57, 82–84, 109, 120, 143, 166, 180–84, 186, 195, 197, 207, 212–13, 262
gunsmith, 5, 75, 161
gun society, 4, 6–10, 14, 20–23, 29, 51–59, 62, 81–82, 87, 93, 101, 113, 121–22, 149, 156, 177, 187, 194, 218, 227, 257–59

Hastings, A. C. G., 66, 119, 126–27, 130–33
Hermon-Hodge, H. B., 126–33
hippopotamus, 63–64, 66, 68, 131–33
homicide, 194, 209, 217, 227, 231
horse, 41, 128, 207
horse racing, 23, 135, 139, 149
human rights, 165, 172, 268
Hunter, David, 124, 144–45
hunter guards, 24, 71, 203–4, 206–8, 218
hunters, x, 14, 21, 24, 32, 48, 56, 61–63, 65, 67–69, 71, 74, 78, 83, 85–86, 95, 101, 107, 124, 126, 129–32, 143, 163, 203–16, 230–31, 259–60, 267
hunter's guild, 62, 75, 79, 124, 210, 212, 214, 216
Huntsglen, SS, 96

Ibadan, 34, 37, 43, 45–47, 59, 67, 83, 98, 101, 104–5, 110, 121, 136, 140, 145, 179, 182, 197, 204, 216, 245, 246–48, 257–58, 269
Ibadan Division, 101, 105, 140, 205
Ibadan Rifle Club, 140
Ibibio, 59, 84, 162
Ibikunle, Balogun, 46
Iddo, SS, 98
Idowu, Folarin, 269
Igala Division, 108
Iganmu, 70, 211
Igarra, 86, 231
Igbeti, 70
Igbo, 37–38, 42, 49, 57, 62, 66, 69–70, 78, 177–78, 193, 204, 213, 242
Ijaiye War, 35, 37, 43
Ijala, 48
Ijasi, 98
Ijebu Igbo, 69
Ijebu Ode, 103, 182
Ijebu Province, 64, 105–6, 182
Ikeja, 80
Ikemefuna, 194
Ikenne, 102
Ikirun, 60
Ikorodu, 197, 208, 262
Ikoyi Club, 142–43
Ile-Ife, 44
Ilesa, 60, 78
Ilorin, 95, 109, 197, 235, 237, 243
immigration, 122, 159
Imperial Chemical Industries, 99
imperialism, 121, 123, 156
imports, 3, 9, 13–14, 94
innovation, xii, 12–13, 29, 268
international trade, 10–11, 13, 22, 32, 49, 60, 94, 260

invention, 14–15, 44, 83
Iseli, Susanna, 120
Iseli, Theophilus, 120
Iseyin-Okeiho uprising, 61, 158, 163–64
Iva valley mine, 155, 168
ivory, 66–70, 132
Iwolabo, Aston, 212
Iyamu, George, 265

Jannuzzelli, Messrs., 96
javelin, 31, 33
Jebba Locomotive Shed, 243
John Holt Company, 71, 74, 81, 94, 104, 107, 109, 195, 197, 209, 228, 239, 242, 248
Jonathan, Goodluck, 270
Jones, Arthur Creech, 138
Jos, 112, 113, 136, 156, 177–78, 182, 236–37, 244, 248
Jos Province, 178
journalist, 56, 72, 77, 198
juju, 62, 71, 86, 131, 163, 190, 199, 204, 214–15, 259, 269

Kabba Province, 108, 129
Kaduna, 72, 86, 136, 155–56, 182, 195, 233, 235–36
Kakaki, 44
Kalabari, 42, 180
Kalashnikov, 257
Kano: chronicle, 39; city of, 125, 137, 155–56, 183–85, 234, 237, 248; native authority, 79; rifle club, 135; riot, 183, 184–85, 244–45
Kanuri, 40, 182
Katagum, 40, 125, 129
Katsina, 40
Kerslake, R. T., 127
kidnapper, 255, 267
Kiriji, 43
Kirikiri Maximum Security Prison, 262
Kisch, Martin, 127–28
Kopytoff, Igor, 4

labor, 18, 23, 25, 85, 107, 110, 147, 156–57, 166–68, 172, 175–76, 182, 200, 236, 240, 259
Lagos, 8, 37, 59–60, 66–68, 77, 80–81, 85–86, 96–98, 100, 120–21, 127, 134–36, 138–39, 142, 145–48, 155, 159, 162, 174–75, 178, 182, 185, 195–98, 200, 203, 208, 211, 217, 225–27, 240, 242, 248, 261–63, 268
Lagos Hunters' Club, 80
Lagos Rifle Club, 134, 138
Lagos Weekly Record, 134
Lagos Youth Movement, 80, 182
Lander, Richard, 29, 35
Larymore, Constance, 83, 125, 127–28, 211

Lasekan, Akinola, 157, 179
lawyer, 2, 10, 56, 72, 77, 110, 120, 134, 182, 186, 211, 213, 215, 225, 248
Lebanese, 121, 234
Legislative Council, 80, 158, 163, 232
leisure shooting, 121, 134–43
Leith-Ross, Sylvia, 125
Leonard, Arthur, 84
leopard, 64–66, 68, 127, 129, 214–15, 231, 259
Liberia, 1, 257, 265
lion, 31–32, 39, 43, 64, 66, 68–69, 126, 129–30, 148, 182, 194
lioness, 84
Liverpool, 1, 96
Lloyd Commission of Enquiry, 186
Lokoja, 66, 81, 129, 136
London Daily Mirror, 175
loudspeaker, 14
Lugard, Frederick, 58–61, 132, 162, 164, 231–32

machine gun, x, 8, 19, 23, 31, 49, 71, 87, 157–58, 162, 164, 200, 227, 257, 261–62, 272
Macpherson, John, 85, 170, 172, 184–85
magazine: of explosives, 111–13, 166, 168; of gunpowder, 94–97, 99, 109; of guns, 5, 55, 159, 201
Maiduguri, 178, 262
Maitatsine uprising, 270
Makurdi, 81
Makurdi Division, 128
Mamu, xi, 105, 259
manslaughter, 206–7, 210, 215–18
Maraba, 61
marksmanship, 35–36, 40, 45, 64, 73, 80, 214, 259
marriage, 85, 120, 171, 226
Marx, Karl, 11
masculinity, 3, 18, 21–22, 45–46, 48, 74–75, 79, 123, 193–94, 266
matchlock, 30
material culture, 5, 21, 71
Maxim, Hiram, 49
maxim gun, 49, 51, 59, 162–63
Mbadiwe, Kingley Ozuomba, 85
meat, 22, 64–65, 67–68, 124, 128, 131–32, 136, 259
medicine, 40, 64, 67, 182, 204
mental illness, 120, 211–12
Mfon, Edet, 1
migration, 108, 122, 159, 258
military, 4, 7, 15, 18, 21, 23, 29–40, 44–45, 48–50, 57–59, 77, 82–83, 85, 87, 108, 122, 127, 129, 134, 137, 139–40, 145, 149, 159, 162–63, 175, 196, 198, 202, 211–12, 245, 255–56, 258, 261–70

Minna, 136, 156
Mitchell, Henry, 1
monkey, 66, 78, 133
Muoghalu, Stanislaus, 271–72
murder, xiii, 133, 162, 202–3, 206, 210, 212, 215–18, 225–27

National Council of Nigeria and the Cameroons, 167, 183–84, 186
Native Authority Police Force, 16, 58–59, 159, 199, 201, 204–5
New Yam Festival, 194, 210
Niger Delta, 39, 97, 272
Nigerian Air Force, 268
Nigerian Civil War, 195, 255, 268
Nigerian Hunting Society, 80
Nigerian Ivory Trading Company, 66
Nigerian Observer, 255–56, 263
Nigerian Pioneer, 21, 55, 65, 86, 121, 209, 225–26, 250
Nigerian Railway Corporation, 243
Nigerian Rifle Association, 20, 80, 121, 124, 134–43
Nigerian Tribune, 263
Nigerian Youth Movement, 80, 182
Nigeria Police Force, 16–18, 23, 155–66, 171, 177, 179–80, 183, 196, 199, 201–3, 205, 208, 211, 240, 245, 261, 265–66, 272
night guards, 71, 204–5, 207–8
nightlife, 204
Niven, Rex, 129
Nkpa, 42
Nkwerre, 37, 42
Northern Elements Progressive Union, 183
Northern Peoples' Congress, 182
Northern Province, 68, 95, 102, 108, 225, 229–30, 233, 238

Oakley, Richard, 119, 126–27, 129–30, 133
Oban, 70, 215
Odogbolu, 105
Ogbomoso, 60, 196, 204, 207, 214, 269
Ogbunigwe, 268
Ogoja Province, 65, 85, 166, 178, 229–30
Ogunde, Hubert, 155–56
Ogunleye, Ladapo, 196
Ogunmola, Bashorun, 34, 43, 46
Ojiyi, Okwudi, 85, 172
Ojukwu, Chukwuemeka Odumegwu, 77, 268
Okondo, 43
Okonkwo, 193–94
Okoroigbo, E. I., 242
Okoye, Mokwugo, 167

Okuku, 60
Olagbegi, Olateju, 243
Olosan, 70
Omomeji, Lamidu, 148
Ondo Division, 108
Onitsha, 72, 95, 104, 113, 136, 143, 156
Onitsha Province, 95, 166, 231
ornament, 64
Osifekunde, 41–42
Osogbo, 60–61, 81, 140, 197, 201, 203, 206–7, 212
Otan, 60
Owerri, 104
Owo Division, 108, 224
Oyenusi, Isola, 261–63
Oyo Province, 60–61, 139, 164, 206
Oyo riot, 183, 185–86

palm kernel, 43, 101–8, 212
party politics, 20, 74, 181–82, 243
percussion cap, 1, 3, 11, 60
petro-naira, 255, 264
pistol, 5, 8, 10, 40, 42, 55–57, 73, 119, 146, 195–96, 199, 201–2, 213, 227–28, 232–33, 236, 244, 246, 256, 267
Plateau Province, 238
poisoned arrow, 58–59, 61, 145, 164, 230–31, 238
polo, 23, 66, 135–36, 141–42, 149
Port Harcourt, 104, 109, 113, 156
Portuguese, 30–31
poverty, 25, 200, 259, 268
Prendegost, William, 1
prison, 1–2, 99, 146–47, 164, 202, 207, 213, 215–16, 226, 261–62, 269
Pyke-Nott, J. G., 168

race, 3, 6–8, 13, 20–22, 86, 106, 121–22, 136, 143, 203, 230, 239, 241, 244
race course, 86, 139
racism, 122, 141, 173, 211
railway, 147, 159, 233, 234–36, 243
ranger, 70
recreation, 68, 79–81, 121, 124, 134–35, 139, 141–43, 147
Rees-Williams, David, 176
religion, 21, 258, 267, 270
revolver, 5, 8, 10, 49, 55–57, 73, 80, 125, 128, 146–47, 155, 166, 182, 195–96, 198, 201–2, 205, 209, 226–28, 232, 236, 243, 246, 256
rhinoceroses, 126, 129
Ribon Valley Tinsfields Limited, 113
rifle: effectiveness of, 5, 10, 18, 55, 57, 59, 66, 72, 78, 123, 159–66; in hunting, 124, 127–31, 134–43;

prohibition of, 49, 56, 58, 78, 122, 227, 228–36, 246, 248, 256–57, 161; and race, 57, 80, 123; in recreation, 22–23, 121, 124, 157, 211–12; in violence and warfare, 37, 43, 50, 59, 159–66, 168, 172, 196, 202, 261–62, 264–65, 267
ritual, 12, 15, 44, 46, 82, 216, 255
roan antelope, 128–29
rocket, 40, 49, 58, 257, 268
Roosevelt, Theodore, 126
Royal Niger Company, 50, 66, 97, 99, 110
Royal School of Mines, 110
rubber, 70, 101–3, 106–8, 120

Sadare, L. A., 81
sailor, 2, 147
Saint Andrew's Teacher Training College, 77
Saki, 70, 215–16
sand grouse, 124
sanitation, 159
Santa Anna Magistrate, 80
Savage, Richard Akinwande, 173
scramble for Africa, 13
Sebastian, Pedro, 80
Shagamu, 102, 106, 212
Shankland, T. M., 86
Shell D'Arcy Petroleum Development Company, 112
Shepeteri, 70
shooting range, 134, 136–37, 145
shotgun: effectiveness of, 10, 62; for hunting, 63, 129, 144, 216; as marker of class, 13, 17, 56, 72–82, 123; regulation of, 3, 10, 50, 55, 144, 227–28, 233–39, 243–46; in violence and conflict, 19, 25, 42, 124, 144, 167, 182, 184, 199, 204, 216, 230, 232
Sierra Leone, 36, 46, 138, 257, 265
Silverdale, SS, 97
slave, 9, 15, 41, 42
slave-gun cycle theory, 34
slave raiding, 7, 29, 33–34, 39, 50
slavery, 41, 45, 61
Small-Wood, J. M., 144–45
Smith, Harold, 146, 156
Smithsonian Institution, 126
snake, 43, 62
soccer, 136
Société Commerciale de l'Ouest Africain, 103
Sokoto Caliphate, 6, 40, 59, 125
soldiers, x, 35–36, 42, 59, 86, 111, 125, 162–63, 198–200, 211–12, 258, 263, 271
song, 42, 46, 132
South Africa, 6, 9
Southern Nigeria Defender, 21, 83, 98, 110, 119

spear, 33, 44, 125, 176, 218, 225, 263
spirituality, 21, 45–46, 48, 62, 84, 214
sport, 22, 74–75, 77, 78, 121, 124, 127, 135–36, 139, 141–42, 225, 231, 235, 243, 246
stealing, 146, 196, 198, 235, 265
storekeepers, 55, 72
Strike and Hunger (play by Hubert Ogunde), 156
Structural Adjustment Program, 264
Sudan, 40
suicide, 48, 120, 145, 212, 226, 270
Suppression of Armed Robbery Decree, 262
Supreme Court, 1, 170, 218
Surulere, 77

Talbot, P. Amaury, 66, 128, 210
tax, 19, 60, 94, 113, 159, 165, 177, 181, 186, 201, 209, 227, 235, 243, 245, 269
taxation, 16, 171, 235
Taylor, G. Ronald, 142–43
teachers, 55, 72, 77, 167, 198, 233
Teachers' Training College, 77
technology, xii, 3, 6–7, 10–13, 17–18, 20, 23–24, 29, 31, 39, 41–43, 51, 270
telegraph, 2, 85, 109, 144
textile, 8, 13, 77
theft, 99–100, 113, 179, 197
Things Fall Apart (novel by Chinua Achebe), 193–94
tiger, 31–32, 64, 68, 129
Tiger's Empire (play by Hubert Ogunde), 156
Tinubu Square, 225
toys, 13
traditional elites, 42, 56, 69, 79, 83, 123, 228, 233
transportation, 55, 260
trap, 62, 124, 178, 259
trophy, 22, 66, 119, 132, 136

Udobi, Lewis, 79
Ugochukwu, Augustine Obianwu, 243
Ugwu ntili egbe (hills where guns were broken and burned), 57
Umuahia, 42, 197, 205, 210
Umuofia, 84, 193
underdevelopment, 20, 25, 155, 255, 257, 265
Underwood, J. D., 119–20
unemployment, 24–25, 196, 200
Union Jack, 185, 267
United Africa Company, 74, 78, 81, 94, 99, 104–5, 107–8, 195, 228
University of Ibadan, 258
urbanization, 71, 258

veterinary officer, 236
violence: of gun, ix, 18–20, 109, 147, 158, 174, 177, 179–80, 183, 193–94, 196, 209, 212, 215, 217–18, 227, 243, 272; political, 25, 169, 181, 183
voyage, 13

warfare, 4, 6, 32, 35, 37–38, 40, 44–46, 49, 56, 61, 87, 163, 214, 269
Warri, 96–97, 99
warrior, 7, 32, 34, 37–38, 45–46, 48, 56–57, 59, 83, 94, 163, 203
Warri Province, 65, 128, 165, 196, 230
wartime mobilization, 239
weaponization, 20, 36
Weiss, Richard, 120
Wesleyan Olowogbowo, 226
West Africa, 10, 30, 32–34, 36–37, 39, 46, 50, 64, 70, 77, 100–102, 123, 125, 137–38, 145–48, 163, 173, 195
West Africa Household Utilities Manufacturing Company, 262
West African Challenge Cup, 132, 137–38
West African Pilot, x, 21, 64, 67, 77, 85, 87, 98, 145–48, 158, 173, 175, 180–81, 183–84, 203, 205, 244
West African Students Union, 173
West African Supply and Production Board, 101

Wild Animal Preservation Ordinance, 67–70
wild animals, 32–33, 62, 64, 66–70, 78, 93, 123, 126, 128–29, 133, 246, 259–60
wildlife, 22, 57, 65–68, 70, 123, 125–26, 129, 132, 259
Williams, F. R. A., 211–12
women: attack by animals, 64; European, 122, 125–26; gun use, 122–23, 125; of market, 94; sexual relationship with, 121; in violence and crime, 67, 78, 144, 183, 197, 207, 212, 266
Women's War of 1929, 16, 158, 166, 171, 177
World War I, 1, 111, 124, 134
World War II, 13, 22, 70, 84, 86–87, 93–94, 100–101, 110, 113, 121, 129, 139–41, 145, 156, 159, 170, 177, 200, 212, 230, 239, 256

Yola, 126, 133
Yoruba: animal world, 124; gods and spirituality, 74, 214, 226; gun use, 35–38, 42, 43, 44, 46, 51, 61, 75, 83, 163; hunters, x; involvement in crime, 197
youth, 75, 134

Zaria, 81, 126, 156, 197, 233, 235
Zikist movement, 167–69
zoo, 67
Zungeru, 66, 125, 133, 211, 233

SAHEED ADERINTO is Associate Professor of History at Western Carolina University and the author of *When Sex Threatened the State: Illicit Sexuality, Nationalism, and Politics in Colonial Nigeria, 1900–1958.*

www.ingramcontent.com/pod-product-compliance
Lightning Source LLC
Chambersburg PA
CBHW050431240426
43661CB00055B/2344